The Call from Algeria

D1593111

The Call from Algeria

Third Worldism, Revolution,
and the Turn to Islam

Robert Malley

UNIVERSITY OF CALIFORNIA PRESS

Berkeley / Los Angeles / London

University of California Press
Berkeley and Los Angeles, California

University of California Press, Ltd.
London, England

© 1996 by
The Regents of the University of California

Library of Congress Cataloging-in-Publication Data

Malley, Robert, 1963–
    The call from Algeria : third worldism, revolution, and the turn to
Islam / Robert Malley.
        p.   cm.
    Includes bibliographic references and index.
    ISBN 0-520-20300-3 (alk. paper). — ISBN 0-520-20301-1 (pbk. :
alk. paper)
        1. Algeria — Politics and government.   2. Developing coun-
tries — Miscellanea.   I. Title.
    DT295.5.M34   1996
    965.05 — dc20   95-36054
                                                                      CIP

Printed in the United States of America
9 8 7 6 5 4 3 2 1

The paper used in this publication meets the minimum requirements of
American National Standard for Information Sciences — Permanence of
Paper for Printed Library Materials, ANSI Z39.48-1984.

A Gemma
Ovunque tu sia

Contents

Acknowledgments

Quality, it is said, is more important than quantity. Especially in large numbers. Over the many years it has taken me to research and write this book, I have had more than one occasion to verify this adage. The friends who accompanied me along the way were of rare generosity and invaluable assistance. But they also were numerous, for which I am particularly grateful.

Michael Gilsenan, who supervised this project from its beginnings, was a constant source of inspiration and comfort. In more ways than they can know, Jean Manas and Rebecca Haile compelled me to question my beliefs, leading me to others they no doubt would challenge just as convincingly. I also am indebted to Donald Billingsley, Immanuel Wallerstein, David Apter, Ursula Werner, Richard Ward, and Augusta Conchiglia, who read the manuscript in one version or other and offered helpful advice.

I owe thanks to the Rhodes Trust for support I received during my years at Oxford and visits to Algeria. In Algeria, I could not have found my way — in every sense of that word — without the exceptional hospitality and guidance of Mohamed Yazid and his family. Similar gratitude goes to Mustapha and Maha Benabdellaziz and to Hocine Aït-Ahmed. I know how much they gave for their country, and I know the pain that the destruction visited upon it must cause them all.

More than once during these years, in the midst of momentary and not quite so momentary discouragement, I have been blessed with my family's presence. Nadia, Rick, and Kate were persistent in their support, generous with their patience, magnanimous with their affection.

To Caroline, who was always there, encouraging and pressing me on when I needed it most, my everlasting devotion. As for my parents, this book truly is their story. They dedicated their lives to the Third World and to their children. They never lost faith in it, nor we in them. To my parents, I wish to express my admiration, my gratitude, and my love.

Introduction

       Only moments before the gunshot that would take his life, Mohamed Boudiaf was reflecting fatalistically on the brevity of life itself. The Algerian president perhaps was displaying exceptional prescience. But then, issues of life and death, of uncertainty and flux, of violence and chaos, were never far from the minds of ordinary Algerians in the summer of 1992. For by that time their country stood somewhere between Western-style democracy and Islamic fundamentalism, the while hesitating between military rule and civil war. The political and ideological divide that tore the nation apart and caused hundreds of casualties left few families intact. The divisions even affected individuals whose opposition to the government offered them nowhere but the Islamic Front to go yet whose everyday lifestyle and routines defied this commitment and challenged this faith. So that, initially received with a feeling of shock, the murder of the man who had returned after 28 years of exile to become president of his embattled country for 165 days ultimately was absorbed with a sense of the inevitable. As if somehow, in the midst of such intense doubt and radical transformation, he too was destined to pass.

       Regardless of who pulled the trigger, or of who ordered it pulled, Boudiaf was one more casualty of the turmoil experienced by his nation. Directly or indirectly, he was thus a victim of the meteoric rise of the religious organization known by its French acronym, FIS (for Front Islamique du Salut), a group that has challenged the very foundations of the Algerian state. In January 1992 an attempt was made to interrupt its ascent by calling off the runoffs to Algeria's first open parliamentary

1

elections in the face of a seemingly inescapable FIS victory. By then, however, it was too late. The FIS, created in 1989, had several million members. It had triumphed in the 1990 local and municipal elections, attracting over 54 percent of the popular vote. Through a combination of civil disobedience and local control, it had undermined the authority of the state and offered an alternative source of power. Unavoidably, Algeria was nudging its way into the Western psyche, joining the ranks of Iran and Sudan in a category of the Orient—fundamentalism—with which the United States has become so thoroughly obsessed in recent times. Alongside Islamic movements in the occupied territories and in Egypt, Tunisia, and Afghanistan, it stood as confirmation of the authentic nature of Islam, its true face and real design. The FIS, in short, had changed Algeria's complexion.

Lost in this narrative was the fact that for so long, and for so many people, Algeria had embodied an idea very different but just as powerful. I call this *Third Worldism,* a term that I later shall define in some detail but that for now can be summed up, schematically, as the belief in the revolutionary aspirations of the Third World masses, in the inevitability of their fulfillment, and in the role of strong, centralized states in this undertaking. Third Worldism was more than political doctrine; it was all-encompassing ideology that permeated fields of intellectual knowledge and militant activism. It was authoritative, not in the sense of ever being the exclusive ideological referent, but in that it provided the instruments by which to legitimate and discredit, to measure success and decree failure. It was pervasive in that not only Third World statesmen but also Third World and Western sociologists, historians, economists, anthropologists, and political scientists drew inspiration from its outlook.

In the aftermath of World War II, as revolutionary thought and practice faced a dead end in the industrialized world, the underdeveloped nations became the new theater of politics, the new battleground of ideologies. Third Worldism took off where a legacy of left-wing, essentially European beliefs fell both geographically and politically short of explaining the past and forecasting the future. The result was, on the one hand, a radicalization of the national liberation struggle in countries remaining under direct colonial rule and, on the other, a renewal of the "national struggle" in what came to be known as the "formally independent" nations.

To a degree, then, Third Worldism restored a feeling of moral purity that had been shattered by Stalinism, rekindling confident representations of history as a positive and intelligible course, infusing politics with a sense of excitement, as eyes turned in succession to Cuba, Guinea, Algeria, Indonesia, Vietnam, Tanzania, Libya, Mali, Madagascar, Cape Verde, Angola, Mozambique, Yemen, or Nicaragua. For Americans, the reference points might have differed slightly from the Europeans'. None-theless, generations of political activists awakened in the West to the sound of Third World guerrilla fighters. Black militants in the United States identified with the exploited Third World, the ghetto becoming its symbolic equivalent. Eldridge Cleaver selected Algiers as his tempo-rary haven; Carmichael chose Havana, Hanoi, Conakry.

I pause here to note an apparent ambiguity in the concept of Third Worldism. I refer to the tension between Third Worldism as an ideology *about* and as an ideology *of* the Third World. With Third Worldism, Eu-ropean left-wing activists and intellectuals projected their ideals onto the seemingly virgin lands of the less developed nations. This was not un-characteristic behavior: the reader need not look very far back in history for illustration, as colonial expeditions were celebrated by European par-ties of the Left in the name of universalism and as prerequisite to the Third World's own development. In this respect, Third Worldism might be viewed as an outgrowth of the Orientalism that Edward Said so mas-terfully described, the West's enterprise of constructing the Orient. The intrusion, need it be said, was not always welcome. In Algeria the ten-sion was epitomized in the half-tragic, half-farcical fate of the European revolutionaries who, having stood up against colonialism, felt entitled not only to judge but also to formulate national policy. As many ulti-mately were forced to leave the country, they were uncharitably dubbed *pieds rouges* — a cruel pun indeed, since *pieds noirs* was the term used to designate Frenchmen who lived in colonial Algeria, and who were its staunchest defenders.

That said, in contrast to Orientalism, Third Worldism also was an ideology rooted in the Third World, and in my view, the convergence between the two discourses outweighed their differences. My belief, which I will try to illustrate, is that the hopes invested by the European Left in the revolutionary Third World mirrored, to a remarkable extent, the Third World militants' justification of their own actions. In other words, Third Worldism was not a means by which the Third World was created by the West, but a shared representation of the world in which events, processes, and actors were endowed with specific significance. To borrow Said's metaphor, the emergence and consolidation of the ide-ology involved a two-way traffic between the exercise of power and the discourse on power. Third Worldism became a style of thought and a means of coming to terms with the world that was appropriated by political leaders as a language of power, by activists as a vocabulary of dissent, and by historians, journalists, economists, and sociologists as an interpretive tool. The hopes of one were the hopes of all, as would be the case, in time, with their respective disenchantments.

✛   ✛   ✛

I tell the story of Third Worldism from the perspective of Algeria but try, as much as is possible, to formulate questions and draw conclusions applicable to the system of thought as a whole and to the individuals who produced it, believed in it, or simply found themselves caught in its web. I begin with its rise and concentrate on questions of origins: What accounts for its success, for its ability to overcome disciplinary and geographic barriers, for its appeal both to holders and claimants of political power? What confluence of historical, economic, social, and ideological factors — Said speaks of "energies" — contributed to its ascension? How did pronouncements as varied as state propaganda, rebellious harangue, critical study, and detached sociology serve mutually to reinforce each other as well as the system of thought from which they all arose?

I explore, too, reasons for its gradual demise, its fading away, its replacement by other means of apprehending the world. So quickly and abruptly has this occurred that one is almost at pains to recall the atmosphere of Third Worldism in its heyday. With this difficulty comes the temptation to account for the fall by downplaying the ascent. Hence the recent resurgence of the notion of revolutionary Third Worldism as an alien graft imposed by the West, ill adapted to the unchanging "essence" of various underdeveloped countries. The tendency will be familiar to students of Orientalism, for it too depicts Islam as unchanging, describing "modernist" trends in the Islamic world as inimical to its authentic nature. Third Worldism, in this view, was merely an unwelcome, foreign, and short-lived parenthesis. In the case of Algeria, the *turn* to Islam thus becomes a *return* to authenticity.

It should be clear from what I earlier have said that this is a perspective I reject. I have little doubt that the roots of Third Worldism can partially be traced to the developed world, not only intellectually but economically and culturally as well. However, rather than reflecting the imposition of Western models on a passive recipient, namely, the Third World, this indebtedness captures a dynamic process. More generally, international phenomena — chief among them fluctuating power relations, whether military, economic, or cultural — affect the credibility, legitimacy, and overall effectiveness of discursive regimes at any given time, in any given place. Such regimes do not, in that process, become any more or less "authentic," only more or less timely or, as it were, in tune. Stated quite simply, I thus would concede that recent international developments have modified the world balance of power, thereby indirectly devaluating the Third World's revolutionary pronouncements. Indeed, the now fashionable labeling of these pronouncements as alien grafts is perhaps the most obvious manifestation of this trend. But to say that the system of truths called Third Worldism no longer is adapted to the Third World is very different from saying that it never was.

Though by no means a "resurfacing" of a so-called authentic Third World, the apparent replacement of Third Worldism by different systems of representation is another subject of this book. Islam's increasing role in Algeria has its likely counterparts in the strengthening of religious, ethnic, or communal identities and ties elsewhere in the Third World. I devote many pages to trying to come to terms with these phenomena, particularly in the case of Algeria's FIS, and in so doing cast a critical eye on much of the Western media's account—specifically as it concerns "Islamic fundamentalism." For now, it suffices to emphasize that the turn to Islam is often deceptive. The first deception involves terminology, since the religious movements in the Arab world are far from being fundamentalist. The second involves causation: what happens, I argue, has less to do with an inherent appeal of religion than with the fact that religion becomes the most effective vehicle for the expression of social, economic, and political frustration. The most interesting questions raised by this evolution, in short, are the following: Why has protest borrowed religious (or national, ethnic, tribal, etc.) accents, and why now?

❖   ❖   ❖

Three main themes underlie this book. The Third Worldist ideology of the Algerian revolution, its origins, evolution, and, in more recent times, the drift from Third Worldism to Islam (as expressed in the rise of the FIS) constitute the first. The reason for choosing Algeria might not appear to be self-evident to an American audience more familiar with the behavior—some would say antics—of a Gadhafi or an Ortega than with the actions of Ben Bella, Boumedienne, or Chadli Benjedid. But Third Worldism had its own measure of success and prestige. And to the extent that it became a dominant system of knowledge, Algeria was one of its principal surrogates.

Indeed, prior to the recent turn to Islam, Algeria enjoyed a privileged status in the Third Worldist pantheon. The reasons are to be found at every stage of the history of Third Worldism — its origins, its pinnacle, its downfall. As I shall argue, Third Worldism to a large extent was born out of ideological and physical contact with the European colonial powers, principally France. Due to geographical proximity and colonial status, Algeria experienced an especially intense interaction with the metropolis; as a result, its thinkers were at the forefront of the Third Worldist movement.

A colony, Algeria had been militarily occupied by France since 1830; it was home to roughly a million Europeans, mainly of French but also of Spanish and Italian descent, who owned the richest, most productive lands. Considered a part of France, it was divided into three *départements,* enjoying a particular status, to be sure, but French all the same. "The Mediterranean," the saying went, "cuts through France as the Seine cuts through Paris." Simultaneously, relatively large numbers of Algerians moved to France, leading to a peculiar mix of ideological mimicry and resistance: migrant workers experienced both solidarity with their fellow proletarians and the obstinacy of condescending racist attitudes; foreign students were both drawn to the progressive thoughts of their French counterparts and repelled by their Eurocentric instincts.

An important figure at this crossroads was Messali Hadj, arguably the father of modern, revolutionary Algerian nationalism. His efforts as a worker in France are to be credited for much that later would occur to solidify and color the national movement, namely, the fusion of working-class populism, nationalist anticolonialism, and traditional Islam. But his impact extended far beyond. By playing a decisive role in the Union Intercoloniale, one of the first political expressions of Third World solidarity, and at *Le Pariah,* its journalistic equivalent, Messali lay the foundations of Third Worldism as an ideology that, in theory at least, transcended national boundaries.

Next, Algeria's colonial situation, but mainly its harsh and long war of national liberation, magnified its prestige in Third Worldist eyes. As the French geographer Yves Lacoste once put it, the Algerian revolution "politicized thinking and discourse on the Third World."[1] In the seven years from the beginning of the war, on November 1, 1954, to the declaration of independence, on July 5, 1962, a poorly armed, ill-trained group of maquisards evolved into a regular army that enjoyed the support of a large proportion of the population and frustrated one of the world's major military powers. Before the war was over, hundreds of thousands had lost their lives, millions had been uprooted, eight thousand villages had

been destroyed, and millions of acres of land had burned. In the Third
Worldist historiography, such sacrifices—as Gellner's phrase has it—
stood second only to Vietnam's.[2] The North African country's eminence
continued long after it gained independence, for it took a leading part in
challenging the industrialized world and in calling for a new world economic order.

I chose Algeria, finally, because of the extraordinary events of recent
years: the collapse of the Third Worldist organization and justification of
power and the fascinating rise of the Islamic FIS as its challenger. Again,
as in every preceding stage, Algeria amplified trends that could be noticed elsewhere, so that it once again stands as an emblem, a condensed
narrative into which observers can read their favored story: either "the
Algeria of Frantz Fanon—guerrilla struggle, militant Third Worldism,"[3]
or the Algeria of Islam.[4]

Because sense cannot be made of Third Worldism's remarkable fate
without serious investigation of its relation to the colonial and anticolonial experience, or to the challenges that faced the independent nations,
I begin with the ideologies of Algerian political parties before the war of
independence and move to the discourse of the independent state and its
detractors. In the end, a comprehensive system of representation took
shape. It was aided along the way by a remarkable array of academic and
journalistic contributions sharing similar assumptions, preconceptions,
and attitudes. I end with the decline of Third Worldism, both as Algeria's
official discourse and as a dominant grid through which observers—the
historians, economists, political scientists, and sociologists of which I
earlier spoke—interpreted Algeria. I end, too, with the ascent of the FIS,
a formidable foe of the progressive, quasi-socialist Third Worldist outlook. I ask how it is that Islamic radicalism has become the expression of
social discontent and social despair, one that enjoys the appeal of a familiar, reassuring language of solidarity but also the attraction of effective protest and the promise of radical change. For, more than a religious
party, the FIS is a loose conglomerate of the genuine believers, the socially excluded, and, most importantly, a vast section of the youth that
have ceased to have faith in their future.

My second theme is more general; it relates to Third Worldism as a
whole. The belief that conclusions applicable to Algeria can be extrapo-
lated and applied to other, less developed nations is, of course, not uncontroversial. A convenient catchphrase, the term *Third World* also can
be misleading. The Third World exists neither as a political union nor as
a homogenous geographical ensemble, not even as a set of economically

comparable nations. Third Worldism itself, as the self-proclaimed practice of the several states, has its many subvariants, depending for the most part on the level of development, culture, traditions, and political heritage. Between nations that have experienced one or more military coups, such as Somalia, Madagascar, and Burkina-Faso, and nations born of long national liberation struggles, such as Algeria, Vietnam, and Mozambique, lie differences that affect not only their leaders' official discourse but also the appraisal of the Third Worldist intellectual community.

Still, when concessions are made to the uniqueness of historical processes and political characteristics, the fact remains that a belief in the Third World's commonality of aspirations and fate is central to Third Worldism. In this book I deal with Third Worldism, in other words, not with some objective entity called the Third World; indeed, debates about whether such an entity exists are largely irrelevant to this enterprise. Third Worldist activists and thinkers look to similar authoritative writings, exemplary heroes; they see in things analogous signs and meanings. I thus draw principally on the case of Algeria but move freely to other examples. Students of other regions of the Third World will, I hope, recognize in the Algerian experience familiar ways of acting, talking, and being.

I aim at a third audience in this work. To all who are interested in the ways in which a style of thought or discourse is constituted, maintained, and ultimately challenged, Third Worldism offers fruitful material. We can see the dynamic interaction of ideas (socialism, nationalism, etc.), historical events (colonialism and the struggles for independence) and social structures (economic polarization, dependence, underdevelopment) that makes it possible for a discourse to achieve prominence. We can see, too, that such discourse cannot be reduced to a mere rhetorical device for legitimating one group's authority. Third Worldism simultaneously provided tools of domination *and* of resistance, a vocabulary of power *and* of dissent. We can see, finally, how a dominant system of thought can be undermined by inherent as well as extraneous factors. The dismantling comes in ways overt and subtle, involving economic changes on a grand scale as well as minute shifts in the intellectual environment.

❖   ❖   ❖

I set out to write a book about Algeria, intent on scouting the path from ersatz socialism to self-proclaimed Islam, from almost-Cuba to maybe-Iran. Along the way, however, I stumbled across another story, the story of Third Worldism. It manifested itself time and again, for the transformations I saw in Algeria mirrored those that had occurred in more than a handful of Third World countries; they too had followed the same road toward intellectual self-doubt, conversion to economic liberalism, and apparent embrace of multiparty democracy, the turn to Islam simply taking the guise of an ethnic "revival" here, a tribal "awakening" there. It soon became clear to me that understanding Algerian politics required taking a step back to contemplate what was happening around it and that by coming to terms with Algeria one could make far more sense of what was occurring in other Third World lands. The interaction of these twin narratives has had certain implications for the organization of this book, which I think it best to discuss at this point.

The book is divided into three parts, each dealing with a phase in the history of Third Worldism, particularly as it played out in Algeria: its gestation (part 1), its apogee (part 2), and its demise (part 3). The structure is thus roughly chronological, and I hope this semblance of order will provide the reader with a general historical sense. Some might question the pertinence of this approach to an ideological movement that has been pronounced dead, buried, and quickly forgotten. I cannot agree.

We live at a time when ideological belief systems of yore such as socialism and Third Worldism are being disregarded as arbitrary political verbiage and unsalutary dogma, while, in the same breath, the current articles of universal faith — economic liberalism, structural readjustment, privatization, coupled with a dose of political pluralism — are being celebrated as pragmatic, and nonideological to boot. Such cavalier dismissal of yesterday's creed and self-congratulatory adherence to today's are terribly costly, and seriously misleading. The retrospective dimension of this book is of particular interest to me precisely to the extent that it can broaden this depressingly confining vision, showing us the past for what it was worth and the present for what it is not.

I wrote the individual parts with an eye to conveying some of the interplay between Third Worldism and Algeria. Chronology breaks down here, and within each part the book proceeds along parallel tracks. The parts each begin with a chapter devoted to Third Worldism in general. In these opening chapters I attempt to provide a broad outline of the historical period and set out the main themes of Third Worldism as an intellectual current at the time. They are followed by chapters dealing with Algeria in which I explore these themes in far greater depth and test some of my stated claims, for example, on the origins of Third Worldism in part 1; on the role and meaning of the single party, personalization of power, or demonization of dissidents in part 2; and on the rise of reductionist, exclusionary ideologies and tribal politics in part 3.

I do not wish to be misunderstood. By linking the fate of Third

Worldism to the evolution of the Algerian polity I do not intend to suggest a mechanical causal relationship between the two. Causal pulls have existed, to be sure, and they have worked in both directions. For instance, the rise of the nationalist movement throughout the Third World helped loosen the colonial grip and inject a new sense of what was possible, thereby contributing to the effective mobilization of Algerian militants. Too, the success of the Algerian revolutionary struggle radicalized political ideology, chiefly in Africa and the Arab world, but in other parts of the Third World as well, not to mention in France itself. In more recent years, the international debt crisis, the collapse of Soviet-style communism, and the triumph of the Islamic revolution in Iran likewise have had an unmistakable impact on Algeria. But that is about as far as I am willing to go, and it should be apparent that the precise extent to which the Third Worldist movement shaped the Algerian polity is not the principal focus of this effort.

I hasten to add that since this book is not an intellectual history of Third Worldism, much less a political history of the Third World, I do not pretend to cover exhaustively all that has happened to the under-developed world in the relevant time frame. My overriding purpose is to help the reader make some sense of the dramatic move from Third Worldism to the odd potpourri of economic liberalism, multiparty-ism, and the morass of ethnic, tribal, and religious impulses, all of which has been experienced — with what speed, with what intensity, and with what violence — by Algeria. This goal, along with limitations in my own knowledge, has informed my decisions concerning what needed to be discussed and what could be left out.

This point is particularly salient with regard to the chapters that deal with Third Worldism per se. I have written a book about the life cycle of Third Worldism in the case of Algeria, and therefore what I am after in those chapters is more mood than minutiae. I want to set the historical and thematic stage for what was happening in Algeria, to show that it was part and parcel of broader political and intellectual trends, and to suggest that understanding Algeria's contemporary history is one way — a fairly good way, in fact — to understand what has been happening throughout much of the formerly progressive Third World. If my assumptions about the relevance of Algeria's fate to the experience of Third Worldism as a whole hold up, other country studies should confirm my conclusions. By acquainting readers with Third Worldism as it existed beyond Algeria's boundaries, by jumping, as it were, between the generally Third Worldist and the specifically Algerian, I hope to have made this clear.

For one interested in the history of Third Worldism, then, this work presents significant gaps, and I apologize for these in advance. Third Worldism, I will argue, was born at the confluence of the imperial ideology of assimilation (according to which backward, colonized people needed to conform to the standards set by the higher civilizations of Europe), the pull of tradition, and the appeal of the system of thought bequeathed by Marx and Engels. Needless to say, a detailed analysis of assimilationism, traditionalism, and Marxism will have to be found elsewhere. Likewise, the rise of nationalist feeling in colonial territories and the Third World's role in international relations are both critically important subjects, and it is hardly possible to leave either unmentioned. But I take of them only what I deem necessary, and their study is consequently cursory. Other authors have chosen these themes as their focus, and I refer the reader to them.[5]

Additional limitations are also fairly straightforward. Nkrumah and Cabral are counted by many as being among the intellectual giants of Third Worldism, yet I do not assess their individual contributions at any length. This is no intellectual history, as I have said, and therefore I do not consider such detailed discussion essential, advisable, or, frankly, within my means. Instead, I have chosen to summarize the main tenets of Third Worldism as they emerge from these leaders' writings and those of several others.

Finally, I have relied heavily on the Third Worldist connection to France. This has meant ignoring other important linkages, such as to Britain or Portugal. I did this for two reasons. The first has to do with France's relationship to Algeria, and it hardly needs expounding. The second is that France, and its left-wing intellectuals in particular, appears to have taken a far greater interest than others in dispensing political advice (as opposed to charitable aid) to the Third World. There is something deliberate and organized about French attitudes toward Third World politics and also something quite impassioned, which would seem to have much to do with the need for forgiveness after the colonial mess and for absolution after the Stalinist debacle.

In the story of Algerian Third Worldism — from heroic anticolonial militancy to the pinnacle of power and prestige, followed by bleak degeneration into civil war, social dissolution, and economic wasteland — can be read the sorry fate of the contemporary Third World. How we got from there to here, what exactly was the "there" and what is the "here" —

these are the kinds of questions I ask in this book, and to which I try to respond.

But beyond all this a central fact remains. Third Worldism was not simply academic exercise. People throughout the world invested their entire capital of energy, enthusiasm, hope even, in the effort. They had faith in this impassioned but ultimately comforting way of scrutinizing the Third World, a certain way of talking about it; these were the gaze and the prose of Nasser, of Castro, of Boumedienne, of Cabral, and of Fanon. In the name of this idea sacrifices were made, lives shattered, lives lost. Looking back, it is good to remember that ideologies sometimes can do such things.

PART I

Gestation

Even the unimaginable sometimes can be scripted; even the unthinkable choreographed. So it was with the handshake that shook the world: Yassir Arafat, the tamed rebel, generously extending his hand, relishing his moment in the sun; Bill Clinton, the compassionate mediator, gently prodding the Israeli prime minister; Yitzhak Rabin, the old warrior, repulsed, hesitant, then resigned. And finally the crowd, having waited patiently for over three hours, expressing its wonder and amazement at the sight of a miracle all had come to expect. Historical drama aside, an unmistakable staged quality pervaded the scene. As if its meaning had to be immediate and transparent, leaving no room for the observer's independent interpretation.

In its simplicity and immediacy, the snapshot told it all: who had asked, who had encouraged, who had reluctantly agreed. As each participant dutifully played his part, the meaning of the reconciliation between the two foes was forcefully thrust upon us. In his traditional military garb, a kaffiyeh wrapped around his head, Arafat appeared on the White House lawn as a man almost comically out of place. He had been let in, allowed to retain his trademark outfit and native tongue, but with firearm, grand aspirations, and vast dreams left behind. His success, as it were, consisted almost entirely in his being accepted by the powerful of this world, invited to share their stage.

In this odd blend of triumph and disgrace, a striking fact went unnoticed, yet it explains why what so many saw as Arafat's moment in the sun was viewed by others as his twilight: the Palestinian leader had been on that stage not long before, its acclaimed and uncontested hero. The

15

prize then had been to share the platform with Fidel Castro, Houari Boumedienne, Abdel Nasser, or Zhou Enlai. Indeed, the prize at that time was to appear with Arafat himself. Those were different days, of course, and in the meantime the stage had changed, dramatically.

The architecture of that earlier platform, its protagonists too, traced its origins to the beginning of the twentieth century, a time when revolutionary Third Worldism gradually emerged as a dominant system of thought. Its demise has been so swift, its life span so brief, that it requires considerable effort to imagine the appeal Third Worldism once enjoyed, the passions it inspired. What it requires, really, is to look back to these beginnings, to the time when what since has become disenchantment was on its way to being hope.

CHAPTER I

When South Met North

On the Origins of Third Worldism

Third Worldism was one of those heroic ideologies that arise in times of transition, when the old order breaks down under the combined pressure of political, economic, and social mutation. The change affected both the countries of the so-called Third World and industrialized Europe but was most striking at the points where the two met: colonial possessions, where soldiers and settlers set foot, and the metropolitan centers of the North, where migrant workers and students came ashore. At these two critical intersections, vastly different social orders came face to face, leaving neither unscathed, and hostile worldviews clashed, leaving all deeply altered. Third Worldism emerged as a by-product of these encounters.

Without a comfortable box in which to fit such ideological outcomes, observers and thinkers traditionally label them mythical, ill-conceived efforts to impose one's outlook on others. Add to this the fact that Third Worldism grew out of meetings, many violent, between a dominant, arrogant North and a subjugated South, and it is all too easy to conclude that it was an ideology without roots in the Third World, the projection of European ideals, illusions, and hopes onto politically "virgin" lands. Third Worldism, in this view, was merely the failed attempt to graft European left-wing ideologies onto the Third World. What is missing from this analysis, I believe, is the sense of mutual influence between the Third World and Europe. The result of their encounter, rather than expressing one outlook's sway over the other, was a hybrid that borrowed from both. Where there was mutual transfer, in short, people saw unilateral imposition.

Third Worldism, then, was the child of two encounters: the territorial, as Europe foisted itself upon the Third World and the Third World encroached upon Europe; and the ideological, as preexisting modes of thought and perspectives, together with new outlooks born of these contacts, confronted each other. As Edward Said shows, with habitual insight and eloquence, throughout the pages of *Culture and Imperialism,* such links did not translate into cultural dependency; rather, they were made of fluid exchanges and mutual borrowings. Which is to say that if Third Worldism was partially indebted to Europe, it was not imposed by Europe.[1]

In reality, it is only somewhat ironic that the birth of Third Worldism, an anti-imperialist ideology of national self-determination, came about (for the most part) via contact with the metropolitan capitals of colonial Europe. For in attempting to understand the origins of Third World revolutionary movements, it is difficult to overemphasize the impact of the colonial years — 130 years in Algeria, many more in Portuguese southern Africa — on both colonized and colonizer. Colonialism was first and foremost an enterprise of domination and subjugation, but inevitably (and at times deliberately) it generated intellectual and human exchange, thereby putting North and South face to face. As a result, a vast number of future Third World militants was educated or worked in the metropolis; and a vast number of European militants came of age at a time when the critical fault line appeared to divide colony from imperial power, not worker from capitalist.

The following sections are intended as an introduction to these complex ideological, political, and social meeting grounds and to the ingredients that would compose Third Worldism. Of course, the success of Third Worldism in individual cases ultimately was a function of a number of variables: the colonial social structure; the intensity of colonial penetration and settler presence; the degree of economic development, social mobility, industrialization, and education in the dominated land; and immigration politics as well as politics pure and simple. All this, and much else, helps explain why radical nationalism prospered in one country, yet faltered in the next. Developing a satisfactory explanatory model would require a number of detailed case studies and thus is far beyond the scope of this book.[2] My own procedure, instead, is to outline certain broad themes by looking at the intersection between North and South from a number of perspectives: the Third World resident forced to endure the consequences of colonial rule; the Third World migrant worker or student confronted with metropolitan reality; and the European left-wing intellectual torn between national and political loyalties. These hypotheses will be explored in detail in chapter 2, as I turn to the case of Algeria's encounter with France.

❖   ❖   ❖

A recurring motif amidst the variety of settings in which the North-South encounter was to take place at the turn of the century was the quasi-ubiquitous presence of colonial or imperial domination and, never far behind, inescapable feelings of superiority and subservience, cultural narcissism and defiance. Indeed, at the end of the nineteenth century a vast majority of the Southern Hemisphere was under the effective control of the "lords of human kind," to use Hobsbawm's phrase, be it as colony, possession, territory, or mere protectorate.[3] The imperial project and the emblematic figure of the *colon* are central to understanding the emergence of Third Worldism. I mean this not only in the most obvious, direct sense—Third Worldism as anticolonial struggle, the *colon* as embodiment of the villain—but also in its less immediate dimension, as the backdrop for the social restructuring and ideological awakenings that would nourish Third World movements both North and South and shape their respective contours.

This unequal relationship played out in a number of ways. In the South, and although obvious differences separated French, British, Dutch, Belgian, and Portuguese rule, colonial domination almost by definition meant the superimposition of exogenous administrative and social structures upon the "native" populations. Anthony Smith pertinently observed that "the line drawn between these two societies, which often corresponded to the colour-line as well as one or more cultural differentiae, soon assumed (with some exceptions) a caste-like rigidity."[4] Class distinctions among colonizers and colonized, though present, were attenuated, just as imaginable bridges across groups were quietly ignored. In European eyes, the elites of the subordinated populations were possible collaborators, perhaps even potential heirs, but in any event inferior beings. And the peasants or workers of the South generally saw their Northern counterparts (the French *petits colons,* for instance) as pieces of the problem, not parts of the solution.

This point deserves further development. Colonialism was a messy business: on its tail came economic dislocation and upheaval, rural pauperization, the privatization of land, forced resettlement, and anarchic urbanization. The disruption of economic structures inevitably implied the undermining of old power bases and the introduction of novel avenues of social advancement, which in the main were tied to the new urban centers, colonial bureaucracy, and civil service. Colonialism thus encouraged the emergence of an educated local elite, a middle class whose links to traditional economic, political, even cultural structures were severed. Paradoxically, however, and at the same time, the colonial order blocked this ascent, erecting an insurmountable color or racial barrier. "The sole career outlet of any significance available to educated Africans," writes Immanuel Wallerstein, "carried with it an arbitrary (racial) limit of aspiration."[5]

Since this process spanned several continents and numerous decades, such generalizations necessarily are crude. But my point is one that has been noted with some frequency by students of the colonial era: what European rule offered with one hand — dangling titillating prospects of membership in a modern social and cultural universe — it unceremoniously withdrew with the other. For many members of this petty bourgeoisie, or "sub-elite," as Martin Kilson calls it,[6] lower civil servants, clerks, shopkeepers, white-collar workers, teachers, or health personnel, the colonial bargain quickly took on the appearance of a raw deal. They found themselves alienated from their old world, yet unwelcome in the new; socially caught between abilities and professional opportunities that the former far outstripped; culturally estranged both from their traditional environment and from the rituals of modernity, which they were permitted to observe only from afar.

First the Great War, and then the Great Depression would shake this uneasy status and force members of this "sub-elite" to take sides. Both events magnified the gulf that separated imperial power from dependency, the one by freely using inhabitants of the South as cannon fodder during the war, yet brusquely dismissing them at its conclusion; the other by exacerbating the sharp economic conflicts of interest between North and South.[7] Both war and depression "established contact between the politicised minorities and the common people" of what had yet to become the Third World.[8]

The same ubiquitous colonial or imperial equation served as inescapable backdrop to Third World immigrants. Migration to Europe was the other contact point between North and South, and the search for the origins of Third Worldism must take us back to times at once promising and faintly pathetic, when men from Africa, Asia, or the Americas came to the metropolitan centers of the North in search of work, learning, or inspiration. Some believed that change was needed in the colonies, that the road to such change was through Europe. And why not? Europe was the oppressor, but not that alone. For, they felt, it held some of the keys, political and intellectual, to their countries' future: potential alliances with anticolonial forces who could bring about desired political changes in Paris or London; ideological refinement by rubbing against notions of democracy, revolution and equality, socialism or communism. They came a handful, yet must have felt they had millions for company: the millions whom they left home but whose fate they believed, not without a hint of hubris, they held in their hands.

In the end, however, for the immigrants, confronting the metropolis meant confronting disparity and injustice, often more acutely than in the colony itself, where cultural, local, or family ties helped soften the harshness of foreign rule. Though they met, organized, argued, and propagandized, more often than not they were slighted and rebuffed, treated with the arrogance that power, fatefully, induces. The immigrant was treated as all at once socially and ethnically (or racially) inferior. Overall, the experience of this double subordination was to have a long-lasting impact on political outlooks, generating mistrust, suspicion, and skepticism toward orthodox Marxist assumptions regarding the primacy of class struggle. Indeed, the Third World migrant could measure the weight of racist and colonial predispositions, standing in the way of working-class solidarity, dimming the glow of European intellectual enlightenment in all its manifestations, liberal but also socialist or communist. For culprits included not only the anticipated, namely, right-wing circles and apologists for colonial rule, but also the less so, parties of the Left who, out of nationalistic conviction or political convenience, refused to endorse the cause of independence.

But perhaps most important, migration to the metropolis resulted in contact with other Third World exiles. Being of the colonies and in Paris or London or Lisbon often meant enduring imperial domination in similar fashion, looking at things in the same way, and speaking in the same tone, half submissive, half defiant. It is in this sense that Third World solidarity can be viewed as the diaspora's offspring. I will have more to say on this when discussing Algeria, but for now a broad picture of Third Worldism's initial steps on the European continent will have to do. In 1900 the First Pan-African Congress convened in London, with later meetings in Paris, Brussels, and Lisbon. The movement, with its early emphasis on racial solidarity, attracted young activists from the West Indies, South Africa, then East and West Africa. Speaking at the first congress, William DuBois, a prominent Pan-African leader, boldly predicted that "the problem of the twentieth century is the problem of the colour line — the relation of the darker to the lighter races of men in Asia and Africa, in America and the islands of the sea."[9] In 1920 the

Soviet Union, another center of Third World activism, hosted both the Congress of the People of the Orient and the Communist University of Workers from the Orient. Tan Malaka from Indonesia, the Peruvian Carlos Mariategui, and Roy from India attended.[10] Then in 1927 the First Congress of the Anti-Imperialist League met in Brussels. In the eyes of many historians, this was when Third Worldism truly was born. Assembled at the congress were some 175 delegates representing 134 organizations and 37 "dominated or oppressed countries." The significance of the event was not lost at the time: The North African newspaper *l'Ikdam* proclaimed, "For the first time, more than 150 delegates representing a billion oppressed people, have met!"[11] Nor was there much modesty of purpose or of ambition. In a resolution adopted by participants, the congress stated: "One would have to be either demented or a miserable philistine in order to believe that today's civilization and the future of this world are a matter of concern to Europe and the United States alone. The independence movement of Asian, African, and American people, together with its expansion, is a true miracle. It alone can turn our planet into a civilized world. . . . It alone can turn a leaf in the history of the world . . . a history that, for the first time, truly will be universal, a history of all mankind."[12]

I have barely begun to explore the role of these and other metropolitan centers. Further research undoubtedly would underscore the role played by London — Basil Davidson, in his writings on Kwame Nkrumah, starts us on that path[13] — while the lives of Agostinho Neto and Amilcar Cabral point in the direction of Portugal.[14] But this much can be said: these meetings, gatherings of people from the world around, must have had an extraordinary impact and generated abundant enthusiasm. Out of them came some of the reflexes, instincts, intellectual predispositions, and what later would be called *langue de bois* (wooden references to "the popular masses," the "revolutionary Third World," etc.) but must have appeared quite alive, indeed quite new, at the time. For it was one thing to recognize that the peoples of Asia, Latin America, Africa, and the Middle East shared the same foe. It was quite another, requiring men and women of superior vision, to look beyond the unity of oppression to see the unity of purpose.

Oppression and social immobility in the colonial lands, racism and incipient Third World solidarity in the metropolitan centers: such ingredients form part of Third Worldism's peculiar ancestry. This convergence of social, economic, and cultural frustrations, along with a renewed sense of political possibility, was not fertile ground for Third

Worldism alone: it was the cradle of the far broader nationalist movements around whose banner the petty bourgeoisie in time would rally.[15] Which is to say that many other components would be needed for Third Worldism to succeed where and when it did. In all circumstances, however, a prerequisite was this colonial equation and the ambivalence it generated vis-à-vis tradition and modernity, class conflict and ethnic solidarity. The bearers of Third Worldism largely grew out of this environment, and in particular out of the stifling sense of cultural and economic immobility. In both North and South, it contributed to the emergence of a different perspective: on the Third World, its revolutionary potential, its relation to left-leaning European movements, on the role and nature of nationalism, religion, the peasantry, urban classes.

What was this new perspective? And how did it play out in Europe and in the Third World? Let us begin by focusing on Third World activists, those who remained at home to face the foreigners' claims to dominion and those who migrated to the lands of the European colonizers. In retrospect, we can see that in both cases, though to differing degrees, these intellectuals and militants experienced a combination of attraction to Western liberal thought, feelings of foreignness and cultural otherness, and social rebelliousness owing to economic subservience. These sentiments can perhaps best be understood as three powerful pulls, each tugging in a different direction, with Third Worldism emerging, in numerous instances, as the end result. Thus, at the root of Third Worldism, as I propose to show in the case of Algeria, one finds the fecund encounter between three seemingly incompatible ideological attitudes — assimilationist, traditionalist, and socialist. In their unadulterated version, the first strived for equalization between the colony (or dependency) and the metropolis via cooptation; the second called for separation between the two through an affirmation of the former's identity (e.g., by taking refuge in religion or custom); and the third aimed at transcending the dichotomy by engineering a universal working-class revolution.

As is apparent, each of these intellectual attitudes was defined in reaction to the colonial situation as described above and to the colonizer — by way of mimicry or by way of rejection — and each, therefore, had strong ideological links to Europe. Less apparent in hindsight is the *nature* of the relationship the three outlooks enjoyed both with the metropolitan centers and with each other. It is this, I believe, that helps account for the fact that none of the three was entirely discredited or thoroughly glamorized during the colonial period; instead, each, in some measure, influenced and shaped the contours of what ultimately was to emerge as Third Worldist ideology. Let me put this somewhat differently: assimilationism, traditionalism, and socialism offered three potential systems of representation to colonial subjects located at the various points of intersection between Europe and the Third World. And yet, none of these systems provided a fully satisfactory frame of reference to Third World militants, for each was encumbered by ambiguous relations to the European oppressor. At the same time, overt and covert affinities between the outlooks meant that Third Worldism not only could but would develop as a crossbreed of all three.

The relation to Europe first. In their respective dealings with the continent, of course, assimilationism, traditionalism, and socialism displayed varying degrees of proximity and cooperation, the "assimilationists" appearing closest, the "traditionalists" furthest away. The assimilationists had much to overcome in order to appeal to the Third World activists. They saw themselves as agents of progress but often were perceived as instruments of colonial domination; they preached democracy and constitutionalism, but what was heard was the traitorous voice of collaboration. Still, in its call for equality, assimilationism implicitly rejected one of the central tenets of colonial rule, European superiority, and appealed to those in the Third World whose social aspirations had been stifled on ethnic grounds. As such, assimilationism represented a type of threat that traditionalism, by reaffirming the distance between colonizer and colonized, did not.[16] Writing, as he does so well, about African responses to colonialism, Basil Davidson evokes this unbridgeable gap between the colonizer and what I have called the assimilationist: "Yes, to become civilized Africans they must cease to be Africans, but in order to ensure that this should duly and completely happen, they should never be allowed to become Europeans. They should wander in some no-man's-land of their own until the trumpet of destiny, at some unthinkable time in the future, should swing wide the doors of civilization and let them in."[17]

One would imagine that, in their radical opposition to colonial mores, the men of tradition enjoyed a more unsullied appeal than did the assimilationists. Yet they too were unable to fully capture the loyalty of Third World activists. I do not mean that the traditional chieftains, kings, or za'ims, did not possess the authority and prestige to stand up to the colonial masters; not at all.[18] Tradition and custom remained robust, but a simple return to the past could not successfully mobilize anti-European sentiment at the time, for it was the past, precisely, that

Europe so thoroughly had vanquished.[19] Plus, the ambiguity of the traditionalist response was such that European powers at times manipulated, massaged, and stroked the sentiments, power structures, and loyalties it inspired. This allowed them, intellectually, to justify colonial domination (in the name of Western civilization) and, politically, to perpetuate time-honored societal divisions (along, say, ethnic or tribal lines) that prevented the colonized from effectively challenging it. As Davidson observes, in opposing demands for equality, Europe increasingly relied on "the 'savage backwoods' for the purposes of colonial rule."[20] Likewise, in later times, with the end of their rule in sight, the British and the French would turn ever more ardently to hierarchies of "ancestral powers," in some cases going so far as to create, nourish, and strengthen them.[21]

The interaction between socialism and European colonialism exhibited similar ambiguity, dampening the ideology's appeal in the eyes of Third World activists. While in some respects the most radical challenge to the colonial order of all, for it called for social transformation not only in the colonial possessions but in the metropolitan centers as well, socialism also was the most familiar. Born and bred in Europe, it was at once threatening and strangely comforting, the mirror image of an enemy one had come to know, if not to enjoy.

Nor should one forget the uneasy coexistence between Marxism and socialism, on the one hand, and the Third World, on the other. I use the term *Marxist* guardedly in this context, for there is no single Marxist viewpoint to speak of. Still, I believe it fair to say that the perception of a superior, more civilized Europe was never far beneath the surface of Marxist thought. Some of Engels's least felicitous writings drew on the supposed distinction between the "energetic yankee" and the "lazy Mexican."[22] Not to mention his depiction of the colonial conquest of Algeria as "an important fact and favorable to the progress of civilization." The Bedouins, after all, were nothing but "thieves"; and "the modern bourgeois, with the civilization, industry, order, and 'enlightenment' [*lumières*] that he carries, is preferable to the feudal lord or the plunderer, and to the barbaric condition of the society to which they belong."[23] Lastly, behind the concept of "Oriental despotism" lay the belief that the "Asiatic mode of production" was synonymous with "stagnation and eternal misery, an incomplete entry into 'civilization'—incomplete, and partially failed."[24]

This equivocal tradition lingered on, affecting the socialist and communist parties' perspectives on colonialism. For with military conquest came a capitalist mode of production, which was viewed by many on the

Left as indispensable to the ultimate socialist revolution. As the Egyptian economist Samir Amin later would comment, this Eurocentric version of Marxism, by "claiming the universality of the succession primitive communism–slavery–feudalism–capitalism–socialism," suffered from "the temptation to extrapolate from the European example in order to fashion a universal model."[25] Undoubtedly, this Eurocentrism weakened Marxism's attractiveness to Third World militants.

Characterized as dependent on Europe for their economic development, poorer nations of the South also were depicted as politically dependent on European socialists for their eventual freedom. Speaking at the First Congress of the Third International in 1919, Trotsky summarized this position as follows: "The liberation of the colonies is possible only if preceded by that of the metropolis. . . . Capitalist Europe led the backward regions of our planet in its wake. Likewise, socialist Europe will come to the aid of the liberated colonies, with its technology, its modes of organization, its spiritual influence. . . . Colonial slaves of Africa and Asia, the hour of the dictatorship of the proletariat in Europe also will be the hour of your own freedom."[26]

Then there is the question of Marxism's apparent inhospitality to national, religious, or cultural factors. Especially to later-day exegetes, Marx's theory explained all of history's evolution as resulting from the conflict of classes possessing differing economic interests. Other explanatory factors that once had been deemed critical were reduced to mere expressions of underlying class consciousness or (but this was really the same thing) to instances of false consciousness. "The theory of nationalism," as Tom Nairn once put it, "represents Marxism's great historical failure," for "it is in dealing with the enigma of nationalism that 'Marxism' is inexorably thrust against the limits of its own western origins, its Eurocentric nature."[27] Claude Liauzu's analysis is in rough agreement: "The colonies," he writes, "were never one of the revolutionary categories of communism," precisely because of its mishandling of the national question.[28] For illustration he points to the French Communist Party's reaction to early manifestations of national sentiment in French North Africa, which it dismissed as archaic and inspired by the local bourgeoisie. The struggle for ethnic and cultural self-preservation thus became, in communist eyes and in fine colonial candor, little more than the rearguard fight to maintain outdated social structures.

In part because of these ambivalent relations vis-à-vis the colonial enterprise, none of the three most readily available systems of thought would command sufficient support to become the dominant mode of resistance, each proving far too easy a target for the other two. But just as none prevailed, none was thoroughly disqualified. Indeed, between the three outlooks were unexpected bridges and connections, a complicity of sorts, which helped preserve the legitimacy of all. More important, such links made possible the ideological blend to which we owe Third Worldism. Both socialists and assimilationists were seduced by systems of thought, whether Marxist or liberal, that were European in origin but universal in aspiration. Both took for granted the urgent need for Africa, Asia, or Latin America to break with their stifling past, and both identified the North with progress and modernization. Leaders of the assimilationist movement and men of tradition also enjoyed a sense of familiarity: both tended to come from similar conservative backgrounds, members of their society's sociocultural elite and intent on remaining there. The connection between the socialist and traditionalist perspectives, though perhaps more subtle, existed nonetheless, as the two provided the intellectual tools with which to reject the relations of subservience that one attributed to economic, the other to cultural, imperialism. The ideological trajectory of Amar Ouzegane, an Algerian who advocated communism before promoting Islam, is one illustration of this subterranean affinity. The path of Sultan Galiev, dubbed by his biographers the "father of Third Worldism," is another: a prominent Tartar who rose through the ranks of the Soviet Union's Communist Party before falling in disgrace, he attempted to unite Muslim populations under the twin banners of socialism and Islam.[29]

❖   ❖   ❖

That the omnipresent background of colonial domination in the South and ethnic and racial intolerance in the North should have shaped the mindset of Third World militants is hardly surprising. Less immediately obvious is the impact this mingling between North and South had on European thought. In the early twentieth century, left-wing Europeans were drawn to the essentially communist and socialist ideologies of radical social change that would find their most concrete expression in the Bolshevik revolution of 1917.[30] Yet Europe's colonial ventures and the Third World's resistance to them brought into question assumptions that had formed the kernel of communist and socialist thought—regarding the "natural" development of societies through predefined stages (feudal, capitalist, socialist) and the dominant role played in this development by economic, as opposed to cultural, forces. More precisely, colonialism posed the questions whether capitalism was an agent of progress or, rather, of racial and national dominance when it was thrust upon less developed societies; whether it was a necessary stage of economic development in all circumstances; and whether it ultimately would serve to check the revolutionary aspirations of the European working class by offering it new and vast possibilities for economic exploitation of a common enemy — the alien. To European left-wing movements, colonialism (and, it must follow, imperialism) thus proved highly unsettling. The destabilization of dogma can lead to various reactions. Some left-leaning activists or thinkers fended off the challenge, taking refuge in what remained of certainty, embracing the colonial endeavor wholeheartedly, albeit in some cases with misgivings concerning the means employed. Though it undoubtedly played a significant, if indirect, role in shaping Third Worldism, this nationalistic reaction is not one I am principally interested in here.

Third Worldism grew out of another type of reaction on Europe's soil, more open, some would argue, less sure-footed in the beginning to be sure. To many on the Left, the colonial and imperial experience exposed their rigid materialism and economic determinism to the national, cultural, ethnic, linguistic, and religious challenge. Among both colonizers and colonized, class solidarity faded when confronted with these other affinities. The French bourgeois and worker were united against the colonized, just as the Algerian *fellah* and the traditional landowner found common ground against the *colons*. Later the influence of the Third World would become more pronounced still: the concept of a cultural revolution, renewed emphasis on political voluntarism and on the role of the state as autonomous actor, and the search for new social foundations for the revolutionary project — the lumpen-proletariat, the socially excluded, and what many tellingly dubbed the "Third World within the First" — all were offshoots, to some degree, of the North's encounter with the South and of the ensuing questioning of the Left's long-held beliefs. Repression and resistance in the colonies had other unintended effects as well, leading to a reassessment of violence as a political tool, the legitimate violence of the oppressed being contrasted with what appeared to be the concealed, euphemized violence of the oppressor. At the risk of oversimplification, we might say that dealings with the Third World smoothed the rough edges of European left-wing thought, emphasizing novel variables — nationalism, religion, culture — and suggesting new attitudes toward power and dissent. When the certainties of old were severely tested by the experience of Stalinism and Soviet intervention in Eastern Europe, this new, some would say "virgin," ideological perspective would enjoy even greater appeal.

The point here is worth summing up. Third Worldism resulted as much from geographic as from ideological crossbreeding. To many Europeans who fashioned themselves as leftists, dealing with the Third World as colonial oppressors meant confronting old tenets with the power of nationalism and cultural identity. For Third World activists who found themselves at the crossroads between Europe and the less developed world, traditionalist sentiments, assimilationist aspirations, and socialist ideologies each exercised a powerful pull. Yet each bore the weight of perturbing questions (some more obvious than others) regarding its relation to the colonial enterprise at the same time that it represented a challenge (again, the degree varied) to that very enterprise. Ambiguous relations with Europe were duplicated by ambiguous relations with one another, each outlook having enough in common with its two counterparts to make possible the compromises, unforeseen alliances, and ideological conversions of which an Ouzegane or a Galiev offered illustrative examples.

❖   ❖   ❖

I have left out an important, some would say central, ingredient of the Third World's encounter with imperial Europe. It is a peculiar legacy, in some sense, for it was neither entirely material nor precisely intellectual. It was, rather, territorial: the space, or frame, within which Third Worldist activists would conceive of their efforts. I am referring to the paradoxical coexistence within Third Worldism of a broad, universal outlook and of the narrow, national confines it would run up against and, ultimately, embrace. Third Worldism at its very source was ecumenical, generated in part by feelings of solidarity among the oppressed. Europe's domination of all united all in reaction, and the capitals of the North were fruitful meeting grounds for generations of future leaders of the South. Ironically, contact with Europe also cultivated another territorial dimension, one whose ascendancy ultimately would overshadow the ecumenical promise of the beginnings. I am speaking here of the nation-state, the curious notion that territorial, cultural, and political identities, in order to reach the highest order of civilization, must exactly overlap. The term *nation-state* reflects this outlook, merging as it does the institutional arrangement of power (the state) with the source of its authority (the culturally or ethnically homogenous inhabitants of a given land).[31]

I have set this aside because nation-statism (as Davidson calls it) came closer to being blindly mimicked and imported by Third Worldists than practically any of the other intellectual paradigms with which Europe influenced the anticolonial, then post-colonial, Third World. Many historians and social scientists of the underdeveloped regions have explored the roads, tortuous and twisted, that nation-statism followed, taking it from nineteenth-century Europe to the twentieth-century Third World. And there appears to be widespread agreement: "Nationalism is a doctrine invented in Europe"; it is a "product of Western conditions" and "spread in Europe's train," so that people of the Third World have been "governed on European models." [32]

Nation-statism is one of the more vexing puzzles. The principal equation upon which it rests — between individuals, identity, and land — is both unquestioned and utterly arbitrary. Indeed, we have come today to accept, unreflectively it seems, the axiom that a land *belongs* to a people as a constituent part of its identity. Territory, in other words, has become thoroughly imbued and macerated with meaning, with "identity," so that there is now a specific Algeria, a specific Mexico, a specific France, as central to the being of their respective inhabitants as is their language, religion, or culture. Manas calls this the "territorialization of attachments," and it alone explains why Palestinians will fight for Palestine, Jews for Israel, Armenians for a land they call Armenia — and no substitutes will do. [33] This phenomenon is a riddle, for it was not always so: the feudal order, nomadic cultures, and religious empires, to name but a few examples, hinged on allegiances and affiliations that transcended land. Accordingly, in the case of the Christian empire the only territorial limits were those set by the scope of religious conversion; in the case of Islam, the ever-expanding *dar al-Islam* (land of Islam) by definition lacked predetermined territorial boundaries; up until the end of the eighteenth century the Kurds' identity was unattached to land; the predominant allegiance of the nomadic Tuaregs in Africa, as well, was anything but territorial; and so on. [34]

This is not a book on nationalism or the birth of the Third World nation-state, so it will do justice to neither. That said, some discussion of the roles nation-statism has played in the Third Worldist consciousness, intermittently as ideal, political necessity or as booty, yet at all times as the unquestioned, "natural" framework of politics, is needed. I use *ideal* to evoke the sense, apparently deeply ingrained in the minds of Third World activists at the turn of the century and afterwards, that the modern age belonged to nation-states. Davidson describes this conviction in the case of African nationalists: "They studied the portents and examined the entrails of Europe's national-liberating struggles; and they found in them sure prophesies for colonial Africa and for the nations that Africa must build if it was to realize its destiny," for "they had lived through a time when nationalism glowed with the brilliance of a manifest destiny, and spoke with the tongues of the angels."[35] Only by forming nation-states, in other words, could the Third World emerge from backwardness and realize its full destiny. Nation-statism would be smuggled out of Europe despite the fact that Europe was the imperial power—indeed, *because* it was the imperial, which is to say more successful, power.

But nation-statism was more than a goal; it was viewed as the only possible means for challenging colonial rule. Again, as a result of European domination, the legitimacy of anticolonial movements was measured in terms borrowed from the imperial continent—national awareness and nation-building. Here we move into the arena of political necessity or expediency, the idea that to contest the colonial order, "no other instrument of liberation was thinkable" but the assertion of a homogenous national identity and the aspiration to create state structures in order to represent and defend it.[36] This was of particular importance to anticolonial movements, for they would try to oppose Europe's enterprise in the name of the very territorialization of identity upon which rested the European order. Hence, it was by "claiming a territorial affixation that dominated units . . . would succeed in asserting the legitimacy of their cause."[37] Algerians, Guineans, and Indians, among so many others, would call for more than political equality or social justice; they would demand territorial restitution, a "restoration" of their privileged attachment to land. Colonization, in other words, could (and would) be challenged on the ground that it severed the sacred bond that linked a people to its identity and to the land on which it lived.

European powers, who remained the holders of authority and distributors of legitimacy, felt comfortable only when seated across from other nation-states. Speaking of the Arab nationalist movement at the turn of this century, Albert Hourani aptly captures this process: "The idea of Europe as the exemplar of modern civilization . . . was powerful. . . . To be independent was to be accepted by European states on a level of equality, . . . to be admitted to the League of Nations. To be modern was to have a political and social life similar to those of the countries of western Europe."[38] As different roads were ignored—some that would respect ethnic or cultural diversity, others that would strive for vaster federations, Pan-Arabism, the Islamic *umma,* or the contemplated federal unions in Africa—the nation-state was viewed as "the only feasible route of escape," for all "knew what happened to persons 'without a nation.'"[39] Whether this was a correct assumption—and there is considerable argument that it was not — is beside the point. (In any event, it cannot be dismissed simply as an irrational assumption. By the recognition it confers and the benefits it bestows, the North in myriad ways has elevated and continues to elevate the status of nation-state above all else. One need look no further than to the standards of membership in the United Nations or other international institutions to grasp this point.)

Third Worldist militants, like other, ordinary nationalists, would feel the need to appeal to a national consciousness, with independence being simply its recognition and the emergence of a nation-state its just reward. In an irony few at the time fully appreciated, they welcomed Europe's artificial territorial carving up in the same breath as they purported to reject its legacy. I turn again to Edward Said: "That is the partial tragedy of resistance, that it must to a certain degree work to recover forms already established or at least influenced or infiltrated by the culture of empire. This is another instance of what I have called overlapping territories: the struggle over Africa in the twentieth century, for example, is over territories designed and redesigned by explorers from Europe for generations."[40] This helps explain the Third Worldists' tendency, so often encountered, and later described in some detail in the Algerian case, to discover nations and national structures in their distant past. Proof of such a history was seen as the ultimate anticolonial argument, evidence that — like Europeans — Africans, Asians, and Arabs were entitled to their nation-states.[41]

Finally came the era of national spoils. Even if the ideals that irrigated early nation-statism were severely contaminated, and even if the achievement of independence logically should have diminished the need to appeal to European territorial or political categories, nation-statism was doomed to survive. For by that time certain groups had conquered positions of power within the new administrative and political structures, and they were not about to abandon privileges and prerogatives merely because the nation-state had been imported from the North and proved a less than satisfactory arrangement. Far too much was at stake now. The nation-state had made its way into the Third World, with importers probably not fully aware of its consequences. But it was there to stay.

But to return to Third Worldism. The search for its origins takes us back, for now, to one of the intersections where Europe and the Third World came face to face. I look at the encounter between Algeria and France not in its totality — far from it — but to the extent that it sparked a set of novel ideological positions on both sides of the Mediterranean, and insofar as it generated a Third Worldist web of individuals, ideas, and, not least important, taboos. I have chosen the cluster formed by Algeria and France, not because it necessarily is the finest example of what I am describing, but because it constitutes an inviting observation point, full of bravado, drama, and a healthy sense of self-importance, without which history is more difficult to recapture. A number of actors in Paris and some of their counterparts in Algiers felt strongly that destiny was in their hands, and the feeling was concealed neither in writing nor in speech — of which there was plenty.

CHAPTER 2

On the Origins of Algerian Third Worldism

The telling of history is always, in some sense, an act of creation and an act of power. Narration coats orderless and entropic events with layers of meaning. It connects past to present where continuity is desired or severs the two where rupture is in demand. The teller, at day's end, is master of historical legitimacy, here recognizing the inevitable and authentic, there decrying the deviant or treacherous.

Witness the official chronicle of the Algerian war of national liberation: nine men frustrated with partisan political maneuvering and intent on putting an end to indecision and inaction (the rupture), guided by the everlasting will of the Algerian people and firmly anchored in its midst (the continuity), launched the Front de Libération Nationale (FLN). Weaved into this narrative, as its structure, plot, and characters proved again and again, were the negation of the country's most recent political history and the idea that the break with the present was but a resumption of ties with Algeria's authentic past. This was the tale of a people's unyielding, monolithic aspirations finally at one with its leadership, with bridges to ancient times and references to historical protagonists (the emir Abdelkader, Boumaza, El Haddad, Mohammed el-Moqrani, and others), all the more revered for being politically harmless. At best, assimilationists, traditionalists, and communists, who until then had occupied the center of the political scene, made fleeting appearances, and then only as roadblocks on the path to national liberation. In this context, Mohamed Harbi, a keen observer of Algeria and a participant in its anticolonial war, evokes the FLN's "myth of the tabula rasa," the notion that it represented a clean break with the political parties that pre-

34

dated it.[1] The assimilationists, led by Ferhat Abbas and generally known as the *évolués* or Jeunes Algériens; Ben Badis's *ulémas,* who belonged to a wider Arab movement for Islamic reform; the Algerian Communist Party (PCA); and Messali Hadj's populist and proindependent Mouvement pour le Triomphe des Libertés Démocratiques (MTLD), were depicted in the FLN's and then the independent state's self-serving narratives as irrelevant or, worse, harmful. That this was more legend than reality was there for all to see, but then who was going to say so?

Non-Algerians gave it a try. William Quandt, C. H. Moore, Elbassi Hermassi, and Janet Zagoria, for instance, wrote extensively on the dominant political parties of the pre-1954 era.[2] Yet, hampered by a lack of original sources and by the independent state's rhetorical flourish, most observers disregarded the ideological links between these parties and the FLN, instead accepting the view that the founding of the FLN represented a fundamental break with the past and the triumph of a new breed of nationalist militants, not liberal, modernizing, assimilationist, or Islamic, but "radical."[3]

The myth that the FLN represented a new beginning, and all other political parties a discarded past, had a purpose, which was to discredit the FLN's potential rivals and, ultimately, erase them from Algerians' memory. The Front, like the independent Algerian state to which it gave rise, worked hard at refashioning the nation's history. In the official discourse, history began with the FLN or with Algeria's faraway past. Abbas, Messali, and, to a lesser extent, Ben Badis belonged to the silenced in-between.

The myth had many less intentional effects. One was to create the impression that the FLN lacked any degree of ideological coherence. Observers who viewed the emergence of the FLN more as a quantum jump than as an incremental change were prone to describe it as pragmatism bereft of conviction. And with good reason: if, as Algeria's official historians asserted daily, the founding of the FLN was unrelated to the efforts of its predecessors, it was hard to understand how its members could share much beyond copious impatience and an itch for action.[4]

Later, another consequence would be to strengthen the notion that the FLN's Third Worldism was an alien graft. Indeed, when things were going reasonably well, the FLN's self-proclaimed novelty was cheerfully acclaimed. Radical innovation was an occasion for celebration, an end to partisan bickering and the promise of a different future. But let decay and disillusion set in, and novelty quickly becomes aberrant, unnatural.

Of decay and disillusion there had been plenty, to put it mildly; hence the tendency among Algerians and foreigners alike to denounce Third Worldism as an unwelcome import.[5]

The effort to conceal the nation's history also deprived subsequent generations of Algerians of any real understanding of political pluralism and political competition. Ultimately, this perhaps was the most damaging effect of all. The occultation of the role played by Abbas, Messali, and Ben Badis in drawing the contours of Algerian nationalism narrowed the scope of imaginable alternatives to which Algeria's youth could turn once the FLN had lost their favor. Raised with the legend of political uniformity, they naturally would substitute one orthodoxy for another, the Islamism of the FIS for the Third Worldism of the FLN.[6]

My own view is that the creation of the FLN is best understood, not as a sudden revelation or the outburst of pent-up frustration, but as the logical product of existing political parties. Algerian Third Worldism grew out of a dual process: the surface disqualification of existing political parties, followed by the subterranean integration of much of their apparently contradictory discourses into the ideology of the FLN. The move from multiple parties to single front occurred, in short, not by mere successive elimination but by ideological evolution, the circulation of ideas, ideological exchange. As the French historian and political scientist Jean-Claude Vatin argues, pre-1954 parties and movements were "elements that, in various degrees and at various times, have helped reach a more acute political awareness. They also have favored the spread of national demands, less fragmented and divided than traditional analyses have led us to believe."[7]

Little by little, the buried history of pre-1954 political parties has reemerged, thanks in large part to the painstaking efforts of historians and to Algeria's skittish version of glasnost. Books and articles have reassessed the role of the various branches of the nationalist movement and engaged in a more realistic intellectual genealogy of the FLN. Participants in this enterprise include Ali Mérad, whose study of Ben Badis's reformist movement attests to the lasting impact of the *ulémas* on the FLN.[8] His views received further confirmation in Mustapha Benabdellaziz's work on the history of education in Algeria and in Ernest Gellner's investigation of Algerian puritanism.[9] The task of reevaluating the communists' actions was undertaken by Henri Alleg.[10] Abdelkader Djeghloul and Gilbert Meynier provide us with new insights on the role of Algerian intellectuals, whether religious or Westernized, as does more recent work by Benjamin Stora and Zakya Daoud.[11]

Among the most interesting efforts have been those focused on the various political parties formed by Messali Hadj, the Étoile Nord-Africaine (ENA), the Parti du Peuple Algérien (PPA), the MTLD, and the Mouvement National Algérien (MNA). The historical documents, political studies, and biographical works suggest two main conclusions. First, as Harbi has shown, there is a marked similarity between *messalisme* and the contemporary ideology of the Algerian state.[12] Second, the evolution of Messali's own organizations illustrates the powerful influence of other intellectual outlooks — religious, communist, and reformist.

How did these parties come to articulate the policies, ideas, or cultural proclivities that, once spirited away and altered by the FLN, would come to dominate the Algerian scene? To make sense of this process, some history is necessary. I begin, for context, with an overview of the colonial enterprise and then move to an examination of the political movements of the period between the two world wars. What I most want to show is how Third Worldism emerged, not by outside imposition or domestic import, but gradually, through the natural dynamic of social, economic, and political influences.

❖   ❖   ❖

Sheathed in a rhetoric of rank and honor, impelled by the prosaic calculus of economic and political interest, the French conquest of Algeria began in 1830. The government spoke grandly of avenging the insult suffered by its consul, stricken with a fly whisk by the dey of Algiers in 1827; it spoke loudly of securing maritime commerce, allegedly disrupted by piracy along the Algerian coast; yet it thought more quietly of domestic popularity, economic expansion, and competition with other European countries for colonial acquisition.[13] The occupation's initial years were marked by ambiguity and confusion, as advocates of an expansionist policy locked horns with those harboring second thoughts about the invasion itself. By 1834 a compromise of sorts — known as *occupation réstreinte,* or "limited occupation" — had been reached: France would control the main coastal towns, and the country's interior would be left to native rulers. But the policy was wholly divorced from local realities, opposed both by Algerian Muslims and by European *colons* (five thousand out of a total Algerian population of roughly three million), fierce partisans of greater French control.

Continued resistance to colonial conquest and pressure from the *colons* gradually led to a policy of thorough occupation. The most effective opponent to this strategy in its early period was a young marabout, Abdelkader, who at the age of twenty-four had been designated emir by a number of tribes from the western part of the country. Although initially cooperating with him, going so far as to recognize his sovereignty over western and central Algeria, France soon would see in the emir a vexatious obstacle and potential threat. French forces under General Bugeaud fought a fierce and crucial war against Abdelkader from 1840 to 1847, when the latter finally surrendered. While resistance to the occupier never ceased, as the insurrections of 1864–65 and 1871 demonstrate, the emir's struggle arguably was the most significant prior to 1954.

John Entelis possibly overstates the case when he remarks that Abdelkader "successfully united the many warring tribes under his command, and he succeeded in creating a Muslim state in the interior."[14] At the very least Abdelkader came the closest to establishing a "national" Algerian state prior to the war, for which he can thus accurately be described as a "state-builder and promoter of the public realm [la chose publique]."[15] Nonetheless, his legacy remained a mixed one: on the one hand was the embryonic state, or "tentative d'état," as historians Ahmed Koulakssis and Gilbert Meynier nicely put it;[16] on the other hand was the unstable balance between competing centrifugal forces (religious brotherhoods, tribes, clans), which the emir alternately sought to suppress or to manipulate.[17]

Militarily conquered, Algeria would undergo a series of more profound social and economic changes. One was the widening expropriation of land and the growing European presence; another was the undermining of traditional social structures (tribe, religion, etc.); a third was the set of discriminatory practices put in place by the French, both in Algeria and in the metropolis. The combination of these factors was a prescription of sorts for Third Worldism: the alien presence led Algerians to seek refuge in comforting sanctuaries; at the same time, the corrosion of more traditional settings and intensified feelings of discrimination paved the way for urban organizations that blended tools of cultural identification with those of social revolt. The impact of these processes in France was lesser, of course, especially in the first half of the century, but it was not negligible. The colonial mores that infected even socialist and communist parties alienated a number of militants. In contrast, the emerging Algerian nationalism, particularly when combined with a strong social agenda, enjoyed an unblemished appeal that some in France (Algerians in exile as well as left-wing Europeans) would find hard to resist.

The raw physical impact of colonialism was paramount. The emergence of Algerian nationalism and Third Worldism can be understood only in the context of this territorial, human, and cultural encroachment that, although probably magnified in Algeria because of the duration of colonial rule, was duplicated in countless other Third World countries. In 1870 the settlers owned 480,000 hectares of land; by 1900 they owned 1,480,000.[18] Eventually, French colonists would appropriate approximately 2.5 million hectares of the country's most productive land.[19] The European community, which numbered 109,000 in 1847, reached 272,000 in 1872, 578,000 in 1896, and 829,000 in 1921. In 1954 about 984,000 Europeans, most of them French, lived in Algeria. Officially, Algeria had become an integral part of France.

The expropriation and privatization of lands forced impoverished Algerian peasants to work, indeed overwork, the land they managed to retain. As a consequence, the ecological balance of extensive regions was upset, leading to deforestation, land erosion, and further economic trauma for the rural classes.[20] But it was the new legal regime imposed by the French that more directly undermined and destabilized traditional rural society. The Sénatus-consulte, established in 1863 under Napoleon III, broke up many ancestral social structures, particularly the power edifice of prestigious religious families. The effects, as Eric Wolfe explains, were double: "On one hand [the Sénatus-consulte] destroyed in one blow the entire pyramid of over-right which had guaranteed the livelihood of the lowly cultivator but which had stood in the way of making land a freely circulating commodity. On the other hand it threw all land held by Muslims upon the open market, and made it available for the purchase or seizure by French colonists."[21]

The Warnier Act, which replaced the Sénatus-consulte, had a similar intent, including the "suppression of common lands (*arsh*) and the disruption of family holdings still remaining undivided."[22] As Larbi Talha shows, this transformation contributed to the "monetarization" of exchanges and the growth of a rural proletariat that possessed either no land or so little that it could not survive on its meager resources.[23]

Most important for our purposes, the pauperization of rural areas and the disruption of traditional power bases severely crippled the old dominant classes, precipitating the political and economic decline of the once powerful rural aristocracies and religious brotherhoods. The monetarization of the economy, which went hand in hand with "the constitution of individual property and the authorization given to everyone to sell lands which are given to him as shares[, was] the death warrant of the tribe."[24] Moreover, as society was being urbanized, most of the relatively small urban bourgeoisie, intellectuals, *cadi,* tradesmen, and shopkeepers, were ruined by the disruption of traditional commercial channels and the decline of the craft industries. At the same time, sizable sections of the poorer rural strata reacted to their predicament (made worse by increased French taxation, known as the *impôts arabes*) by fleeing the countryside, migrating either to Algerian cities or, especially after 1920, to the French metropolis. Kielstra notes that "in the 1930's, about half the Algerian 'peasantry' . . . consisted of underemployed rural proletarians, while most of the migrants to the cities and to France had also been recruited from this group."[25] They became part of the ever-expanding world of the new urban space — the slums, the ghetto, the inner city.

As habitat and geographic environment were radically altered, so were the structures of cultural sustainment. Traditional educational and religious networks were a privileged target of the French *colons:* mosques became churches, hospitals, or museums; religious lands were confiscated; and the teaching of Arabic was severely curtailed.[26]

There were more blatant forms of ethnic or cultural discrimination. To be a Muslim meant having unequal access to the franchise, employment, education, citizenship, or justice. Such inequity affected rural and urban dwellers alike, members of the working classes as well as members of the elite, and would play a critical role in the (relative) unification of the nationalist front around a moralistic vision of social equality.

In short, the nature of Algerian resistance to colonialism was shaped largely by five distinct features of French rule: (1) disorganization of conventional social bases of authority; (2) economic pauperization, especially affecting the rural areas; (3) systemic socioeconomic discrimination; (4) migration, both to the cities and abroad; and (5) disruption of the country's cultural foundations. As Michael Gilsenan puts it, such radical changes "combine to transform life in different ways and different rates and rhythms, sometimes with brutal suddenness, sometimes in modes that are not immediately directly perceived but, as it were, creep up on a society, setting in train processes whose nature and outcome neither colonizer nor colonized can grasp."[27]

✤   ✤   ✤

For the purposes of this work, we need to focus on those processes set in motion that would modify the practice and experience of political power. That such modifications would occur is not difficult to understand: by undermining traditional power structures — political, ideological, and economic — and imposing alternative forms of domination —

more central, more uniform, generally subordinate to the interests of France and French capitalism — colonialism could not but affect Algerians' traditional attitudes toward authority and resistance.

These traditional attitudes were composed, generally speaking, of the dual legacy of Ottoman rule and a particular practice of Islam. During the period of Ottoman dominion, power was largely decentralized, highly dependent on tribal organization, and conducive to fragmentation and infighting. The degree of central political control declined gradually as one moved away from Algiers, with forms of public regulation, such as taxation, varying considerably from region to region. As Vatin remarked, "*Le pouvoir* does not have the same content, nor the same expression, in Algiers, Constantine, Médéa, or Oran."[28] Authority was "diluted,"[29] scattered over a space that was central in name only. Simultaneously, attitudes toward power were shaped by Islam, or more precisely by the particular religious practices of the time. France conquered an Algeria whose piety was essentially rural, organized along tribal lines and religious lodges (or brotherhoods) that were dominated by spiritual masters. These were not so much unstructured as they were structured to coincide with the diffused character of power in precolonial North Africa.[30] Of particular relevance to our inquiry, the brotherhoods embodied attitudes toward politics and authority in which the source of power was viewed as thoroughly extrinsic to the body politic itself. In other words, legitimacy was perceived as a function of religious designation and lineage and bore no relation to, say, notions of popular sovereignty or popular will. Political appeals therefore would be addressed to this external authority, to the Muslim community, the *umma muhammadiyya*, the *dar al-Islam*, or, at a more prosaic level, to the family, tribe, region, or professional group — and not to popular legitimacy, the people, or the nation per se.[31]

This dual heritage of Ottoman rule and rural Islam was reflected in the early, aborted efforts to resist the colonial onslaught. Predictably, the practice of opposition and the practice of power had developed in tandem. Decentralized authority had fostered localized resistance, grounded in regional religious brotherhoods, tribes, and the like. Likewise, the character and pervasiveness of religious beliefs inspired chiliastic forms of rebellion, reliant on the anticipated coming of a savior. Writing of pre-twentieth century revolts against the French, Gilsenan argues that they all "featured the annunciation of the coming of the deputy (*khalifa*) of the Mahdi or the Mahdi himself. All of them were framed by the conviction of an ultimate crisis of the community, an ultimate crisis of the end of time, beyond everyday time, just as action to confront it would transcend everyday action and its rationalities."[32] Thus, throughout the nineteenth century, resistance to the French endured, stubborn, tenacious, yet inevitably fragmented, disorganized, and hovering somewhere between the political and the transcendental, never quite sure whether to confront or retreat into isolation.

Such dissent no longer could prevail. French colonialism introduced novel forms of centralized domination and control against which traditional modes of resistance were thoroughly ill suited. As Gilsenan put it, the religious (Sufi) brotherhoods "did not, and could not, transform a series of social units whose character was defined by internal opposition and particularistic patterns of rights, identities, and allegiances into a unified social movement capable both of defeating the French and of grasping the full nature of colonialism and its outworkings."[33] Political decentralization and the otherworldliness of sources of legitimacy amounted to a colossal mismatch between forms of resistance and the exercise of colonial power. Moreover, French colonialism itself had severely strained and undermined the political, economic, and social structures upon which such resistance had been based, thereby compounding the maladjustment of traditional resistance to colonial oppression with the incapacitation of the resistance itself. With the authority and economic position of the brotherhoods in decline and no alternative power structures yet in a position to replace them, economic and even political competition between them intensified. The disorganized dissent thus was plagued by, and in turn perpetuated, Algerian social divisions and dislocations produced by French rule.

In retrospect, Algerians' failure throughout the nineteenth century to turn back the *colons* is hardly cause for surprise, a result of sharp technological but also political imbalance. Reflecting on the common features of Algerian revolts during this period, Belkacem Saadallah writes: "All of them were led by a *murabit,* head of a politico-religious fraternity; all of them failed to achieve their main goal: driving the *roumi* (foreigner) out of Algeria; . . . all lacked discipline and organized action, and relied on individual leadership."[34] In the end, "'rebellious' Algeria took refuge wherever it could, in plains and gullies, on plateaux and peaks."[35] If "rebellious" Algeria was to triumph, it would have to adapt.

By the early twentieth century, signs of change were becoming increasingly discernible. As tribal society and its network of domination, hierarchy, and support deteriorated, as the relationship to work, land, and neighbor underwent profound alteration, notions of power and dissent — Gilsenan calls them "patterns of hierarchy and authority"[36] — could not remain stable. Koulakssis and Meynier note that by 1916–17 a different kind of insurrection was taking place in the southern part of the Constantinois: "Indeed, and this is a completely new factor, the religious brotherhoods were not at the origin of the insurrection. . . . Resistance to the French is, among the rural population, proportional to dissatisfaction with overly subservient religious leaders. . . . If young men linked to the brotherhoods take up arms against the French, it is precisely in order to restore their political image [*se donner une virginité politique*] vis-à-vis the rural population."[37]

For the transition to Third Worldism to take place, however, what needed to occur next was a relocation of the political center of resistance from countryside to city, where intricate and strained interactions with the French were paving the way for a reorganization of Algerian society and for the development of a radical nationalist outlook. For there, under the contradictory influence of the assimilationists, the *ulémas,* and the communists, radical nationalism, new notions of political legitimacy and power, and novel ways of interpreting relations between civil and political society took root.

Such reconstruction of course takes time. It involves redefining the space that is occupied and the individuals within that space over whom authority is being exercised; it involves, indeed, renaming them: Is the pertinent space the village, the city, the Algerian nation, imperial France, the *umma?* Are the individuals fellow believers, comrades, compatriots? New and different ways of contemplating holders of power also are required. The question then becomes to whom to appeal — to the family, the *za'im,* the military commander, God? And does one even appeal? Or does one pray, supplicate, petition, demand, or summon?

The events that took place in Algeria in the interwar period and thereafter affected all of these categories. Turning the colonial discourse against itself, assimilationists would speak in the name of an Algerian identity that, in the image of its French counterpart, was territorially defined. Even as they accepted the premise of European presence, they developed an ethnonational narrative in which Algerian soil was peculiarly Algerian, possessing its own identity, its own interests, and, it followed, its own representatives (who, of course, were the assimilationists themselves).[38] In short, the assimilationists (along with others) contributed both to the territorialization of identity and to the notion that legitimate power meant the proper representation of the Algerians' common interests.

To the assimilationists' contribution, communists and followers of Messali Hadj (commonly referred to as *messalistes*) added a social component, more romantic and moralistic than scientific, but social nonetheless. In their narrative, what brought Algerians together was not only a common religion, language, history, or territory but also a common social agenda. More than compatriots but not quite comrades, Algerians — and most notably their legitimate representatives — were being defined by their common dedication to the pursuit of social and economic justice.

Finally, the job of harmonizing the emerging political and social outlook (though not necessarily subscribing to it) with the tenets of Islam would largely be left to the *ulémas*. Rejecting the "tribal and peasant" Islam of the brotherhoods,[39] the reformists introduced an essentially urban, middle-class religious perspective within which the FLN's Third Worldism could fit quite comfortably.

Assimilationists, communists, Messalists, and *ulémas* had different intellectual pedigrees, yet they were offspring of the same set of sociopolitical conditions — rapid, disordered urbanization; worsening economic conditions; and persistent frustration of political and social ambitions — and precursors of a single, Third Worldist outlook.

❖   ❖   ❖

Third Worldism came to Algeria as ideologies often do. It erupted with suddenness, and so one scrambles for explanations having to do with men or women of exceptional vision, the cathartic power of violence, or historical whimsy. But the apparent abruptness conceals the long simmering. By the time Third Worldism emerged victorious at the end of the war of national liberation, its silent march had already rearranged old assumptions and made way for the new. The starting point for much of this was the period immediately after World War I, among city dwellers and within political parties.

The war had sent several thousand Algerians to the front and taken the lives of some twenty-five thousand. Service in the military, while it brought together colonized and colonizer, did not resolve the tension inherent in their relationship, as native Algerians faced forced conscription with lower pay and longer years of service than their European counterparts. But the conditions Algerians experienced upon their return made things far worse. Witnessing intense poverty and Algeria's unchanged subservient status, returning soldiers would fuel sentiments of hostility toward the French.

Paradoxically, native members of Algeria's elite saw these contradictions, coming on the heels of joint victory in the war, as providing an opportunity to appeal to reason and to France's sense of justice. In this sense, the early years after World War I were a turning point, the moment between brutal colonial conquest and the routinization of colonial rule, when violence ceased being the privileged means of contact and the promise of equal status had yet to be wholly betrayed, when many viewed accommodation with the French as a chance to be seized and separation as a fate to be avoided. Accommodationist sentiment was particularly strong among members of Algeria's urban elite, a group that has come to be known as the "reformists," assimilationists, *évolués,* or Jeunes Algériens, who fashioned themselves the occupiers' deserving partners (*interlocuteurs*).[40]

Two men symbolized the reformist movement: the emir Khaled and Ferhat Abbas. To mention them together is to invite controversy, for their places in Algeria's official historiography hardly could be further apart. History, seldom kind to the vanquished, has treated Abbas with particular scorn. So long a political leader in his country, Abbas would be branded a collaborator, described as a Gallicized elitist. In contrast, Khaled would be hailed as a father of the nationalist movement.[41] The difference, however, has far less to do with beliefs and actions than with age. Khaled died in 1936, his reputation untarnished by the merciless intra-Algerian political battles that would surround the war of national liberation. Abbas had no such luck. Named president of the FLN's first provisional government in 1958, he found himself at the center of ruthless power struggles, from which he never fully recovered.

Politically, Abbas's and Khaled's approaches to France were remarkably similar. Neither was a nationalist as that term now is defined, and neither advocated Algeria's outright renunciation of her cultural identity. Indeed, as Vatin has argued, "There never was, strictly speaking, an integrationist current, aimed at the absorption of the Algerian by the French community."[42] Khaled's rallying cry was equal citizenship for Muslims, not independence. As for Abbas, he fit very well the French mold of the petty bourgeois, provincial republicanism of the time.[43] He believed in social justice — but in a "noblesse oblige" sort of way — in the virtues of moderation, and in the importance of remaining in touch with "the common people."[44] Above all, he was a reformist through and through who had faith in the power of persuasion, in compromise, and in the possibility of a Franco-Algerian understanding under which France would retain her possession and Muslims, their identity. Abbas, it should be noted, steadfastly refused to be naturalized, for that would have implied abdication of his "personal," Muslim status.[45]

In other words, the reformists understood assimilation to mean equal political rights under French rule but also fidelity to one's Algerian identity. Symbolic means helped express such sentiments, as headdress and wardrobe revealed the quiet endurance of one's identity amidst colonial turbulence. This clearly was true in Khaled's case, photographs of whom illustrate his "miraculous resemblance to [the emir] Abd-el-Kader," his grandfather. This was a studied, calculated likeness, which he underscored by wearing traditional garb — a white *gandoura,* a pair of *burnous,* a *gannur* on his head, and a pair of red leather boots covering his feet.[46] But it also was the case for the latter-day Jeunes Algériens, such as Ferhat Abbas, who generally wore the Ottoman fez and met for conferences or lectures on the Islamic day of prayer.

Although the question whether Abbas and his followers were "authentic" nationalists, colonial puppets, or naive dupes is not unimportant, I would rather leave this debate to others.[47] I am interested in different matters, such as how the reformists' discourse played out on the anticolonial stage, what portion of their outlook was retained by the FLN, and what portion the Third Worldists discarded.

Khaled, Abbas, and the other *évolués* influenced the Third Worldist ideology of the FLN in various ways. The first was in their role as conduits for French ideals, those very same standards to which they would hold the colonial power: freedom, equality, justice. Torn between, on the one hand, their loyalty to Algeria and recognition of an irreducible Algerian identity based on Islam and the Arabic language and, on the other, their attachment to a certain idea of France, they vacillated between resistance and dialogue, rejection and mimicry.[48] The tension comes through vividly in Khaled's words, striking today for their submissiveness, noteworthy then, no doubt, for their audacity: "The people of Algeria are all, without distinction as to religion or race, equally children of France and have an equal right in her home. . . . The desire we have to create within the bosom of France a status worthy of us and worthy of France is the best proof that we are good Frenchmen and wish only to strengthen the bonds that attach us to the mother country."[49]

Like Abbas years later, Khaled honored the France of 1789; yet both asked how in the twentieth century it could "reconcile ideas of freedom, of equality, of brotherhood, of human rights . . . with practices based on oppression, arbitrariness, and racial discrimination."[50] The most loyal image of France inspired its most uncompromising rejection, for such practices belied the ideals of progress while tarnishing their natural venues: democracy, equality, the enlightened state. Emir Khaled experienced the contradiction with special keenness, having suffered discrimination in his military career, in which he never rose above the rank of captain.[51] But the limitations were painfully felt by the *évolués* as a whole, so that rather than becoming the "body of communicators between French and Algerian communities" that some had envisaged, they became "the most visible victims of a blocked system organically incapable of permitting the merger of the two peoples."[52]

The reformists' discourse, all intention aside, had the effect of putting France face to face with its own contradictions. In Jacques Berque's phrase, Abbas proposed to take France at its own word: "prendre au mot, si l'on peut dire, l'histoire coloniale."[53] The assimilationists, as it were, did not favor assimilation with just any France, but with the mythical France of 1789, and thus France would never view assimilationism as a trustworthy ally. And, indeed, inconsistency between ideals of equality and freedom and the oppressive reality of colonialism led Abbas and his followers on a path from moderation to quasi-nationalism. Years later, he would write that "by agreeing to locate the struggle on the field of 'legality,' [I] had chosen the road that seemed to me the shortest."[54] France having littered the route with countless obstacles, emancipation would have to take place without it — in other words, against it.

Second, the reformists opened Algerian politics to new questions of legitimacy and power. To begin with, they believed their legitimacy derived from civil society. Viewing themselves as members of the same social and cultural caste as the French, they first offered themselves as partners, expecting recognition to derive from sameness. But they soon would realize that there was little to expect from France, certainly not treatment as coequals in the governance of the Algerian people. And so they would turn to the national social body as the foundation for their political power. Like the French, they belonged to the social and intellectual elite, or as Djeghloul put it, capturing the European filiation, "diffuseurs de lumières."[55] Unlike the *colons,* they represented Algerians, and this was what entitled them to a share of power. Speaking in 1926, Khaled claimed that "to deny [my] status as authorized representative [*mandataire*] of indigenous Algerians is to try to stop the rays of the sun."[56] Likewise, Abbas held that only the educated Algerian elite could "interpret the genuine feelings of the masses."[57]

By proclaiming themselves legitimate representatives of "indigenous" Algerians, they implicitly accepted two postulates: first, that identities could be territorially circumscribed (recall our earlier discussion of nation-statism); second, that Algerians enjoyed not only a particular attachment to their territory and specific characteristics but also shared interests. Add to this the notion that the people must be sovereign and the job of a political leader was cut out: to decode and then to further those interests. To the ethnonational equation between land, people, and identity was thus added a fourth component, the representative, the presumed embodiment of the other three, the virtual sovereign-in-waiting.

Nor was this just any kind of political representation. It was one that owed far more to Rousseauesque, Jacobin notions of a univocal general will than to ideal-typical American conceptions of pluralistic democracy in which "the word 'people' retained the meaning of manyness."[58] Of this Jacobin political understanding, Hannah Arendt wrote, "The very word 'consent,' with its overtones of deliberate choice and considered opinion was replaced by the word 'will' which must indeed be one and indivisible. . . . The enduring unity of the future political body was guaranteed not in the worldly institutions which these people have in common, but in the will of the people themselves."[59]

In short, for assimilationists to speak of the representation of indigenous populations was implicitly to collapse the concepts of popular sovereignty and popular will into one. The exercise of popular sovereignty would mean, then, the translation of the people's unanimous aspirations. In the discourse held by the *évolués,* political legitimacy no longer was exclusively a function of the divine word, or even of social and economic rank. Rather, opposition to the French grew out of the people's will, deciphered and decoded by its representatives. Whether or not the claim that the assimilationists represented the Algerians' will was supported by fact — in all likelihood it was not — is far less interesting than what it presupposed and, in due course, made possible. To borrow Clifford Geertz's dichotomy, legitimacy was moving from its "intrinsic" to its "contractual" variant, from "one which sees authority inherent in the ruler" to one in which authority is "conferred upon [the ruler] in some occult and complicated way, by the population he rules."[60]

The art of political leadership became a form of ventriloquism: the people spoke through their representative. In Khaled's plebiscitarian approach to political activism, the people were "convened" to "enthrone" their leader; by so doing, they were supposed to "enthrone the enthronement."[61]

The political shift had its semantic expression. Khaled, far more than his predecessors, made use of a resounding, emphatic "we," never encompassing but often opposing "France" or "the French." A grammatical object in its antagonistic relation to the colonial power (as in "France opposed us"), the pronoun was used chiefly as a grammatical subject exemplifying the invigorated, unified community (as in "we demand"). In other words, it is not only in its objective, passive relation to France but also in its active presence and political activism that the Algerian community came to life in Khaled's rhetoric. Koulakssis and Meynier conclude that Khaled's discourse "gave birth," symbolically, to an Algerian citizen whose attributes were a sense of purpose and of national unity. Within this ethnically and racially polarized setting, Algerian society emerged from Khaled's "transclassist" language as essentially unified.

Yet it would be a mistake to disregard the social component of the *évolués'* outlook. The discourse of the Jeunes Algériens transcended class distinctions, quite obviously, but in ways that prefigured the Third Worldist conception of a solidarity based on shared experiences of injustice and oppression and a common yearning to do away with both. Conduits for French Republican ideals, for notions of popular sovereignty and popular will, the *évolués* thus also provided a passageway for social awareness. This is the third point, namely, that emancipation from colonial rule, even if it did not mean full independence, was to incorporate a social dimension, in other words, to fulfill the social aspirations of the people as a whole.

Koulakssis and Meynier call this an implicit populism, and the description fits rather well. Colonialism, with its racist underpinnings, produced a kind of *peuple-classe,* which the assimilationists called upon and invoked. At a time when the term Third World had yet to appear, the Algerian reformists made repeated reference to the French Revolution of 1789. The cultural and social elite began to think of the country as an "ethno-cultural Third Estate," indiscriminately exploited by colonial rule.[62] In the early 1920s Abbas went so far as to write, "The native cannot forget the hell from which he came and in which live his brothers. If that is to be a communist, then I am a communist."[63] Years later, when asked whether the Moroccan resistance to the French could be likened to French resistance to the Germans, Abbas pointedly replied, "It is not on the French resistance that we should model ourselves, but on the stubborn struggle of the European proletariat against omnipotent capitalism."[64] Significantly, barely a year after the French economist Alfred Sauvy coined the expression *tiers monde,* Ferhat Abbas would paraphrase Sièyes' famous statement: "Le Tiers-Etat comme celui de la France de

1789 sait qu'il n'est rien alors qu'il devrait être tout. Il demande aujou-rd'hui au Ministère de l'Interieur de ne pas entraver sa ferme volonté d'être quelque chose" [The Third-Estate, like that of France in 1789, knows that it is nothing even though it should be everything. Today it asks the interior minister not to stand in the way of its firm intention to be something].[65]

Consider as well Khaled's earlier condemnation of "colonization" as a form of "capitalist expansion using the most illicit and barbaric means"[66] or his support for "Lebanese, Syrians, Algerians, Tunisians, Moroc-cans . . . people of all races, enslaved by a handful of roughnecks and bourgeois."[67] Never mind that this was not intended as a class discourse or that there was much that separated the reformists' outlook from the overtly proletarian and communist ideology professed by someone like Messali in his early years. The point, rather, is that the assimilationists' painful awareness of their subordinate status nudged them toward the idea of the *peuple-classe,* which the FLN later would articulate with such success. Lurking close by the reformists' project, though hidden by considerable haze, was thus the Third Worldist image of the world proletariat.

I do not mean to downplay the significant differences between the FLN's Third Worldism and Algerian intellectual reformism. They mani-fested themselves at various times and in various circumstances, some-times acquiring particular acuteness, as when the debate turned to the ultimate end of the anticolonial struggle and to the choice between vio-lent and nonviolent means. In many instances they led to overnight con-versions; Abbas, for example, was a remarkable political contortionist, unable to pronounce the name Algeria in the 1920s yet willing to become the first president of the Algerian government in exile in 1958. Equally as important as the nature of these differences between reformists and Third Worldist activists, however, is the extent to which the disagreement af-fected the relationship between the FLN and Algerian intellectuals. As Djeghloul comments, "For the intellectuals of latter generations, their predecessors' inability to . . . comprehend the national question created a guilt complex of which they are more or less aware. . . . The position of Algerian intellectuals remains largely . . . subordinate."[68]

Thus, while much was borrowed from the intellectuals' discourse and practice, and while they played an important role in shaping Algeria's modern political landscape, their political status was undermined by their cautious inaction and, at times, their embarrassed silence. In his memoirs, Messali Hadj recalled with bitterness that whereas "in Morocco and Tunisia the students . . . and the intellectuals took the people's destiny in their hands . . . in Algeria this honor fell upon the workers, the peasants, the 'modest' classes of our society."[69] This perception, perhaps as much as anything the intellectuals in fact did or did not do, would have profound repercussions on the Algerian ideology and praxis of power.

❖   ❖   ❖

Although Algerian intellectual reformism, with its ambiguous stance toward colonialism, was treading on dangerous ground, it contributed to the introduction of a new conception of authority. In addition, as I have suggested, it intimated the outlines of a social dimension to political power. But these were only outlines; it was up to others, namely, the French Communist Party (PCF), its local affiliates, and, chiefly, the populist movements of Messali Hadj to fill them in. I referred earlier to the role played by the immigrant community and the international communist movement in adding a social and internationalist component to the Third World's national awareness. In the Algerian case, the junction between the immigrant community and European left-wing thought occurred through the Messalist movement, the vast turnover in the immigrant population ensuring that the impact was not restricted to France, but rapidly made its way to Algeria.[70]

My argument is twofold. First, *messalisme* must be viewed through the lens of its complex relation with the Communist Party, made up in equal parts of thankful dependence and proud defiance. Second, this double-edged relationship, together with the rough congruence between nationalist and communist thought, gave rise to the Messalists' equivocal discourse on the social question. The nationalistic outlook of Messali's organizations, principally the ENA and the PPA, embodied ambiguous social concerns, reflected both in the source of grievances (heartless colonialism viewed as an avatar of capitalism) and in the ultimate goals of political activism (social transformation to help the anonymous "little man").[71] Dampened and dulled, the Messalist version of class conflict in turn would be ideally suited to the populist project of the FLN.

As for the first point, between 1914 and 1918 some 900,000 people were brought from the colonies to France, 525,000 as soldiers and 220,000 as workers. While most left as the war came to an end, several thousand subjects of the colonial empire remained on French soil by 1925. French factories and cafés became meeting places for persons from various continents; workers shared their woes and students, ideas.

Claude Liauzu, in a rare account of the origins of Third Worldism, observes that France became the "colonial political center of the '20s." "Despised or enticing," he writes of the French capital, "it is fascinating, for it is where history makes progress. Imperialism appears as the master of time." He concludes, "Paris is one of the stages and one of the keys of [the Third World intellectuals'] march to power."[72]

Although they may have had a stage, Third World immigrants still lacked a script. For the road to postcolonialism was fraught with uncertainty. So many questions paved the way—what alliances to strike, what objectives to pursue, let alone whether it was even worth going there at all. Anticolonialism, in short, was not a natural venue; nor, for that matter, was it a straightforward one.

At the outset, communist and other left-wing organizations offered many appealing answers. They offered hospitality, some material assistance, and at times a half-listening ear. While various French associations tried to take charge of colonial migrant workers, the PCF's heavy presence and activism in the workplace gave it an obvious advantage. Moreover, the Russian Revolution continued to generate awe and enthusiasm within the immigrant community.[73] The commmunists offered, as well, suitable ideological reference points from which Third World militants could make sense of their purpose. Their struggle became an extension of the battle for social justice and equality, and racial segregation another expression of economic exploitation. The politicization of the colonial émigrés thus coincided with their social *prise de conscience,* Third World cultural and social awareness thereby becoming early partners.

Finally, early linkage with the PCF exposed immigrants from French possessions in North Africa, Indochina, and black Africa to one another. Emigrés admittedly were setting up their own groups, independent of the communists. But these were more sociocultural networks of aid and assistance than they were political organizations. In addition, they tended to be strictly geographically based: the Second Pan-African Congress, which met in Paris in 1919, Fraternité Africaine, the Association Pan-Africaine, as well as a number of groupings for émigrés from French Indochina. In contrast, the PCF sponsored political organizations that transcended geographic boundaries. The gathering together of individuals from various areas of the Third World made possible, in time, the emergence of a global Third Worldist vision.

The communists' record of solidarity with Third World militants nonetheless was mixed. Their assistance to migrants was unmatched, and they often were the only organization to which émigrés could turn.

At the same time, they insisted on maintaining ultimate control, pater-nalistically limiting the autonomy of their Third World allies. The PCF never quite viewed the colonies as having interests of their own; rather, they were considered peripheral to the central fight against capitalism, periodically useful, frequently irksome. As a result, communist support for the anticolonial cause—splendidly rhetorical yet painfully fluctuat-ing—was a function of broader geopolitical considerations. In France these vacillations paralleled quite faithfully the Party's and Moscow's shifting stances toward the French government. When a Popular Front strategy was in vogue, Third World activists were urged to temper their positions; as class struggle resurfaced, radical anticolonialism was cham-pioned once again. An exchange between Nguyen Van Tao and the PCF is revealing of the communists' state of mind: In 1920 Nguyen Van Tao complained to the Party's Central Committee that "during all this past period, our colonial work has been absolutely defective. While crucial events are taking place within the various colonies of the French Empire, we have not been able to achieve our aims: to support the struggles of our oppressed brothers; to unmask the colonialists' acts of pillage and murder." The PCF dryly replied that indigenous populations were "po-litically and ideologically weak."[74]

Similar ambivalence was manifest in the PCF's attitude toward the several organizations it helped set up. The Comité d'Études Coloniales was established in 1921 and became a point of contact for several promi-nent Third World activists, including Nguyen Ai Quoc (better and later known as Ho Chi Minh); Hadj Ali, the Algerian; and Hetza, from Ko-rea. But as the Comité began to stray from the conventional idea that the North would pull the South out of dependency and underdevelop-ment and to advocate the radical view that the South would free the North of capitalism, the PCF took matters more closely into its own hands. The Comité was replaced by the Commission Coloniale (1924–34), an organization whose ties to the Soviet Union and to the PCF were far tighter. The Party's interests were the Commission's guiding princi-ples at all times, so that the anticolonial struggle generally was relegated to the background.

The most successful Third World organization was the Union Inter-coloniale. Founded in 1921, it included immigrants from Indochina, Madagascar, Guadeloupe, and Martinique as well as from black and North Africa and would succeed in attracting revolutionaries, national-ists, and assimilationists.[75] Though it too was strongly influenced by the Communist Party, it enjoyed far more autonomy than either the Comité or the Commission, and its relationship with the PCF would be accordingly strained. Assessing the Intercoloniale's impact, Liauzu explains, "The exchange of experiences, expressions of solidarity among dominated people, the awareness of a link between the destinies of metropolitan workers and colonized people, added a new dimension to national liberation movements."[76]

With the Intercoloniale came its news organ, *Le Paria*. The newspaper was of paramount importance, a molder of Third Worldism in its formative years, fashioning and spreading certain themes, as well as a forecast of things to come. Here, already, were the makings of a Third Worldist mythology, different from, if inspired by, the communists' own. First, by linking in a single paragraph or thought areas ranging from Indochina to the Maghrib, Black Africa, and the Middle East, *Le Paria* contributed in no small way to the political geography of Third Worldism. Third World solidarity, the interconnectedness between national movements locked in a struggle against the same foe, at once became necessary, desirable, and, most of all, natural. Second, and equally noteworthy, *Le Paria* introduced its readership to a new inventory of idols to worship and heroes to imitate: Gandhi, Emir Khaled, Sun Yat-Sen, Abd el-Krim. Finally, and in sharp contrast to its communist counterparts, it exalted the history of Third World "nations," contrasting today's wretched colonial status to the golden age of yesteryear. All along, of course, the militants' efforts could not escape a sense of paradox and ambivalence. Ambiguity began with the setting itself: here were members of the colonial possessions pleading in the language of the oppressor and on his soil, laboring for attention, clamoring for joint action. Ambiguity also was reflected in the newspaper's name itself: Was the pariah the social outcast seeking economic equality, the ethnic untouchable demanding fair treatment, the political exile striving for acceptance and assimilation, or, depending on the circumstances, all of the above?

The Intercoloniale's tense interactions with the PCF were another indicator of the limitations inherent to the relations between communists and Third World activists. French communists could not bring themselves to wholeheartedly embrace the anticolonial cause and in particular were deeply reluctant to espouse the call for independence. This recalcitrance had many possible sources — the subordination of the colonials' interests to those of the Soviet Union; remnants of a French nationalism they never fully overcame; or, more simply, shrewd political calculations. Its consequence was to render impossible an effective alliance between the PCF and the nascent movements of the Third World. Touching on

the case of Algeria, Albert Hourani, the renowned Arab world special-
ist, nicely sums up this attitude: "Even French communists would have
thought rather in terms of a more complete and equal absorption of
Algeria into another kind of France, although they could hope for a different relationship with the Muslims and could lend their weight to protests against specific acts of injustice."[77] Another element must be added,
and that is the Party's evident discomfort with the influence religion
continued to exert on many Third World activists, notably those of the
Arab world. In the Party's view, the Koran was simply "a system aimed
at preserving reactionary social relations."[78]

Messali and, in a broader sense, Messalism were offsprings of this
rich, tangled environment: the migrant community, the early attraction
and link to the Communist Party, the frustrations this entailed, the contacts it allowed with other Third World militants, the ultimate split to
which it led. Messali Hadj himself was a migrant worker, and his favorite source of information rapidly became *L'Humanité,* the Communist
Party's daily.[79] Reading through its columns, he learned of the 1920 rail-
way strike, which, he gleefully noted, united "Indonesians, Indochinese,
Chinese, Egyptians, Syrians, members of the [Tunisian] Destour, and
many others." It was, he explained, a "small revolution."[80]

In 1926, the PCF and the Union Intercoloniale were instrumental in
the founding of Messali's Étoile Nord-Africaine. Although the origins
of the ENA are uncertain, Jean-Claude Vatin convincingly maintains
that "there is no doubt concerning the affiliation with the internationalist anti-colonial movement. The first groups that composed the Étoile
came directly from the Union Intercoloniale, from the Ligue contre
l'Oppression Coloniale, and from the Internationale Syndicale Rouge."[81]
By 1929, according to Emmanuel Sivan, sixteen of the ENA's twenty-
eight-member Central Committee belonged to the PCF.[82]

Yet, as suggested above, relationships between Algeria and the French
(later Algerian) Communist Party turned sour. From the outset, French
communists saw assimilation as the indigenous population's best chance,
the fable being that it was their passageway to civilization, history, socialism, or whatever else the PCF could dream up. Thereafter, the chronology of the relations between the Party and the colony at times read
like the story of a crumbling marriage.

The 1920s were marked by the Sidi Bel-Abbes incident, during which
an Algerian section of the PCF rejected one of the eight requirements
for membership in the communist Third International, namely, "to support, not in words but in deeds, every emancipatory movement in the

colonies; to demand the expulsion of metropolitan imperialists from the colonies."[83] This was by no means an epiphenomenon; rather, it was an index of the PCF's "colonial socialism" and, more generally, of its indifference to the colonial question. At times, silence would have been preferable to words. In 1921, for instance, the Algerian Federation of the Party asserted that "French civilization, the highest expression of humanism, can be the instructor of all races who genuinely want a guardianship [*tutelle*]."[84] As Harbi acidly comments, "'L'internationaliste' algérien sera le frère jumeau du nationaliste français" [The Algerian internationalist will be the French nationalist's identical twin].[85]

Nor did this condescending attitude spare Messali, whose radical nationalism was received with growing suspicion and distrust. Gradually he emerged "not as a partner of the PCF but as a political leader," autonomous and active. Clearly annoyed by this trend, the PCF chose to reduce its material assistance to the ENA and, in the case of its general secretary, Messali, to suspend aid altogether. Torn between its procommunist and "Messalist" wings, the ENA became embroiled in a power struggle whose outcome foreshadowed the decline of communist influence in Algeria.[86]

In the 1930s, squabbles turned into open conflict. The PCF first used its influence to bar the ENA from access to anticolonial meetings. Then it began issuing *El Amel* as a counterweight to Messali's *El Oumma* and established a supposedly "Algerian" party, the Parti National Révolutionnaire (PNR), to counteract his growing influence.[87] In 1933 the ENA general assembly passed a resolution forbidding dual membership in the ENA and the PCF. Finally, in 1937 the PCF approved the government's banning of Messali's party, a warm-up for its decision to grant French Prime Minister Guy Mollet special powers in the war against the FLN some two decades later.

Such proximity and betrayal provide background for my second observation, namely, that Messali served as a conduit for a bleached version of Marxism to enter Algeria and, further along the way, the FLN. First, tension with French communists caused Messali and his followers to become disillusioned, leading them to distance themselves from the PCF's rigid ideological tenets and contributing, in turn, to an "Algerianization" (by which I mean an emphasis on the religious and the ethnic) of the ENA and successor parties. From its inception, the ENA had insisted on its religious identity but had remained quite vague about its role.[88] In contrast, its Algeria-based successor, the PPA, repeatedly drew attention to the indivisibility of the Algerian nation and the Muslim community.[89] Second, and conversely, the potency of nationalist and Islamic feeling among Messalists accentuated the rift with the PCF. In the end, the allegedly ecumenical project of internationalist socialism was seriously imperiled.

Even to the untrained eye, Messali's vision did not look particularly Marxist: the exploited classes had become the *peuple-classe,* and the toiling proletariat, the faceless masses of the Third World. As Mohamed Harbi put it, "Revolution rests not on class struggle but on the people in its plebeian sense, the working class being amalgamated with the poor in general, without a specific identity or specific interests."[90] Indeed, as time went on, and with the Communist Party's influence diminishing, Messali's discourse would become less and less class-oriented. The central figures ceased to be the factory worker and poor peasant; the core demands no longer were "the confiscation of large properties monopolized by feudal landlords allied to the conquerors" or "the return of the seized land to the peasants."[91] With the move from France to Algeria, the sociological basis of the Messalist movement would turn from migrant worker to the intermediary social strata (the urban petty bourgeoisie), the lumpen-proletariat, and the peasantry as a whole.[92] The very name of the party that replaced the ENA in 1937, the Parti du Peuple Algérien, betrayed its social and political goals. It aimed to be the party of the united people, casting aside class struggle in favor of the struggle between colonizer and colonized and substituting vague, broadly phrased demands for the ENA's more programmatic approach.[93] As Harbi describes it, the Messalist outlook consisted of a confused mix of "anticapitalism wrapped in nostalgia for an Islamic golden age and use of a socialistic verbiage."[94]

Still, Messali's lasting influence imparted a sense of social commitment to the FLN that was passed on to the independent Algerian state, though at times more as rhetorical packaging than substantive policy. The early collaboration between communists and Third World militants, of which he was an ardent proponent, undoubtedly was important to the future of Algerian national movements. After all, there was nothing obvious in the ideological path of Third Worldism; and contact with social convictions, a class discourse, a socialist agenda, and men and women who held all of the above was far from inconsequential. Third Worldism retained a respect for the centrality of social struggle and social justice and a reverence, often bordering on the burlesque, for the so-called urban proletariat. Much of this might have been little more than political chatter, but even chatter can influence, mold, and — why not? — subvert policy.

As it were, Messali's masses were defined in social terms; they bespoke the unanimous aspiration for social justice and dignity. Various names have been given such Third World composites of national (or religious, ethnic, or other) sentiment and quasi-socialist conviction — "marxist nationalism" (Anthony Smith), "nationalisme marxisant" (Maxime Rodinson), "objective Marxism" (Abdallah Laroui) — and each more or less does the trick.[95] In the case of Algeria, Messali (though not him alone) made it impossible *not* to think of politics as the attempted resolution of the social question. From beginning to end, as Messali once put it, "poverty speaks one language, and wealth another."[96] Messali could achieve this because, probably more than that of any other prominent Algerian of his time, his life was braided into the everyday existence of his people — the bitter and the sweet, the routine and the daunting.

Yet the influence of communist or socialist modes of thought extended beyond social awareness. One area concerns the vision of history, the seductive, if paradoxical, wedding of human willpower to historical necessity. Messalism offered its followers, in a rough and simplified form, the Marxist-Leninist project of a world in which one's political actions were part of history's predesigned course, or in François Furet's nice phrase, in which one could "participate in history without the uncertainties of history."[97] Nor was the future that was contemplated at the end of history's road just any future. Drawing a parallel between communism and the Third Worldist variant of nationalism, Smith writes that "they both present a tripartite historicist vision of humanity's progress: a present state of oppression, a period of transition and transcendence, and a vision of the messianic future." Through struggle the conditions permitting oppression will be superseded, the end result being a state in which "man will realise his true social nature and identity. . . . The nationalist sees the true state as one in which the nation has become a regenerated community, a genuine fraternity."[98] Thus, in the ENA's newspaper, *El Oumma,* romantic references to the past stood side by side with utopian images of the future.[99]

Another parallel with the communist movement has to do with concepts of power and the role of the party. Self-proclaimed representative of the people's aspirations and interests, the Messalist party replicated in rough fashion communist partisan structure: ideologically, in the search for a general will (of the working class in one case, of the people in the other); organizationally, in its unanimous expression and channeling via democratic centralism. In the ENA, the *comité directeur* was the equivalent of the political bureau, sections were clones of the Party cells, and the Central Committee was elected from a single list presented to the

Congress.[100] The charismatic leader, it is true, had replaced collective leadership. But, for that matter, could not the same be said of countless "orthodox" communist parties?

The third point of convergence relates to the chosen instrument of social emancipation and progress. Practically speaking, both the communist and the Messalist perspective, each in its own way, focused on the state (existing or yet to be) as the expression of the popular will and guarantor of its attainment. The state was a demiurge that, in Messali's familiar language, would grant social rights, ensure progress, and guide each and all.[101]

There is a price to pay for failure and the disenchantment it sparks. For Algerian Third Worldism the penalty has been a comprehensive reassessment of the experience itself. I have described one form of reevaluation, namely, the notion that Third Worldism was an ideology imported from the West that, once it had been thoroughly rejected, gave way to the more authentic system of thought that was Islam. There is another, though it may be no more than a subtle variant. It is the view that the socialist discourse of the ENA, the PPA, and the FLN was nothing but an adroit camouflage, one that probably deceived some of the protagonists themselves. When the misleading verbiage is dusted off, there can be no mistaking the true inspiration behind the nationalist movement: it too is Islam.

Many Western observers appear comfortable with the latter version, partly, I guess, because it comports with their impression of Islam: conquering and manipulative, omnipotent yet conniving. But even putting aside such pointless stereotyping, the argument gives reason to pause.[102] Khaled made extensive use of religious symbols and rhetoric. The Messalist movement too contained many of the ingredients that are commonly identified with an Islamic conception of the social order: dreams of an Islamic community and consensus, belief in the primacy of the group over the individual, or the use of a religious language of exclusion. The enemies are *manfouqiin* or *manhourfiin,* those who doubt or those who deviate. As Stora remarks, "the slogan becomes a religious mandate; the final aim, a prophecy; the propagandist, a preacher."[103] For his part, Ferhat Abbas once described the PPA as a "politico-religious sect."[104]

Nor should one too eagerly dismiss the idea that the Algerian masses might have reinterpreted Third Worldist discourse in their own, pious way, so that it might have meant one thing to the Western observer and another to them. Maxime Rodinson points out that during the anticolonial struggle foreign dominators were infidels, just as the glory of the Algerian nation, in whose name the struggle was waged, was, for the most part, the glory of Islam.[105] Thus, Algerian Third Worldism, shrouded as it was in quasi-socialist language, may well have been seen through religious lenses. Confirmation of this thesis might be found in Messali's discourse, which not only had religious overtones but explicitly and loudly affirmed its Islamic lineage and faith. The same can be said of the discourse of Ahmed Ben Bella or Houari Boumedienne, the first two presidents of the independent state.

Is there, then, such a thing as Islamic political thought? A project that, beyond socialistic bombast and adornment, constituted the Algerian revolutionaries' true agenda? In my view, the answer to both questions clearly is no. I will have far more to say on the subject in subsequent parts of this book, but some form of explanation is warranted now. Western observers — those who have been called Orientalists — are so entranced with Islam, so willing to view it as monolithic, that they tend to confuse reality with their phantasms. Hence the talk about Islamic polities or political organizations, as if that sufficed to identify and characterize the polities or organizations involved.

Yet Islam no more prescribes a given political attitude or project than do other religions. It is, rather, a set of beliefs, some of which touch on issues of social organization, political action, legal mores, or morality but which overall do not impose strict limitations on action. It is, in other words, a system of loose constraints, which is to say a system one can invoke to justify a wide assortment of policies, at times even wholly contradictory ones. Islam, to be sure, does not leave politics unchecked, and some political opinions or attitudes might quite plainly transgress the religious code. More often, however, it acts as a rough frame of reference and provides the vocabulary to explain and vindicate political action. The point being that the restrictions Islam implies are for the most part malleable, leaving considerable room for maneuver, and that it does not dictate a definite stance toward state power or popular rebellion.

Consider, for example, the two stances that historically have been dominant in the Muslim world, justified by reference to the same Islamic texts. On the one hand is the "argument of necessity": the earthly order by definition is not a divine order, *mulk* (legal authority) is not the *califate* (legitimate Islamic government), *amr* (order) is not the *qanuun* (law), nor the *sultan* (physical authority) the *qur'aan* (moral authority), yet it is necessary to obey the existing political authority. While fundamentally evil, ethically illegitimate, based on the "mere enjoyment of power . . . through the use of brute force," on "extortion, servitude, and immorality," the postcalifate state is the only realistic order. "Islam, as ethical requirement, and the state, as natural organization, belong to two different orders," the one legitimate but "utopian," the other based on coercive force, but necessary. In this view, the relation between religion and politics is one of exteriority. As Laroui writes, "The state and the community [the religious *umma*] do not contradict, but rather totally ignore, each other."[106]

On the other hand, thinkers and activists have defended opposite attitudes by reference to the very same system of beliefs. Here, religion is by essence rebellious, since the nonreligious state is by essence amoral, devoid of the califate's ethical dimension. The conservative obedience of the first school of thought gives way, in this instance, to a radical critique on religious grounds. "Utopia" is the reverse side of "realism," and only the immediate imposition of an "Islamic" government (still to be defined) can be legitimate. Such an attitude can be highly destabilizing, since any order, including one that claims to be religious, can be challenged on these grounds. Here the political and the spiritual come face to face, implacable opposition taking the place of neutral disregard.

That Khaled, Messali, Ben Bella, and Boumedienne continuously professed their religious allegiance and even cast their actions in religious terms is therefore of little practical significance. A more useful effort is to look at the *type* of Islamic discourse in which they engaged, and this brings us back to the question of the origins of Algerian Third Worldism. For although Algerian Third Worldism was not a convenient cover-up for Islam, it grew out of and expressed a specific conception of religion and of its function.

My argument has two parts: first, the social and political conditions faced by Algeria at the turn of the century led to the rise of religious reformism in general and of the *ulémas* in particular, an evolution that had serious implications; second, the *ulémas* in turn influenced the nature of religious and political discourse in Algeria. Their conceptions of power and authority implied what could be taken as a secularization of Algerian politics but more accurately represented a modification of the interaction between the religious and the political, between religion and state power.

Reformism was Islam's response to European colonialism. With Europe's intrusion, Geertz writes of the Arab world, "the symbols of legitimacy, the loci of power, and the instruments of authority were rudely dissociated," so that the religious leadership was directly undermined. The challenge was met with a combination of reform and return to the past, an attempt to "assimilate the great achievements of modern European civilization, the while reviving the classical Arab culture."[107] Rejecting both the utopian and the realist attitudes outlined above, reformists invoked the tenets of Islam in an attempt to reconcile the moral and the pragmatic functions of political power. Al-Razeq (1888–1966), one of the most prominent reformist thinkers, thus argued that political power should be assessed in terms of "reason, the experience of other nations, and political rules. . . . Nothing forbids [Muslims] from . . . coming up with the rules of their kingdom and the organization of their government in conformity with what human minds have invented recently, and with what the experiences of nations have proved to be the most solid principles of government."[108]

The religious reformists' contribution to the emergence of a new conception of the state and political power has been variously interpreted. Whereas Albert Hourani evokes an "Islamic positivism," a progressive concept of the "rights" of the people "vis a vis their rulers," Laroui proposes the notion of an ethical, or "moral," theory of the state, and Badie of the transformation of the state into a locus devoted to the "creation" of "the common good."[109] But all three agree that for the reformists the state need not be patterned after the religious califate in order to be legitimate and that it need not be obeyed simply because it exists. Legitimate and illegitimate rule can thus be of this world, a function of popular will, a manifestation (or betrayal) of popular sovereignty.

In Algeria, religious reformism, or *salafiyya,* made its way through the Association des Ulémas. The movement faced formidable obstacles, for, as Gellner observes, "probably no Moslem country was more completely dependent on the rural holy men than was 19th-century Algeria."[110] Sufi lodges, or *zawiyas,* saints, and marabouts were dominant in the early years of the French conquest. They embodied both syntheses of the spiritual and the political referred to above (utopia and necessity), alternating awkwardly between the two in an attempt to adapt to the colonial presence. At times the full force of religious conviction would propel the lodges into absolutist opposition; at other times they would withdraw into quasi seclusion, opting for the detachment befitting those scornful of the things of this world. But neither comportment provided adequate defenses against the colonial onslaught: militarily outgunned, the brotherhoods also were culturally unable to mount a long-term resistance to the French on their own terms.[111]

The *colons* ruthlessly undermined the material bases of the religious groupings' authority, directing their efforts primarily at the "dislocation of a whole series of relations and practices of production and property rights that are the basis of social life."[112] Rural pauperization, the disruption of tribal landowning patterns (recall in particular the role of the Sénatus-consulte), among other acts of societal mutilation performed by the *colons,* contributed mightily to the marginalization of the religious orders and to their decline as a meaningful language of resistance. They were losing their basis of economic and cultural power and, it follows, their instruments of social and political leverage.[113] Gilsenan calls this "reach[ing] for the heart of society," and the expression is well chosen.[114]

The inability of lodges and brotherhoods to effectively resist had a good deal to do with the articulation of Islam and politics within which they operated. "All of these movements failed," writes Gilsenan, "not only in the mere fact of military defeat and disintegration. They all failed to resolve the contradictions inherent in attempts to achieve both a permanent revolutionary state or condition outside time, in which mundane actualities are irrelevant if indeed not treated as nonexistent, and at the same time to act in the world by subordinating it through the force of the apocalyptic vision, which must take on physical, military form yet which at root anticipates that it is the vision itself that will guarantee the destruction of the unbelievers."[115] By the end of World War I, the religious lodges and brotherhoods were caught in the midst of a spiraling, inexorable decline. Between the two world wars, the Rahmania in the east, the Taibia in the west, and the Tidjania in the south lost approximately a third of their membership.[116]

These deep transformations were conducive to the advent of a new political expression of faith. This was the shift from an "islam refuge," a sheltered, sanctuarylike Islam, to an "islam jacobin," a centralized, urbanized Islam, national in scope, that, as its name indicates, bore the imprint of European contact.[117] "For an atomized, mobile, uprooted population [the saints'] usefulness was limited, at best," writes Gellner. "Sufism," he concludes, "is the opium of the tribesmen, reformism of the townsmen."[118]

The result was not that Islam, its intellectual resources, moral suasion, or social authority abruptly came to an end. What I argued earlier is of special pertinence here: Islam is a codified system of signs, but a loose one, versatile and generous in the uses it permits. God, the Word, and the faith remained the same, but their relation to the mundane, that is, to the political, was to change radically. The whole of the *ulémas'* work —

and, in his capacity as their chief spokesman, Ben Badis's — was to offer a different interpretation of religion and its rapport with the temporal, yet one still consistent with the principles of Islam. At first, sermons and addresses were framed in exclusively theological and doctrinal terms, the statutes of the Association des Ulémas professing a distaste for politics. The aim, it was solemnly proclaimed, was to achieve "spiritual leadership"; and Ben Badis pledged that the movement had nothing but "respect" for France's "government and laws."[119] The *ulémas'* main concern was to maintain Algeria's Muslim identity, not to achieve its independence. Ben Badis, particularly in the 1930s and 1940s, insisted on the distinction between "ethnical nationality" [*jansiyya qawmiyya*] and "political nationality" [*jansiyya syassiyya*], the former expressing Algeria's timeless identity, the latter the vagaries of history.[120]

Soon, however, the *ulémas* would turn to the political realm. And there they would stay, battling the Messalists and the Abbasists for legitimacy and leadership. Ben Badis once lamented that "today there is not a single orator who . . . speaks without claiming that he represents the entire Muslim community . . . that his words are the very expression of the *oumma*," an insightful observation made all the more revealing by his comment, which followed almost without a pause, that he spoke "in the name of the majority."[121]

Unlike the declining religious orders, the *ulémas* brought the earthly and the spiritual into direct contact, spreading the view that a national, political legitimacy was consonant with Islamic precepts. Hence, to a large extent, the reconciliation between religious discourse and nationalistic practice, between traditional religious culture and, as the slightly misleading expression has it, "secularized" political practice. Religion remained a vibrant part of politics, which was "secular" only in comparison with the practice of the Sufi lodges and only insofar as political power was now framed in terms of popular legitimacy. Throughout, however, harmony with Islam was proclaimed by Abbasists, Messalists, and *ulémas* alike.

The true irony of the *ulémas'* contribution, then, was not so much that they removed religion from politics but rather that they saw the opening presented by the decline of rural Islam, adjusted to the colonial situation, exploited it to their advantage, and then, in the thick of the anticolonial struggle, were forced to remove themselves from the center of the political scene.[122] Islamic reformism was borrowed and then integrated into the discourse of revolutionary Algerian nationalism — first that of the PPA and later that of the FLN. Third Worldism Algerian-style took for granted that religion, far from being the masses' spiritual narcotic, was, or could be, their ideological energizer. So began the notion of a "socialist Islam," an Islam that enjoyed an objective complicity with revolutionary systems of thought both because it was oppressed by the West and because, in its appeal to justice and its reflection of the ultimate will of humankind, it was consonant with the project of Third Worldist militants.[123]

More generally, in the Muslim universe of Third Worldism, the convergence between revolutionary and religious talk was made plain in all sorts of ways. To jump slightly ahead of our story, Egyptian president Gamal Abdel Nasser asserted that "our religion is a socialist religion. . . . In the Middle Ages, Islam successfully implemented the first socialist experience in the world."[124] With characteristic braggadocio, the Indonesian leader Sukarno proclaimed, "I am a follower of Karl Marx, but, on the other hand, I am also a religious man, so I can grasp the entire gamut between Marxism and theism. . . . I have made myself the meeting place of all trends and ideologies. I have blended, blended, and blended them until finally they became the present Sukarno."[125]

Let me quickly recapitulate: Like assimilationism and Messali's brand of socialistic populism, Islamic reformism evolved out of violent exchange—not only military but cultural and social as well—with the French occupiers. In the words of Stora and Daoud,

[The] three towering figures who emerged in the thirties . . . complement each other. Messali, self-educated, born amidst the migrant community, possessed of exceptional oratorical and leadership skills, is the plebeian expression of Algerian social *déclassement*. He knows how to exhort rupture and confrontation with the colonial state. Ben Badis was—or rather would become—the emblematic figure of Algerian Islam, the father of Algeria's Muslim personhood. He grows out of the immutable depths of society; he knows how to manage the autonomous cultural space. The third, Ferhat Abbas, personifies the *évolué,* bred in the French tradition, a symbol of social mobility among the elites and the *notables*. A lucid intellectual and brilliant polemicist, he advocates reconciliation and compromise. . . . All three spring from the colonial state's obstinate refusal to mature, and from the Algerian masses' aspirations.[126]

Each outlook would set foot in the other two. Each would seep into its counterparts, infiltrating them, altering them ever so slightly, to the point that traces of democratic Jacobinism, of social activism, and of a "secularized" religion could be found in all three. Each would gain a measure of legitimacy from being attacked by the French, "Ben Badis by means of ostracism, Messali by means of repression, and Abbas . . . by means of defamation."[127] More importantly, these outlooks smoothed the path for Algerian Third Worldism, a mélange of radicalized representative democracy, diluted Marxism, and revolutionary Islam. Jeunes Algériens, Messalists, and *ulémas* met at this intriguing crossroad, which would be roughly replicated throughout the Third World, in Africa, Asia, and Latin America.

I spoke of Amar Ouzegane earlier on. His life is a fitting metaphor for the volatile and ambiguous relations between communism, religious reformism, and Algerian Third Worldism. Ouzegane was born to a peasant Kabyle family that was ruined after the insurrection of 1871. His family's fate reflected the violence and disabling capacity of French colonialism, as well as the Algerians' inability to transcend ethnic or geographic divisions. In 1930 he joined the communists' youth organization, the Jeunesses Communistes, one of the few groups that appeared capable of forming a unified social movement. Rising rapidly, he became secretary of the PCF's Algiers region in 1934 and in 1936 was appointed to the Central Committee. Yet twelve years later, he was expelled from the Party ranks on charges of "nationalism." By the time Algeria achieved independence, he was in the habit of sharply attacking his former communist comrades, extolling the primacy of the national over the class struggle. From his "Cité Communiste," the communist haven he evoked in his early years, to his later "Cité Musulmane de 'caractère socialisante'" the line is tortuous yet intelligible. Exploited by Western imperialism, Islam had become an oppressed religion, the emblem of the people's national identity, cultural aspirations, and social goals.[128]

My focus so far has been on the origins of Third Worldism among Algerians, not on its emergence among the French. This is not meant to detract from my argument that Third Worldism was an outlook both *of* and *about* the Third World and that it spawned converts in North and South alike. Rather, it reflects the fact that, in their infancy, notions of Third World radicalism encountered far less success in the North than in the South. Even in the thirties and forties, the Russian revolution retained luster among European left-wing militants, appealing to their sense of universalism and, particularly in France, to their desire to complete the revolutionary cycle begun in 1789.[129] There had been no time for disillusionment and thus no need to search for a new source of revolutionary inspiration. Then there was the ideological baggage carried by both socialists and communists, which was hardly receptive to Third World activism.

Still, if support was to be found for the early anti-imperialist and anticolonial movements, it came from the Left. During the interwar period, three distinct visions of the Third World began to develop among French leftists.[130] The first saw Algeria through the prism of the French Revolution; its priority was that France live up to republican ideals of equality and justice. The second, which had as its central reference point the Russian Revolution, assessed activity in Algeria in terms of its usefulness to the communist movement; the efforts of the PCF and the Intercoloniale belonged to this cluster. The third vision projected onto Algeria its hopes for a different form of socialist development, less bureaucratic and less Eurocentric than its European forerunners. In many ways, this eclectic assortment of Trotskyists, pacifists, and trade unionists was the most hospitable to the anticolonial movement, more genuine in its solidarity than the Communist Party, less hampered by domestic or international political consideration. Indeed, when relations with the Communist Party soured in the thirties, North African and Indochinese militants joined with members of this loose grouping. Paradoxically, though, the strength of these movements, namely, their rejection of nationalism as an inspiration for political action, also constituted their most conspicuous weakness. For their anticolonialism was an outgrowth of internationalism, an aversion to things patriotic that they applied with equal fervor to French and to Third World nationalistic sentiment.[131] Uncomfortable with the appeal to tradition or national solidarity, the extreme Left ultimately would not become a full-fledged partner of the Third Worldist revolutionary movement.

The Third Worldist perspective spawned by the Algerian revolution would build on these three visions, just as it would build on the assimilationist, traditionalist, and communist outlooks prevailing among Algerian militants. All in all, however, in the absence of a successful alliance between the organized Left (socialist, communist, or other) and Third World militants, French commitments to Third Worldism would be less orderly and less structured, emanating more often from individual French activists or intellectuals than from the parties themselves. But even this unstructured alliance was not unimportant: thanks to the Third Worldist movements' early ties with the metropolitan Left, there existed the semblance of a common language, precisely, the language of social revolution I have just evoked. Third Worldism would thus have its vocal advocates in the heart of the colonial capital. And although the commitments were slow to come at first, the path was clear for them to come in droves once, owing to the macabre revelations about Stalinism and to the Hungarian, Czechoslovak, and Polish uprisings, many left-wing militants saw in the Third World utopia's last remaining sanctuary. At that point, indeed, detachment from traditional communist parties was viewed as a blessing, not a curse, holding out the promise of novelty— that is, the promise of purity.

Conclusion

Ornamenting the spacious conference room at the Washington, D.C., offices of the National Democratic Institute (NDI) is a vast map of the world. It is dotted with pins of various colors, some in South and Central America, one in Haiti, a few on the Asian and European continents, the bulk in the southern half of Africa. These are, so to speak, recycled pins, slightly faded and worn-out, once used to designate the whereabouts of oil wells, colonial possessions, recipients of economic assistance, or revolutionary uprisings. Today, mended and refurbished, they serve to identify the targets of the NDI's "governance project," the attempt to introduce a semblance of democracy and collective national identity in the still-undemocratic world. Promoting self-governance, otherwise known as "nation-building," is the latest fad, and it is all the rage.

Between North and South, the First World and the Third, there have been countless such encounters, countless ways of meeting. In each case, a corpus of authoritative texts, a gallery of heroes, and a reservoir of symbolic events help define how the two sides will see each other. Indeed, the very terminology I employ—North versus South; First World versus Third—is a product of just such an encounter, so dominant, in fact, that we have come to take the territorial (and political) division it assumes for granted.

Thus, we have had developmentalism, a view according to which the Third World's task was to play catch-up with the economies of the "developed" world by duplicating their industrial revolutions, fostering the growth of a market economy, and spurring the emergence of an entrepreneurial class. The exemplary references in this narrative were the so-called NICs, the "newly industrialized countries," success stories of world capitalism that included countries such as Taiwan or Singapore. On other occasions, relations between North and South have been perceived through the prism of international aid, or charity. In this view, the Third World became above all a repository of famine, the First a depository of abundance. The interaction took on aspects of a morality play, bursting with urgency and good intentions; politics were to step aside. And then there have been more unforgiving times, when the "underdeveloped" world was viewed as just that: a stockpile of militarism and pathological misrule, a gathering of despots, ghastly dictators, or uncivilized barbarians, pure and simple. In this model (in which fits colonialism, for the most part), interacting has meant essentially forceful intervention — against Nasser, Gadhafi, Castro, Noriega and, most recently, Saddam Hussein.

The American operations in Somalia and Haiti are the latest incarnations of these encounters. Somalia was a peculiar one, a hybrid of economic charity, military confrontation, and nation-building; or more precisely, an example of charity having lost its compass and gone amok. But at its core it depended on and promoted the image of the Third World as a lawless universe, disorderly and unruly, unprovided for and, most of all, in need. The state has given way to the tribe, economic exchange to dispossession, central command to warlords. (How exactly does one become a "warlord?" And how is a warlord to be distinguished from a general or a tribal leader — all of which titles the American press, at one time or another, has used to describe Somalia's Aideed?) Prodded by distressing CNN broadcasts, the United States would unleash its forces in the vain hope of assembling the unfastened parts and creating a nation.

In Haiti the American purpose was democracy, and the measure of democracy, elections. Within fifteen months of the U.S.-led intervention, Haitians were to have voted for new local representatives, a new parliament, new senators, and a new president. This intoxicating electoral fever was fed by a series of assumptions about the virtues of democracy, the moderating influence of what has come to be known as "civil society," and the cleansing role of the ballot. The key ingredient to the Third World's recovery, its political cure-all, had become free and fair elections, and this would be illustrated in the Western Hemisphere's most destitute nation.

The dominant perceptions associated with each of these encounters are never wholly invented — Somalia undoubtedly did produce its share of famine and political anarchy — but they are never wholly disinterested either. We could take time and identify the means by which these paradigms, these selective and partial ways of apprehending North and South, have taken root, generated a body of knowledge and a hefty literature to back it up, and then endured or collapsed. In each case, powerful intellectual, political, and commercial interests are at work — on both sides. Aid, nation-building, even military intervention, have their constituencies and lobbyists in Washington, Paris, or London, but also in the capitals of Africa, Asia, and Latin America.

Consider the case of economic aid. On one hand, the process of "tied aid" mobilizes enthusiastic European and American exporters of goods behind the assistance program, simultaneously spawning a bureaucracy and network of scholars thoroughly associated with that program. On the other, meanwhile, local groups in the Third World, more often than not urban, always members of the elite, race for the spoils and become, for all practical purposes, the North's amenable clientele. Or consider the image of Third World countries as patchworks of rival tribes. Africa provides numerous examples, for nowhere has that conception been so widely and so successfully disseminated. What elsewhere might be viewed as a struggle between a repressive and exploitative state on one side and politically motivated rebels on the other inevitably comes to us packaged as manifestations of age-old, indomitable tribal hatreds. In Sudan, Somalia, and Ethiopia, for example, warring parties organize raids in areas where their opponents enjoy support, depriving them of their livelihood and creating regional famine. With the arrival of international assistance, relief organizations in turn become targets, as food is diverted and "protection money" is extracted. Yet, when all this is conveniently disguised by the veil of ungovernable tribal warfare, an image frequently accepted by the North, political violence can be presented as natural disaster, justifying continued assistance. The politics of tribal warfare thus has its victims, of course, but also its winners, such as "the traders and army officers who helped finance and organize the raids" or governmental and rebel forces who diverted the aid shipments.[1] The same analysis could be replicated for each of the dominant paradigms mentioned above and for the many that are not.[2]

What occurred at the turn of the century and in succeeding years, and what I have attempted to describe in some detail in the Algerian instance, laid the groundwork for the encounter between North and South that I call "Third Worldism." Though it never was dominant, and though it proved short-lived, it too managed to frame particular images of North and South — especially South — highlighting certain aspects, covering up others; and it too commanded wide respect, inspired devoted loyalties, and generated thinkers and a multitude of texts. Its rough outline can be gleaned from what has been discussed above, namely, the equivocal relations with the European Left and its ideologies of social progress; a tendency to both mimic and reject Western notions of democracy; a reappropriation of traditionalist (or religious) modes of discourse as instruments of the anticolonial struggle; and, overall, an adherence to nation-statism.

How all this translated into a more or less coherent intellectual whole on both sides of the North-South divide is the subject of part 2. But certain themes should be apparent. In the Third World this particular encounter with Europe would give rise to political movements with the following traits in common: first, they would characterize the "popular masses" of the Third World as revolutionary, the social underclass of a world economy dominated by the North; second, they would view history as an intelligible and inevitable evolution stretching back to traditional, egalitarian structures of the precolonial era and heading toward the utopian society of tomorrow; and third, they would put faith in the centralized, Jacobin state as the representative of these masses and the agent of that evolution. For Europeans, such movements in time would offer a welcome harbor for their hopes, so utterly abused by the experience of Stalinism. Revolutions of the Third World thus would serve as political and cultural reference points for the rebellious youth of the First. The origins of Third Worldism, particularly the influence of socialism, liberalism, and nation-statism, meant that what Europeans saw was sufficiently familiar to reassure, yet sufficiently novel to inspire.

PART 2

Apogee

In the summer of 1984, I sat on the porch of President Thomas Sankara's rather undistinguished residence. We spoke for roughly an hour—or, rather, he spoke; I listened—about the problems faced by the little West African republic he then led, the ambitions he entertained, the fears he tried to suppress. Sankara, it was clear, was a man of extraordinary courage, rectitude, and determination. Suddenly, and for no apparent reason, the conversation shifted to the United States. President Sankara seemed obsessed with a single question: how had the American people, particularly its youth, reacted to news of his country's revolution?

How one is to respond to a presidential query, especially one so peculiar, I am far from sure. A polite pirouette probably is called for, and I suppose that is what I attempted to do. But of course the response was far less significant than the question that prompted it. In its self-assurance and self-importance, in what it revealed about my host's perception of his nation's role and image around the world, the president's inquiry was vintage Sankara, and vintage Sankara meant quintessential Third Worldism. I had come to a country called Upper Volta, a name coined by the French *colons,* yet a month later I was exiting Burkina Faso, "land of upright men," and that name change itself was quintessential Third Worldism. To re-name was to redefine; with that simple, symbolic act the Burkinabés, as they would be known from then on, would obliterate their colonial past, thereby taking decisive possession of their future. But more than a name had been changed: revolutionary committees had sprung up, town meetings were being held, as ordinary citizens ardently and restlessly discussed their undecided destiny. There was much goodwill in the air, and considerable excitement, a belief in the inevitability of social and political change when desired and if fought for, a conviction that inventing new men and new women was not only necessary but possible.

Inventing a new way of governing also was part of the agenda. What had brought me to the country was a project to work with the minister to the environment. Yet days prior to my arrival the president had dissolved his government and sent all of its members to do "field work." Forget the fact that the "fields" looked suspiciously like urban offices, or that the cabinet, practically unmodified, would be renamed a month later. For the message was clear: the government too had to change its ways. Such energy, raw enthusiasm, and refreshing naiveté all were ingredients of Third Worldism.

The revolution had its caricatural side as well. Newsstands in Ouagadougou, the capital city of this essentially rural country, were overflowing with radical political pamphlets bearing such unlikely titles as *Le Prolétaire* or *Les Cahiers du Prolétaire* and engaging in arcane debates about the relative merits of Maoism, Stalinism, or Trotskyism. But that too was quintessential Third Worldism. In the midst of so much feverish activity, little wonder that Sankara would imagine the American masses spellbound by events in Burkina Faso, rather than gripped by the latest episode of *Dallas* or *Dynasty*.

Sankara had a vision for his country, and while there were considerable differences, it was not unlike Sékou Touré's in Guinea, Nkrumah's and then Rawlings's in Ghana, Machel's in Mozambique, Manley's in Jamaica, or Neto's in Angola. A few years later, Sankara remarked that "you cannot carry out fundamental change without a certain amount of madness."[1] And indeed, madness there was, enough to go around. It was the madness, or fever, of Third Worldism, and at various times, in various places, it looked as though it might really make a difference.

Eventually, Sankara would succumb, gunned down by the man who until that time had been considered his closest companion, the man in whose house I had resided in 1984, the man who had driven me to the president's abode. In its unpredictability, its dramatic flair, and its sense of tragic betrayal, that too, perhaps, was vintage Third Worldism.

CHAPTER 3

The Making of a World

In the end, there really had been no beginning. Events were taking place at a swift pace, bruising preconceptions and battering the existing order. But they were taking place somewhat disjointedly—the birth of an anticolonial movement here, a declaration of independence there—not quite unnoticed, not yet feared. Only later were the dispersed images gathered, given a chronology and a name, and described as part of a single, coherent historical phenomenon: the Third Worldist revolution.

The act of assembling was mythmaking, but in the way that the creation of any system of thought is. I use the term *myth* to evoke not so much distortion or manipulation (though certainly there was much of that) as the systematic organization and interpretation of events in order to imbue them with meaning, to replace their seeming arbitrariness with irresistible logic. I use it roughly as Edward Said does in his celebrated *Orientalism*. "A myth does not analyze or solve problems," he writes. "It represents them as already analyzed and solved; that is, it presents them as already assembled images, in the way a scarecrow is assembled from bric-a-brac and then made to stand for a man."[1] Or, as Roland Barthes defined it, "Myth has the task of giving a historical intention a natural justification and making contingency appear eternal." To which he added: "The world enters language as a dialectical relation between activities, between human actions; it comes out of myth as a harmonious display of essences."[2] At bottom, that is what ideologies are all about.

Mythology commenced with the object of discourse itself, the Third World. To be sure, Third Worldism was not the first thought system to posit the globe's division into North and South. From the colonial proj-

77

ect to developmentalism, ideological constructs have been premised on this sharp distinction between two worlds. (This is not to say that it is immutable: witness the fate of Japan.) But it arguably was the first in the modern era to view the South as the lead historical actor and screenwriter: Europe had brought not development but underdevelopment; independence in Asia, Africa, and South America would signify not their countries' ruin but the world's emancipation.

The term *Third World* captured this intellectual reversal, or *retournement*. The French economist Alfred Sauvy coined the term in 1952, and the choice of expression was knowing. By suggesting a parallel between the emergence of the nations of the South and the awakening of the *tiers état* that had led to the French Revolution of 1789, Sauvy gave words to the feelings of humiliation and appetite for international recognition that animated colonies and dependencies: "Nous parlons volontiers des deux mondes en présence, de leur guerre possible, de leur coexistence, etc., oubliant trop souvent qu'il en existe un troisième, le plus important et en somme le premier dans la chronologie. . . . Car enfin ce Tiers Monde ignoré, exploité, méprisé, comme le Tiers Etat, veut lui aussi être quelquechose" [We speak freely of two existing worlds, of their possible confrontation, of their coexistence, etc., forgetting all too often that a third one exists, the most important and indeed the first in chronological order. . . . For this Third World, ignored, exploited, scorned, like the Third Estate, also wants to be something].[3]

Later, Lacoste would describe the quasi-mythological impact of the expression, recalling the "extraordinary fate of a formula that made a discreet appearance in a Parisian weekly magazine. How, why was it adopted in Cairo, Havana, Beijing? . . . It is not solely a change in words but a change in our representation of the world. . . . 'Third World' evokes [the geopolitical group's] unity and turns it into a force, a huge historical entity, the champion, but also the victim, of titanic struggles."[4]

What I call Third Worldism, in other words, was a political, intellectual, even artistic effort that took as its raw material an assortment of revolutionary movements and moments, weaved them together into a more or less intelligible whole, and gave us the tools to interpret not them alone but also others yet to come. It is a system of representations that resolutely rejects the clichés, dogmas, and preconceptions of the past, only to replace them with clichés, dogmas, and preconceptions of its own. In part 1, I tried to describe and explain the conditions that made this effort, or rather its success, possible. Part 2 focuses on the ideology and institutions of Third Worldism as they developed, par-

ticularly in the wake of World War II. In this chapter, I begin with the
raw material, that is, the ever-expanding anticolonial or anti-imperial endeavors, and then turn to the intellectual edifice that surrounded it in
both the Third World and the First. Chapter 4 attempts to illustrate the
above with a more in-depth discussion of the Algerian case.

In 1945 Ho Chi Minh proclaimed Vietnam's independence; India's followed in 1947; and the Dutch were forced to leave Indonesia in 1949. At
roughly the same time, anti-European movements developed in Palestine, Malaysia, Kenya, and Cyprus. A breed apart, Mao Zedong's victory
in China in 1949 appeared to signal the dawn of a new era. Land reform,
wealth redistribution, "thought reform" (rather innocuous-sounding at
the time) — all this was happening with unforeseen abruptness in a land
inhabited by about one-fourth of the world's population.[5]

After a brief lull, the pace picked up in 1954. That year, as France was
being defeated at Dien Bien Phu, a new battle front burst forth in Algeria. Recapturing the significance of these twin events some forty years
later is no easy task. But here was France, one of the great Western powers, militarily humbled in Asia, militarily challenged in North Africa —
that is to say, in its own backyard — seemingly losing its grip on history.
Everything at that point must have seemed possible and all within reach.

The "rebels" were still working without a map, so to speak, but they
certainly had a different representation of the world in mind. This they
made clear in 1955, when twenty-nine African and Asian heads of state,
"representing some 1,300 million people," met at the Bandung Conference.[6] Significantly, the Algerian Front de Libération Nationale was invited to attend, and the conference unanimously adopted a resolution
calling for Algeria's independence. Bandung at once presupposed and
symbolized renewed pride. It signified that world leaders no longer resided exclusively in Paris, Washington, or London, that there would be
new names to pronounce and new faces to recognize: those of Nehru,
Nasser, or Sukarno. An insightful observer of the Egyptian scene, Jean
Lacouture, wrote that Nasser returned to Cairo as a man invested with
a revitalized sense of purpose, about to begin his "Bandung period."[7]

To the West, and particularly to France and Great Britain, Nasser's
hard-won respect looked very much like provocative insolence. The
worst affront of all was the Suez crisis, another turning point in the
Third World's emergence.[8] The incident, and above all its outcome,
came to stand for the nascent division of the world: on the one hand was

the old imperial guard, resolved to overthrow the brash Egyptian leader, desperately clinging to its evanescent power; on the other was the youthful and impetuous *rais,* who had dared to nationalize the canal, had bought arms from pro-Soviet Czechoslovakia, refused to obey the former masters' injunctions, and, politically at least, would get away with it. There was more than humor or sarcasm in the distinctive laugh that permeated Nasser's Suez radio address: it reverberated with the defiance of "Goha the clever and Sinbad the prodigious."[9]

Winds of change were blowing southward, toward sub-Saharan Africa. In 1957 the Gold Coast became the first black African country to gain its independence. It called itself Ghana, and it was led by Kwame Nkrumah, a man about whom Basil Davidson would write that his "name and significance signalled the beginning of a new life . . . at the heart and centre of the whole great process of primary decolonisation."[10] A year later, Ahmed Sékou Touré led Guinea in rejecting the French community. The arrangement had been imagined by French President de Gaulle as a means of replacing the cumbersome ties of colonialism with looser neocolonial bonds, the while preserving French interests basically intact. Guinea's resounding "no" would be heard throughout the continent, one in a series of firm, rebellious, and inspiring new voices. Ryszard Kapuscinski, the renowned chronicler of Third World revolutions, lent them his ear, and it is worth quoting him at length:

I have heard how Nasser speaks. How Nkrumah speaks. And Sekou Touré. And now Lumumba. It is worth seeing how Africa listens to them. You have to see the crowd on the way to a rally, festive, excited, with fever in their eyes. And you need strong nerves to endure the moment of ecstatic screaming that greets the appearance of one of these speakers. It's good to stand in the crowd. To applaud together with them, laugh and get angry. Then you can feel their patience and strength, their devotion and their power. . . . Nasser speaks tough, forceful, always dynamically, impulsively, imperiously. Touré banters with the crowd, winning it over with his good cheer, his constant smile, his subtle nonchalance. Nkrumah is turgid, intent, with the manner retained from his days preaching in the American black churches. And then that crowd, carried away by the words of its leaders, throws itself in exultation under the wheels of Gamal's car, lifts Sekou's car off the ground, breaks ribs trying to touch Kwame's car.[11]

To return to our chronology: in 1959 Fidel Castro rose to power in Cuba, and it seemed as if the rest of Latin America soon would join in this "collective honeymoon" and follow in his revolutionary footsteps.[12] The prediction was nurtured by faith in the elusive, already mythologized figure of Che Guevara, who had confidently asserted that "a nu-

cleus of thirty to fifty men . . . is sufficient to initiate an armed struggle
in any country of the Americas" and disingenuously apologized that "we
cannot promise not to export our example, as the United States is asking
us, because it is a moral example, and moral examples know no borders."[13] A member of the comfortable middle class, Che was not just
another hero; he became "the icon of the armed Latin American left"
and, even more, "a symbol . . . of the extreme difficulty, if not the actual
impossibility, of indifference."[14] Then, in 1962 came the FLN's victory
in Algeria, a defining moment in the history of Third Worldism, for the
battle had lasted so long, had been so violent, and had been won by a
movement so acutely aware of its international dimension. Equally momentous would be the war in Vietnam, which began in 1965, conjuring
images of a battle between David and Goliath and bolstering the conviction that success was preordained against an arrogant, murderous, but
crippled American giant.[15] Finally, armed resistance in Angola (starting
in 1961), Portuguese Guinea (1963), and Mozambique (1964), along
with the emergence of Yassir Arafat's Fatah movement in the Middle
East, all contributed to a confident Third Worldist representation of the
international arena, a romantic one perhaps, certainly one imbued with
a passionate, unshakeable faith in the future.

That momentous events were occurring in the South hardly could be
questioned. Recounting the history of what he dubs the "short twentieth century," Eric Hobsbawm emphasizes the striking fact that so
few Third World nations were spared a revolution, left-leaning military
coup, or protracted social and political instability. "It seemed to be
a global volcano waiting to erupt, a seismic field whose tremors announced the major earthquakes to come."[16]

All myths need their share of heroism and martyrdom, and Third
Worldism had a copious supply of both. There were glorious struggles,
like those of Algeria, Angola, and Mozambique; there were those, leg-
endary, that seemed to go on endlessly and with a touch of stoic despair,
as in East Timor and, increasingly, in the Sahara. There were tragedies
too (recall Indonesia), and mourned victims: Patrice Lumumba, Amilcar
Cabral, Che Guevara, Samora Machel. All of these episodes, epics, and
vignettes formed, to borrow David Apter's terminology, a "retrievable
legacy" for Third Worldist militants, enabling them to "generate [their]
own mythology."[17]

Third Worldism had its scriveners as well, who played a pivotal role in
bringing the scattered together and in chronicling revolution wherever

they believed it might be. They enjoyed the support of a Third Worldist press (*Tricontinentale, Partisans, Tiers Monde, Afrique Asie*) and a publishing house (Maspero). But there also were individual folk heroes: Wilfred Burchett in Asia, Regis Debray in Latin America, René Dumont in Africa, Jean Ziegler practically everywhere, to mention but a few. They included historians (Basil Davidson, Abdallah Laroui, Jacques Berque), economists (Pierre Jalée, André Gunder Frank, Samir Amin, Arghiri Emmanuel, François Perroux), political scientists (Anwar Abdel-Malek), philosophers (Jean-Paul Sartre), sociologists (Pierre Bourdieu), anthropologists (Georges Balandier), poets and fiction writers (Pablo Neruda, Gabriel García Márquez, Kateb Yacine, Jean Genet), even movie directors (Costa-Gavras).

Some recorded events lyrically, as did Ania Francos upon visiting Cuba: "A revolution is possible, even in the worst conditions, even fifty kilometers from the American coast, even in a poor country. . . . Here, legend is made not of noise, rumors, myths, but of active, young, laughing faces. . . . Cuba is alive. The crowd can feel its leaders—the vast meetings are not stilted ceremonies: Fidel and his people embark on a kind of unending duo, speaking, singing, dancing."[18] Others, like Dumont, chose a more moralistic tone; more austere, like Amin; more romantic, like Debray; or more sensual, even bordering on the erotic, as in Jean Genet's account of obsessive infatuation with young Palestinians.[19]

Of these, many, it is fair to say, would be surprised to see themselves featured on this list, if indeed they thought they belonged on any list at all. And yet, the ideas they helped to propagate, the rough visions of the world to which they subscribed, the political affinities that, as if by instinct, they displayed, were familiar to Third Worldism and facilitated its dissemination. This made eminent sense, since their approaches were largely by-products of precisely the same historical events and historical context to which we owe Third Worldism, namely, the anticolonial and anti-imperialist struggles of the Third World. While there were nuances and differences between thinkers, they all started from the premise that the so-called Third, or underdeveloped, World consisted of more than a litany of despotic rule, perverted economic policies, or recipients of Western charity. They thereby offered an effective counterweight to the monotonous monologue that had portrayed the Third World as the passive receptacle of economic advice and political tutoring.

The counternarrative took the form of a series of abrupt reversals. The first concerned the representation of economic relations between North and South. Traditionally, and until the early 1960s, literature on the

Third World had been dominated by "developmentalism" or "modernization" theory, both of which assumed that overcoming underdevelopment meant following Europe's and North America's economic lead. The view, schematically stated, was that underdeveloped countries consisted of "dual societies," segregated between backward hinterlands and more modern urban centers. The solution to poverty, like the road to development, lay in the "trickling down" of prosperity: internationally, from the developed to the underdeveloped world; internally, from modern (i.e., European-like) to traditional regions. Thus, in Gabriel Almond's vision, to understand development means to "master the model of the modern, which in turn can only be derived from the most careful empirical and formal analysis of the functions of the modern Western polities." [20] This view is repeated in Eisenstadt's argument that modernization is "the process of change towards those types of social, economic and political systems that have developed in Western Europe and North America from the seventeenth century to the nineteenth and have then spread to other European countries, and in the nineteenth and twentieth centuries to the South American, Asian and African continents." [21]

This relationship is turned upside down in the works of the intellectuals mentioned above. To them, far from developing the Third World, Europe had underdeveloped it. The North's economic growth was no more a strictly endogenous phenomenon than was the South's pitiful stagnation, for they were two sides of the same coin, namely, Europe and North America's imperial exploitation of the Third World. Frantz Fanon is perhaps best identified with this outlook: "This European opulence is literally scandalous. . . . It has been nourished with the blood of slaves and it comes directly from the soil and from the subsoil of that underdeveloped world. The well-being and the progress of Europe have been built up with the sweat and the dead bodies of Negroes, Arabs, Indians and the yellow races." [22]

Many others within the so-called dependency school of thought would further elaborate upon this idea of the "development of underdevelopment." Osvaldo Sunkel and Pedro Paz, for example, explained that "both underdevelopment and development are aspects of the same phenomenon, both are historically simultaneous, both are linked functionally. . . . This results . . . in the division of the world between industrial, advanced or 'central' countries, and underdeveloped, backward or 'peripheral' countries." [23]

The economic reversal was connected to other attitudes that would become prevalent among Third Worldists. When these rather sophisticated economic analyses were transferred to the less subtle realm of political discourse, they conveyed a sense of the world as polarized between two irreducibly antagonistic foes, the South against the North, the periphery against the center, the *zones des tempêtes* against the arena of the status quo. Such coarse generalizations left little room for intranational class divisions and in this respect proved a valuable political tool for Third World elites, who could appeal to national unity against the common adversary. From this representation of the world order would also derive the popularly held view that international relations reflect the conscious stratagems of omnipotent decision makers, principally the states. The Third Worldist world is intelligible, and it is shaped by a whole set of calculated moves, systemic strategies that are reified by use of such terms as *world capitalism, imperialism,* and so on.

Key questions were left unasked, the most obvious being what, besides serving as a convenient catchphrase, *imperialism* meant in the minds of Third Worldists. Bandied about with abandon, the term became so familiar a fixture of the political landscape as to escape serious probing. Inquiry appeared unnecessary, since at some level people thought they knew what they were talking about. A policy was labeled "imperialistic," and therefore condemned, when motivated by a European or American (principally American) desire to control and take advantage of less developed nations.

Yet the assumptions behind the exercise of such rhetorical censure are debatable, to say the least. Either it presupposes that some states act out of sheer altruism, whereas others (the imperialist ones) act in order to maximize their respective position — in which unlikely case imperialism would hardly be a useful concept at all — or, more probably, it agrees that all states use forms of persuasion and influence to maximize their interest but then assumes that normative distinctions somehow can be drawn between such efforts, those of the North generally being castigated as "imperialistic," while others are applauded in the name of the national interest. Alternatively, imperialism may be merely a matter of degree: the power imbalance between North and South is such that what otherwise would be the legitimate pursuit of the national interest becomes illegitimate imperial design.[24] Of course, also underlying the idea of imperialism is the political topography in which nation-states — as opposed to individuals, classes, and so on — are assigned identifiable collective "interests," so that little room is made for intranational differentiations, distinctions, or conflicts.

In short, the first reversal involved the belief that the Third World's

economic woes originated in the North and that the Third World's economic salvation would require separation from it. Imperialism, the representation of the world it implied, and the central role it assigned to
states in the struggle for economic development were spin-offs — with
the particular virtue to Third World leaders of justifying the strong centralized states they were resolved to build. As a theory, then, Third
Worldism was at once *structural* and *functional:* structural because it portrayed the world as an organized system divided strictly among nation-
states and governed by specific rules and mechanisms; functional because international relations were believed to serve the capitalist system's
frantic drive for domination.[25]

The second main reversal was in the realm of politics. The counterpart to modernization theory, "political development" had been equally
dominant in the 1950s and 1960s as a prescriptive model for the Third
World.[26] That countries of the South needed to replicate Western political arrangements was considered logical, almost unquestionable. Generally speaking, members of this school of thought advocated a type of
constitutionalism that focused on process, equilibrium, and checks and
balances on the institutional side; and elite political culture and the assimilation of modern values on the attitudinal side.[27] As Samuel and Arturo Valenzuela remark, "The literature assumes that the values, institutions, and patterns of action of traditional society are both an expression
and a cause of underdevelopment and constitute the main obstacles in
the way of modernization."[28]

As in the case of modernization theory, the political development
view acknowledges little, if any, of the influence colonialism and imperialism had on political conditions within developing nations. Against
this essentially Eurocentric vision of the world, the new intellectual current argued that the Third World could not simply follow Europe's democratization. For it too, like the capitalist development with which it
went hand in hand, had been made possible by the North's domination
over the South. Such rethinking opened the way for the notion, so popular among Third Worldists, that stability and legitimacy in the Third
World was not a function of abstract institutions, which could be replicated as if in a vacuum, but of a political economy of power, which very
much hinged on a state's position within the world system. In other
words, more important than electoral fairness was the leader's representativity as measured in terms of his or her position on issues of social
justice and foreign domination. Articulating such views, the Tanzanian
leader Julius Nyerere had this to say about Western insistence on pro-

cedural guarantees: "The system of 'checks and balances' is an admirable way of applying the brakes to social change. Our need is not for brakes. . . . We need accelerators powerful enough to overcome the inertia bred of poverty."[29] It is not difficult to discern, lurking below the surface, arguments in favor of the centralized state, the single party, and a plebiscitarian style of politics — all hallmarks of Third Worldism.

There was another powerful political tradition in the postwar period: socialism. Yet we observed earlier how little it had done to lessen the predominant Eurocentric bias: first, the revolution's nerve center was in the industrialized nations of Europe, and that is where it was meant to stay; second, any Third World revolt would follow the path scientifically and rigorously plotted out in Europe. Rarely was there any mention of the Third World as having an independent say in the overall revolutionary strategy (for instance, in its capacity as foremost victim of capitalist oppression) or an independent role in its ultimate outcome. The intellectual outlook I have been discussing would subvert these equations as well.

To begin with, it countered the traditional and dominant view that the world revolution, were it to occur, would start in Europe and North America. As scholars like Samir Amin or Pierre Jalée explained, as of the late nineteenth century and the dawn of the imperialist era, the "center of gravity of capitalist exploitation had been displaced," and with it the heart of anticapitalist resistance.[30] The exploitation of the peripheral countries of the Third World had, as it were, modified the political arithmetic, promoting the workers of the European cities — for so long portrayed as the progressive vanguard of the world — to privileged status. As a result, they had become "either passive or active accomplices of imperialism, so thoroughly corrupted that they have become historically insignificant as a revolutionary force."[31] Hence the shift to the Third World masses, and in particular to the unsullied and uncorrupted peasantry, as the new revolutionary class. In this respect, China's role was central. With great assuredness, it proclaimed the three A's (Africa, Asia, and the Americas) the heart of the world revolution. The main contradiction, as Lin Bao put it, pits the "revolutionary people of Asia, Africa, and Latin America against the imperialist countries, led by the United States."[32]

Consider the ironic and formidable perversion of classical Marxist analysis: the proletariat of the metropolis having been co-opted, the periphery having become the principal target of economic exploitation, capitalism's "weak link" (as Mao had put it) had become the rural, undeveloped Third World. This notion of the displacement of the revolutionary axis is revealed clearly in the works of Sukarno, Cabral, and Nyerere, who, while stating that "Karl Marx was right," proclaimed that "today it is the international scene that is going to have a greater impact."[33] The notion is also apparent in Amin's analysis: "The argument of those who constantly remind us of the fundamental bourgeoisie/proletariat contradiction hardly contributes to the debate; the proletariat exists here and there, on a world scale. . . . Quoting Marx can hardly help, since imperialism developed after his death; quotations from Lenin are slightly more useful, since he gave us the first decisive analysis of imperialism . . . but he died in 1924."[34]

Some would take the argument a step further and assert that revolutionary movements in the Third World "will bring about not only their own liberation, but also the world-historic destruction of the power-apparatus oppressing all humanity," thereby "permanently alter[ing] the 'human condition.'"[35] This view is expressed full-blown in Jean-Paul Sartre's comment that "we in Europe too are being decolonised: that is to say that the settler that is in every one of us is being savagely rooted out."[36] Or in Angolan president Agostinho Neto's hopeful assessment that "the importance of the national liberation struggle is much greater than is generally admitted, because through their [the revolutionaries'] activity they are transforming themselves into accelerators of history. . . . They are an important factor for the positive transformation of our entire continent and the whole world. The national liberation struggle is also a means of overthrowing a whole unjust system of oppression existing in the world."[37]

The final political reversal had to do with the revolutionary model. Once again, Europe's fairly familiar mix of conceit and self-centeredness meant that it had looked to the Third World as at best a passive location in which to play out revolutionary patterns fabricated in the West. Yet, as disenchantment grew both with workers' movements and social democracy in Western Europe and with the Soviet Union, so did the underdeveloped nations' independent appeal. In this context, China, with its emphasis on cultural renovation and mass participation and because of its contrast to the austere, stagnant model of the Soviet Union, played a special part. I mentioned Wilfred Burchett, but countless others within the Third World and the European Left were enthralled by Maoism, among them Maria Antonietta Macciochi, Louis Althusser, and, in its terrorist travesty, the Peruvian Shining Path.[38] Albeit with somewhat less zeal, individuals from North and South would look to Algeria as an exemplar of revolutionary struggle, to Cuba for the romance of guerrilla warfare, to Mozambique for the administration of "liberated zones," to Somalia (at one time) for the promise of mass participation, or to Tanzania for an experiment in grass-roots socialism.

Third World nations, it suddenly seemed, could themselves be examples for the "developed" world, places where revolutionary ideas, such as a new kind of mass-based politics and new forms of economic or social organization, might be tried out and replace the failed recipes of capitalism and Soviet-style socialism. This view led to the boldly novel idea that they had more to teach to the North than they had to learn from it. As Jean Ziegler, once one of the more impassioned of European Third Worldists, explained, revolutionary Third Worldism was a "specific social formation, radically unexplored by Western human sciences."[39]

In sum, regardless of whether they were all what I call Third Worldist, the scriveners blazed the trail for Third Worldism. They did this by capsizing what until then had been the natural and dominant representation of the Third World as an idle recipient of everything from material aid to economic advice and political tutelage. In the emerging counternarrative, the nations of Asia, Africa, and Latin America challenge material dependency, advocate novel economic policies, and constitute the potential vanguard of the revolutionary movement. In short, the scriveners spoke about the Third World differently, which allowed others to think differently, which allowed others to act differently.

Strategy is a name we like to give to happenstance when it is viewed in hindsight. The string of successful independence movements and prolific ideologues of Third Worldism did not develop by pure chance, of course. Victory invites victory, and innovative thought has a way of infecting like minds, but it would be something of a stretch to speak of a coordinated effort at this level. Besides, the unity and effectiveness of the Third World should not be overstated. At all times there were internal divisions: on the economic front, between, say, producers and importers of raw materials; politically, over the meaning of nonalignment, the role of the Eastern Bloc and its Third World allies, and so forth.

Yet, divisions and happenstance notwithstanding, the Third World achieved remarkable success in forming a united front. Out of the disparate developments that saw its rise, there issued a whole set of gatherings and meetings of newly independent states, nationalist organizations, and Third World leaders. The institutional expression of the Third World displayed a deliberateness of purpose that bore witness to a well-calculated strategy. So effective was the effort that by the mid-seventies one could hardly speak of the state of international relations without at once thinking in terms of North and South, the New International Economic Order, nonalignment, and so on. As Stephen Krasner correctly notes, in the 1970s "the agenda was being set by the Third World," with "Northern countries . . . generally reacting to, rather than initiating, proposals.[40] That so much effort was put into building and maintaining a sense of cohesion in spite of the disagreements goes far to show that the ultimate prize was deemed to outweigh the discomfort the company produced.

A point to note is that the Third World that burst onto the global scene was by no means Third Worldist. Neither the political nor the economic positions it put forth faithfully reflected what I call the Third Worldist view. It generally was less radical in its prescription for change, less interested in the domestic policies of Third World states, less prone to call for self-reliance or a de-linking of Third World economies from the dominant (capitalist) international system. The overlap between the objectives of the more radical members of the Third World coalition and those of the more conservative nonetheless was impressive. The Bandung Conference, nonalignment, and the Group of 77 might not have been Third Worldist, but the desire to provide exploited countries with a unified voice and to compel the North to deal with them as a coherent bloc as opposed to a scattered crowd—as a trade union rather than a fragmented group of workers—certainly was.[41]

The Third World's attempt to frame the terms of the international debate and coalesce into a coherent political force capable of altering the world balance of power proceeded along two (at times converging) tracks. On the one hand was the creation of organizations in which Third World countries would be able to adopt common approaches; on the other was the infiltration of existing international institutions as a means of occupying strategic positions of power. The latter built upon the former, for it was the unified positions reached at southern fora that ultimately found their way into the international arena.

The first method by which the Third World made its entry onto the world stage has its origins in the Afro-Asian Bandung Conference of 1955.[42] Much of what has been written since that time on the "spirit of Bandung" borders on the lyrical: Leopold Senghor, the president of Senegal, viewed it as "the most important event since the era of the Renaissance," one that spelled the "end of the colonized peoples' inferiority complex"; for Odette Guitard, Bandung symbolized the "awakening of colonial people"; and Jean Rous described it poetically as "history's dress rehearsal."[43] Hyperbole aside, there can be little doubt that Bandung was pivotal. That the eclectic group of twenty-nine delegations participating in the conference — pro-Western countries like Turkey, Iran, and Thailand rubbing elbows with more militant Egypt or India, to say nothing of communist China — had seen a reason for getting together was remarkable in and of itself.

Divisions at the conference were not without consequence. Participants were able to agree on a list of vague or overly general principles — respect for territorial integrity, nonaggression, noninterference in another's domestic affairs, the right to individual and collective self-defense, anticolonialism, the need for economic development, disarmament, and so on — setting aside more contentious issues, such as membership in military alliances. Yet they laid the foundations for the dominant themes of Third World diplomacy in the seventies and early eighties: "(1) nonalignment with either East or West, (2) an international self-assertion of former colonial countries, and (3) a militant anticolonialism,"[44] to which one might add a call for economic development.

Bandung had no direct descendant, largely because it lacked ideological focus and a clear sense of purpose, but it had many heirs, each of which accentuated one theme or another. The more radical offshoot was the collection of African and Asian progressive movements known as the AAPSO (the African-Asian Peoples' Solidarity Organization).[45] Created in Cairo in 1957, the AAPSO differed from Bandung in its character — it was a "transnational association of political parties"[46] — and in its stance vis-à-vis the East-West conflict, inviting delegations from both China and the Soviet Union. Nor, despite the convening of several other meetings, did it enjoy Bandung's long-lasting impact. In the end, it suffered both from intensification of the Sino-Soviet feud and from success of the more mainstream Non-Aligned Movement. The most accurate epitaph probably is that the AAPSO helped keep the Third World idea alive at a time when, in the aftermath of Bandung, the Third World was in need of some sorting out.

Nonalignment was Tito's fixation, and though, strictly speaking, he was not of the Third World, he was instrumental in carrying it in that direction. Yugoslavia could not afford to antagonize Moscow nor bear the thought of yielding to it, which is largely why Tito turned to Asia and Africa (Latin America somewhat less) in order to preserve his independence. The first meeting of nonaligned countries took place in Belgrade in 1961 with the Yugoslav leader at its helm. Unlike Bandung, which Tito had not attended, this conference was closed to states that had entered a military alliance with one of the superpowers. The emphasis was on neutrality, the world's geography being viewed very much through an East-West lens.[47]

The Non-Aligned Movement gradually drifted away from Tito's original concept and his underlying political mapping of the globe. Subsequent conferences on the whole had a keener interest in the North-South division, in part because the threat of a superpower confrontation appeared to recede, in part because the Third World had concerns of its own. At the second meeting, held in Cairo in 1964, the emphasis shifted to anticolonialism and broader issues of global power distribution. No longer satisfied with being a buffer between East and West, the South sought to take an active role in challenging Northern intervention.

The third phase of the Non-Aligned Movement saw greater focus on economic issues, though the political agenda — denunciation of South Africa, Israel, and various forms of imperialism — never was far behind. If one era was Yugoslavia's, and the other Egypt's, this one belonged squarely to Algeria. The culmination was the Fourth Conference, held in the Algerian capital in 1973 (the third had taken place in Lusaka three years earlier), which "became the point of departure for an unprecedented burst of Third World diplomatic action."[48] If the Third World was to survive at all, President Boumedienne proclaimed, it would have to achieve genuine economic independence. That would require nothing short of a radical change in the organization of the international economy — a New International Economic Order (NIEO). His message was all the more forceful for being echoed concurrently in numerous international fora.

Adding to its weight were the simultaneous efforts of the Organization of Petroleum Exporting Countries (OPEC) to restructure the oil market following the 1973 Arab-Israeli war. OPEC's brief embargo and its decision to quadruple the price of oil were, in Robert Mortimer's words, "a concrete expression of the demand for economic change," "at once a symbol of Third World assertion and a model of collective action."[49] More than ever before, the Third World was able to present a coherent message and then to press it on a variety of diplomatic fronts.[50]

The second method by which the Third World asserted itself involved its involvement in the various international institutions set up for the most part after World War II. It is useful here, I think, to stop to consider Krasner's intriguing discussion of this strategy. Krasner begins his

analysis with the assumption that, given the existing distribution of resources, the Third World preferred an international regime sanction-
ing authoritative modes of resource allocation (i.e., modes determined
by political authority) over market-oriented modes. This is a difference
that, as a whole, is supposed to separate North from South, though it is
clear, and Krasner acknowledges as much, that there are exceptions on
both sides.

This one difference implies several more, of which the principal for
our purposes is that the Third World became increasingly active in those
institutions premised on authoritative modes of allocation (and, not
without significance, on the principle of one country, one vote), seeking
to modify the rules of the game rather than simply to master those already in existence. Not for nothing, then, did the South do its best to
play a role in the U.N. General Assembly (responsible for the allocation
of political resources), the United Nations Economic, Social, and Cultural Organization, or UNESCO (for cultural resources), the United
Nations Conference on Trade and Development, or UNCTAD (for the
economic), and the International Labor Organization, or ILO (for the
social), as opposed, say, to the World Bank or the International Monetary Fund (IMF). At the same time, the Third World pressed an ideological agenda whose natural consequence was to invigorate those very
institutions: the NIEO, questions relating to the flow of technology and
information, and the law of the seas, to name but a few.[51] All offered the
Third World an opportunity to refashion the global arena in a manner
more consistent with its interests.

In the 1970s, Krasner argues, the Third World was able to achieve its
objectives (partially, that is) thanks to a combination of circumstances.
By presenting a clear ideological alternative, the South broke the North's
grip over the terms of the debate. In many ways, in fact, it put the North
on the defensive, unable to justify the vast inequity in resources and life
standards. To this one must add that the institutions in which the South
was able to exploit its comparative advantage, those that had both the
capacity and the willingness to reorder the international allocation of
resources, had been set up by the North at a time when it enjoyed clear
preeminence, both cultural and political; times had changed, but the developed world was not willing to walk away — not yet at least.[52]

There was an interesting synergy between the two methods to which
I have alluded. Having elaborated a relatively coherent language in its
own arena, the Third World then did what it could to bring that language consistently and resolutely to those international institutions best

suited to its purposes. Nowhere was this synergetic relationship more steadily pursued, and more effective, than in the instance of UNCTAD, the U.N. General Assembly, and the Non-Aligned Movement. To gauge this coordination, one need only look at the sequence of their meetings and the remarkable frequency with which the Third World groups referred to each other's documents.[53]

One example: On the heels of the 1973 summit of nonaligned countries, Algeria urged, and obtained, the convening of a U.N. session devoted to issues of economic development. Many have suggested that the landmark session, known as the Sixth Special Session on Raw Materials and Development, was the climax of the Third World's efforts to coalesce and be noticed. The expression "New International Economic Order," first introduced in the economic declaration adopted at the 1973 summit, was repeated here emphatically, soon to become an effective catchword. The General Assembly called for the establishment of an NIEO "based on equity, sovereign equality, interdependence, common interest and cooperation among all states irrespective of their economic and social systems which shall correct inequalities and redress existing injustices, and make it possible to eliminate the widening gap between the developed and the developing countries."[54]

Another illustration involves the Group of 77, a coalition originally made up of seventy-seven less developed countries within UNCTAD — in a sense the Third World's "caucus" in the conference. In tandem with the Non-Aligned Movement, the Group put together an economic platform that it vigorously urged upon the U.N. organization.[55] Broadly speaking, it began with the premise that "unequal exchange is . . . the defining characteristic of the world economic system, and authoritative, rather than market, modes of allocation are . . . the prescription for rectifying this inequity."[56] The themes raised by the group echoed those voiced by the Non-Aligned Movement, particularly as of 1973: terms of trade, transfer pricing, the news flow, technological appropriation, financial lending conditions, and so on.

In 1975 the Group presented a list of demands to the United Nations' Seventh Special Assembly on Development: to index the price of raw materials on the price of imports from developing countries; to institute a generalized system of preferences for Third World countries; to reform the international monetary system, and others. Simultaneously, the United Nations became a platform for thunderous denunciations of colonialism and what often were viewed as its variants, Western imperialism, Zionism, and apartheid.

What had all this achieved? Much of the sympathy for the Third
World in fact was generated out of this strategy of ideological consolidation. Fully armed with a baggage of fairly coherent positions, the
Third World was able to carry it to places where it could be heard. As a
result, the South was revealed to the North, for the first time in many
instances, as something more than a medley of impoverished nations
and failed authoritarian states. Roger Hansen made the point concisely
when, writing in 1979, he noted that "it is because the heterogeneous
countries encompassed by the term *South* have forcefully coalesced over
the past decade as a diplomatic unit that we examine them as an actor
in global politics."[57] By the mid- to late seventies a number of the issues put forth by the Third World had acquired an urgency, an obvious-
ness even, that it was difficult to ignore. "Slowly, the rhetoric has its
effects on the norms and values of the international system and North-
South relations if only because constant and adamant opposition [by the
North] can be and often is perceived as reflecting a selfish and self-
serving desire to retain 'inequitable' rules of the game."[58]

Third Worldism was only a part of all this. The themes just canvassed
served, to a degree, as common belongings to the traditionalist, conservative, and progressive Third World. But one cannot fully understand the success of the Third Worldist movement without an appreci-
ation for the broader shift in intellectual perspectives in whose context it
developed.

❖   ❖   ❖

The witchcraft of ideology consists in the dissemination of presuppositions and premises that go either unnoticed or, if noticed, without saying. I have already mentioned a few that characterized Third Worldism — the polarization of the world; the self-explanatory quality of terms
such as *imperialism, world capitalism,* and *revolution.* But of these there
are many more. They were the undergirding of Third Worldism, a lexi-
con and code of orthodoxy that belonged to, and at the same time
helped to define, Third Worldists.

The enterprise of cataloguing some of the key concepts or images of
Third Worldism is not without risk, for there is no uncontested doctrinal
text or program. I am convinced, however, that one can extract in rough
form the assumptions that, with various degrees of awareness, were
shared by Third Worldist activists and thinkers and constituted their
common denominator. My focus is on three central themes that explain
the thought and practice of Third Worldism. First is the perspective on

history, viewed as an inexorable march toward progress. Leaders, guerrilla fighters, journalists, and others represented history as a logical and meaningful unfolding, and it became common practice to assail opponents for standing "in history's way." Another element is the depiction of the historical actor or subject. Third Worldism took as its premise the existence of a general will, successively labeled "revolutionary" or "popular." It thereby created a highly manipulable yardstick, since all political positions were measured against this elusive standard. And elusive it was, for who has ever heard of "unpopular" masses? The third motif was the image of power, viewed as something one either possessed or endured, and imagined as the ultimate aim of all political struggle. Of equal importance was the related belief that once in the right hands (the hands of progress, of the revolutionary masses, and so on), power would be benign; indeed, the more of it, the better.

Before rushing to conclusions about the utopianism, naiveté, or even bad faith of the thinkers and activists who propagated such ways of thinking, one should remember that much of this intellectual production coincided with the heyday of the Third World's national liberation struggles. At that time there seemed to be clear moral choices — for or against colonialism; for or against the Third World's autonomous economic development — and the thrill of victorious insurgency movements, coming as disillusion with the prospects for socialism in Eastern and Western Europe gradually set in, made all the more credible some of the more outrageous-sounding claims of the day. Third Worldism in many ways was a material reality, witnessed every day and everywhere. The political muzzle its ideology imposed was not seen as a muzzle at all; it was envisioned as the faithful translation of events into thought, not the molding of facts to fit some prearranged intellectual grid.

Every ideology has its favorite exegete. In the case of Third Worldism, it was the historian. This had nothing to do with his or her status as a social scientist or in the academic community; rather, it is a reflection of the role of historical narrative in the Third Worldist discourse. And it is a reflection of the first unspoken assumptions behind this discourse: that history has a meaning, that it follows a precise course, and that particular events are its logical outcome. Central to Third Worldism, then, was the interesting combination of human agency and historical inevitability, the notion that by their free actions human beings accomplish, and therefore bring to pass, history's predetermined course. As Hannah Arendt wrote of Marxism, "Every old society harbors the seeds of its successors in the same way every living organism harbors the seeds of its offsprings."[59] With the difference that here, human deeds remain the trigger. Leaders, militants, ordinary citizens — all are thus either on the side of history (which is to say, on the side of revolution) or against it and are to be judged accordingly.

As the gauge of political legitimacy becomes loyalty to history's revolutionary course, so the arsenal of political struggle includes competing claims to history's legacy. One is charged with betraying not only his party, his cause, or his word; one has betrayed the past, and there can be no more serious crime. Through all this, historical narrative, the process by which the past is decoded, emerges as the critical form of discourse. For it alone can speak and understand the language of revolutionary destiny; it alone is entitled to discredit and legitimate. In the words of Michel de Certeau, the writer of history does not "tell facts," he "expresses meaning."[60]

This phenomenon can be seen in several contexts. Earlier I alluded to one that is hardly generic to Third Worldism, namely, the Third World's effort to invoke the past in order to justify the anticolonial struggle in the era of nation-statism. The safest (perhaps only) route to independence having taken the shape of the modern nation-state, leaders of the anticolonial movement scrambled to portray themselves as beholden to the undying national spirit, and the boundaries of historical narrative followed closely those of the once and future nation-state. History was being manufactured, so to speak, for the purpose of gaining entry into the Western-dominated world. The discourse of the Algerian FLN is a case in point, and I will have more to say on this later. To quote Said, the construction of the past occurred "when decolonization encouraged Algerians and Muslims to create images of what they supposed themselves to have been prior to French colonization."[61] The development of a politicized Palestinian counterhistory is another example. Focusing on this quasi-mandatory "rewriting" of history, Tarif Khalidi describes the "projection, and frequently the justification, of a particular communal self-image."[62]

With independence, the process simply continued. The past was the story of a monolithic people sharing national characteristics and affording little, if any, cultural, linguistic, or religious dissent. The "national tale," as it were, is the modern Third World state's autobiography, an account of its coming into being as the inevitable consequence of *national* aspirations. One way of achieving this is by dismissing the manifestation of any ethnic difference as a mere relic or artifact, the object of curious observation, perhaps even preservation, but certainly not the genuine expression of a collective identity. In the words of Lucien Levy-Bruhl, "Once folklore surfaces, it means that traditions are dead."[63] What gets conveniently left out is the diversity, heterogeneity, and richness of any social formation. But anticolonialism came at this cost, and it was deemed well worth the price.

Third Worldism carried this practice one step further. In Third Worldist rhetoric, history recounted the exploits not just of the nation per se but of its socially progressive, revolutionary element. Out of the depths of the past came the mythic tale of a common political will that had guided the people throughout the centuries. In other words, if history is the preferred discursive category, its privileged object is the revolutionary people. The aim thus becomes to give a voice to the "people," the "popular masses," that is, to "the truth of history — a truth that has existed since the beginning of time, but that, as of yet, has remained speechless."[64]

A curious dialectic is at play here: historical continuity and revolutionary fracture; retrospection and anticipation. It is explained by another unquestioned Third Worldist assumption, the notion of a revolutionary invariant, a popular will always in existence and impervious to time, a revolutionary spirit released by the past and into the future. In the end, Third Worldist politics involves this dizzying oscillation between yesterday and tomorrow, for projections into the past are the surest guideposts for the future, and revolutionary change the most faithful tribute to ancient times.

An important consequence follows. With its nostalgic references to a "golden age"[65] and its systematic choice of the terms *people* and *masses* over *class,* Third Worldism often has been characterized as a depoliticized ideology, part populist, part religious. Neither description is fully accurate. In the pronouncements of leaders and writings of historians and essayists, we find "the people" appearing not merely as a descriptive concept but as a social construct, and their social struggle as the engine of history's progress. The word *mass* itself has several meanings. It might indicate sheer number and brute quantity, as in the Latin *massa* or the French *amas* and *tas.* But there developed a qualitative connotation as well, as in "popular masses." Then, as is the case with Third Worldism, the designation gains power as a sociopolitical label, as if to render homage to the laboring and toiling segments of society. The masses are no longer capitalism's individual monads, not simply the nationalist's homogenous anticolonial entity, not quite Marx's social classes. They are, rather, the multitude of individuals brought together less by social condition than by social purpose, a class less by status than by will—which is why I find the expression *peuple-classe* so fitting.

This rather curious notion of a subjective social class willing itself into being can be seen, for example, in the writings of Nyerere, Cabral, and Sékou Touré. Note how the description of social groups is bereft of any mention of economic condition, how much it appears to turn on political consciousness rather than objective material interest: socialism is "an attitude of mind"; [66] the "agent" of history is "*all* the social strata since unity of all the social strata is a prerequisite for the success of the national liberation struggle." [67] At the same time, the people's enemies were "the entire social strata of our country . . . who do not want the development of our people, but only their own development, the development of their families, of their class." [68] The "contradiction," in short, needs to be put "back to its rightful place: between the people and those who wish to freeze its revolution," between the *classe-peuple* and the *classe anti-peuple*. [69] On the Third Worldist grid, the *classe-peuple* has replaced Marx's proletariat as the universal revolutionary class. Third Worldism, in its own way, has reverted to Rousseau as opposed to Marx, or perhaps to the Rousseau in Marx. With Rousseau, it tends to say *corrupt* where Marx said *capitalist,* to speak of moral effort where he would have preferred class struggle. [70]

Third Worldism's masses thus symbolize a somewhat original entity, at once united and divided along quasi-social lines, transcending narrow partisanship yet beholden to a clear ideological mission. In the modern era, they manifested themselves first in opposition to colonialism, for colonialism, as Sartre's *Critique de la raison dialectique* and Albert Memmi's *Portrait du colonisé* were quick to point out, is a form of social discrimination. In Memmi's words,

C'est que le privilège est affaire relative. . . . Il lui [le colon] suffit de paraître pour que s'attache à sa personne le préjugé favorable de tous ceux qui comptent dans la colonie. . . . C'est qu'il possède de naissance une qualité indépendante de ses mérites personnels. . . . Le colonisateur participe d'un monde supérieur dont il ne peut que receuillir automatiquement les privilèges.

[For privilege is a relative matter. . . . The *colon* need only make an appearance and all favorable notions that attach to those who count in the colony will be attributed to him. . . . That is because from the date of his birth he possesses a quality unrelated to personal merit. . . . The colonizer belongs to a superior world, and he cannot but automatically reap its privileges.] [71]

Evoking the African nationalist movements of the 1950s, Basil Davidson goes so far as to state that they "had far less to do with any national cause than with demands of a social nature and content. . . . Like the European movements of the 1840s, it was always the 'laboring poor' whose involvement and effort in the 1950s gave the tribunes of the 'national struggle' . . . their ground to stand on."[72]

This was more than mere nationalism, then, or so it claimed to be. It was the struggle for "authentic independence," of which freedom from colonial rule was but a prerequisite. In the words of Anouar Abdel-Malek, who perhaps best articulated this view, to fulfill the people's historical aspiration meant to "guarantee the different popular social classes and categories access to the material and cultural resources of the nation and . . . the exercise of state power."[73] Abdel-Malek's essential theme, echoed by countless Third Worldist leaders, was that there exists a distinction between the nationalist struggle and its radical offspring, what he called the "processus nationalitaire." With Third Worldism would come the time of "national fronts," the gathering of all "progressive" — the label enjoying a kind of incantatory, entrancing aura — social forces. For Ben Barka, the prestigious Moroccan opposition leader, independence was "the condition, the promise of liberation, not liberation itself."[74] Angola's former president, Agostinho Neto, put it this way: "I am very pleased by the formula adopted by some political parties in power in Africa when they say that they too are national liberation movements. This expresses the full significance of the phenomenon of liberation."[75] And the same point would be made by Nasser, Ho Chi Minh, and Mozambique's Dos Santos.[76]

Third Worldism, in other words, thinks in terms of history, but its entire premise is social. For, as Cabral had it, not all individuals are "agents" of history; it is, rather, those infused with a sense of social consciousness and social responsibility. The labor of enlightened leadership is to be on the proper flank of history, which means the side of the people's revolutionary will. Central to Third Worldism, then, is the absolute power granted the political functions of interpretation and representation — interpretation of the past and the popular will, first and foremost, but also representation of the history and the people in whose name political demands are made. The legitimate Third Worldist leader possesses absolute knowledge and flawless vision; he is the loyal translator, caretaker of the popular will, and slave to aspirations he alone can identify. Consider these words of Eduardo Mondlane, formerly head of FRELIMO, Mozambique's liberation movement: "FRELIMO and only FRELIMO knows [and] understands the real motivations of the People . . . [only FRELIMO knows how] to organize, to unite, to educate the people politically. . . . FRELIMO [therefore] appears as the incarnation of the will and aspirations of the Mozambican masses, the depository of national sovereignty and leadership for the fatherland."[77]

For this overall relation between leader and led, and between leader and opposition, the dominant metaphor, encountered time and again in Third Worldist rhetoric, is organic or biological: the image of the national "body" governed by a single purpose, composed of myriad elements, independent yet motivated by the sole desire to serve the common good, is a piece of pure Third Worldism. It captures the dialectic between the parts and the aggregate, between an overriding unanimity and its local agents. In short, there are healthy cells to be strengthened, ailing ones to be cured, and in extreme cases of open deviance or dissent, antibodies to be disposed of. Most of all, the metaphor conveys the notion of biological necessity. In one of many examples, Sékou Touré stated that the "individual and society form a single identity. Just as one cannot separate an element from the body to which it belongs, one cannot consider man independently from the society to which he is beholden."[78]

What also emerges from all this is a particular conception of power as a group attribute and the ultimate trophy of social competition: social groups have it, seek it, resist it, or are subjected to it. Third Worldism attaches so much importance to "power" as an object of desire because it is the lens through which historical progress is measured. In other words, Third Worldism envisions history as political attempts to conquer power by people representing predefined interests, and, from then on, as the vindication and promotion of those interests. Power, moreover, is an all-or-nothing proposition, so that there is, literally, a seat of power, the state. In short, when the neocolonial elites or the popular masses are said to be "in power," what actually is meant is that their interests will preside over the state through the intermediary of representatives, who are there simply as executors.

It is easy to see how in this context historical discourse became a language of power. Third Worldist rulers attach a particular significance to history, for it (and often it alone) can endow their reign with legitimacy, conferring on the present the prestige of the past and establishing the present as the sole caretaker of the past's dreams. Because the rulers believe they are accomplishing the promise of the past, or at least present themselves as such, they seek to connect each current aspect of policy to an unchallenged and idolized past as if to borrow some of its luster. The year is punctuated with memories of sanctified revolutionary moments as the state literally manages the telling of time: August 4 in Ouagadougou, October 21 in Mogadishu, September 28 in Conakry, July 26 in Havana, November 1 in Algiers. Selecting such official celebrations is no mere bagatelle; it is solemn and serious business precisely because they serve to define the state and the heritage it claims as its own. "Transposing the past into the present," the celebrations "bestow upon the latter the virtues of the former," allowing the state to offer itself as the past's legitimate heir.[79] History thus occupies the space blood lineage occupied in earlier social formations, so that in the end the state's authority is portrayed less as a function of raw power than as one of historical, and revolutionary, necessity.

The discourse also is a language of protest, as Third Worldist dissident groups proclaim their higher allegiance to revolutionary tradition. The past is then solicited to challenge current holders of power, branded as usurpers if they do not so much as claim to be upholding that tradition, as traitors if they do. Fundamentally, this rebellious discursive strategy operates in the same way as its state counterpart, as an affirmation of connection with remote times, of faithfulness to distant struggles. Witness the names of such revolutionary movements as the Sandinistas and the Farabundo Martí Front, to name just two.

The end result is this: two sides scuffling for power and for the mantle of historical legitimacy. For an ideology that prided itself on its focus on the future, Third Worldism was extraordinarily and intensely backward-looking. Ironically, the texture of this revolutionary politics was thus passionately historical, the past having become the sole standard against which to assess political power. But so it was, translating the most brutal and cruel political contests into the innocuous language of historical allegiance. Thus, President Ben Bella would be overthrown in the name of revolutionary continuity. And, apparently without giving a thought to shame or ridicule, those who would have President Sankara murdered would invoke his own memory to justify their senseless act.

Being the bearers of history and the caretakers of the people's revolutionary will is no small task. Political leaders of the Third World, in power or in dissent, experienced this awesome responsibility acutely; then again, they made the most of it, concentrating authority, silencing opponents, cultivating flatterers and sycophants. They had become Third Worldists, with swollen rhetoric to justify their mission and an ornate myth to light their way.

The mission was closely bound up with the myth. There was a revolutionary historical path to discover, a revolutionary will to which to be true, popular aspirations to identify and ultimately to concretize. Indeed, the goal of political leadership followed naturally from the Third Worldist representation of the world, the mission being to achieve perfect harmony and concurrence between the genuine popular will, the people's perception of their own interest, and the exercise of political power. Various obstacles might stand in the way of what Starobinsky called the coveted "transparency,"[80] which I use in this context to mean the desired congruence between the three elements. Removing such hurdles became the solemn business of politics.

For one thing, there might exist a mismatch between the popular will and the people's imagined aspirations. Recall that it is not to the demands of the majority one must bow, but to the *revolutionary* will. There is a difference here, and it is far from insignificant: it implies, for example, that elections are not the chosen vehicle of politics, that the problem for the Third Worldist leader is to unearth the pure being beneath the corrupted surface, the general will below narrow self-interest. In short, heroic Third Worldist leaders were the mold and all who followed were to be cast in it.

Again, it is worth insisting that with such experiences as "people's power," or *participacao popular,* in Cape Verde or Guinea-Bissau and "popular" liberation struggles in Angola, Mozambique, Namibia, Eritrea, Vietnam, or Nicaragua, the ideology of Third Worldism appeared not so much to shape reality as to be shaped by it. Its legitimacy, authority, and credibility drew heavily from the state of the world surrounding it. And what "the world" suggested, and Third Worldism rapidly ratified, was that the people's will could be unleashed, power could devolve to the masses, and new forms of popular democracy could be set in place.

Two principal roads leading to the unadulterated "people" — that is, to the absolute coincidence between general will and popular awareness — were identified. One was by means of political education or indoctrination. It is an ambiguous one, for the educator or leader — the *mualim,* or teacher, as Nyerere was known — must never forget that in the end he or she is subordinate to the people's revolutionary will. To educate is not so much to bestow knowledge as it is to extract what already is there: the people's unpolluted, unspoiled political awareness. In countless texts — by Sékou Touré, Nkrumah, Nasser, and so forth — the Third Worldist political pedagogue is portrayed as torn between leading and following. The tension comes through clearly in Nasser's comparison of the Egyptian masses to "a caravan lost on a wrong path" and in his subsequent admonition that "it is our duty to lead the convoy back on the correct road" in order to "allow it to keep on its way."[81]

The tension helps make some sense of the awkward relation, composed in equal parts of admiration and distrust, between the military and intellectual vanguards of Third Worldist movements. In an indirect and convoluted fashion, as I earlier explained, Third Worldism is a child of nineteenth-century European enlightenment, from which it inherited fairly romantic ideas about the virtues of knowledge. But against this idealized vision are the constant fear that education might distort popular perceptions, the belief that it should be aimed strictly at removing impurities bequeathed by colonialism, and the conviction that at some point it adds impurities of its own. Mao Zedong once remarked that the Chinese people should be well-read, but he cautioned that "to read too many books is harmful. . . . We should read Marxist books, but not too many of them either. It will be enough to read a dozen or so. If we read too many, we can move towards our opposites, become bookworms, dogmatists, revisionists."[82] We can recognize the same ambivalence at play in the 1960s debate between Mozambique's independence movement, FRELIMO, and its student organization, UNEMO. Vying for a leadership position, UNEMO advanced the claim that the decisive criterion should be one's education level. In the process, it invoked a maxim neither too subtle nor too charitable: "A flock of sheep commanded by a lion is worth more than a pride of lions led by an ass." To which FRELIMO replied, essentially, that in order to direct the masses, one had to be directed by them: "The revolution also needs and cherishes its students, leaders and revolutionary intellectuals, but they can get more of an education in the revolution than in the university."[83]

The other road is, precisely, revolution. "Revolution" is not a particularly useful category, and I know of no meaningful way of distinguishing the revolutionary from the nonrevolutionary. But Third Worldism viewed it as the process of standing up to the dominator (generally foreign) and of taking up arms against the established order. More than that, the faith in revolution was so robust that it was apprehended as the best catalyst for, as well as the most truthful expression of, the popular will. As noted above, faithfulness to "revolution" becomes a political criterion by which to judge, to endorse, or to condemn; indeed, in the case of France, as Arendt remarks, "it turned out that it was not even the people and its 'general will' but the very process of the Revolution itself which became the source of all laws."[84]

Perhaps the greatest significance is attached to revolutionary violence as the process that will awaken the masses to their true will. The theme typically is associated with Fanon, and just as typically misunderstood. Fanon sees violence as an act of overcoming, a rebellion against the picture of the passive native painted by the *colon,* a triumph over colonial enslavement. In an insightful analysis, Said thus explains Fanon's notion of violence as the act "by which the native overcomes the division between whites and natives," overcomes, indeed, the division between the native and the image of the native and joins his or her true self.[85] Violence, Fanon wrote, "introduces into each man's consciousness the ideas of a common cause, of a national destiny, and of a collective history."[86]

As in so many other Third Worldist accounts, Fanon's central metaphor is biological: violence helps resume life's natural course. "The appearance of the settler has meant in the terms of syncretism the death of the aboriginal society, cultural lethargy, and the petrification of individuals. For the native, life can only spring up again out of the rotting corpse of the settler. . . . But it so happens that for the colonized people this violence, because it constitutes their only work, invests their characters with positive and creative qualities. The practice of violence binds them together as a whole, since each individual forms a violent link in the great chain, a part of the great organism of violence."[87]

Such assumptions about violence, hallmarks of an assertive Third Worldism, were nourished principally by successful wars of national liberation, in Algeria, Vietnam, Guinea-Bissau, Nicaragua, Mozambique, and elsewhere. Struggle is presented as the key not only to resistance but also to popular awakening in the words of the Algerian FLN, of Cabral in *Unité et lutte,* of Nasser, or of the leaders of the Palestinian movement.[88] Armed struggle, in Cabral's eyes, is a "*determinant* of culture," enabling the "mass of workers and in particular the peasants . . . [to] understand their situation as decisive in the struggle. They would break the fetters of [their] village universe and integrate gradually with the country and the world."[89] In the wake of the Franco-British expedition in the Suez Canal, the Egyptian *rais* asserted that resistance had helped the people "recover its revolutionary will . . . discover its capacities, its potential."[90] One of the more celebrated moments in Palestinian history is the first direct battle between Israelis and the *fedayeen* in the town of Karameh. *Karameh* is the Arabic word for "honor" or "dignity," and the Palestinian leadership made much of the symbolism.[91]

The assumptions also are echoed, at times twisted, in the writings of various historians, political essayists, even lawyers and philosophers.[92] In Jean-Paul Sartre's *Critique of Dialectical Reason,* we can discern Fanon's influence clearly. Sartre's account of social polarization and the temporary formation of revolutionary groups gives violence a place as a chief catalyst, allowing individuals to emerge as "agents of a common *praxis*" in a normative universe.[93] Along similar lines, the Algerian historian Slimane Chikh wrote about the cathartic effect of the war of national liberation, lifting the *fellah* from the despairing life of occupation into the enthralling existence of collective armed resistance.[94] Other examples abound, such as Algerian novelists Mimouni and Ouettar, about whom I will have more to say later; or the Palestinian poet Mahmoud Darwish, whose most celebrated work, *Identity Card,* oscillates between ironic resignation and a threatened violent reprisal that is intimately interlaced with the question of Palestinian identity.

In such a crowd, the singular French lawyer Jacques Vergès might seem odd company. Yet in his courtroom strategy one becomes intensely aware of the opposition between the hypocritical, embarrassed violence of the hegemonic North and the conspicuous, creative violence of the South (or of the marginals generally). Where the defendant is an Arab terrorist, it is French brutality in Algeria or Madagascar that he puts on trial. In his narrative, no choice is left but to side with the terrorist, whose act of defiance embodies courage and restored dignity, the individual defendant expressing the people's covert frustration and obfuscated will.[95]

Vergès's views of terrorism and violence belong, of course, to a more extreme version of Fanon's theory. The same is true of myriad groups in the First and Third Worlds, the Red Brigades, the Bader-Meinhof gang, Action Directe, Sendero Luminoso, and so forth. But to attribute to Fanon a "baffling" and blind "glorification of violence," as Arendt does, is to permit the caricature to take hold of the original.[96] To Fanon and others like him, violence is not everything, nor is it a virtue in and of itself so much as it is a temporary *necessity,* for in its absence colonial subjugation lingers on in the minds of the native in the form of cultural subservience. Davidson evokes Cabral's "distrust of violence," accepted only because it is indispensable.[97] And as Edward Said rightly observes, "for both Cabral and Fanon, the emphasis on 'armed struggle' is at most tactical";[98] it challenges the relationship between colonizer and colonized and introduces the possibility of equality where subordination once reigned. Whether or not one agrees with the assumption is, evidently, an entirely different matter. What is of interest to me, beyond terrorist travesty or excess, is that the *idea* of violence played an important part in Third Worldism, coinciding with the objective of conforming popular self-perception with the general will.

A second potential obstacle to Third Worldist "transparency" is a lack of fit between the popular, revolutionary will, on the one hand, and the nature of political power, or the state, on the other. This too is capable of being realigned. For there is hardly a sense of inherent and unavoidable tension in Third Worldist politics; instead, civil conflict and contradiction are conceived of as symptoms of a curable disharmony. The Third Worldist visions of power come into play at this point, the focus being on whether power can be "possessed" by the people and whether "revolutionary power" can be fixed in an orderly, stable, and institutionalized site.

The answer to the first question — whether the people can possess power — clearly is yes: because power is little more than a delegation of authority and a representation of clearly defined interests, the "revolutionary people" can seize it by putting one of their own in its seat. At that point, political power becomes the perfect expression of the popular will, itself the exact embodiment of the revolutionary interest. In true Jacobin spirit, "the problem of the elimination of evil from the world comes to coincide with the problem of revolution." [99]

The state is crucial in thinking about Third Worldism because it is the space where people and power either meet or miss each other as well as the space where power takes on concrete, physical meaning. In practical terms (though there is nothing very practical about all this), politics ends where state power and popular will become one. Then, as Sékou Touré once put it, since society "has fused with the state, it cannot dissolve the state, for it is the state. The people administers itself, the people manages itself . . . organizes and directs society." [100] The state is therefore not an alien entity, foreign and domineering, or at least it is neither inherently nor irremediably so. Nor indeed is the state the mere reflection of underlying socioeconomic conditions — again, quite a departure from classical Marxist thought. Running through Third Worldism is the certainty that control of the state is the paramount goal and that all else will eventually follow. The French anthropologist Georges Balandier sums up this view as follows: "Modern relations of production have not acquired [in Africa] the determining role they have had and still have in Europe. One must look elsewhere: at the locus where relations concern *power*. . . . It is access to power that leads to control over the economy, far more than the other way around." [101]

If power is a tool that can be possessed by the virtuous and sinful alike, then it should be judged not by its intensity but by its direction. Inverting Benjamin Constant's illustrious aphorism, one might say that under illegitimate rule the weapon is not too heavy, but the arm is unjust. In turn, progress hinges on the possession of, not freedom from, state power, absolute freedom growing out of absolute authority. The personalization of rule and the role of the army in the "progressive" Third World were understood in these terms. It was characteristic of military takeovers in Egypt, Libya, Sudan, Burkina Faso, and Ghana that they were greeted not as manifestations of authoritarian tendencies but as revolutionary events, rectifications, or accelerators.[102] The point being that when power lies in the hands of representatives of the popular will, it is more efficient when it is concentrated than when diluted.

An obvious tension is manifested here, and it runs throughout Third Worldist pronouncements. I come now to the second question — whether revolutionary power ever can be fixed in a stable, institutionalized site — and refer to the dichotomy between popular power (since that is the objective) and centralized, almighty authority (since that is the means). Again, the answer that is offered is yes, and the effort to match popular power and centralized authority can be seen in numerous attempts at such reconciliation, both as an intellectual and as a practical matter. The recognition that rigid hierarchies of governance might thwart the expression of the popular will thus has led, in one way or another, to such constructs as the Comités de Défense de la Révolution in Burkina Faso, Gadhafi's Popular Committees in Libya, self-administration by local assemblies in the "liberated" zones of colonial Cape Verde or Guinea-Bissau, even to the myriad political organizations existing for the most part as single parties (insofar as there was but one will to represent) but that professed to be bastions of popular vigilance.[103] More often than not, the "popular" (the committees, the party cells, and so on) faded, abandoning the stage to the central state authority — the fate of Algeria's FLN or Egypt's Arab Socialist Union immediately comes to mind. Still, debate and tension lingered, and this friction is an important intellectual element in the structure of Third Worldism.

Another attempt at reconciliation took the form of political schizophrenia, a response to the contradiction between the perils of administrative deviation from the general will and the promise of the revolutionary state as that will's guarantor. I have in mind the general tendency of Third Worldist regimes to promote a split image of political power. On the one hand, there is the state-as-revolution, voice and inspiration of the revolutionary will; on the other hand, there is the more dreary state-as-administration, everyday practitioner of governmental policy. The former, embodied in the solitary leader, charismatic soldier, or inspired politician, oversees the latter, alternatively encouraging, lecturing, or castigating. Think, for instance, of Egypt's 1962 Charter, cautioning the people to beware of "the numbing of the revolutionary zeal by the wheels of the bureaucracy"; of Nkrumah's stinging attacks against party bureaucrats and careerists; or of President Sankara's annual dissolution of his cabinet, a choice example of split politics if ever there was one.[104]

More subtle, but partaking of the same spirit, are the ritual ceremonies of self-criticism. Through them, the speaker simultaneously distances him- or herself from what is condemned, reaffirms the existence of a proper path, and reiterates his or her ability to identify it. The leader who has the authority to perform such acts is all at once exonerated and confirmed in his or her priestly position as ultimate custodian of the revolution. Bourdieu thus framed it judiciously when he described self-criticism as the "supreme form of self-celebration," providing "additional evidence of the difficulty and necessity of the sacerdotal function."[105]

One final note concerning the Third Worldist attitude toward political opposition: an image of power is always, in one form or other, an image of dissent. Symmetrical visions of state and rebellion ensue, the one being simply the flip side of the other. Raoul Girardet, in a study of political mythology that is full of insight, put it as follows: "Is the power we ascribe to our enemy not the very one we wish to possess? Does its ever-extended capacity of social control, the mastery of events and of minds it is supposed to exert, not correspond to the kind of power we claim in defense of our own cause?"[106]

In the case of Third Worldism, the totalistic theory of power thus gives rise to totalistic theories of dissent. Third Worldism views itself as omniscient, the impeccable proxy of the popular masses, capable of reordering the world, and that is how it comes to view all who would oppose it as well — as almighty representatives of the planned counterrevolution. To the supposed enemies of Third Worldism — international capitalism, imperialism, Zionism, the IMF — are thus ascribed not intrigue and wiliness alone but also unbounded resourcefulness, influence, and control. Third Worldism and its dissenters are conceived as thoroughly different and yet thoroughly the same — thoroughly different *because* thoroughly the same.

Which leads to yet another consequence: if revolutionary leadership represents both the popular will and the compelling march of history, there can be no such thing as minor disagreement, or even disagreement over a particular policy. Instead, all forms of opposition, from the petty to the grand, are traced to a uniform center of resistance. As in France in 1789, debates on issues of domestic policy thus become, literally, debates on "foreign affairs," objections become disloyalty, and protest, treason.[107] As Lynn Hunt put it, "On the one side . . . the people's will, the Revolution; on the other, the plot, the anti-principle, the negation."[108] Hence the outbreak of political paranoia, international conspiracies — real or imagined — cropping up in endless succession in Guinea, Benin, Congo-Brazzaville, Libya, or Burkina Faso.

The point, of course, is less to challenge the veracity of such accusations than to explain what underlying ideological environment enabled them and, in turn, what ideological activities they enabled. It seems to me that the explanation is simple, namely, that an all-embracing conspiracy is the sole qualified foe for Third Worldism. International conspiracy fits naturally in the structure of Third Worldism because it corroborates the Third Worldist mapping of the universe, polarized and at war. It also supports Third Worldism's claim to being the surrogate of revolutionary forces seeking to rearrange the world order. If Third Worldism meant all that it said it did — radical political reform and sweeping economic change — then surely it must have threatened the interests of world capitalism, and just as surely it must have prompted a hostile reaction. What better gauge of the seriousness of one's ambition than the seriousness with which it is taken by presumed adversaries? In this sense, indeed, Third Worldism *depended* on the idea of conspiracy: with its lofty designs and exalted goals, Third Worldism could afford no less of an adversary. As François Furet correctly notes, "The plot is, for the Revolution, the only worthy adversary because it is modeled after it."[109]

States, as I have tried to show, are prolific storytellers. They recount the story of their origins, of the identity of their inhabitants, of the nature of the individuals who have come to be their rulers. Politics thus can be seen as a process of perpetual self-vindication, the self-legitimating tales edging their way sporadically into official pronouncements or into society's diversified intellectual productions. At more or less regular intervals, however, states deliberately mobilize cultural resources and political energies to perform the founding story, to repeat the gestures that provide meaning. The episodes contain, in highly condensed form, the essential ingredients of state mythology, reaffirming the nation's identity, characterizing its people, vindicating its leadership. We call such dramatic moments elections.

The narrative culminates with elections because that is the point at which the state openly projects its ideological vision of society and social interactions onto a different—let us call it political—plane. The exercise of the franchise is thus doubly revealing. On the one hand, by choosing precisely what it will project or transfer onto the political realm, the state tells us how it constructs its people—as a constellation of individual monads, as clusters defined by ethnic, religious, or linguistic similarity, as an assortment of social classes, or, for that matter, as a homogenous whole. The problem in each instance is to identify the lens through which the state reads and filters society. On the other hand, electoral procedures are the state's way of indicating whence the authority of political leaders derives and what their legitimacy actually means.

The electoral process offers a privileged angle from which to examine (briefly) a number of the concepts discussed so far. Third Worldist countries were predominantly single-party, their elections either noncompetitive or, at the very least, lacking in openness, partisanship, and the resulting accountability of leadership. Why, one might ask, did they bother with the preordained plebiscites, ritualized celebrations, and fastidious enthronements to which, at set intervals, their citizens were summoned? Chiefly because elections are where society turns into politics, which is where, in turn, the often indiscernible process of ideological reproduction is at its most visible.

To begin with, the notion of national homogeneity and oneness lent itself naturally to a single-party structure. As Julius Nyerere put it, "Politics in a country ruled by a two-party system is not, and cannot be, national politics; it is the politics of groups whose rivalries have generally little interest for the great majority of the people. . . . When there is one party, and when that party is identified with the Nation as a whole, the foundations of democracy are more solid."[110] In theory, the Third Worldist popular will had little use for partisan politics and equally little use for territorial, ethnic, linguistic, or religious divisions. (I say "in theory" because, though it was dominant, the unitary reading coexisted alongside competing ones that acknowledged here socioeconomic cleavages, there ethnic or regional splits, and territorial divisions most everywhere.)

Nor is that all, for Third Worldist electoral systems also evinced the particular understanding of leadership previously described. By positing the existence of a latent revolutionary will, Third Worldism was led to judge political representativity in terms less of procedure than of substance. As a result, Third Worldist elections dealt only marginally with issues of choice. I concede that this is a somewhat a crude generalization, since single parties often presented more than one candidate per seat, whether in Tanzania or Algeria.[111] But, certainly in relation to Western democracies, picking leaders was hardly the principal concern in Third Worldist elections. In Hanna Pitkin's interesting typology, Western democracies can thus be said to espouse an "authorization" view of representation: elections are honored primarily as techniques designed to empower state officials. In contrast, a "recognition" view permeates the Third Worldist approach: representation is all about the alignment between the people's interest and the officials' beliefs.[112] The plebiscitarian character of Third Worldist elections is thus significant, inasmuch as they are not avenues for choosing leaders but confirmatory rites. They celebrate the identity of view between the popular will and revolutionary aspiration, between revolutionary aspiration and state policy. Gone is the grave, at times austere atmosphere of secret balloting; Third Worldist–style elections would exhibit a "festive, ritual, almost magical character."[113]

One final point. All electoral systems, I have said, reflect and reproduce the organizing principles of the political regime they happen to serve, particular techniques of selecting elites (including those in which the elite is *self*-selecting) betraying particular interpretations of the people to be represented and of the very function of representation itself. In Apter's words, they are "periodic and highly ritualized spectacles of combat that reenact and celebrate both the myths and theories of the state."[114] Which means that when the rules of the ceremonial change, one must ask what has happened to the theories and what has become of the myths — but that is to get way ahead of our story.

A list of so-called Third Worldist countries and movements may make my meaning of Third Worldism easier to understand. By the 1970s and 1980s the Third Worldist universe could be said to include (or at some point to have included) the following: Angola, Mozambique, Tanzania, Madagascar, the Seychelles, Zimbabwe, Algeria, Benin, Congo-Brazzaville, Cape Verde, Guinea, Guinea-Bissau, Nicaragua, Burkina Faso, Ghana, South Yemen, the ANC, the PLO, the Polisario, the Salvadoran rebels, Somalia, Ethiopia (for some), the Eritrean independence movement (for many more), Libya and Iraq (grudgingly), Syria (barely), Grenada (under Bishop), Jamaica (intermittently), Chile (briefly), Cambodia (agonizingly), Cuba, Laos, and Vietnam.

An important point bears stressing. It would be ludicrous, to say the least, to claim that these events or political regimes were without distinc-

tion, that they were the culmination of identical social or political aspirations, or that the men and women who managed to seize power all
were cut of the same cloth. There were individuals of superior virtue and
vision alongside individuals of exceptional cunning and deceit. More
often than not, the latter survived (for survival was what they were all
about), while the former were ungraciously swept away.

As deep as these differences were, however, they never quite eclipsed
the sense that self-proclaimed revolutionary states and organizations
were part of a single historical process. It may appear strange to yield to
a claim that we know to be inaccurate. But once we begin to think of
Third Worldism as an ideological construct, as a vision of history backed
by political leaders, sustained (wittingly or not) by academics, embraced
by militants, and denounced by critics, the links between dissimilar
events become less difficult to accept. What matters here, in other words,
is the existence of a system of thought in which Gadhafi's erratic goings-
on and Neto's persevering dedication can be viewed (at some level) as
similar and placed in the same category by friend and foe alike.

Doubtless some will brand the classification as arbitrary and irrational, but that is essentially to miss the point.[115] Like all groupings, this
one is part of what the French sociologist Pierre Bourdieu dubs a "classification struggle," the battle to "impose the legitimate definition of
the divisions" of the world "and through that, to make and unmake
groups[,] . . . to impose a vision of the . . . world through principles of
di-vision."[116] For the vision of a world comprising a group of industrialized nations lending their civilizing and developing hand to less fortu-
nate counterparts, Third Worldism sought to substitute the picture of a
globe polarized between a revolutionary Third World symbolizing the
future and an imperialistic, exploitative, and decrepit West. Neither was
more or less inherently arbitrary than the other; both required overlook-
ing certain subtle nuances, even flagrant discrepancies, and both were
aided in their effort by true believers as well as more detached observers
(for instance, the scriveners of which I spoke), who, intentionally or
not, entered into alliance with them, providing them with an idiom, instruments of knowledge, and broad political or economic explanatory
theories.

The asserted similarity, or to put it more circumspectly, the shared
political space in which both Gadhafi and Neto were made to fit, was
thus intrinsic to Third Worldism and to the worldview it sought to promote — on many levels. For Third World leaders, to begin with the more
obvious, it offered international backing and a means to escape the uneasy political tête-à-tête with the West. Support at times would become

more tangible, as when Cuba sent its troops to shore up the MPLA's regime in Angola or when material, financial, and other types of assistance were offered to the PLO, the ANC, the Polisario, and others. Domestically, the image of an allied front provided both ideological and rhetorical support for the notion that the country belonged to a far grander and therefore far more powerful historical process. In this context Philippe Braillard speaks of the international arena as "an instrument of domestic legitimation."[117] Consider the pomp surrounding visits such as Castro's to Algiers, or these words from Amilcar Cabral: "Our hearts beat in unison with the hearts of our brothers in Vietnam . . . with our brothers of the Congo . . . with our brothers in Cuba . . . the refugees, the martyrized refugees of Palestine . . . and most seriously and painfully with our brothers in South Africa."[118] Of course, the most illustrious symbol of the universal character of the Third World revolution remains Che Guevara, the man who claimed to have led people "of another language in an unknown land."[119] He is the "revolutionary phoenix," literally everywhere: spotted in the Dominican Republic one day, in Venezuela, Columbia, Peru, Chile, or Guatemala the next, perhaps even in Tanzania, the Congo, or Vietnam.[120]

Third Worldism was also used as a basis for discrediting or neutralizing internal opponents, by accusing the opposition of being aligned with the forces of imperialism against the universal forces of progress or, more subtly, by appropriating the opposition's own discourse only to project it onto the international scene: a "class enemy" existed, to be sure, but it was "outside," beyond the national borders.

At yet another level, many among the Third Worldist intelligentsia—journalists and scholars alike—would partake in this enthusiasm and look to these various countries as laboratories for land reform, state-building, industrialization, cultural renewal, or grass-roots democracy. Among European students, many of whom had lost faith in the possibility of domestic revolutionary change, "calls for Mao, Castro, Che Guevara and Ho Chi Minh" at times resembled "pseudo-religious incantations for saviors from another world."[121] They too had been fascinated by utopian visions of Che's "two, three, abundant Vietnams," captivated by Debray's romantic notion of the *foco* as the starting point for the "revolution in the revolution." As Hobsbawm remarks, "It was support for Third World guerrillas, and, in the USA after 1965, resistance against being sent to fight against them, which mobilized the Left more than anything else, except hostility to nuclear arms."[122]

But even Third Worldist intellectuals who did not share in the euphoria, those who were keenly aware of the differences between a Neto and a Gadhafi, often would speak in terms of faithfulness to, and betrayal of, the Third Worldist cause; and in so doing, they inevitably contributed to the mythmaking. Betrayal is a key concept here, as is deceit. For it presumes that there is something to which one can be disloyal, that there is a true Third Worldist path, a path the renegade, in some manner, was meant (or claimed) to follow. Leaders of Zaire, Thailand, or Guatemala never fooled anyone, and they were all they were ever meant to be; not so leaders of Syria, Ethiopia, or Kampuchea.

Finally, among those in the North who reacted with trepidation and unconcealed disgust to any talk of the coming Third World revolution, Third Worldism was a concrete reality, and lumping Neto and Gadhafi together came effortlessly. To quote Said, "Westerners [became] aware that what they have to say about the history and the cultures of 'subordinate' peoples is challengeable by the people themselves, people who a few years back were simply incorporated, culture, land, history, and all, into the great Western empires and their disciplinary discourses."[123] Europe had learned how to deal with localized armed resistance, but it was not used to a collective "talking back," let alone to a transnational counternarrative that not only challenged its traditional discourse but literally reversed it, blaming Europe for the Third World's backwardness, poverty, and other afflictions — indeed, blaming Europe and its societal models for *Europe's* own political, economic, and social decay and turning to the Third World as the path to a rejuvenated future.[124]

And so it was that Third Worldism, understood as a system of representation, a radically new angle of vision on North and South, took root. At all times, it would remain mutinous in relation to Europe and North America; yet by and large it would achieve a localized dominant status within a certain political, cultural, and intellectual sphere. There would reign its language and its norms, its forms of censorship and forms of discipline.

CHAPTER 4

Algeria in the
Age of Third Worldism

When we last left it, Algeria was a country bearing the full weight of foreign occupation, tugged by various ideological currents — traditionalist, assimilationist, and socialist — and lured by competing political parties. By World War II the process of synthesizing the three currents was well under way. Traditionalism assumed the guise of justifiable opposition to Algerian cultural decimation; out of allegiance to France came intellectual tools of resistance — liberty, democracy, equality, and the like; and economic radicalism, once transferred to the international arena, lapsed into less threatening anti-imperialism. Though movements bringing Abbasists, Messalists, and *ulémas* together, such as the Amis du Manifeste et de la Liberté (AML), had surfaced, it was becoming increasingly clear that the chief beneficiary of this blend would be Messali Hadj.[1] For Messali, it would be fair to say, felt ideologically, culturally, even temperamentally closer to radical nationalism than did his political peers.

In hindsight the force of Messalism appears unmistakable. Messali's populism, the intellectual nimbleness of his cadres, and the organization's roots among the immigrant proletariat all enabled the Messalist movement to exploit the openings (few as they were) allowed by the French. Messali brought to anticolonialism a personal charisma whose appeal resonated with rural and urban masses and yet did not drive away — not entirely anyway — urban elites and rural chieftains. For all its allure, however, the Messalist movement could not meet its objective — achieving independence, providing equal rights to the Algerian population, or simply establishing hegemony on the domestic political scene —

by political means alone. An additional impetus was needed, and that impetus would be violent uprising and the war of national liberation. The irony is that the war would remove Messali from the political stage once and for all. He was not about to give up what he regarded as his due of his own accord, but others would do it for him — gladly.

This chapter discusses Third Worldism in the Algerian context as a way of providing added depth and detail to the matters touched upon in chapter 3. From a historical standpoint, it takes us from the end of World War II to the heyday of Algerian — and international — Third Worldism (roughly the mid- to late 1970s). Woven into this narrative are the themes that characterize Third Worldism as a whole: the emphasis on historical legitimacy, the sacralization of the people, the identification of political power with popular will, and so forth.

To repeat a point I tried to make at the outset: I am interested in Algeria in its own right, of course, because present and likely future developments make an understanding of its past all the more necessary. But I am also interested in what its evolution tells us about the significance of left-wing ideologies in the Third World, about whether they were "genuine" or merely "imported" thought systems, and about trends that can be observed with depressing regularity throughout the formerly progressive underdeveloped world.

The first significant outburst of violence in the aftermath of World War II took place on V-E Day, May 8, 1945, in the city of Sétif. It was as if the entire injustice of colonialism had crowded in on that one fateful day: Algerian soldiers who had been sent to the front, many never to return, had helped vanquish Nazi Germany, ceremonies marking victory were being held, and yet Algerians remained under foreign rule, oppressed and victimized. The parallel between France's recent liberation from German domination and its continued control over Algeria was obvious — and painful. Most troubling, perhaps, was that the parallel, let alone any contradiction, barely crossed the minds of the French, who were far too enamored of the image of their own *mission civilisatrice* to grasp the significance of the comparison.

If the celebrations were the immediate trigger, deeper motives also were at play. As a result of the war, economic conditions in the countryside had so deteriorated that by 1945 famine had become a serious threat. Politically, the success of the AML, Messali's forced confinement and subsequent transfer to Brazzaville, and France's timid, ill-timed reforms combined to aggravate the situation.[2] The V-E Day ceremonies simply provided the spark.

As the celebrations were under way, demonstrations rapidly turned into protest against colonial occupation. Members of the crowd, mainly Messalist sympathizers, brandished banners "bearing such provocative slogans as 'Vive Messali!' 'Free Messali!' 'For the Liberation of the People, Long Live Free and Independent Algeria!' They were also flourishing, for the first time, the green-and-white flag that had once been the standard of . . . Abd-el-Kader."[3]

What happened next remains unclear. The protests somehow degenerated into bloody riots. Some Europeans were murdered indiscriminately—according to Harbi, roughly 28; according to Alistair Horne, slightly more.[4] The French *colons,* soldiers, and policemen responded in kind, and then some. And then some more. The official *Rapport Tubert* estimated the toll of Muslim dead at between 1,020 and 1,300. Algerian nationalists claimed that it was closer to 45,000. Today, French historians believe it was approximately 7,000.[5]

The events ruffled certainties on both sides of the colonial frontier. For French officials, the comforting division between those Arabs with whom one could deal and those with whom one could not became far less reliable. Messalists, as well as Abbasists and *ulémas,* had joined the AML, and the AML itself was now being blamed for the disturbances. While Algerians were asking for greater autonomy, local *colons* seized on the opportunity to demand greater French firmness. In the ensuing political confusion, Paris made token gestures to Algerians, banned the AML, imprisoned many of its leaders (including some of the more moderate ones), and organized local elections, the most noteworthy aspect of which was the scale of electoral fraud.

On the Algerian side, the sense of disorientation was, if anything, more profound. In 1946, Ferhat Abbas established the Union Démocratique du Manifeste Algérien (UDMA), but its influence rapidly waned, moderation proving an unsuited response to French inflexibility. The *ulémas* were unable to articulate a coherent political approach; they kept returning—reflexively—to the cultural question even as the urgency of the moment, violence now unleashed, seemed to clamor for more. The communists continued to be plagued by their ambiguous attitude toward nationalism. Finally, although Messali Hadj's newly formed MTLD had become Algeria's most dynamic political organization, internal divisions tore it apart. On the one hand, many of the party's cadres resented Messali's authoritarian leadership style; on the other, the party's younger members, weary of political games and maneuvering — they dismissively called it *boulitik* — favored immediate action.[6]

Hanging over all this was an expanding sense of irrelevance. Political parties born and bred in turn-of-the century colonialism were unprepared and ill equipped to handle the mounting frustration and anger. This was less true of the Messalists, whose culture had always included a good deal of activism, but even they gradually had become bogged down in the drab routines of politicking. Messalism and its counterparts had provided a coherent ideological outlook with which to confront the colonial power; yet at the organizational level, disconnectedness between stagnant political parties and a restless rank and file could hardly have been greater. Fastening the latent ideology onto a structured but nevertheless activist movement would be the nationalist movement's challenge and, ultimately, its crowning achievement.

The history of Algeria from 1945 to 1954 thus grew out of Messalism but also away from it. Future leaders of the FLN were steeped in the Third Worldist ideology of Messalism, passionately nationalistic, attached to a "messianic vision of an egalitarian society"[7] and to a traditional, albeit politicized vision of Islam. Neglecting social divisions for the most part, they emphasized unifying elements: religion, culture, and colonial status. At the same time, they sought to break ranks with the more bureaucratic tradition of Messalism. Most were former members of the Organisation Spéciale (OS), a clandestine offspring of the MTLD created in 1947 and designed to conduct violent operations against the French. Although the OS was discovered and dismantled in 1950, the common experience shared by its members helped forge the bonds that would be instrumental in the creation of the FLN. The FLN's founding fathers were young (their average age was thirty-two), they had a visceral dislike for the political debates that had divided their elders, and they worshiped direct action.[8]

Thus, France's fierce repression in Sétif had invigorated precisely what it had sought to suppress. By radicalizing the nationalist movement, the massacres had an "incalculable" and "ineradicable" impact.[9] Algerians "understood the power of collective actions" thanks to the revival and rejuvenation of past mythologies of armed resistance.[10] For instance, Kateb Yacine, the renowned Algerian poet, said that at Sétif "my sense of humanity was affronted for the first time by the most atrocious sights. I was sixteen years old. The shock I felt at the pitiless butchery that caused the deaths of thousands of Muslims, I have never forgotten. From that moment my nationalism took definitive form."[11] And Rabah

Bitat, who soon would become a leader of the FLN, asserted that from then on he "knew without the shadow of a doubt that he was one of the colonized." [12]

Indeed, upon returning home from the front lines at the end of World War II, a number of future FLN fighters would be outraged by accounts of the massacre. How could it have been otherwise? Soldiers had risked their lives for France, and France had expressed its gratitude by shooting their brethren on armistice day. There was enough in that tragic asymmetry alone to nurture lifetimes of wrath, resentment, and vengeance.

On All Saints' Day, 1954, the FLN finally launched its revolt. In pamphlets distributed throughout the country, it proclaimed:

> To the Algerian people,
> To the militants of the National Cause!
> . . . After decades of struggle, the National Movement reached its final phase of fulfillment.
> . . . A group of responsible young people and dedicated militants, gathering about it the majority of wholesome and resolute elements, has judged that the moment has come to take the National Movement out of the impasse into which it has been forced by the conflicts of persons and influence, and to launch it into the true revolutionary struggle at the side of the Moroccan and Tunisian brothers. . . .
> Our movement of regeneration presents itself under the label of
>
> FRONT DE LIBERATION NATIONALE
>
> thus freeing itself from any possible compromise, and offering to all Algerian patriots of every social position and of all parties . . . the possibility of joining in the national struggle. [13]

This amounted to healthy rhetorical overkill for what in reality was a rather inconsequential initial sally. The FLN, of course, saw to it that the space between promise and delivery would be amply filled with mythology, but even so the French must not have had too much to worry about at first. The *colons* suffered relatively few losses, and the Algerians recovered relatively few weapons. [14] With the exception of the Messalists, all Algerian political parties condemned the violence. Communists, Abbasists, *ulémas,* even centralists (members of the MTLD's Central Committee, who had broken with Messali) referred to it scornfully as a "provocation" or as "suicidal operations." [15] To make matters worse, the FLN's first attacks revealed a lack of organization and a pronounced geographic imbalance. It showed its strength in the mountainous Aurès and Kabilya, traditional strongholds of anticolonial resistance; elsewhere, in the Constantinois, the Algérois, or in Oranie, the FLN suffered initial setbacks.[16]

Yet neither disappointment nor temporary defeat would prove fatal to the Front. The difference between the nineteenth-century movements of Abdelkader or Moqrani, which were not entirely unsuccessful insurrections but eventually petered out, and the FLN's uprising was not, certainly not principally, a matter of superior material resources. Of greater significance was that the FLN drew its power from the far-reaching political, social, and ideological restructuring that had taken place in the intervening period. That out of the modest achievements of November 1, 1954, would come the triumph of 1962 suggests just how profound that restructuring had been and the extent to which the various and converging currents of Algerian anticolonialism had prepared the way for the FLN's Third Worldism. To these one must add the influence of the international context, described above.

In 1955 the subprefect of Tizi-Ouzou, Kabilya's capital city, noted that "not even three months have gone by [since November], and already [the Algerians'] vocabulary has changed."[17] Then, in August 1955 an FLN assault in the northern Constantinois caused the death of seventy-one European civilians, thirty-one French soldiers, and twenty-one Algerians. By the time the French had finished exacting revenge some twelve thousand Algerians lay dead.[18] Of equal magnitude was the political toll, though in this case the victim was the colonial power. By intensifying the confrontation, the FLN and, less willfully, the French had forced Algerians to take sides, shattering the illusions of a "third force." Now there could be no more neutrality, and no more innocence. For moderates on both sides the dilemma reached truly agonizing proportions.

There is little doubt, for instance, that Camus was not insensitive to the misery nor oblivious to the injustice that colonialism had meant for Algeria, where both he and his family had long lived. But his perspective was above all that of a *French* Algerian, his feelings toward French *colons* at all times drawing from disappointment rather than opposition. In the colonial effort, as Said perceptively remarks, Camus saw waste, not error.[19] When push came to shove, loyalty to France could not but prevail:

As far as Algeria is concerned, national independence is a formula driven by nothing other than passion. There has never been an Algerian nation. . . . The size and duration of the French settlement, in particular, are enough to create a problem that cannot be compared to anything else in history. The French of Algeria are also natives, in the strong sense of the word. Moreover, a purely Arab Algeria could not achieve that economic independence without which political independence is nothing but an illusion. However inadequate the French effort has been, it is of such proportions that no other country would today agree to take over the responsibility.[20]

The process of taking sides, which Camus evokes here as logical deduction, the Algerian writer Mouloud Feraoun expresses in the language of overpowering inevitability: "From now on, [my compatriots] belong to one clan, and they know that the other is the enemy. . . . Violence on the field has awakened a large number of us. . . . Slogans have become decrees."[21]

By polarizing the situation in this manner, the events of 1955 helped spread the revolution. Geographically, the cycle of repression came at a tremendous cost to the local population. Four hundred thousand Algerians were confined in one way or other, three hundred thousand sought refuge in neighboring Tunisia and Morocco, and approximately seven hundred thousand found their way to the cities in what became a massive urban migration. By 1961, according to Pierre Bourdieu, one out of every three Algerians "no longer lived in his former place of abode."[22] Sociologically, the revolution affected the lower and middle classes, in both rural and urban areas. The FLN sponsored and controlled various socioprofessional organizations—for students, the Union Générale des Etudiants Musulmans Algériens (UGEMA); for workers, the Union Générale des Travailleurs Algériens (UGTA); and for merchants, the Union Générale des Commerçants et Artisans (UGCA). As Harbi comments, "L'Algérie toute entière va basculer dans la guerre."[23]

And politically, virtually all of Algeria's nationalist cadres would soon join the FLN. Again, there was no longer room for choice, and little time for hesitation. Even Abbas, whose nephew had been killed by members of the Front in the course of its operation in the Constantinois, realized that he had to join them. This he did in 1955. Likewise, *centralistes* and *ulémas* closed ranks. Vainly trying to resist the FLN's hegemony, in March 1956 the communists set up their own military organization, Les Combattants de la Liberté. By July the Combattants had been integrated into the FLN's armed branch, the Armée de Liberation Nationale (ALN). Though the Algerian Communist Party refused to disband, in 1957 it formally recognized the FLN's leading role in "the Algerian people's struggle for independence."[24] By 1958 the FLN had established a provisional government, known as the Gouvernement Provisoire de la République Algérienne (GPRA), headed by Ferhat Abbas.

Not all opposition to the FLN had been quashed, however. Even

though it believed both in the Front's goal of total independence and in
the means it chose for achieving it, Messali Hadj's Mouvement National
Algérien rejected the FLN's attempt to monopolize the political arena.
Their competition for supremacy turned fierce and deadly, and it became
in many ways the forgotten war of the Algerian revolution. The MNA
claimed the right to represent the Algerian people during the war, at the
negotiating table, and during the transition to independence. Since both
parties were driven by an ideology whose notions of popular representativity and power demanded exclusivity, they did not take well to opposition or dissent. Hence, the FLN's supremacy came about as the result of considerable effort, and at a very heavy price indeed.[25]

But come about it did. By the early 1960s even the French government was forced to bow to this reality. Of course, it insisted on holding
a national referendum, and it refused to formally recognize the FLN's
provisional government until the very end. Yet the cumulative effect of
years of struggle had already taken Algeria out of France's hands and put
it in those of the FLN. Arguably, this was not the case in strictly military terms. But military terms had by then become of only marginal
interest. What mattered was control over the inner world, that is, control
over the minds. As Jean Leca, one of the preeminent specialists on Algeria, observed, "Self-determination resulted from a 'predetermination'
through which the French government admitted that the FLN represented the Algerian nation. . . . Beyond legal subtleties, a fundamental
truth emerges: neither independence nor the FLN's legitimacy derives
from a popular vote, however solemn it may have been. They are the
outcome of the history of national liberation."[26]

In more ways than one, the study of Algeria's revolution takes us to the
heart of the Third Worldist enterprise. My aim here is to read the FLN's
revolution, or *thawra,* not solely as an attempt to (re)conquer land but
as an effort directed at the cultural, ideological, and intellectual fields as
well. The wartime Front employed itself systematically to establish certain ways of thinking — about the revolution's relationship with the past;
about the revolution's relationship to the people; and about the people's
relationship to political leaders.

The historical discourse of the wartime FLN thus was marked by a
selective amnesia of sorts, a decision to reject one legacy while embracing
another.[27] There is November 1st as "mystique," as "la source, le geste
qui détérmine tout," a radical rupture with the past;[28] and then there

is November 1st as outcome, the culmination of a long historical process in which not only Algeria but the Third World as a whole participated. In the end, a story was assembled comprising both of these outlooks, neither incompatible nor fortuitously brought together. What gave them unity were the purposes they served: to characterize the FLN as the legitimate representative of the Algerian people; to delegitimize all other groups; and to bestow upon the FLN the virtues of the Algerian and Third World national movements.

As part of this endeavor, the FLN portrayed pre-1954 political groups as stagnant or sluggish. From its very first proclamation, the Front sharply distinguished itself from all other parties, calling for a thorough "political purification." "Our national movement," it declared, "overcome by years of paralysis and routine, poorly directed, lacking public opinion's necessary support, overwhelmed by events, is disintegrating. . . . L'heure est grâve!"[29] In other words, the FLN was novel and all else was obsolete, ineffective — out of commission.

Things were not as simple as that, of course. The FLN pirated much of the Messalists' ideology and raided their personnel, along with those of practically all other partisan groups. As Harbi describes the effort, "the function of the historical discourse of the FLN is not to reconstitute the truth, be it relative, but to unite the forces that have joined it, to ensure the hegemony of its founding group, and to exclude all other candidates to society's leadership from the national body."[30] He adds: "The revolutionary legitimacy claimed by the FLN's leaders is not the legitimacy of practice, judged, politically, by its effects, but the legitimacy of a date: 'The combatants of November 1st.'"[31]

A creative use of history also helped establish the FLN's affiliation with a more general, more distant — hence less contentious and less threatening — tradition. Temporally, the association was with the perennial "spirit" of the Algerian nation; spatially, it was with the global anticolonial movement, the FLN's revolution being characterized as the natural outgrowth of the two. In the first place, Algeria was revealed to the FLN's audience both at home and abroad as a succession of nationalist or revolutionary moments. Thus, the Front chose to revive the memory of precolonial Algeria and the struggles of Abdelkader, Moqrani, and others rather than evoke the divisive and politically charged history of modern Algerian nationalism. As head of the provisional government, the GPRA, Abbas explained in 1958 that the aim was to "restore the Algerian state that the vicissitudes of military conquest in 1830 had brutally and unjustly erased from North Africa's political map." Also in 1958, in an article entitled "Les origines de la révolution algérienne," *El Moudjahid* proclaimed that "the Revolution of November 1, 1954, is the outcome of the Algerian people's secular resistance to French domination."[32] Indeed, "the roots of the Algerian revolution lie in the depths of [our] past."[33]

The figure of Abdelkader is central. I wrote earlier on that he was presented as the first nationalist, the first anticolonialist, the first true Algerian statesman. Much of this is pure fiction, but the image itself is revealing. The FLN was in search of an appropriate pedigree, and Abdelkader was a fitting (i.e., uncontroversial) historical figure. In one of the previously mentioned 1958 articles in *El Moudjahid,* a picture of the emir was accompanied by the following caption: "He was in a sense the forerunner of the Algerian revolution." The story went on to make the link even more explicit: "Abd-el-Kader's surrender in 1847 did not put an end to a resistance that . . . lasted until 1881. . . . Behind an apparent resignation, the French easily recognized the indomitable character of the Algerian nation."[34]

The FLN's historical discourse also relied heavily on the international motif. To an extent, I have tried to illustrate, the FLN's Third Worldist outlook was made possible by the existence of anticolonial movements in the Third World; in the Front, one sees the deliberate effort to embrace such movements, to link them together in a single grouping, and to establish the Algerian revolution's membership in that ensemble. Participation in the Bandung Conference was one instance, and "the spirit of Bandung" soon would become a familiar refrain.[35] But *El Moudjahid* made the point more generally: "The Algerian people have experienced concretely the interdependence of historical phenomena. To say that the local destruction of colonialism magnifies its destruction as a system is no longer to express an abstract, academic principle understood by intellectuals alone."[36] Indeed, "the struggle of the Algerian people is neither isolated nor unique; it is but an episode in the universal struggle . . . against European colonialism. . . . The Franco-Algerian conflict is part of the gigantic battle pitting colonial forces against the aspirations for emancipation of subject people."[37]

Leaping freely over temporal and geographic barriers, the FLN therefore delivered a selective, or rather politicized, history to Algerians and Europeans alike. The enduring resistance of the Algerian people, the exceptional character of the revolution, the concurrent radicalization of Third World politics — all formed the ideological underpinning for the Front's discourse on history.

The second core component of the FLN's ideological effort had to do with the people. It had two aspects. One was the construction by the Front of a "revolutionary" people, which slowly supplanted all others. I am referring to *le peuple,* featured prominently in *El Moudjahid*'s subtitle: *La révolution pour le peuple et par le peuple.* We are dealing here with an almost sacred being, part *moudjahid* (the fighter, or more precisely, the fighter of the *jihad,* loosely translated as "holy war"), part *fellah* (the ordinary Algerian peasant), but first and foremost socially and politically homogeneous. Algerian Third Worldists were heavily influenced by Frantz Fanon, and his way of apprehending the peasantry is much in evidence. Indeed, the ALN's chief of staff, Colonel Houari Boumedienne, reportedly founded a "revolutionary club" in which Fanon offered courses in political training.[38] In the quasi-Marxist language of which Third Worldists were so fond, Fanon taught his atypical students that "the peasants alone are revolutionaries, for they have nothing to lose and everything to gain."[39] Paradoxically, this image of a uniform, undifferentiated peasantry was supported by the French image of a dual Algeria, the one modern, fully dominated by the *colons,* the other backward, still in the hands of the traditional peasant. That both were highly misleading, that both overlooked pronounced inequalities among the peasantry—between the expanding underclass (landless rural workers, rural proletariat, and city migrants) and the emerging rural bourgeoisie[40]—was barely noted and, as the images served the interests of those on both ends who had crafted them, skillfully avoided.

Quite literally, the revolution thus gave birth to a new actor on the national stage, one patiently pieced together, chiseled, and polished by the FLN. In the Front's methods the reader will not fail to notice familiar Third Worldist attitudes and convictions. The FLN's vision of the people implies the existence of a pure, unsullied, popular core that needs to be extracted. Beneath the precious surface of colonial rule lies the common man, uncorrupted, "pragmatic," and "full of common sense."[41] The theme can be found in Fanon's contrast between the "well-lighted European city and the dark, fetid, ill-lit casbah"; in novelist Kateb Yacine's reference to authentic Algeria as a "cave"; or in Jacques Berque's evocation of Algeria's "interiorité explosive," the explosive inwardness.[42]

The FLN also emphasized the ability of the leadership and of the war itself to bring to the fore the people's latent revolutionary aspirations. As early as 1948, Hocine Aït-Ahmed, then a member of the MTLD and soon to be one of the FLN's *chefs historiques,* argued that while the "revolutionary potential is very powerful," it must be "sharpened and deep-

ened." Indeed, "to deepen their [the people's] revolutionary consciousness is to make explicit . . . their social aspirations."[43] Amar Ouzegane,
for his part, compared the effect of the insurrection to "social biochem-
istry," explaining that it had "ripened national awareness."[44] Notably, it
was while writing about the Algerian war and lecturing to the FLN's
leaders that Fanon developed the idea that violence could awaken men
and women to their being. The revolution was apprehended as a process
of purification thanks to which the authentic *peuple* would burst forth
and rise to the surface.

Throughout there is an urge for political and cultural redemption. At
its most explicit, the phenomenon involved human metamorphosis, a
thorough reversal of signs: the impure became the pure, the sacrilegious the sacred. Ouzegane thus finds himself claiming that "nonsense
can be latent truth. What is judged as evil can be metamorphosed into
good. Chimera becomes audacity; madness, lucidity; ignorance, science."[45] Characters who once had belonged to the underworld, the
shady universe of crime and villainy, were rehabilitated and portrayed as
revolutionary heroes: Ali la Pointe, Ali-Z'yeux Bleux, Petit-Maroc, Said
Touati dit le Balafré.[46] Recent novels on the war underscore the expia-
tory role of popular violence. In Rachid Mimouni's *Tombéza,* the hero is
an illegitimate child, fraught with ambiguity, fallen and then redeemed
through political action.[47] L'As, the title character in Tahar Ouettar's
story, also carries the burden of the original sin of illegitimacy and the
vagaries of marginality, but the revelation that his father is a prestigious
revolutionary leader awakens his dormant qualities: "L'As," he is told,
"you carry the seeds of life . . . like the ocean! No! You are the people
itself."[48] Being a peasant, or a combatant, was a reality, of course, but
it had become more than that: it was a pivotal trope in the FLN's discourse, with specific social codes to follow and a particular political role
to play.[49]

We come now to the second aspect of the Front's effort to create and
perfect the *peuple,* that which enabled the FLN to invoke it as its social
and political power base. The Front's leadership had essentially urban,
middle-class origins; Kielstra describes its outlook and aims as "mainly
urban and unpeasantlike."[50] Yet the abstract "people" suddenly became
the public in whose name all political demands would be made. Algerian
leaders never confronted the difficulties of reconciling their interests
with those of other segments of society and coming to terms with the
people as an assortment of diverse, sometimes hostile social classes.
There was no need to, since a far more docile and obliging *peuple* was at

hand. National unity meant the unity of "progressive forces," and all else was supposed to fall into place. Thus, all serious analysis of the land tenure system was avoided; feudal landlords were reduced to charlatans of recent origin; and so-called peasant virtues were summoned to disqualify any potential opponent. Political *fanonisme*, as Harbi nicely calls it, was a lethal ideological weapon, serving to indict militants for excessive "individualism" or for their so-called bourgeois tendencies.[51] In like manner, the future was discussed not in terms of specific class interests, which might disrupt the meticulously preserved unanimity, but rather in terms of a vague "social justice," "decent wages," a "fairer distribution of wealth" — uncontroversial claims of an illusory people.[52]

Alongside the role of history and the definition of the *peuple* was a third, closely related component of the FLN's discourse. Amidst the talk about a people animated by shared interests and a shared will emerges the Third Worldist notion of revolutionary power, that is, the ability to recognize and articulate popular aspirations. As I have attempted to show, certain institutional arrangements are likely to ensue, and they can be laid out as follows:

1. *Single-party politics.* With a single will, only a single party would be needed. This notion ran counter to the tradition of partisan diversity, but it was well suited to the FLN's claim that it represented a fundamental break with the past and that it would transcend all preexisting parties and their never-ending squabbles. "November 1, 1954, sounded the knell of political pluralism."[53] The Front's statutes, for instance, forbade its members from belonging to any other political organization. In 1962, with the end of the war in sight, the FLN's governing body presented a program asserting that "the party determines the general axis of the nation's policy and inspires the State's action." It also required that "a majority of the government be composed of party members; that the head of the government belong to the Political bureau; that a majority of the Assembly be members of the party."[54]

2. *The centralization of power.* The form of the Algerian revolution led to a confusion — also somewhat of a trademark of Third Worldist politics — between party and army, both of which, in any event, were seen as emanations from the same political will. The war endowed the ALN with considerable ideological authority, and soldiers were held up as models to be emulated. So that while the FLN's political platform emphasized the primacy of the "political" over the "military," this view rapidly would be contradicted by discourse and by practice. "The army," reported *El Moudjahid,* "draws from the people, with which it forms a

single entity, its creative force and its inspiration. . . . The people see in it the expression, . . . the instrument of their own will to freedom. The ALN does not merely express or reflect popular virtues. In the course of its struggles and the sacrifices it makes, it enriches them, brings them to their apogee. More than a mirror of the people, the ALN is a reliable model, an example to be followed."[55] To speak of a conflict between military and political functions was "to forget that at every hierarchical level, the leaders of the FLN are politico-military leaders. Every officer and leader, being a genuine revolutionary, must conceive of his role under a dual light: military and political."[56]

A further point that needs to be made concerns the nature of the military force that acquired such prominence. It would be misleading to look at this phenomenon simply in terms of a struggle between civilians and soldiers, for political clashes occurred within each grouping as well. There was a vast difference, for instance, between the professionally oriented army based on Algeria's frontiers with Tunisia and Morocco and the more disorganized, guerrilla-like forces of the interior. Professional soldiers and guerrilla fighters clashed throughout the conflict (as did, incidentally, various political leaders of the FLN), and alliances were formed across lines, joining certain *politiques* with certain *militaires*. To speak of a "militarization" of Algerian politics, though not entirely inaccurate, is to tell only half the story. Algeria's eventual slide, beginning in 1954, toward the ALN and, within the ALN, toward the better-organized "army of the frontiers," also ought to be looked at as part of the overall propensity of the political field to lean toward the more centralized and the more authoritarian.

Indeed, a theme that recurs with some frequency in the history of Third Worldism (we considered it earlier in the context of the personalization of rule) is the natural gravitation of authority toward spheres of concentrated power. This may be explained in part by Third Worldism's approach to power as an object to be possessed — absolutely or not at all — by particular social groups.[57] Thus, in the Algerian case, Harbi notes the degree to which the more centralized and organized branches of the national movement eventually supplanted their rivals. In 1954, and again during the war, the main organization of the Algerian resistance — first the MTLD, then the FLN — broke up. In each instance, the split resulted in the reinforcement of the more centralized nucleus: the heirs of the OS (the MTLD's clandestine branch) in 1954 and then the ALN's army of the frontiers in the midst of the liberation struggle.[58]

3. *Hegemonic politics*. Scattered throughout the FLN's rhetoric are ref-

erences to the body politic as a human body,the parts apparently operating independently of one another yet all regulated by a single consciousness, the general will. The depiction had its institutional translation,
moreover, and it is on this aspect that I would like to focus. Most historians of the war have looked at the struggle through the lens of the
Franco-Algerian conflict. Yet a closer look discloses another side. Indeed, the countersociety gradually established by the FLN, even though
it lived in the shadows of colonial rule, aimed at being all-encompassing,
scrupulously muzzling all that did not emanate from its political will or
belong to its symbolic order. The effort at times would acquire a dominant, almost obsessive status in the FLN's actions. Not content with its
de facto political hegemony, the Front sought a similar monopoly over
the social field. This could be witnessed, for example, in the fierce
struggle between the FLN-sponsored workers' union (the UGTA) and
the procommunist Union Générale des Syndicats Algériens (UGSA)
and in efforts undertaken to establish the preeminence of the students'
and merchants' unions. The FLN went even further, extending its presence to the prison camps, where it set up parallel administrative, judicial,
political, and educational structures. But then, that was perhaps the ideal
location in which to ingrain the idea of the Front's supremacy. Prisons
offered a mix of generations, social classes, and regional backgrounds;
most of all, they offered a particularly receptive audience: in all likelihood hostile to the French, on the whole impressionable, and literally
captive.[59]

The FLN also annexed portions of the cultural field, and that effort
cannot be detached from the rest of its deeds. In the forms of action it
chose to perform, the language it deployed, and the symbols it used, this
Algerian countersociety was quite deliberate and, it seems, culturally
self-conscious. Most important in this respect are the uses to which tradition was put. Tradition was reappropriated and, in Bourdieu's words,
"*purposely* adopted," in essence elaborating a rhetoric of resistance.[60] For
example, intra-Algerian vendettas were carried out not with modern
weapons, emblems of a distasteful and alien order, but with local dag-
gers.[61] Then there was the FLN's decision to order its militants to boycott products such as wine and tobacco, with the promise that action
would be taken against all who disobeyed. Punishments were at once
eminently symbolic and painfully corporeal, the FLN going so far as to
cut off the offender's nose. Finally, there was the increased use by Algerian women of the Islamic veil, or *haik*. With Michael Gilsenan, we can
agree that when such a turn to tradition is invoked against foreign domi-

nation, it is "a language, a weapon against internal and external enemies, a refuge, an evasion."[62] But the grammar of the language can itself be full of surprises. During the war, and behind the veil, one might well have found more than a face. The *haik* had evolved into an instrument of camouflage, concealing a grenade, or a bomb.[63]

4. *The suppression of dissent.* In the Third Worldist system of knowledge, we have seen, a special place was reserved for political dissent, and the Algerian case is as good an illustration as any. The problem was not with the existence of political competition but with the perceived stakes of the struggle, its all-or-nothing quality, the self-importance, the rhetorical devices, the ferocity of it all. The practice began with pre-1954 parties over the question of national representation. Thus, in 1936 the alliance of communists, *ulémas*, and Abbasists known as the Moslem Congress accused the PPA of being "the most servile agent of imperialism," to which Messali promptly replied that the Congress was made up of "the friends and servants of colonialism." As Messali put it, there was "no alternative": one was either an "ardent nationalist" or a "guilty traitor." To strive for a midway position, he added, was like trying to turn "tar into pure milk."[64]

The war, of course, only added to the intensity. The FLN, it now appears, had its own prison camps and centers of torture.[65] The Front's chief target was Messali's MNA. As Harbi aptly put it, "In the Algerian universe, Messalism occupied the place assumed by Trotskyism in its Stalinist counterpart: absolute error, absolute betrayal." In the past Messali had "already . . . broken the unity of the national movement. Today, he is colonialism's auxiliary force."[66] Conversely, the MNA accused the FLN of being a "traitor" to the national cause and of having joined forces with the French by "sacrificing the authentic aspirations of the Algerian people."[67] When, in 1956, Messali attempted to bridge the rift — perhaps all too aware of his impending defeat — the FLN replied: "You do not ally yourself with traitors. You kill them."[68]

Minor strategic disagreements aside, Messali and the FLN shared the same objectives, and that, paradoxically, was the crux of the problem. The struggle between the FLN and the MNA drew its fervor less from ideological differences than from political similarity, not from distance but from proximity. The uneasy coexistence between competing claims to popular representation played out for all its worth in the intra-Algerian feud. Buoyed by Messali's historical prestige and authority, the MNA hoped to circumvent the FLN as France's *interlocuteur privilégié*. Ultimately, Messali was unable to accept that "the new power emanated from an organization created to oppose him. . . . Messali was not opposed [by the FLN] in 1954–55 because he was a counterrevolutionary. Rather, he was branded a counterrevolutionary in order to get rid of him."[69]

Relatively limited in Algeria, the MNA's support was widespread among migrant workers in France. According to Horne, by 1960 the "French" version of the war between the MNA and the FLN had claimed hundreds of victims: "In 1960 the killings reached a crescendo as the F.L.N. stepped up its campaign to achieve total ascendancy. Barely a day went by without a corpse fished out of the Seine, or found hanging in the Bois de Boulogne. A favourite place of reckoning was the quiet Canal Saint-Martin . . . which with hideous regularity yielded its crop of sacks containing the disfigured bodies of Algerians."[70]

The Front's approach to history, to the people, and to power — in describing all of these, I have tried to bring forth a set of beliefs and a set of practices that link the FLN to the wider Third Worldist movement. Yet a truly remarkable feature of the Algerian experience is how profoundly self-conscious the connection was. On all sides. What makes the Algerian revolution so interesting is this acute, even wearying perception by actors engaged in the conflict — Algerians, French who supported the war, French who opposed it — that their every deed carried far more than its own weight and the exaggerated sense of self-importance that thereby was heaped upon such deeds. The FLN's first proclamation set as one of its aims the "internationalization of the Algerian conflict," and by that it meant identifying with struggles elsewhere in the developing world. Actions on national soil had immediate repercussions on the international front; diplomatic successes automatically were translated into "domestic" triumphs. Significantly, the FLN planned its most spectacular actions with an eye to international events, staging strikes or demonstrations to coincide with sessions of the U.N. General Assembly.[71] The Front sent its most able spokespeople to Bandung (Aït-Ahmed and Abdelkader Chanderli), to New York (Aït-Ahmed, Chanderli, and Mohamed Yazid), or to Ghana (where Fanon was dispatched to represent the provisional government). Fanon, in fact, put it as follows: "Between all colonized people, there seems to exist a kind of illuminating and sacred communication. Every freed territory is, for a certain period, promoted to the rank of 'territoire guide.' . . . In this process . . . the Algerian war occupies a privileged position. There is not a single piece of occupied African land that has not been affected by the war."[72] The battle, so to speak, had been joined.

The French saw things in quite the same way. They believed that they were fighting in Algeria to preserve their territorial integrity but also, as

Chikh points out, to halt the spread of revolution (which they sometimes called communism).[73] The French, by their actions — hijacking the
plane that carried four of the Front's historic leaders (Ben Bella, Boudiaf,
Aït-Ahmed, and Khider) in 1956; using the Algerian conflict, and Nasser's support for the revolutionaries, as partial justification for the Suez
expedition; bombing the Tunisian village of Sakiet Sidi Youssef in 1958 —
magnified the importance of the Algerian war, thereby contributing to
the image of the FLN as beacon of the Third World.

The French nationalist fervor had a measurable impact, both on the
many who succumbed to it and on the few who did not. I am thinking
in particular of the attitude of French socialists and communists, whose
silence, equivocation, at times even outright chauvinism, strengthened
the belief among many that revolutionary hope had completed its migration from developed to underdeveloped lands. When the conflict began, the French government was headed by Pierre Mendès-France, an
"unorthodox leftish radical" who had come to power on the promise of
ending the war in Indochina.[74] Yet barely two weeks after All Saints' Day
the prime minister declared: "One does not compromise when it comes
to defending the internal peace of the nation, the unity and the integrity
of the Republic. The Algerian departments are part of the French Republic. . . . *Ici, c'est la France!*"[75] The statement was echoed by then minister of the interior François Mitterrand: "L'Algérie c'est la France. La
seule négotiation, c'est la guerre." Until the late 1950s the communist
themselves were on board, going so far as to grant then prime minister
Guy Mollet "special powers" to send conscripts to Algeria in 1956.

To disillusionment with the "official," chauvinistic French Left must
be added, first, the more general inertia of domestic politics, especially
in the wake of de Gaulle's 1958 presidential victory, and second, the simultaneous de-Stalinization and demystification of the Soviet Union.[76]
When all is added up, little remained by way of organizational support
or ideological outlet for French men and women in search of a cause,
with the exception of individual commitment to and/or fervent solidarity with the FLN, and this too contributed to the importance the
Algerian struggle gradually took on. In France, the Algerian revolution
would thus give rise to a "Third Worldist euphoria."[77] The anticolonial
activist Daniel Guérin likened Fanon's work on Algeria to an "inexhaustible source of reflection." "With Fanon," he wrote, "we witness the internal revolution of a people . . . an altogether bloody and magnificent
birth."[78] Also, as the first conscripts returned from the war front, awareness grew of the war's brutality. In 1957 the "Dossier Muller" was published in *Témoignage chrétien,* soon to be followed by Servan-Schreiber's

Lieutenant en Algérie and, in 1958, by Henri Alleg's highly controversial *La question,* all of which described numerous and harrowing incidents of French torture. The Algerian war also constituted Sartre's "great political moment."[79] His prefaces to Albert Memmi's *Portrait du colonisé* and to Fanon's *Wretched of the Earth* are expressions of solidarity with the embattled Third World, of faith in its ability to reshape, to regenerate, to renew. He addressed the following words, impassioned and stirring, to his French compatriots: "You condemn this war but do not dare to declare yourselves to be on the side of the Algerian fighters; never fear, you can count on the settlers and the hired soldiers; they'll make you take the plunge. Then, perhaps, when your back is to the wall, you will let loose at last that new violence which is raised up on you by old, oft-repeated crimes. But, as they say, that's another story: the history of mankind. The time is drawing near, I am sure, when you will join the ranks of those who make it."[80]

It is not a belittlement to remark that the passions generated by the Algerian war had something to do with the dearth of political hope existing in France. In the main, I am talking about men and women of genuine devotion, of unfeigned commitment. Nor was this a mere ideological workout. French Third Worldists organized networks of individuals who assisted the FLN in concrete ways, offering shelter to Algerian militants who were on the run and, most important of all, carrying money from France to Switzerland at great personal risk to fund the FLN (hence the term *porteurs de valises*).

Upon learning of the signing of the Evian accords between France and the Algerian representatives in 1962, one of the *porteurs,* Robert Davezies, turned his eyes to his Algerian prison inmates. "That day," he later would recall, "I understood that men had the power to make their own history. History was there, in their hands."[81] Hamon and Rotman conclude their remarkable book, *Les porteurs de valises,* with the following words: "The Third Worldist eschatology . . . was not, at least for the *porteurs de valises,* a gratuitous inclination. . . . The price was forced exile — many of them had to wait until 1966 to be amnestied and allowed to return to France. The price was months of imprisonment . . . shattered professional careers. At such a cost, hopes and myths are precious."[82]

Out of war came independence, a proud state, distinguished statesmen, and an inexhaustible supply of memories, some joyful, many sad. A new dance invented for the occasion was called the "independence twist."

The street named Anatole-France was dubbed Anatole-Algérie. And when the referendum on independence finally was held, 99.72 percent of the Algerians who participated voted yes, thereby apparently endorsing the FLN, the ALN, the GPRA, and the way they had led the country to victory. Algerians could look back with the full wonder of what they had accomplished, against what odds, and against whom.

Peace came as well, though not quite, and not right away. Although French and Algerians signed an agreement at Evian in March 1962, "the week after the cease-fire brought the bloodiest interlude that Algiers had yet seen." [83] The capital was home to the final convulsions of a colonial conflict that had outlived its purpose. Fighting opposed the FLN to a group of obdurate French settlers who had formed the Organisation Armée Secrète (OAS). During the next few months, the OAS conducted a campaign of terror in Algiers and in the Western city of Oran. Justifying the violence, an OAS leader matter-of-factly explained: "You have to remember Arab mentality — to impress the Arabs, you've got to make a solemn performance of killing a man. . . . We had to do something that would really make them understand the significance of what was happening." [84]

By the time a truce had been signed between the two protagonists, the OAS had killed some 2,360 people and wounded another 5,000. According to some calculations, "in the Algiers zone alone [the OAS's] activities over the last six months of the war had claimed *three times as many civilian victims* as had the F.L.N. from the beginning of 1956 onwards." [85] As Charles Gallagher would remark, "The only fitting epitaph for this ending was that the colonial period died as it had lived, in violence and incomprehension." [86]

Algerians dealt with one another with only slightly more civility and compassion. Political dissension surfaced in the Libyan capital of Tripoli, where the FLN's governing body convened between May 25 and June 7, 1962. It spread into Algeria itself, where a civil war of sorts, ashamed and embarrassed, was under way. On one side was the "Tlemcen group": Ahmed Ben Bella and Mohammed Khider, recently freed from years of imprisonment in France, Ferhat Abbas, and the army's General Staff (EMG), headed by Boumedienne. On the other was the "Tizi-Ouzou group," composed of Hocine Aït-Ahmed and Mohamed Boudiaf (both of whom had just spent five years in jail in the company of Ben Bella and Khider) and members of the GPRA. On June 30 the GPRA dissolved the General Staff and removed Boumedienne. The EMG challenged this decision and began returning its soldiers — until then stationed in Tunisia (21,000) and Morocco (15,000) — to Algeria. Side by side with the forces of *wilayates*, or regions, 1 and 6 (Aurès and Sahara), they fought the forces of the pro-GPRA *wilayates*, 2, 3, and 4 (Constantinois, Kabilya, and Algérois). Behind the confrontation was a ruthless power struggle. Some of the antagonisms were deeply rooted, as many of the *wilayates* had long resented the wartime attitude and demands of the Army of the Frontiers, which fell under the authority of the General Staff. Blocked at the Moroccan and Tunisian borders by barriers set up by France, Boumedienne's army had become more of a political force than a military one, indeed the country's most (if not only) organized political unit. With victory now in sight, the militarily idle army engaged in what it knew best: politics. On a more personal level, relations had become strained between Ben Bella and other historic leaders who had spent years together in jail after their arrest by France in a dramatic mid-air kidnapping in 1956. As one witness put it, "It was just like a scene out of Sartre's *No Exit*." [87]

In the end, Ben Bella prevailed, though in truth it was less he than Boumedienne's army. The military forces, Harbi explains, "had an advantage over all other organs of the revolution, including the GPRA, because the GPRA was subject to myriad particular interests. The army could transcend regionalisms and take the shape of a centralized political instrument at a time when the forces of the national revolution were threatened with dispersion and demoralization." [88]

The country over which Ben Bella was to rule was in sad shape. While the exact number of casualties remains unknown, roughly five hundred thousand refugees from Morocco and Tunisia had to be resettled in Algeria, and about 2 million peasants returning from French *camps de regroupement* had to cope with ravaged land and devastated herds. About 1 million hectares of the most productive lands had been abandoned in the aftermath of a massive exodus by frightened Europeans. The country's livestock herds had been cut in half. [89] All in all, approximately 4.5 million Algerians were considered to be living in poverty. [90]

And yet, with a Third Worldist at its helm, one whose politics were more sentimental than ideological, more instinctive than deliberate, enraptured with the *idea* of revolution rather than with its details, Algeria rapidly would become "the pivotal Third World state," a "haven for the struggling and the oppressed of the world," an "example for the non-European continents, a model, bright and entrancing." [91]

For, indeed, out of war also came the stuff of legend and the stuff of myth — about the Algerian people, whose unbreakable unity was said to have been illustrated anew; about the Algerian leaders, a close second, whose ability to harness that popular energy was viewed as an assurance of representativity and a gauge of legitimacy. There emerged, to put it differently, a vision of Algeria that had been fabricated, then refined, then maintained by Third Worldism in its myriad, uncoordinated manifestations: Algeria as surrogate for the revolutionary masses; Algeria as proxy for the progressive state; Algeria as model for the developing world. Whatever the country was in reality going through had been overlaid with these visions, and with these expectations.

Much of this was self-imposed, or self-inflicted. Algeria was indeed the main source of production for the mythology, its everyday discourse, pronouncements, behavior even, requiring the images of which it had become captive. The state was the most visible and vigorous of participants, in part out of conviction, in part out of interest. Algerian leaders narrated history, the people, and their own power, each narration an attempt to confirm their ideological purity. The Third Worldist seduction found its way to the nation's dissidents as well, echoes being heard in their own discourse: if Algeria was to exist as a symbol, its heroes now gone, its past now betrayed, it would have to do so by finding its way back on history's track, reinspired by the sacrifices of the *mujahideen*, reenergized by their memory. The Third Worldist ideology was, so to speak, reversible: *historiques* on one side battled *historiques* on the other, with similar determination, similar arguments, similar logic. In everything, from the issues it addressed—Who did the state represent? Was power really "popular?"—to the promises it made and the language it used, the opposition was an exact mirror of the state.

Not all the visions originated in Algeria, however. Many French came out of the war with considerable guilt about what they had done, not done, or allowed done. Some looked to the newly independent state with inflated hopes regarding the future. Guilt and hope can be formidable emotions, especially in tandem, and that combination helped suffuse Algeria with added symbolism. The Third Worldist gathering that formed around the North African state thus little by little came to include a foreign press, economists, political scientists, not all of them blindly supportive by any means, but each coming at Algeria with elements of the ideological tradition we have been talking about. In addition to the names I mentioned in my general discussion of Third Worldism, others who made and remade Algeria in their own image include Paul Balta; Gérard Chaliand (author of *L'Algérie est-elle socialiste?*); Henri Alleg; Ania Francos (co-author of *Un algérien nommé Boumediène*); André Mandouze (*La révolution algérienne*); Philippe Lucas (*Problèmes de la transition au socialisme: Le transformisme algérien*); and the periodicals *Afrique-Asie* and *Africasia*.

How all this operated is quite difficult to describe because of the different levels at which Third Worldism presented itself—more or less sophisticated, but also more or less "official," that is, having varying ties to the regime. One way is to focus on the representation of Algeria as an economic model. At one level, outsiders converged on the country, rich with its oil and gas reserves, as a kind of experimental ground for new developmental policies in the Third World. Behind much of the economic thought involving Algeria was the model of a world polarized between rich and poor nations, in which colonialism had "underdeveloped" the Third World and neocolonialism was helping to maintain it in that state. Since domination was exercised by countries possessed of an industrial basis, that too must be Algeria's ambition, even if it meant (temporarily) neglecting the nation's agricultural economy. Chief among advocates of this view was the so-called father of Algeria's economic policy, Destanne de Bernis, who summed up this "industrialization first" program as follows: "[The industrializing industries] act as the 'motor' of the development process, producing raw materials and machinery for other sectors of industry engaged in the production of finished goods. . . . In turn, the products of the new industries will contribute to the modernization of the more backward sectors of the economy, notably agriculture, forging new linkages that will eventually create an integrated economy reducing Algeria's dependence on the world capitalist market."[92] (Of course, that the proposed economic policies were grounded in such ideological presuppositions does not thereby attest to their fallacy. Theories often begin with their author's initial predispositions. The scientific inquiry regarding empirical validity is another, vastly different affair.)[93]

Next came political activists and sympathetic journalists, who translated the theoretical model into a simplified political warfare between a progressive Algeria and the conspiracy-driven center of imperialism—located somewhere between Paris, Wall Street, and the Pentagon. Critical Third Worldists, both foreign and Algerian, played their part as well. Authors like Tahar Benhouria, Kader Ammour, Tarik Maschino, and Fadela M'Rabet, come to mind, not as one voice, but as conveyors of the idea of an Algerian departure from the genuine Third World road to socialism. The notion of state capitalism, having acquired familiarity through the Soviet and Chinese examples, was central to their approach:

not only did these critics view Algeria as a typical instance of the state interrupting or hijacking the process of economic development but they also experienced a firm sense of betrayal, of Third Worldism having been stabbed in the back. Third Worldism gained in credibility this way too, as the prize deferred.

Finally, at the core was the state's own discourse, which built on the same ideological premises. Then-president Boumedienne emphatically rejected "a system of thought that sanctions the world's division into two categories: on the one hand, the countries that enjoy all privileges and claim to rule the world; on the other, those that are condemned to underdevelopment and submission." As he explained in 1967, the aims of his domestic policy were "first, to free our economy from foreign dependence and to recover our national wealth; second, to build an independent national economy on a solid foundation."[94]

The economic policy advocated by the regime also reflected a companion core tenet of Algerian Third Worldism, namely, that there were no class contradictions (or any others for that matter) within Algeria, since the main dividing line ran between North and South.[95] It followed that to strengthen the entity called "the state" was to empower the nation as a whole in its struggle against world capitalism. Banks, insurance companies, and some mines were "socialized" — as official parlance would have it — in 1966. The nationalization of oil and gas properties, begun in 1968, was completed in 1971.

Layer upon layer, Third Worldism thus organized itself as a vision of Algeria, by Algeria, sometimes even against Algeria — against, that is, its regime and official policies. The nation was converted from country to case study: everything was to be dissected, judged, celebrated, villified.

❖   ❖   ❖

Before we can examine the ideology of the independent Algerian state, a question proposes itself: Can one properly speak of a single revolutionary Algerian ideology? Did Algeria's romance with Third Worldism last any longer than Ben Bella's short reign, or did it end after a mere three years, at which point Ben Bella was summarily removed from power by the man who had put him there in the first place, Houari Boumedienne?

As put forward by some, the argument runs essentially as follows: Ben Bella was a romantic, verbal politician whose tenure coincided with the influence of leftist Europeans intent on building in Algeria what they could only dream of at home. Trotskyists such as Guérin or Raptis had imagined an Algeria reflecting their hopes, mirroring their ideals.

Thus, when in the aftermath of the French departure workers and peasants began to take over abandoned property, the French militant Daniel
Guérin was quick to speak of an "irreversible" movement, the embodiment of his own socialist utopia. In 1963 he tellingly commented that
"in France in June 1935, we were at the threshold of self-management.
We had to take only one more step. We did not dare. Faced with the
unknown, we retreated. . . . Here, in Algeria, the threshold has been
crossed. . . . Self-management will survive . . . because it has one advantage: it follows the course of history."[96] The following year, while attending the Congrès de l'Autogestion Industrielle, Guérin once again
thought he saw workers defending a socialist revolution and heard the
"authentic voices of the working people." "What dominated the congress," he said, "was the emergence . . . of a working class, of a socialist
awareness."[97] Guérin's idea of Algeria from 1962 to 1965 was that of a
country torn between a genuinely socialist line — backed by the proletariat, intellectuals, and students — and a right-wing current. The ensuing class struggle would determine Algeria's future.

As a result, when on the night of June 19, 1965, a group of officers
dressed in army fatigues broke into Ben Bella's residence, rifle barrels
pointed at the president, many lamented the end of an era. Impatience
with flowery rhetoric, amateurish governance, and utopian politics, it
appeared, had gotten the better of the army. The days of quixotism were
over. Ben Bella's fall meant the end of self-management, the end of socialism, the end of the dream. By 1965 the European socialist "pilgrim"
might well have felt, as Gellner put it, that "Fanon is for export only."[98]
Now was the time for rigorous leadership, the triumph of conservative,
Islamic, bourgeois forces.

Yet, even allowing for a substantial difference in leadership style, political instinct, and background, the vision of a "Thermidorian" Boumedienne is just as misleading as that of a socialist Ben Bella. This is not to
deny that there were two phases in the Algerian revolution, though in
many ways they were more a function of rhetoric or temperament than
of actual policy. Enthusiasm, excitement, and quite a few illusions were
tempered, mitigated, sometimes betrayed. But all that was to be expected. There were exaggerations on the part of European activists, exaggerations or naiveté on the part of many Algerian ideologues. But in
reality there were very few essential differences between the two regimes,
for both Ben Bella and Boumedienne were heirs to similar political lega-
cies. Guérin had not heard the voices of the "authentic" people, whoever
they might be, or even of the "authentic" elite. Rather, he had listened

to the voices of brilliant, young Algerian intellectuals such as Harbi and Zahouane, both of them close advisers to Ben Bella yet never representing more than a marginal political current.

As for the shift in the discourse on self-management, to which Guérin attributed such importance, we must put Ben Bella's own conviction in proper perspective. From the start, self-management was a peripheral aspect of public policy. It had not been mentioned in official pronouncements prior to 1962, and it touched a mere two hundred thousand workers. In truth, self-management was a matter less of choice than of necessity, a reflection of the state's absence rather than its self-imposed disengagement. French *colons* had fled Algeria, first in order, eventually in panic, and the resulting vacuum was one not even the state could fill on such short notice. Little by little, the state reaffirmed its authority, President Boumedienne merely continuing a trend begun by his predecessor.[99] All in all, as Chaliand concludes, "there never existed a 'rightist'-'leftist' split in Algeria," and the country did not move overnight from "a 'period of transition toward socialism' to 'fascism.'"[100]

Chaliand does not stop there. He argues further that the *pieds rouges,* the European political activists who became Ben Bella's "internationalist advisers" only to lose favor under Boumedienne, had essentially misread Algeria's revolution. Not only did Boumedienne's regime represent more a continuation of Ben Bella's than a break with it but their common left-wing rhetoric also concealed the less glamorous ideology of religious nationalism. Victims of their own ethnocentric bias, the *pieds rouges,* or so the argument goes, had failed to see beneath "socialist verbiage" and outright "mystification" this more prosaic reality.[101] Indeed, with the current crisis of socialist and Third Worldist systems of thought, such analyses have been gaining increasing currency.

What are we to make of this view? There is some truth to it, of course, as Guérin's mistaken dismissal of the influence of Islam and Arabism in the conduct of the Algerian revolution amply proves. Muslim traditions and belief constituted key ingredients of the revolution, as the cultural elements of nationalism did in all colonized countries of the Third World, to a greater or lesser extent. However much Europeans of the Left may have wished to think otherwise, this fact has reasserted itself time and again. Yet we need not minimize the influence of nationalism or religion to acknowledge the pull of Third Worldism. The apparent paradox ceases to be if one bears in mind that Islam has far less political significance than the specific uses to which it is put and, Western illusions notwithstanding, can no more explain the whole of Arab history than

Christianity can account for Europe's. Algerians of the wartime FLN and then of the postcolonial state subscribed to a Third Worldist representation of the world, not because it was a convenient cover-up for some dark Islamic design, nor because they underwent a sudden ideological conversion, but because the elements of that representation corresponded to conditions experienced by large segments of society (polarization between colonizer and colonized before independence; polarization between developed and underdeveloped nations thereafter) and partially addressed profound social needs and wants (how to survive as a group oppressed by a foreign entity, how to organize as a society, how to maximize the group's material benefits, etc.).

Thus, many of the policies adopted by the Algerian state grew out of its original ideological vision of a new, more egalitarian and self-sufficient society, aspirations that the vague notion of *arabo-islamisme,* at times invoked to justify them, hardly conveys. Before and after Boumedienne's coup, policy choices included agrarian reform, industrialization, state planning and takeovers, economic development, and social redistribution, in addition to progressive educational and health-related measures, all of which belong to the Third Worldist agenda.

As for Algeria's foreign policy, predictions to the contrary notwithstanding, it remained highly visible and militant during President Boumedienne's tenure. This is of particular significance, for so much about the Third Worldist era involved the international sphere. Boumedienne retained Ben Bella's minister of foreign affairs, Bouteflika, and it was under Boumedienne's rule that Algeria came to be considered a "montreur de conduite," or catalyst, for the Third World.[102] Its active role in the emerging Non-Aligned Movement, the nationalization of the oil industry in 1971, support for a New International Economic Order, and solidarity with national liberation movements all pointed to an aspiration to become the "best, the most progressive, in a word, the Third World's guide [*aiguillon*]."[103] Under both Ben Bella and, especially, Boumedienne, Algeria developed what Lucas describes as a "politique de l'expérience," aware of its responsibility as symbol of an epoch in the Third World's awakening and transformation.[104]

Third Worldism was, to borrow Karl Mannheim's useful typology, essentially a "utopian" ideology, that is, one directed toward the realization of a desired future.[105] As such, it constituted a representation of the world geared toward social and political action and was ideally suited to the efforts of dissident groups, who could attribute to the governing strata responsibility for all social ills and to their own program the potential for the ultimate cure. No such easy contrast can be invoked once the former rebels start to occupy the places of power, and for that reason some have questioned whether the Third Worldist sobriquet could well be applied to states.

Yet, as we began to see in the field of economic policy, the same ideological sets of beliefs that had proved effective against the French were called upon by the Algerian state. An imperative and lasting grammar of conflict and defiance, Third Worldism thus also constituted an effective grammar of power. This was achieved, essentially, by depicting power itself as an enduring state of resistance. By this I mean that Algerian leaders approached their own power oppositionally by invoking a procession of enemies: internal ones, of course, but primarily external ones — Europe, the capitalist world economy, imperialism, and so forth. This was not too complicated a task, for in a world of unevenly distributed resources and economic power the strongest and wealthiest nations naturally strived to maximize their position at the expense of the weakest and more destitute. The Algerian state was quick to interpret this blunt reality of global economic relations as the devious design of villainous neocolonial conspirators.

Foreign policy was the natural arena for such depictions. Paul Balta correctly observed that the country's leaders, long after they had come out of the maquis, conducted a "diplomatie de maquisards."[106] Areas corresponding to the distribution of independent Algeria's political interests on the international scene — identical interests, complementary interests, and conflictual interests — were thus defined in terms of attitudes dating back to the colonial period and in accordance with the predominant Third Worldist perspective. Algeria designated the Western bloc as a sphere of hostility in large part because of the latter's overall opposition to national liberation movements. The self-proclaimed "socialist" camp, which had been an objective ally of the FLN, constituted the sphere of complementarity. Based on a convergence of opposition (to the Western bloc, essentially), it was more a solidarity of interests than an absolute identification. In contrast, Algeria saw itself linked with the Third World by a shared history of oppression and liberation.[107] Algeria welcomed representatives of South Africa's African National Congress and Pan-African Congress, of Mozambique's FRELIMO, Zimbabwe's ZAPU, and Arafat's PLO, which made its capital a "veritable breeding ground of revolutionary movements."[108]

In fact, few countries could rival Algeria in the consistent and single-minded pursuit of foreign policy goals. Baghat Korany speaks of an Algerian "fixation," and this is only a mild overstatement.[109] Algerian diplomats were known around the world for their discipline, the extent to which they planned, organized, and delivered. From the outset, independent Algeria carried forward two central objectives: to multiply political, economic, diplomatic, and cultural exchanges between countries of the Third World in order to unite them around a set of coherent propositions; and to gradually move these propositions in the direction of an all-out assault on the existing economic world order. As a corollary, Algeria sought to enhance the Third World's bargaining position, which its OPEC strategy makes clear. Much of that particular mix between building new institutions for the South and infiltrating existing ones set up by the North is to be found in Algeria's relentless efforts. Political harmonization was the stuff of the former; with the latter came opportunities to confront the developed nations and move the terms of the debate ever closer to the Third World's views.

So obvious was Algeria's leading role in each of these institutions that it is worth turning to them once more. As far as Third World institutions are concerned, the independent state quickly focused its efforts on four fronts: the Afro-Asian group, as manifested in the Bandung Conference; the Group of 77; the Non-Aligned Movement; and OPEC.[110] In the end, as John Entelis notes, Algeria's identification with the Third World "reached mythological proportions."[111]

Bandung had been important to the FLN as a means of acquiring international legitimacy and recognition. A decade later, Ben Bella stood ready to host a commemorative event of sorts, the second Afro-Asian summit. As it happened, the 1965 coup, which took place ten days before the conference was scheduled to open, put a halt to preparations, and repercussions of the deepening rift between China and the Soviet Union frustrated its occurrence altogether. But this setback for Algerian diplomacy was merely temporary, and Boumedienne quickly shifted his focus to the economic field, which tied in more closely with his domestic objectives and from which he believed he could derive greater Third World unity.

In October 1967 the first ministerial conference of the Group of 77 was convened in Algiers to prepare for the second round of UNCTAD. These "Estates-General of the Third World," as *Le Monde* dubbed the conference, in many ways represented the first occasion less developed countries had had to articulate a common economic stance, and the conference bore Algeria's heavy fingerprints. Adopting what came to be known as the Algiers Charter of the Economic Rights of the Third World, a "detailed codification of the policy objectives of the developing states," it set the tone of the North-South debate for years to come.[112] President Boumedienne summed it up when he said that the central problem of the existing world order was the "odious exploitation" and "pillage" of Third World resources.

Of still greater importance was the Non-Aligned Movement. Between 1967 and 1973 Algeria spearheaded efforts to move nonalignment from an essentially neutral, nonpartisan posture to an activist, positive stance.[113] In Algeria's eyes, it meant more than simply refusing to take sides in the East-West conflict (sometimes it did not mean that at all): it meant confronting the North-South divide. To a degree, the confrontation between North and South was political, and Algeria made clear its support for anticolonial movements in southern Africa, for the Vietnamese revolutionaries, for the PLO, and so on. Algeria also challenged what rules there were governing the international legal system.[114] But in Boumedienne's eyes, the main dividing line was and would remain economic. "If politics can divide [the Third World]," he once said, "economics will unite us."[115] His goal thus would be to move the Non-Aligned Movement, the Group of 77, and eventually the U.N. General Assembly to take a common position on issues of technology transfer, resource distribution, terms of trade, the debt, and so forth. His agenda was simple, if far-reaching: "More and easier credit terms, better access to Northern markets for goods manufactured in the Third World, higher and more stable prices for the primary goods the Third World exports."[116]

Algeria's moment—and Boumedienne's—came in 1973, when it played host to the Fourth Summit of the Non-Aligned Movement, which Algeria was determined to turn into a watershed event. In Mortimer's words, the summit "marked a new elan in Third World affairs and laid the groundwork for several of the international conferences on development that have been held ever since."[117] Sixty-five states representing some two billion people attended the summit. Resolution after resolution and speech after speech echoed the central message put forward by the Algerians, namely, that the priority was to achieve genuine independence, which meant closing the gap separating the rich from the poor, which, in turn, meant radically altering the rules of the international game. For a time at least, Algiers became the capital of the Third World, and Boumedienne would exploit the opportunity for all it was worth during the three years he presided over the movement. That the oil crisis was just around the corner, and that it provided Algeria with the financial and political means to match its ambitious foreign policy objectives, evidently did not hurt.[118]

We now come to another forum of Third World initiative, OPEC. For Algeria, OPEC not only provided a means of acquiring additional monetary resources but also constituted a first step in challenging the North's control over the world economy and a model organization (part trade union, part cartel) for other less developed countries. From the time it joined OPEC, in 1969, Algeria took the lead in trying to raise the price of oil and in linking that question to broader issues pertaining to the world distribution of resources. Boumedienne seized upon the 1973 energy crisis to promote his views. His central theme was that the increase in the price of oil, which harmed not only developed countries but many less developed nations as well, was not the cause but a symptom of the problem and that the problem was the unfair international order imposed and maintained by the North.[119] Time and again, Algeria would labor to shift the focus from the question of oil to such broader North-South issues.

Boumedienne's efforts in the Group of 77, the Non-Aligned Movement and OPEC ultimately culminated at the United Nations. In his capacity as president-in-office of the Non-Aligned Movement, he called for a special session of the General Assembly on raw materials and energy.[120] Held in 1974, shortly after the summit of nonaligned nations, the session presented a unique platform for President Boumedienne. Delivering the opening speech, he decried the existing economic order, characterizing it as being "as unfair and as antiquated as the colonial order from which it gathers its origin and its substance. Because it sustains itself, consolidates itself, and prospers according to a process that, ceaselessly, impoverishes the poor and enriches the rich, this economic order constitutes the principal obstacle hindering any chance of development and progress for the countries of the Third World."[121] He went on to call for the suppression of the debt burden, improved terms of trade for the Third World, emergency programs to assist the poorest countries of the world, and genuine control by the Third World over its own resources. Perhaps most importantly, the Algerian leader averted attempts by the United States to focalize the debate on the oil question and cause a split between producers and consumers within the Third World. Mortimer describes the process well: "By defining the central issue as the need for broad-based restructuring of international economic relations, rather than as a temporary dislocation attributable to one commodity, the developing countries influenced the conceptual framework which would govern further diplomatic maneuvers on economic questions."[122]

By the end of the session, few could ignore the concept of a New International Economic Order, as the final text adopted by the United Nations by and large reflected Algeria's views. Finally, with the selection of Bouteflika, Algeria's foreign minister, as president of the U.N. General Assembly, "nobody needed reminding that Algeria was the leading actor" in the Third World.[123] Algeria stood as a reminder of the division of the globe between the privileged and the destitute.

This polarized view of the world was aided by the official depiction of the Algerian people as united in their opposition to foreign exploitation. Like the wartime FLN, independent Algeria did not seek a sociological so much as a political, even moral definition of its social basis of support, variously called *le peuple, les forces populaires, les masses.* Paradoxically, the regime's industry-first policies were coupled with an obsessive narrative about the celebrated peasant masses. As Bruno Etienne once remarked, the reason was that the discourse on the peasantry was always, indirectly, a discourse on other social classes, or rather a discourse on the absence of social conflict.[124] The state needed to invent a character that was abstract enough to serve as a symbol of the nation as a whole yet sufficiently concrete to be effective. The *fellah,* in this construct, is a nebulous group, capable of being all things at all times. It is "a myth, a *parole depolitisée,* whose function is to conceal the existence of class struggle. . . . The reason is that, by spreading the mythical image of the *fellah,* the bourgeoisie, urban groups, intellectuals, and politicians establish the illusory lack of differentiation between social classes."[125]

Official programs repeatedly emphasized the unity of Algerian society, making no secret of the existence of various internal "enemies" but failing to name or identify them, or, when they did, holding out the hope of moral and political persuasion.[126] Privileged social "strata" — the word *classes* was avoided when possible — were not to be fought directly; rather, the FLN was expected to "explain to these *couches* that the policy of the revolutionary power . . . will improve their situation."[127] Even the much-vaunted agrarian revolution was justified in nonclass terms. Because it was destined to assist the peasant masses, "in our country, the agrarian revolution is an issue of national solidarity, not the manifestation of class struggle."[128]

The Algerian regime did not claim to represent the interests of any particular social class, but rather of this illusory, docile *peuple* whose aspirations the regime could shape at will. This mythical people was the revolution's normative standard, the political warranty that guaranteed the state's revolutionary credentials. Governmental decisions were justified, in quasi-ritual fashion, with the claim that "the people approve them." For instance, when the oil industry was nationalized in 1971, *El Moudjahid* exclaimed: "The popular masses enthusiastically salute the Revolution's new step forward" and "Algeria unanimously supports the revolutionary power."[129] When the state or party speaks of *le peuple,* in other words, it means people by definition endowed with revolutionary aspirations and a political agenda.

Peuple and *fellah,* in this context, became more selective concepts, odd crosses between the amorphous masses and the politicized avant-garde. "The people of the revolution are less a social stratum or a well-defined social mass than a *couche-signe,* a *masse-signe,* of the forces they reflect. In the end, it is less the people than their deep aspirations that are authoritative within the Algerian polity."[130] Even from this standpoint, of course, the *peuple* remains synonymous with the abstract, mythical "masses." As Henri Sanson nicely put it, the politicized *peuple* belongs to the multitude, only it is "more expressive of this multitude than the multitude itself." In other words, there is the people and, "in its midst, a people that is even more people."[131]

Another characteristic example of Algeria's Third Worldist narrative was the care taken in the presentation of history. I remarked earlier how during the war the FLN drew its power in part from the assumed historical continuity between "Algerianness" and the Front's contemporary leadership; every action today stemmed from the popular yearnings of yore; each told of its origins in the centuries-old aspirations of the Algerian people. If there remained any doubts regarding this intimate connection between political authority and historical legitimacy in the ideological construct of Algerian Third Worldism, the extraordinary sensitivity exhibited by the independent state to all matters relating to the past put them to rest. So routinely intertwined and lumped together were issues of politics, identity, and authority that it often became difficult to tell them apart. The essential components of this ideological interplay can be summarized as follows:

1. *A dizzying list of illustrious heroes and no less illustrious nonpersons.* In the state's official historiography, pre-1954 nationalist parties and leaders remained at best ignored, at worst characterized as "the main obstacles to the people's involvement in open revolutionary struggle."[132] Messali

in particular stood as a constant challenge to the historical legitimacy of the FLN, so much so that when the Front's newspaper, *Révolution Africaine*, commemorated the fiftieth anniversary of the birth of the PPA, it did not once mention the name of the organization's leader.[133] As Ahmed Koulakssis and Gilbert Meynier comment, "The founding myth of the *thawra* [revolution] has yet to reckon with Messali's historical role."[134] Equally unmentionable for the longest time were the surviving "historic" leaders of the FLN who remained in the opposition: Hocine Aït-Ahmed and the deposed president, Ahmed Ben Bella. At the same time, politically innocuous figures (e.g., Abdelkader, Moqrani, and Khaled) were put forward as embodying the people's timeless and unanimous will.[135]

2. *A never-ending celebration of the war and its martyrs.* The wartime martyrs were, of course, the regime's true "constituents," the source of its legitimacy and inspiration. Articles published in the official press made this clear: "Those of 1954 back the nationalizations [of 1971]"; "The former *moudjahid* is capable of occupying a vanguard position, as he did in the past"; "Continuing the struggle begun in 1954";[136] and there are many more.

3. *A counterdiscourse, or to use Mohamed Chérif Sahli's pertinent expression, a "decolonized" discourse.*[137] The state offered a point-by-point refutation of the French characterization of precolonial Algeria as a stateless, stagnant, ethnically fragmented and culturally backward (non-)nation. As the former minister of information and culture, Ahmed Taleb-Ibrahimi, explained, "Every Algerian must be aware of the fact that he is a ring in a long chain going back to the remotest times in history."[138] The terms of this new historical version were spelled out by others as well, each emphasizing that Algeria's history was to be thought of as that of an eternal nation—a nation-in-being, to be precise. Any such statement about Algeria automatically invites a conclusion about its ethnic homogeneity. Problems between Arabs and the minority Berber populations, even the very notion of a multicultural makeup, were thereby conveniently swept away.[139] Again, Taleb-Ibrahimi: "When reading all that has been written [by the French] on Arabs and Berbers, one realizes that a real process of undermining was organized in order to divide the Algerian people. . . . From an ethnical standpoint, Algeria is not a juxtaposition of Arabs and Berbers."[140]

Algerian Third Worldism, then, saw its task as reversing the French image of Algeria, since that image was at the basis of domination, subjugation, and exploitation. In a strange game of reflecting mirrors, the picture of Algeria projected by France — a fragmented mosaic full of *caïds* and *marabouts* — was counterbalanced in the independent state's discourse by an Algerian image of Algeria that, in many ways, was a replica of the French nation-state: centralized, uniform, and ethnically one.

What did Third Worldism look like once the garbs of power had been donned? This occurred in many Third Worldist countries — in Guinea, Madagascar, Angola, Burkina-Faso — but in few places was the power as institutionalized, as systematic, as long-lived as in Algeria. Algeria's economic situation was a principal reason. The availability of gas and oil reserves, coupled with the rise in their price on the world market in the early seventies, made possible a policy of industrial development and social benefits. Oil revenue financed modest but real forms of social welfare and income distribution, both of which were critical to the regime's stability. Viewed in retrospect, there was much to fault in the Algerian economic model, from its excessive reliance on export revenues to its vulnerability to world market prices and disregard for the agricultural sector. As Lahouari Addi has remarked, Algeria was subsidized by revenue created abroad that, in turn, financed an artificial domestic growth. Yet from the very start one of the principal rationales behind Algeria's economic system had been to keep the social peace. Measured by that standard, it was successful for quite some time.[141]

But even conceding that independent Algeria benefited from a relatively privileged economic station, the regime's success in institutionalizing its power needs to be explained in terms of political skills as well. This achievement was particularly noticeable during Colonel Boumedienne's leadership, for he was a firm believer in methodical organization, which he took to be the key to political success and longevity. By the late 1960s, after an initial period of consolidation, the state organized local and regional elections. Only after the elected assemblies were in place did the president consent to reestablishing constitutional government. In 1976 a nationwide referendum gave the country its first constitution since Boumedienne suspended an earlier version in 1965. Finally, in 1977, elections were held for the Assemblée Populaire Nationale (APN), thereby filling another void caused by Boumedienne's suspension of Parliament in 1965.

Step by deliberate step, Boumedienne established the institutional foundations of his rule, which at first glance seemed to have all the earmarks of a Western constitutional regime. Indeed, the constitutional idea enjoyed a venerated tradition in Algeria's modern history. In the years prior to the revolution it had "captivated" Algerian nationalist parties.[142] From the ENA to the MTLD and the UDMA, all had insisted on the need for universal direct suffrage, the election of an *assemblée constituante,* and the establishment of democratic rule. Thus, when they finally met in Evian to settle the conflict, French and Algerian negotiators agreed on the need to set up "constitutional" institutions.

Yet, despite such surface similarities, Boumedienne's approach to Algerian organs of government was typical Third Worldism. Sovereignty, in his mind, was predicated on belief in a common will reflecting shared popular aspirations. It followed that the supreme law of the nation, instead of deriving from the choice of individual citizens, sprung from the revolution itself. Political legitimacy remained at all times "historical" as opposed to "democratic": "The political actors of the coup have no use for legality; they demonstrated their legitimacy . . . by carrying on the national destiny" suggested by the revolution itself.[143] Indeed, the revolution transcended the strictly historical to take on a life of its own in the present. The revolution had its own "logic," its own "determination"; it "makes important decisions" or "triumphs."[144] "We are a revolution," exclaimed Boumedienne. "Our revolution must be everywhere."[145] Appropriately, the supreme authority created in the aftermath of the coup was called the Conseil de la Révolution.

The trademark of such a system of power, in which each action is justified in terms of a revolutionary spirit, was manifested in the regime's tendency to codify its own overarching philosophy. I am referring here to the Algerian habit of "self-chartering," of writing grand expositions, not in the form of legally binding constitutions or laws, but in the form of political promises to past generations of martyrs and to an eternal "spirit" of the revolution. As Leca and Vatin correctly observe, these national charters did not really "impose obligations or create rights," for that, indeed, would have been the province of a constitution; rather, they represented attempts to equate political power with an already constituted body of revolutionary knowledge and tradition.[146]

In other words, one must be careful to distinguish between Western constitutionalism and constitutionalism as a response to colonialism, which is what the Algerian case was all about. The FLN, like its predecessors, borrowed the concept only to turn it into a weapon against French domination. Far from implying adherence to constitutional philosophy as a whole, it became strictly synonymous with national emancipation, the right to self-determination and, eventually, to independence:

insofar as there could be no democracy under foreign rule, democracy necessarily presupposed independence; insofar as the popular will was identified with the struggle for self-determination, independence automatically accomplished (fragments of) democratic rule. Yet ultimately, "Algerian constitutionalism sets forth a system that has nothing to do with the regimes from which these techniques are borrowed."[147] As one author put it, the Algerian regime professed a democratic constitutionalism that it immediately "dissolved."[148]

A multitude of political techniques and attributes helped distinguish Algerian Third Worldism from ideal-typical Western democratic constitutionalism. Corporatism, a single-party or no-party system, the regime's presidentialization, a bicephalous state structure, and the regime's Manicheanism — in all this one sees replicated the Third Worldist system of legitimacy, historical rather than democratic, driven by power rather than by government, focused on the executive rather than the legislative functions of governance.

Let us look first at Algerian corporatism, which can be summed up as the radical separation between notions of election and notions of representation. For Algerian Third Worldism, representation is linked not with plural interests but rather with the unanimous national interest, of which the revolution was the finest example and manifestation. This was formalized in practice by the requirement that all candidates be nominated by the FLN. As Leca and Vatin explain, "To those who would note the omission of the characteristics of Western ideas of representation (designation by those who are represented and the representatives' quasi-contractual responsibility toward them) we would respond that these traits belong to the liberal version of the concept. This version is linked to a conception of society in which social actors can autonomously and directly translate their social demands into political ones. . . . [In Algeria] the people are not a constituency . . . and 'political professionals' do not have a contractual but a 'historic' responsibility, that of guides who must express the people's aspirations clearly."[149]

The corporative state, by ignoring conflicts among the *peuple,* tends to depoliticize society and to "neutralize" potential disputes. Elections for the National Assembly are meant to select the most capable individuals, not representatives of diverse viewpoints. Debates within the Assembly are attempts to uncover the nation's will, not exercises in political pluralism. This can be seen clearly in Boumedienne's tortuous comment on the family code: "We will let the debate open in order to enable us, as a last resort, to adopt the opinion of the majority, as soon as it will be in harmony with the country's political options."[150] The idea is familiar enough: it suggests the habitual Third Worldist propensity to reconcile political representation with the idea of the general will.

More generally, the corporatist state aims to achieve a monopoly over all social and political forms of communication, and in that it readily evokes the organic metaphor discussed above. In Boumedienne's own rhetoric, the "solicitous" state extends its authority throughout society as "the vascular system carries and breathes life into [the human body's] furthest extremities." Likewise, he described the regime's "enemies" as "intruders who have penetrated the body of the revolution"; they are an "excrescence," a "gangrene."[151]

The partisan structure of the Algerian regime was another of its essential features. The FLN was the conduit through which the general will was to be expressed and channeled. Contrasting Algeria's single-party structure to Western multipartyism, the *Charte d'Alger* made this plain: "The multiparty system allows all particular interests to organize into different pressure groups. It frustrates the general interest, that is, the workers' interest." On the other hand, a single, vanguard party creates a "democracy in which the workers' general interest is expressed."[152] As the Algerian journalist Zoubir Zemzoun wrote in 1987: "In countries marked by a multiparty system, their society's historical development has not allowed the emergence, let alone the preeminence, of a national ideological consensus. . . . Lack of this consensus . . . sharpens the struggle between antagonistic socio-political forces. . . . In Algeria, the history of our national revolutionary movement led to a national consensus in the ideological sphere."[153]

In various ways, the country's organizational structure reinforced this understanding of the role of the party. In 1962 candidates for the Constituent Assembly were chosen by the FLN's political bureau. Article 22 of the 1963 constitution designated the party as one of the cornerstones of national legitimacy, with one congressman going so far as to assert that "above the Constitution, there is the party."[154] Under Boumedienne's rule, the 1976 constitution reaffirmed the FLN's position as sole political party. Finally, the president also was secretary-general of the FLN, and up until 1982 all candidates to the National Assembly had to be nominated by the Front.

One can accept these facts and yet at the same time recognize that the single-party system was essentially a no-party system. The FLN occupied a significant, central ideological space, serving to prevent the emergence of competing organizations. Beyond that, the Front was "of very limited practical importance."[155] In its strength lay its weakness: in order to remain the symbol of national unity, the embodiment of the general interest, it had to avoid day-to-day administrative tasks. The party could not be the locus of conflict management or of bargaining over resource allocation since its values were the property of the community as a whole. In the country's ideological equation, it was reduced to the status of symbolic leader, which amounted to political impotence. It could not "disappear as long as the state more or less depend[ed] on its symbolic ability. . . . And it [could] not really be reconverted as long as the political system as a whole compel[led] it to fulfill this allegorical role."[156] Thus, at every critical moment of Algeria's contemporary political history the party has been striking by its absence.

The partisan weakness of Algerian Third Worldism was more than compensated by the weight of the presidency. This personalization of rule cannot be accounted for merely in terms of an excessive craving for power, though that too certainly had a part. Rather, it should be viewed as the outcome of political-ideological constraints. "The president's 'personal' legitimacy is also ideological insofar as his designation perpetually re-creates the founding model of the Algerian revolution": the dedicated militant's awakening to the general will; personal devotion to the unanimous, national cause.[157] The president personified the revolution (and, as such, enjoyed whatever legitimacy the FLN retained) and symbolized active decision making (thanks to which he gained credit for governmental action), while avoiding criticism for the shortcomings inherent in both functions, namely, inefficiency and bureaucratic mismanagement. In this context, some have drawn parallels to Weber's "sultanism," in which "the presidential dynamic makes it possible for a political choice to appear neither as the victory of one group over another nor as the result of a bargaining process, but as the rational outcome of the revolutionary power's efforts to satisfy popular needs."[158]

Another factor made the situation even more obviously ripe for personal power. The president stands as a constant reminder of the dual source of authority in the Algerian system: the state-as-administration (principally the bureaucracy) and the state-as-revolution (principally the president). This bicephalism manifested itself through the practice of self-criticism, the regime attempting to present itself as the most reliable barrier against its own deviations. Leca and Vatin thus reflected that "nothing escapes the eyes of Power. Its knowledge extends to its very deficiencies."[159] No one living in Algeria needed to be reminded of the flaws in the disreputable state bureaucracy, denounced as early as 1962 in the FLN's Tripoli Program. The 1976 charter continued this trend by castigating "the use for personal ends" of public goods, "personalization of authority, misuse of power, opportunism . . . corruption . . . demagoguery," bureaucratization, remnants of a "feudal ethic," and "clanishness." The president, more than anyone or anything else, was depicted as the revolution's protector against such deviance. More power to him meant less power to the enemies of the revolution, of the nation, and of the masses.

In reality, far from being impediments to be removed, the administration, the bureaucracy, and "feudalism" served as convenient ideological buffers between rulers and ruled. Criticism of the regime was redirected against an administrative apparatus that either was inefficient or, worse, had strayed from the chosen path.[160] Thus, social criticism and protest were transformed into (presidential) support, the culprit being identified as incompetent administrators. And as previously observed, self-criticism implicitly reaffirmed the existence of, and the regime's ability to identify, the national will, which opposed the practice subject to criticism.

We come, finally, to the last political instrument of Algerian Third Worldism, political Manicheanism. Almost without exception, Algerian political actors equated criticism (of the non-self-directed type) with conspiracy. To criticize was to condemn, to condemn was to betray — and that meant taking the other side, the other's side, the only one left to take. This was true of the state, and it was also true of Algeria's opposition. Both were rooted in the same historical epoch (1945–62); both were indebted to the same ideological legacy (essentially the war of national liberation); and both reflected the same paradigm of political practice (centralized and personalized power).[161] In short, the archetype of political debate remained the war of national liberation and its theoretical underpinnings regarding the course of history, the definition of the people, and perspectives on power. The opposition, "incapable of revising its ideas, socially identical to the very system it fought, sought refuge in messianic prospects and dreamt of repeating November 1. . . . In terms of its practice and political style [this] opposition was a miniature replica of the FLN."[162]

That there were internal disputes within the Algerian polity surely should come as a surprise to no one. Tensions had been manifest during the war, at the time of independence, and afterward. Former FLN *historiques* created their own organizations: Aït-Ahmed formed the Front des Forces Socialistes (FFS), and Mohamed Boudiaf the Parti de la Révolution Socialiste (PRS). Ben Bella was quick to rid himself of some of the FLN's most prestigious leaders, and Boumedienne would follow in Ben Bella's footsteps, albeit at Ben Bella's expense.

Yet, more interesting than the chronology of these internal splits was their ideological justification. How far was Aït-Ahmed's vision from Ben Bella's (or, subsequently, Boumedienne's) when he aspired to a legislative body that would be the "authentic expression of national cohesion and the spirit of the unity of the people," when he said that "every parliamentarian must think of himself as the representative of the entire nation," or when he appealed to the "forces les plus vives de la Nation," the impassioned and politicized masses?[163] Because the existence of a popular will was treated as an axiom by all, political conflict centered around issues of legitimacy on which there could be no compromise: power was either in harmony with popular interests or hostile to them, if not "for and by the people," then necessarily without and against them. All social virtues, like all social vices, were attributed to the state or the regime; all change would have to occur at their expense. Political speeches were codas on purification, authenticity, and revolutionary legitimacy, monologues on historical origins and loyalty. The opponent became a traitor, the regime a dictatorship; and in this organically interdependent universe, the enemy by definition was an instrument of foreign agents, or of their local relays.

Boudiaf, Khider, Abbas, and Aït-Ahmed all, in turn, denounced Ben Bella's regime and then Boumedienne's as "dictatorships."[164] In the nation's relatively brief history, heroes who became villains overnight are legion. Abbas, Khider, Boudiaf, and Aït-Ahmed were the main victims of Ben Bella's presidency, Zbiri and Ben Bella himself the victims of Boumedienne's. Abbas, the first president of the provisional government, was branded a "traitor."[165] Aït-Ahmed, one of the *historiques,* was a "puppet" of foreign powers. As Ben Bella bluntly put it, "The sole reason for the conflict between Aït-Ahmed and [ourselves] resides in our refusal to submit to those located outside our country."[166] As for Ben Bella himself, he remained in power "with the manifest help of *l'Etranger,*" claimed another *historique,* Mohamed Boudiaf.[167] Next it was discovered that Boudiaf was part of a "Zionist-Kabyle" conspiracy.[168]

So steeped in the FLN's Third Worldist mentality were Algerian opponents that even those at the helm of opposition parties continued to support the principle of a single party, merely criticizing the Front's version of it. Mohamed Boudiaf's PRS thus stated that such a party "can be a valuable tool, a melting pot for the nation's militant forces as long as

certain conditions necessary for its birth, development, and, more particularly, its success are met. . . . Given its past, its evolution, and its
present reality, the FLN cannot become a [genuine] party, let alone a
single party. . . . This party can only be the PRS because from the very
beginning it learned from the FLN's history and avoided the decrepi-
tude and inevitable death experienced by all our national parties."[169]

The reliance on historical legitimacy, that is, on faithfulness to the
past, explains why for so long the only credible opposition came from
former "historic" leaders or, at a minimum, from prominent participants
in the war. In everything they said the logic of historical legitimacy was
dominant. Referring to his cell companions, Khider declared that "I,
Khider, detain a portion of legality, just as Boudiaf, Aït Ahmed, or Bitat
does."[170] Abbas carried the logic to its absurd chronological conclusion:
"In all modesty," he said, "we had already defended Algeria at a time
when Boumedienne was not even born. Our right to speak was politically more legitimate than his."[171] Aït-Ahmed's case is interesting because, of all the dissident leaders, he is one who has come closest to calling for democratic pluralism. Yet he too claimed that "one must proceed
with psychological shocks. . . . The names of the *historiques* have not been
forgotten. . . . They still count in Algeria."[172]

In an odd way, it was as if tacit rules of the game, an unspoken understanding, regulated who or what the opposition legitimately could
be. This is not to say that there were no systemic "mishaps": Abbane
Ramdane, Chaabani, Khider, and Krim all were done away with by the
state. But on the whole, Algeria was marred by fewer political assassina-
tions than other countries of the Arab world—such as Iraq, Libya, or
Syria. Until the 1990s, that is.

Conclusion

Some years ago I came upon an article in the Third World-ist magazine *Afrique-Asie*. Only days before, Angola's then president Agostinho Neto had survived an attempted coup led by a populist politician named Nito Alves. The title read: "The Revolutionary Masses Did Not Take to the Streets!" [Les masses révolutionnaires ne sont pas descendues dans la rue!]. At the time it struck me as a peculiar choice of words. Clearly, a certain number of individuals had marched in Alves's support. Did they not constitute a "mass?" They also seemed seriously angry, with change very much on their minds. But perhaps they were not quite "revolutionary" enough, though the distinction between revolutionary and counterrevolutionary mobs, or popular and unpopular masses, has eluded the finest of minds.

Yet such was the idiom of the day, and besides, there was a level at which it all made perfect sense — the revolutionary masses, history's inevitable course, the progressive state, and so forth. Words were clumsy and prose stilted, but beneath them was a code, a vocabulary that gave meaning to them all. If nothing more, that is the true function of ideologies: to make it possible to say what one means to say without having to fret about it very long.

Even today that way of talking comes out to teach us something about the unspoken assumptions that once held sway. With decolonization, wars of national liberation, nonalignment, or dependency theories came the notion that the revolutionary people were the source of legitimate authority and that revolutionary power was popular power mediated by the revolutionary state. This state, in turn, was institutionalized

157

around a single party, or more often a single leader who alone could identify the state's weaknesses, recognize the true path, and denounce traitorous opponents. How the rhetoric became natural, how its meaning went without saying, is what I have attempted to show in part 2, focusing particularly on Algeria, where a long, violent war and the subsequent establishment of a strong independent state were instrumental in building a Third Worldist idiom.

In one way or another, such themes came to pervade the ideological outlook of Third Worldist militants worldwide. Even the more lucid and critical among them expressed the hope that in the future a new state would arise and that it would adequately reflect genuine national unity. If Third Worldist experiments had failed, they could claim, it was because rulers did not represent the unanimous popular forces, not because such representation or unity was unfeasible. Abdel-Malek, to take one example, held the view that the failure of so-called progressive Arab regimes stemmed from the "distance separating the popular masses from the exercise of state power." "Let the people . . . led by urban and rural workers and by revolutionary intellectuals be responsible for the entire social system through control of the state. Only then will the problem of liberation and revolution be looked at in a radical fashion."[1] Indeed, "the problem of the nature of the state apparatus" was "central." Thus, Abdel-Malek envisioned the future in terms of an "inexorable deepening" and "radicalization of the political course." Borrowing from organic imagery, he predicted a "profound and accelerated mutation." The aim of this "long march" was primarily to "transfer the ruling core of the national movement . . . from the generally conservative privileged classes . . . to the popular classes and radical forces."[2]

Mahmoud Hussein and Michel Kamel evaluated Nasser's rule in similar fashion. Denouncing the new military-civilian political elite, they too saw in the state, or rather in its capture, the key to "authentic liberation." This task befell "the forces of the working people, led by the industrial workers, peasants, and revolutionary intellectuals, the principal forces of the revolution . . . invincible, unshakeable."[3]

This line of analysis was also implicit in official state Third Worldism, of course. In that case the state was regarded as "schizophrenic," divided between revolutionary and bureaucratic branches, with the former blaming the latter for any political imperfection. The Third Worldist paradigm, I have said, was "reversible," as demonstrated by the Algerian opposition's discourse. Viewed from a position of power or of opposition, the state was held to be liable and accountable, the arena and stake of all struggles, the ultimate architect of social transformation. Not surprisingly, a functionalist indictment is also, surreptitiously, a functionalist prescription for political change. To denounce a political power as being responsible for all social ills is implicitly to call for a different policy by a power of equivalent magnitude. In the Third Worldist discourse, the state preserved its alleged managerial capacity, whether for positive or negative ends. Third Worldist states, either real or hypothetical, were "true successors of Jacobin political messianism."[4]

Talk of "revolutionary masses" was thus no cause for stupefaction. It had a context, it had antecedents, it had roots in a way of thinking. How easy it is today, in the name of a new pragmatism, to dismiss it all as mere political babble. That would be done, of course, and part 3 is devoted to a study of this linguistic and ideological shift. Not so fast, though, and not without a last look back. For we would be neglecting the extraordinary power Third Worldism once possessed and the loyalties it once commanded.

The story of Nasser tells it all. Popular grief in the aftermath of Egypt's defeat in the Six-Day War and the president's short-lived resignation "was surely the apotheosis of the special rapport between this leader and the masses, a rapport of personification and incorporation." "I no longer claim to be the leader of my people," exclaimed the *rais*. "At the very most, I would wish to be the expression of one phase of its struggle."[5] Yet such grief paled in comparison with the sense of loss that followed Nasser's death in 1970. Here we touch on something almost inexplicable, almost magical. Some of this has to do with Lacouture's rich, evocative language; the rest lies with Nasser, Egypt, and their mutual, and secret, pledge.

The solemn ceremony had become a vast primitive rite, and the leader's coffin was seized and borne aloft by the crowd. Before being laid in the earth, Gamal Abdel Nasser's body was buried in the living masses of his people. . . .

A strange reconquest. He who had held Egypt like a familiar prey . . . now found himself . . . seized and devoured by his spellbound people. The personification of power, the identification between the leader and the masses, had led to an epic reincarnation. The mandate which they had granted him they now took back along with his mortal remains. The people reclaimed the rights they had given up to their leader a little over fifteen years earlier. . . .

Over whom were these orphaned people really weeping—over their vanquished chieftain, or themselves?[6]

PART 3

Demise

Hands shaken, speech delivered, and the Israeli-Palestinian agreement signed, Yassir Arafat headed out, a man in a hurry, a man with a mission—several, in fact. En route, he would stop for meetings with the U.S. secretary of state, where promises of support would be made, as magnanimous as they were vague; for talks with various Arab-American or Jewish groups, replete with slogans of continued solidarity and newfound fraternity. But these were mere compulsory exercises in a fastidiously scripted peregrination, sideshows to the main events, which were to take place elsewhere.

The first, and the highlight: only hours after laying the necessary groundwork, Arafat had a televised appointment with the ultimate maker of American (that is to say, world) opinion, CNN's Larry King. The last-minute arrangement had meant postponing King's interview with General Norman Schwartzkopf. Put to the side, if you will, the fact that the general's Gulf expedition, and the Palestinian leader's opposition to it, had very nearly sent Arafat's career into oblivion. In our world of instant celebrity, substituting one for another was simply a matter of gauging public interest. Nor did Schwartzkopf have any legitimate grounds for complaint: his reputation had been entirely a televised one, his war "the most covered and the least reported war in history."[1] Who will live by the media will perish by the media: in CNN time, two years was an eternity—and 1993's handshake was well on its way to eclipsing 1991's War of the Year.

The second: a round of meetings with world financial institutions and donor countries. Arafat no longer touted self-reliance, nationaliza-

tion, or state-run industries. This is, after all, the age of economic conformity and orthodoxy, of IMF austerity, devaluation, privatization,
"conditionalities," "stabilization," and other "structural adjustment programs." As Arafat well knew, the best economic plan is now a loan. I
am reminded here of an episode that took place a few years back. At
the time, a colleague and I had been asked to draft a speech to be delivered by Ghana's president at the August 1986 summit of the nonaligned
nations. Jerry Rawlings was a brash, defiant young leader, and we set out
in search of words to suit his daring temper. In the speech, Rawlings was
to attack "neoliberal theses," which "thoroughly fascinate" the world, to
the detriment of socialist models of economic growth. "Every effort in
every case is made to have us believe that these theses are the key to
economic success or that they are the conditions sine qua non for receiving Western financial aid." At the last minute the speech was canceled. It
seemed, ironically, that the "fascination" had taken hold of the Ghanaian
leader himself.[2]

The third came only weeks later, as scores of U.S. advisers descended
upon Tunis, Jerusalem, and Jericho. In his speech, the Israeli prime minister had asked fighters to trade in bullets for ballots; in seeming echo,
Arafat repeatedly invoked American democratic values; and the peace
plan itself called for the election of a Palestinian governing body. With
such intentions in the air, the National Democratic Institute, the Carter
Center, and other, similar organizations were quick to offer advice and
dispense wisdom on how to conduct fair elections and build democratic
institutions. That was bound to happen, Palestine being just the latest in
a lengthening series of exotic locales in which Western political models
would be exported, tested, and applied.

Much of this flurry of activity, this sense of urgency, was due to fear
of the alternative to Arafat. If not the PLO, then Hamas, which was just
another way of saying Islam, fundamentalism, fanaticism, and terror.
Time, in other words, was in short supply and running out. Better yesterday's brute than today's demon.

Westernization, economic pragmatism, political pluralism, and the
fear of religious (or ethnic or tribal or nationalist) revivalism—these
are the ingredients of the dominant contemporary reading of the Third
World. The story goes something like this: An alien graft and fairy-tale
ideology, Third Worldism is at long last being displaced by values reigning in Europe and the United States. The result is a Westernized Third
World bowing to the irresistible power of economic realism and popular representation. For the citizen of Africa, Asia, or Latin America, the

range of options offered is free-market liberalism and representative democracy, on the one hand, or the prospect of oppressive, repressive, and backward allegiances, on the other. The two are really flip sides of each other, the debilitating, disintegrative power of exclusory loyalties serving to highlight the appeal of the West's nonpolitical, impartial, all-embracing universalism. Never far from the surface, moreover, is the notion that the parochial, exclusionary discourses of identity (or, as Badie calls them, "les discours identitaires") [3] are the Third World's "natural" language, from which it can be rescued only through the successful appropriation of the West's universal, nonideological value system. Such are the terms of today's debate: the economic, political, cultural aesthetic of the West versus the ominous nostalgia of coarse essentializations — religious, ethnic, tribal.

My own sense of the problems facing the Third World, as the reader may suspect, is very different. I have been insisting that systems of thought are assemblages of individuals (e.g., militants, theoreticians, intellectuals), tools (books, newspapers, and other modes of cultural communication), and institutions (associations, states, parties) and that their ascent or collapse is a function of historically specific conditions providing the assemblages with greater or lesser evocative power. So-called material conditions are the nursery of ideological movements in the same way that the movements themselves are the cradle of all we consider to be political, social, and economic. As it is currently recited, the story of Third Worldism's demise departs from this understanding by dissociating ideologies from the conditions in which they were born, labeling some systems of representation "ideological" but not others, divorcing a subjective world of ideas from an objective universe of facts. With obvious consequences: Third Worldism, as ideology, is set against a so-called immanent, objective reality comprising the stubborn facts of economic life and the underdeveloped world's deeply ingrained identity (Islam, tribalism, etc.). Ideology is thus relegated to the status of expendable or, worse, harmful illusion; it is viewed as "grafted" onto an extrinsic social world, free to accept it for a while, bound to reject it in the end.

In contrast, if one chooses to look at ideology as a constant actor in the dynamic interplay between political, social, and economic elements, the decline of Third Worldism does not indicate that it was from the outset either alien or ill adapted. Rather, it has become increasingly dysfunctional. A set of factors, some international, others domestic, have contributed to rendering Third Worldism — the individuals, the tools, the institutions — progressively irrelevant, with a diminishing connection to the way the world is being grasped and understood. It has, in other words, experienced a legitimation crisis: it no longer can provide states and political actors with needed rationales of social regulation.

This is not simply a matter of the failure of Third Worldism, of the persistence of poverty, malnutrition, inequity, and repressive rule. For we deal here with the complex link that exists between the world and ways of seeing it. Students of anthropology, of science, and of law in recent times have questioned the assumed independence of the observer from the observed, suggesting instead that the very process of observing can alter the object being examined.[4] The same holds true for the study of ideological processes. Neither the ideological pronouncements of Third Worldist regimes or scriveners nor the critical discussions by Third World and Western scholars were mere backdrops against which the fortune of Third Worldism could be viewed. Instead, they have had a significant impact on its fate by providing the criteria for its assessment — Third Worldism being condemned, as Ernest Gellner might have put it, "by a judge of its own choosing."[5] In other words, the notion that progressive Third Worldist regimes have failed also is a reflection of the ideological criteria observers have used to measure success.

What I have written about Third Worldism is meant to carry over not only to its ideological predecessors but to its successors as well. Therefore, the vogue of "managerial" liberal economics and representative democracy, vaguely defined, cannot be explained as reality's revenge. I take it, rather, to be just another system of thought, an instance of shared convictions accomplished through shared beliefs, shared interests, or some combination of both. It too is shored up and sustained by a confluence of energies and tireless efforts. It is, to quote Said, "a kind of *willed human work.*"[6] Arafat, in other words, was not dodging ideology to take refuge in detached objectivity. Political, cultural, and intellectual circumstances had led him to where he was.

A word of caution: scholarly advances, the contribution of structuralism and other similar academic endeavors, have rendered us far more adept at studying ideological reproduction and stability than at understanding change. We know something of the processes by which systems of thought endure, cooperate with forms of power, and make their way into the daily routines of culture and behavior, enlightened as we are by the works of Edward Said, Pierre Bourdieu, and several others. We are far less comfortable with the kind of phenomena involved in the demise of Third Worldism. As the reader no doubt will notice, I am quick to dissect and criticize interpretations of this evolution and of the rise of economic liberalism or notions of pluralistic democracy or of Islam; I am somewhat slower to come up with alternative narratives.

But these trends are taking place nonetheless, and some sense still needs to be made of them. A central question is whether there is a coherence, a unity, to such occurrences as the convening of "national conferences" in the Congo, Togo, or Niger; the holding of multiparty elections in Algeria, Nicaragua, Cambodia, or Benin; the reactivation of tradition; the growing allure of Islamism in Algeria, Egypt, Jordan, Sudan, or the occupied territories, of communalism in India, of churches and sects in sub-Saharan Africa ("God's revenge" is how Gilles Kepel described all this),[7] of privatization and state disengagement in the Third World and Europe; the influence of the IMF, CNN, and *Dallas* the world around, and, in the same breath, the global persistence of anti-Western feelings. Here and there, in the concluding part of this book, I try to catalog these trends under various rubrics and to relate the Westernization of culture, the turn to economic liberalism and to political pluralism, to the reinvigorated expressions of primordial faiths and fundamentalisms of all shades. If I have succeeded in pointing to possible paths, indicated potential directions of thought or inquiry, I have achieved my purpose.

CHAPTER 5

A Farewell To Utopia

By the 1980s Third Worldism had all but expired. What happened later was mere survival—something very different, even if sometimes under a very similar name. There was no proper burial, in part at least because so much else around it was dying as well: the Soviet Union, the Eastern bloc, socialism, communism, and all that had accompanied them. But in the end Third Worldism too had lost its *lettres de noblesse,* the power of the Word along with the nobility of those institutions (states, parties, etc.) that had produced and maintained it.

The institutions first: Examples of hope turned sour were in abundance. In the economic sphere, Third Worldist strategies had fallen depressingly short of satisfying basic human needs, let alone sustaining solid growth levels, achieving self-sufficiency, or putting an end to material inequity.[1] With the fall in oil prices and the onset of a new global economic crisis, it became painfully obvious that little had changed in the Third World's dependency on the First.

Meanwhile, rural sectors throughout the "progressive" Third World had been devastated, treated as "politically irrelevant,"[2] while the bloated urban areas had produced their own dismal assortment of poverty, unemployment, and homelessness. With angry disenchantment and considerable bitterness, Basil Davidson says it well: "Social revolution . . . had vanished into a verbiage become absurd by empty repetition, even though, in practice, a revolution of existing structures of stagnation remained ever more urgently desirable."[3]

To illustrate what he means, Davidson proceeds with a caustic, scathing overview of the Congo's experience with "African socialism," one

168

example among far too many. He shows with what great harm this Third World version of the myth has been kept alive, sustained by "an Alice-in-Wonderland level of eloquence matched almost nowhere to the realities of foreign dependence and rural decay. . . . The aims may have been admirable, vowed to self-development; the reality has induced an ever-larger bureaucratic parasitism."[4] We could go on, as Davidson in fact does, relentlessly.

The skyrocketing debt was perhaps worst of all, a cruel metaphor for a new, ineluctable dependency, often on Northern states, always on the omnipotent international financial institutions (IFIs). In Africa, governments that once proudly asserted their economic independence and socialist beliefs are forced to plead for financial help.[5] In exchange, they must accept painful economic prescriptions, slash government payrolls, cut back on subsidies, devalue their currency, privatize. They have had to sell themselves out of what they so willingly had talked themselves into — self-reliance, a New International Economic Order, egalitarianism, state ownership, socialism.

In a sense, the debt crisis and collapsing economies spelled the end of the Third World's overall strategy. In part 2, I introduced Krasner's idea that underdeveloped nations sought to infiltrate and beef up those international institutions premised on authoritative, as opposed to market-based, resource allocation. The International Court of Justice, the U.N. General Assembly, UNCTAD, and UNESCO were the organizations favored by the more militant Third World. As previously discussed, the strategy met with some success, the North refusing to give up on institutions even long after they had ceased to serve its interests. As the underdeveloped world aggressively pursued its agenda, its developed counterpart found itself on the defensive, politically and morally incapable of justifying the imbalance between the two.

The financial drought and economic failures in the South changed all that. A sense of urgent despair came upon the Third World, leading to a go-it-alone attitude in which immediate pursuit of favorable individual treatment took precedence over long-term collective goals. Competing with each other for resources that grew scarcer every day, countries of the Third World were in no position to chart a united course of action. Instead, each one tried to persuade the IMF and the World Bank, foreign governments and private investors, that theirs was the best bet. Where once there was talk of curbing the power of multinational corporations and promoting self-reliance, now one hears only of lifting restrictions and increasing trade. The best example of all is Ghana, which went from

Third Worldist model to showcase of the World Bank. Little time is left for changing the rules of the game when so much time is spent playing it.

Overall, the debilitating effect the crisis has had on the Third World lessened its bargaining power with the First. More confident and self-assured, countries of the North began to dismiss as irrelevant institutions that had grown hostile during the seventies. Krasner writes, "By the 1980s, the North, especially the United States, took universal international organizations less seriously, depriving the Third World of its most telling point of access." In some instances, says Krasner, the organizations were abandoned altogether, as in the case of UNESCO, from which the United States withdrew in 1985, or the World Court, whose jurisdiction the United States rejected in the *Nicaragua* case.[6] The Third World had conquered positions of power, only to realize that the power had slipped away soon after the conquest.

The political assessment was strikingly similar, regardless of where one looked. In Latin America, how many failed guerrilla wars, aborted *focos,* ersatz Ches? As a reconverted Third Worldist lamented, "In the course of years, one was compelled to conclude that it was impossible to coordinate the revolutionary forces throughout Latin America, that there was no revolutionary Third World capable of exerting its influence on a world scale and willing to engage in a continental revolution," and that there was no "revolutionary state as preoccupied with the Latin American revolution as it was with its national interest."[7]

Guerrilla warfare was to Latin America what a form of state socialism was to Africa: The cradle and coffin of Third Worldist hopes.[8] The fate of leaders such as Kwame Nkrumah, Modibo Keita or Sékou Touré were the first apparent signals of this failure, some leaders being overthrown, others surrendering to political paranoia, or worse. As if by contamination, things would spread, and deteriorate. In Ethiopia, Somalia, Madagascar, or Burkina Faso, euphoria, short-lived, gave way to disillusionment, and all that remained was, in Davidson's words, "a debilitating sense of waiting for transport to the future which simply refused to come, of waiting in a byroad of history, as it were, through which no traffic flowed. Or of standing still while, at the same time, slipping irreversibly back. . . . It was as though these nation-statist structures had functioned and must function so as to rob the best-intended wielders of power—and these, here and there, were far from lacking—of any real capacity to share their power with those it was supposed to benefit."[9] All of which amounted, by any measure, to rude awakenings.

Yet even that was passable by comparison with the appalling crop left behind in the Arab world. With a bountiful oil supply and lavish rhetoric to rival it, many had believed the region would give rise to a generation of revolutionary models. Instead, it yielded its variants of militaristic absolutism, parodic tyranny, tribal and clannish authoritarianism, its Nassers, its Gadhafis, its Husseins and Assads. To which one might add pathetic scenes of fratricidal violence in what once was South Yemen and what still is the Palestinian movement. A powerful nationalist movement had been hijacked, as Said appropriately put it, leaving sad debris for all to witness.[10]

Then there was Asia, and the once-celebrated Chinese model, ostensible antidote to the Soviet Union's decrepit bureaucracy and unforgiving political repression. It too faltered, as the country moved in dizzying succession from the excesses of the Cultural Revolution to a glum "capitalist restoration."[11] Few were those who remained attached to an idealistic picture of Kim Il Sung's communist dynasty, and fewer still those who were willing to venture into things Cambodian in the wake of the Khmers Rouges' estimated killing of some two million citizens, and thus the Asian chapter rapidly came to a close. Even hopes invested in Vietnam, once the Third Worldist beacon, foundered on its lack of peacetime success, the oppression, the persecution, ceaseless, disheartening.

For a brief moment, it is true, Iran offered a glimmer of hope. A surreal sight it was, European and Third World left-wing, secular intellectuals rallying around a bearded cleric who embodied cultural archaism, theocratic rule, and divine justice, all of which he used the latest tools of political repression to promote. And yet, there it was: Michel Foucault, returning from a visit days before Ayatollah Khomeini would prevail, speaking enthusiastically of the realization of a "political myth," of the "collective will" he had finally "encountered." He offered visions of a popular unity in which religion was merely "the vocabulary, the ceremonial, the timeless drama within which one found the historical drama of a people weighing its existence against that of its sovereign. . . . One has to take the word *demonstration* in its literal sense: a people untiringly *demonstrating* its will. . . . The streets of Teheran witnessed a collective act . . . accomplished according to religious rites — the act of deposing a sovereign." "I wonder," he concluded, "where this singular road will lead [the Iranians], against the stubbornness of their destiny, against all they have stood for century after century, in their quest for something *other*."[12] Alas, as we know too well, both the centuries and the stubbornness were quick to return. With a vengeance. Discussing the reactions of Foucault and others, Maxime Rodinson likens them to symptoms of a collective delirium.[13] I take them, rather, as indicators of how depressed were the moods, how profound the anxiety, and how desperately one clung to hope, any hope, anywhere.

Another casualty of over a quarter-century's worth of Third Worldist quests was the mystique of international solidarity. This had been a constitutive part of the ideological outlook, demonstrated so well in the sequence of gatherings and summits that gave Third Worldism a further concreteness, a sharper focus. Yet what became of this unity when wars raged between China, Cambodia, and Vietnam, Somalia and Ethiopia, or Iran and Iraq?[14] Who was supposed to represent the historical, revolutionary forces in the war waged by the government of Ethiopia, backed by Cuba, against revolutionary Eritrean movements, long welcome members of the Third Worldist congregation? In Afghanistan, where "feudal landlords" battled imperial Soviets? Or in the Middle East, to mention another pathetic example, where Syrians and Syrian-backed Palestinians, supported by Amal's Shiites, besieged Yassir Arafat's loyalist forces in northern, then southern Lebanon? As one French observer asked, "How can one continue to proclaim the unity of the Third World, evoking it as a Prometheus, stressing the heroic solidarity of some one hundred and twenty poor countries, while witnessing increasingly severe and numerous conflicts within this group?"[15] "Third Worldism," concluded another, "has just died on the Sino-Vietnamese border."[16]

There was more to this than hasty and haphazard reaction to daily events from around the globe. The disjointed events — all, it is true, pointing in the same general direction — triggered a tremendous amount of ideological rethinking among Third Worldists. This brings us to the intellectual environment of Third Worldism, the mind-set, thoughts, and attitudes within which it blossomed. By 1978 *Le Nouvel Observateur* had published a series of articles concerning relations between the Third World and the Left.[17] With Jacques Julliard, Gérard Chaliand, Samir Amin, René Galissot, Jean Lacouture, Maxime Rodinson, and Jean Ziegler as participants, the political conclusions were still too undefined, too diverse, to be described as a thorough reappraisal. But whatever sense of certainty had existed was being displaced by ever-widening doubt. In this regard, Edward Said speaks of a "progressive liberal disenchantment with Third World causes in general, particularly those whose promise seems to have been betrayed." He mentions specifically the "anguished *cri de coeur*" of a one-time Third Worldist, Gérard Chaliand, at the sight of "mediocre, repressive states, hardly worth Western enthusiasm"; he alludes as well to the disturbing question raised by *Dissent* magazine, namely, whether Khmer Rouge horrors "warrant a reconsideration of our opposition to the Vietnam war?" All of which, he concludes, amounted to a radical "withdrawal" from the 1960s.[18] The coincidence with analogous developments occurring within other branches of the progressive movement — another important factor — accelerated the evolution from Third Worldism to what we might call, and this is an awkward designation at best, post–Third Worldism.

I do not wish to be misunderstood. There always had been skepticism, especially on the part of those who refused to subscribe blindly to the assessments, prognostications, and strategies of Third Worldism. The distinction I am making, however, is between those who blamed failure on betrayal of the original aspirations and those who attributed it to the aspirations themselves (often the same people, at different times). Whatever critical thoughts the former harbored, the Third World existed in their minds as a place where the anti-imperialist struggle, political innovation, economic reform, and cultural demystification and reconstitution would — could — take place. There is a critical difference between such beliefs (whose expression and impact I attempted to analyze in part 2) and the notion that Third Worldist aspirations, at bottom, are unachievable.

Even that notion always had been present, of course. Third Worldist depictions of the underdeveloped world had never enjoyed dominant status, and they continually competed with Orientalism, modernization theory, developmentalism, and other such views. But here again there was a contrast: by the mid-eighties there was very little to oppose the latter, certainly very little by way of a powerful, cohesive ideological stance. Where once there had been self-confident, hopeful talk, there was now only despondent silence.

The undoing was very much in the mold of the original making. This to me is a point of some importance, and I wish to make it clear: those who had lived on the sidelines of Third Worldism, on its cultural, intellectual, and political fringe, whose attitudes and reflexes ultimately had made it possible, were the first to sap its foundations. Indeed, quite often they were neither speaking of nor thinking about Third Worldism or the Third World. But Third Worldism depended on, was enabled by, a whole range of political dispositions: ideas about the Third World but also about the meaning of history, the nature of the people, the representative capacity of political power. These were the intellectual surroundings of Third Worldism, the environment in which it grew, then flourished. As they were affected, so too were the central tenets of the ideology itself. Let me add that there is much in this reinterpretation with which I agree, as one must with any serious effort to demystify. But I take issue with a number of the conclusions that were drawn concerning the Third Worldist enterprise and, more significantly, concerning the Third World itself.

Among the first to go was the idea of historical inevitability and its link to human agency. From the start, this had been a problematic proposition, existing as much in the state of subliminal thought as in the form of deliberated judgment. But, as we have seen, it played an indispensable part in the intellectual structure of Third Worldism, in its approach to popular representation and to power. At the same time, it drew authority from a well-defined, if misinterpreted, progression of events: from the fall of the colonial order to independence and then to the victory of "revolutionary" Third World movements. Precisely because the seemingly linear progression went awry, such faith in history was deeply challenged. Jacques Julliard put it succinctly: "We no longer have the right to feed the Third World . . . with the fragments of a progressive philosophy of history."[19]

The evolution was part of a far broader rethinking of history as intellectual rubric. Its nature remains somewhat unclear and for the most part is far beyond the scope of my endeavor. Still, a few comments might help. In trying to explain this rethinking, some have pointed to the emergence of Fernand Braudel's "new history." The governing notion is *longue durée,* a focus on the torpid rhythms of subterraneous change and deeply buried continuity. There is a genealogy to time; instantaneous, visible political evolutions become either irrelevant or superficial, certainly misleading. Braudel's legacy is complex, yet the link to politics, and specifically to Third World politics, is made without difficulty. If history was that which we could not see, revolutions ceased to be the expression of profound social sentiment, the source of fundamental change, or in any sense "inevitable"; they were reduced to surface events, unable, often unwilling, to alter longstanding cultural and economic essences.

A significant contribution to the historiography of the French Revolution — François Furet's *Penser la révolution française* — clarifies this link. Furet makes the point that the telling of the Revolution has been closely weaved into a discourse on origins and legitimacy, the historian provid-

ing, as it were, a political genealogy of the revolutionary leadership. This
he sees as the first step in the modern use of history as ideological medium. The narration of history leads us into an imaginary world "in
which all social change is attributable to identifiable, itemized, living
forces; in the same way as mythical thought, it invests the objective universe with subjective will."[20] As Furet argues, to confuse long-term historical evolution with the people's short-term revolutionary spontaneity,
not to mention the leadership's actual intent, is not to recite but to make
history, not to observe but to participate in its ongoing political effort.

As used by others, these ideas fit in nicely with elements of the anti–
Third Worldist critique. Once discredited, the discourse on the meaning
of history and on the people's role within it, to say nothing of the idea
of historical legitimacy, was depicted merely as a vast attempt at domination. The progressive historian's account is viewed as an intellectual
ordering of something that is basically orderless, the recognition and
celebration of a particular constellation of power — it is, in short, *ideology*
(in the unqualifiedly pejorative sense of that term) through and through.
The French philosopher Bernard Henry-Lévy, one of the early demysti-
fiers of ideologies of progress, is at great pains to make obvious this connection between historical narrative and political manipulation: "To col-
lect is to disrupt and to redistribute. . . . To decipher is to construct a
language, produce techniques, establish signs. . . . Wherever there is History, wherever there is the historian's will to submit the disorder of the
incident to the order of linear time, there is always, one way or another,
the earmark and the label of control. . . . Wherever there is the Master,
domination, and servitude, there is always, one way or another, manipulation of time, methodical management of its development and chronology. . . . The revolutionary is a clockmaker."[21]

Other articles of faith were undermined, for instance, the concept of
a united "Third World." Of course, it is possible to keep the notions of
historical inevitability and of the Third World distinct. But the Third
World's unity was far more political aspiration than empirical reality. It
was sustained precisely by the belief that the less developed world was
moving, in inexorable fashion, toward a common future of social and
political emancipation. The two were intimately connected, historical
evolutionism providing fuel for the Third World's willed homogeneity.

The contemporary outlook, with its pronounced skepticism, its self-
proclaimed political agnosticism, also was unreceptive to the notion of
the "people" as a meaningful, intelligible category. In the system of
knowledge of which Third Worldism was a part, we are constantly re-

minded of the role of permanent and stable collective identities. True, in the case of Third Worldism these identities were part social and part political, that is, part determined and part willed. But there remained a rough representation of society as a structure in which individuals belonged to groups defined by, and understood in terms of, material interest. To put it differently, this was an outlook in which what mattered most in making sense of politics were socioeconomic categories: the bourgeoisie, the working class, the peasantry or, more often in the case of Third Worldism, the popular masses and the *peuple*. Such was the power of this taxonomy that ethnic, gender, racial, tribal, and other such groupings were ignored, dismissed as the divisive legacy of colonial domination, set aside as the sequela of false consciousness.

The view came under steady criticism, again aimed at more than the Third World alone. The sources and angles of attack are too numerous to be cataloged, but the point is that the critique assumed that identities overlap and intertwine, that they cannot, in sum, be fixed in any permanent fashion. The social body (and, it follows, the political map) becomes a fluid, indeterminate mosaic of shifting individual and group identities, national, of course, but also ethnic, regional, gender-based, and religious. As Said comments, "'Identity' does not necessarily imply ontologically given and eternally determined stability, or uniqueness, or irreducible character, or privileged status as something total and complete in and of itself."[22]

Of this there was sufficient evidence in the Third World itself, as Miskito Indians battled Nicaragua's Sandinistas, Ovambos resisted the MPLA's dominion in Angola, Eritreans spurned Mengistu's "Marxist-Leninist" road to salvation, and Kurds rose up against Saddam Hussein's Bismarckian vision. Gone was the notion of a unanimous, homogeneous, transparent people represented in the nation-state. In recent years, various social scientists, many of them concerned principally with the Third World, have turned their attention to the problem of cultural and ethnic minorities.[23] Summarizing this viewpoint, René Galissot argues that invocation of the "people" has served to conceal the "frenzied centralizing enterprise that crushes the people in their diversity," a position echoed by Chaliand, for whom "independence has meant the strangling of all minority demands, including the most basic, by the majority group."[24]

There is to all this an antistatist flavor, a universal retreat from the rigid partitioning of the world into nations, of people into social classes, and so forth. As the work of Edward Said well illustrates, the position can derive from a discerning impulse to restore the multidimensionality of identity against the backdrop of nationalistic and nativistic disfigurement. So conceived, it applies to North and South alike, to America's subtle smothering of gender and racial solidarity, as well as to overt Iraqi suppression of Kurds or Shiites.

But there also is a tendency to see in the persistence of infranational solidarities in the underdeveloped world an immaturity particular to it, a question of essence, even of civilization. Third Worldism, in that view, vainly tried to contain what it could not suppress; hence the persistence of tribalism and sectarianism in the Middle East, of clientelism and parochial reactions in sub-Saharan Africa, Asia, and so on. Endemic to the lands of Asia, Africa, and Latin America, tribalism, regionalism, and ethnic conflict are seen as symptoms of a profound and perennial cultural curse.

In so many contemporary visualizations of the Third World, this reappraisal of history and of the people is merely a prelude to a reexamination of power. I spoke earlier of this link between the three and of the central importance of the latter. The point, to present it succinctly, is this: with historical progress as backdrop, the role of political leaders — in the party or, later, in the state — was to translate, which sometimes meant to decipher or uncover, the people's deepest aspirations. There might be a dissonance between the two (represented and representative), delayed consciousness or bureaucratized leadership, but transparency was within reach, a matter of enlightening one or correcting the other. This I summed up in the dual belief that power could be evil (when its beholders were the delegates of the social elite) and that it ought to be virtuous (as when it embodied the popular masses).

One of the immediate effects of forsaking the concept of permanent collective or popular identities is to frustrate this arrangement in its entirety. If there is no single will, how can a state ever be in a position to express it? How can it be the locus for the realization of a monolithic common good when individuals live in a condition that negates the foundations of that very idea? The answers propose themselves naturally: the site of power is the locus where the imaginary concept of "popular will" is created; the common good is then defined as being precisely whatever that locus has chosen to create. And it is only a slight overstatement to say that in this outlook people's actions and interests are determined essentially by the power they possess and the power they must endure. In fact, groups do not seize power, as if it were a vulgar commodity, to make use of as seen fit; instead, to paraphrase Bourdieu, it is power that "inherits" certain groups, carving them in its own image, shaping them to match its needs.

This outlook has impressive intellectual credentials. Structuralism, the *nouveaux philosophes,* works of Foucault in particular but also of Alain Touraine and many assorted others, driven by a general sense of disenchantment — with Europe, East and West, with the Third World, with politics generally — contributed to this reassessment of ideas that had governed left-wing notions of power. More precisely, power became an important object of study in and of itself, with its logic, its independent modes of action, its overwhelming, and overwhelmingly negative, effect.[25] Such complex theories find their way into other arenas of society, much as prevalent political and social moods succeed in influencing the intellectual scene.

This view of power is usually accompanied by several other features. First, and principally, the goals of traditional rebellion no longer can be distinguished from those of the power against which it chooses to rebel. For if one takes away the possibility of representing certain predefined social interests and transferring them onto the political plane, one is left without the prospect of a popular state. There being no virtuous power, there likewise is no virtuous counterpower, or as Foucault put it, "no single locus of great Refusal, no soul of revolt, source of all rebellions, or pure law of the revolutionary."[26] Revolutions, as it were, simply replicate power, and with it its structure, its inequities. "There is no confrontation of dualistic principles," concludes one of the so-called *nouveaux philosophes,* Bernard-Henry Lévy, "no counterpower that is not in the end the expression of renewed power." Thus, "as long as a rebellious plan aspires to, or touches upon, what we call power, the power it will instate will reproduce" existing techniques of domination.[27]

This means — second — that there can be no social finality to politics, no sense of an ultimate, attainable (and laudable) outcome. In their place is but the haphazard shuffling of power positions, society and the principle of hierarchy remaining intact.[28] In 1987, after many years as one of the leading experts on both the Arab and the Third World, Maxime Rodinson confessed: "Personally, I no longer believe in progress. I did, once. . . . [Today] I believe that certain things do not change, most notably in politics. . . . Men have always been driven by the same passion: the struggle for power."[29] "Domination," Chaliand concluded, half bemused, half resigned, "is the essence of politics."[30]

A third corollary has to do with the aims of political action. The demystification of power, of the state, and of revolution meant that there were new priorities: to divide and circumscribe the power of the state, to guarantee a protected space for individual freedom, and to encourage the development of a civil society distinguished from (opposed to) the political. In this context, to use one example for illustration, elections take on a rather different meaning from what was suggested in the Third Worldist construct. Their purpose can no longer be to identify or unearth a "general will" nor to confirm the leaders' legitimacy. It is, rather, to act as a check and allow for the pluralistic expression of self-defined and shifting private interests. As the French sociologist Alain Touraine explained, "We no longer wish to fight for the 'good' society, we expect nothing of politics and of power other than respect for our opportunities and for our freedom. We no longer wish to change the Prince, but to live without one." [31]

Much of this radical reassessment came from outside the Third Worldist universe, yet so much came from within. For ideologies can be casualties of more than external assault alone. They can be victims of their own internal structure of argument, their expectations, their gauges of success. Third Worldism harbored dreams of a utopian state, an impeccable embodiment of the national interest. Its standards of political purity were those of popular government, perfect equality, and economic development. And yet, inequalities persisted, development stalled, poverty endured. Third Worldism dealt with these failings as most state-centered theory would: by blaming the state, accused of betrayal, deviation, and failure. In its pure, unadulterated form, Third Worldism did not suffer approximations or partial results. It had chosen utopia as its standard, history as its demanding judge. It would have to live with history's harsh and unappealable verdict.

The combination of a model that attributed all facts of social life to the state with the resilience of inequities in the distribution of material and cultural resources resulted in a thorough indictment of the state. All forms of social interaction, up to and including the most minute, were viewed as coarse reflections of the dominant group's strategy to reproduce and entrench its control, social disparities being seen as indicators of a more generalized and centralized hierarchical structure. This was pure functionalism, of course, and like all functionalism, it had some unfortunate consequences. If the character of social interactions and hierarchies inescapably serves the interests and defines the nature of the state, all states can be described in roughly similar fashion. Forms of domination might vary—from the more institutionalized, codified, mediated, and opaque (as in modern capitalist societies) to the less so (as in the Third World)—yet their underlying social meaning is much the same. Given the Third Worldist observer's crude analytic tools, all present societies are in some irreducible way analogous. The point is that when sociological insights on individuals' interactions enter a functionalist model of the all-powerful state, all forms of practice expose the true nature of the social and political order, and all that remain are the various but interchangeable orderings of hierarchy and power. All societies are trivialized as permutable arrangements of a single social logic: exit the bourgeoisie, enter the "new class," the apparatchiki, the state bureaucracy; exit capitalism, enter state capitalism; exit exploitation, enter political domination, enter power.

To speak of the Third World today is to speak with this baggage of disillusionment, sense of betrayal, and theoretical reappraisal. The conclusions encompassed the developed world as well, but they were accompanied by a distinctive intensity when it came to the South—perhaps because there were so many ready stereotypes and conventional beliefs to account for the disappointment. These were, briefly, the following: Third World countries, still divided along vertical (i.e., tribal, ethnic, etc.) rather than horizontal (e.g., class) lines, lacked the necessary engines for social consciousness and prerequisites for national unity; their economic backwardness, combined with this vertical social partitioning, meant that struggles for power were simply struggles for the sources of material wealth and the means to distribute that wealth to one's family, tribe, ethnic group, and so on. This meant, in fine, that politics were reduced to the endless, cyclical pattern of power grabbing and power maintenance, one group replacing another, only to follow the exact same policies—to the benefit of a marginally different group. So much for the notion of a popular will, of history going somewhere and meaning something, of power being the means by which social projects got translated and applied.

The emerging image could hardly be further from the Third Worldist visions of old. We saw earlier how the portrait of popular unity became fractured along myriad—and unyielding—lines reflecting antagonistic solidarities and competing identities. That, to state it mildly, put a serious damper on the hope that "the masses," guided by their unanimous interests, would rise up to radically transform social and political structures. In this context, of course, Third Worldist concepts of politics no longer could survive, for they had depended on the idea of a representation of the popular interest by appropriate leaders. In their place came the ideas that power had interests of its own and that an unbridgeable gap separated rulers and ruled. Whereas Third Worldism had spoken in terms of polarities, the goal being to transfer the state from the negative to the positive, the post–Third Worldist discourse focuses on densities, the aim being to disperse power as much as possible, to decentralize and dilute it. As Julliard remarks, this is in total contradiction to the "postulate of a perfect identity between the people and their (revolutionary) leaders, that is, of the end of the structural distance between rulers and ruled."[32]

Once more, this hostile image of authority was applied to the North, but there is a sense in which power came to be seen as an evil peculiar to the Third World, a distinctive affliction. The view has licensed familiar depictions of Idi Amin and Saddam Hussein as reflections — exaggerated perhaps, but only so far — of the underdeveloped world's endemic pathologies and, worse, of its natural, and inescapable, course. Left and Right, "progressive" and "reactionary" — all states were condemned to replicate the same abuses of authority. Looking through this lens, one could not "choose, in the name of a discredited 'meaning' of history, between a corrupt, unjust, police, often sanguinary capitalist Africa and a 'socialist' Africa, altogether anachronistic, tyrannical and no less sanguinary. Yes indeed, there are two sides in the Third World. . . . They are the sides of repressive states and of martyred people."[33]

To put this another way, Third Worldism was perverted by its own success: as a group came to power, power came to it, shaping, molding, and defining it. In *The End of the Third World,* Nigel Harris argues that "the aspirations of the new ruling orders . . . mean that, once in power, the issue of overcoming mass poverty became subordinate to the growth of national power. . . . Class issues disappear into national ones. . . . The concepts of socialism and popular liberation . . . became entirely absorbed by those of state power, the liberation of governments."[34] Political degeneration, social retrogression, and a general relapse into the hierarchies and divisions they purportedly were designed to eliminate — such is the lot of Third World revolutions. "The trouble with a total revolution," Robert Frost once wrote, is "that it brings the same class up on top."[35] Power simply finds its latest abode.

Essentialism has few virtues but many rewards. The compelling simplicity and neatness of its explanatory arsenal is one: Islam breeds to-

talitarianism, or martyrdom, or political instability; with protestant-
ism comes the energy of capitalism, with Africans sloth; generalizations
abound concerning Japan, the Arabs, Latin America, not to mention
even broader characterizations (and this is what we have just been discussing) about the Third World. Such colossal propositions are immune
to challenge precisely because they are so abstract and so divorced from
the concreteness of everyday experience — another of the advantages of
resorting to a theory that focuses on the "essence" of a society, culture,
or religious grouping.

The demise of Third Worldism invited an overdose of such interpretations. Intellectuals and observers were led to a discourse of disappointment and even exhaustion. It started at the outskirts and moved steadily
toward the core, ultimately inducing a renunciation of some central tenets of Third Worldism. In turn, both the reinterpretations and the
events that precipitated them lent plausibility and a degree of legitimacy
to essentialist accounts. Third Worldism had failed because of the Third
World, because of what it was and would always be.

There was an element of vindication, I suppose, in that the Pol Pots,
the Sékou Tourés, the Gadhafis, and the Assads of this world validated
notions that briefly had been considered off limits (and then only by
some). These beliefs had to do with the force and permanence of nativistic, tribal, or religious instincts on the one hand and the superiority of
Western "pragmatism" and rationality on the other. The simplest explanation for the Third Worldist failure, and also the most widespread, goes
something like this: Third Worldism collapsed because it was misguided,
and it was misguided because it was ideological, which is to say, abstract,
subjective, and divorced from everyday reality. With the breakdown, in
rapid succession, of the grand projects of the twentieth century — socialism, communism, and so on — the Third World finally turned its back
on ambitious ideological enterprises, seeing them for the utopian, un-
realistic, and ultimately damaging illusions that they were. What remained were the forces that Third Worldism had sought to suppress and
that ultimately, by their resilience, had pushed Third Worldism aside.
The first was the people's traditional and multiple forms of primordial
identification, to their family, their tribe, their ethnic group, their religion. In other words, freedom from ideology (imposed from without)
allowed people to revert to identity (experienced from within), which
was far more meaningful, familiar, and real. What are often known as
the "objective" realities of economic life constituted the second force,
one that had condemned Third Worldist projects and one to which
Third World governments were compelled to give in.

Third Worldism, in short, is said to have encountered the insuperable forces of parochial value systems and universal economic truths. Parochialism and pragmatism work in tension, of course, and that is viewed as the stake of today's battles: exclusionary ideologies (religious, tribal, ethnic, racial) are the natural language of the Third World, to be countered only by the weight of economic constraints. There thus exists a story within which ethnic and other fragmentations and the ubiquity of neoliberal economic dogmas come together as a coherent whole to illuminate the decline of Third Worldism. Enabled or facilitated by the more general intellectual questioning outlined above, the story was spread by the media and the academic community alike—though to speak of a consensus is not at all to suggest the existence of a conspiracy.

In fact, neither proposition—the resurgence of old solidarities or the resistance of economic constraints—can readily be dismissed. Both enjoy the allure of what I have referred to as essentialism, and there is a truth to them that it is hard to ignore. Various forms of conflict over primordial identities are ravaging the Third World at this time, with signs (such as the massacres in Rwanda) suggesting their intensification, and not at all the reverse. With them come disorder, lawlessness, and the progressive erosion of the nation-state. The sense of anarchy and potential havoc all this evokes was captured in a recent, widely noticed article by Samuel Huntington. We have moved away from ideological conflict, he concluded: welcome to the far more brutal and primal "clash of civilizations" pitting Hindus, Muslims, Westerners, Japanese, Slavs, and Latin Americans, to name a few, against one another.

Simultaneously, governments have been steering toward economic and social policies frequently, if misleadingly, described as "nonideological," privatizing industry, adopting IMF stabilization programs, slashing public subsidies, and so forth. Just consider Ghana's increasingly close collaboration with international economic and financial institutions, Angola's and Mozambique's retreat from state socialism, along with Algeria's and even, by agreeing to limit state industrial ownership, Libya's, Nicaragua's brusque shift, Vietnam's tentative steps in the Chinese direction, Aristide's overnight Haitian conversion, and Cuba's own agonizing and public soul-searching. Here and there, official voices are heard to lament these policies, to castigate the IMF or the World Bank, to vow resistance.[36] But though the rhetoric might well sound egalitarian and nationalistic, even in those cases the policies, with less fanfare perhaps, have shifted to "austerity," "rigor," and "adjustment." Whatever remains of the populist tendencies is purely ornamental.

I want to discuss both of these notions briefly before offering an alternative account. In speaking of Third World's nativism, my focus is mainly on the idea of a return of Islam, primarily because of my greater familiarity with the issue but also because of the superior attention, much of it superficial and distorting, that it has received in the media and by governments in general. Mention of countries of the Arab world, the Persian Gulf, or Central Asia immediately brings certain images to mind: of menace, of fanaticized mobs, of kidnappings, hijackings, and terror, of social and cultural backwardness, of permanent political instability and (never mind the apparent contradiction) perennial, unchanging autocratic rule.[37] I will have more to say when we turn to the case of Algeria, which so aptly fits this mold, but the essential ingredients of the dominant interpretation — that countries of the Muslim world used the cover of socialism and similar ideologies of progress but that behind these, Islamic identities and Islamic fervor endured — are apparent. Islam and Islamism had waited for their moment, and now it had come.

In so many works, the turn (or return) to religion, tribalism, and so on, in countries that once professed an adherence to various ideologies of progress is viewed as a rejection of an unfamiliar system of thought and a reversion to more natural modes of behavior. Third Worldism, in this perspective, was predicated on Western conceptions of the territorial state, the people, and secular history, all of which were foreign to the underlying essence. The point is forcefully advanced in the case of Islam by Bertrand Badie in *Les deux états: Pouvoir et société en Occident et en terre d'Islam*. Implicitly postulating the existence of an ahistorical Islamic identity, he views it as incompatible with the stable exercise of state power. This corresponds to what I called in part I the inherently rebellious image of Islam, refusing legitimacy to all worldly forms of authority and giving rise to the tyrannical and desperate exercise of power by rulers obsessed with the fear of its loss. Patricia Crone, who exemplifies this school of thought, writes that "politics degenerates into mere intrigues and bickerings for the proceeds of a state apparatus," for no one can be assured of long-term, let alone solid, popular support.[38] Leaders are forced to rely on tribal or familial networks to strengthen their rule, for these are the only links Islamic communities will recognize and to which they will defer. Islam goes hand in hand with more severe and more narrow forms of exclusion and tribal or sectarian domination — as in the case of the Alawite sect in Assad's Baathist Syria, or of individuals originating from Saddam Hussein's Tikrit "tribe" in Baathist Iraq. Regional analyses also have been advanced in the case of Algeria (pitting East against West, the Algérois against the rest of the country), though with somewhat less fortune.

Another component to this Islamic essence is its aversion to "modernity," by which generally is meant secularism, rationalism, and the supremacy of civil over political society. Bruno Etienne, one of the more persuasive observers of the "Islamic revival," thus explains that Third Worldism was "too foreign, doubtless, to the culture of Muslim Arabs," for it was the vehicle for many of these values. "Faced with an intolerable modernity, which they perceived as foreign, Islamic activists . . . refused to modernize Islam, proposing instead to Islamicize modernity."[39]

The problem with these interpretations, as I earlier suggested, has to do with their treatment of Islam as perennial essence. Reviewing Etienne's book, Michael Gilsenan observes that "we are right on the edge of the old Western image of civilization or religious tradition that simply repeats itself unchangingly."[40] In his study of the Iranian Islamic state, Sami Zubaida makes a similar point, criticizing authors such as Badie for "postulat[ing] a cultural essence which underlies and unifies Islamic history and distinguishes it from an equally reductionist notion of the West."[41]

Analyses cast in an essentialist mode cannot really be disproved, and that is one of their main strengths, but it is possible to point to changes in the presumed essence and to a suspicious tendency to shape the essence to fit the reality du jour. Yahya Sadowski's insightful discussion "The New Orientalism and the Democracy Debate" is relevant in this respect. He demonstrates how, in attempting to account for the failure of democratic movements in the Middle East, Orientalists have invoked the "essence" of Islam, all the while modifying the nature of that essence in response to shifting political events. Thus, "classical Orientalists argued that orthodox Islam promoted political quietism." The "essence" of Islam, then, was conducive to a system in which the all-powerful state dominated a docile and ill-developed society and repressed any democratic impulse. All this changed with stunning swiftness in the aftermath of the Iranian revolution, when the "essence" of Islam shifted toward the destabilizing side — the side, as Etienne would say, of "radical Islam." "This new generation of Orientalists [he mentions Crone but also Pipes and Gellner] were uncomfortable with their predecessors' claim that Islam promoted political submission — while sharing the conviction that Islam was incompatible with democracy." It was not that the state was too powerful in Islamic countries; to the contrary, it was society that "consistently withheld its support from political authority" and pledged its allegiance to strong autonomous groups — the tribes, religious sects, or brotherhoods of which we have spoken.[42] "The irony of this conjuncture needs to be savored. When the consensus of social scientists held that democracy and development depended upon the actions of strong, assertive social groups, Orientalists held that such associations were absent in Islam. When the consensus evolved and social scientists thought a quiescent, undemanding society was essential to progress, the neo-Orientalists portrayed Islam as beaming with pushy, anarchic solidarities. Middle Eastern Muslims, it seems, were doomed to be eternally out of step with intellectual fashion." In both instances, Sadowski notes, Islam is portrayed "as a kind of family curse that lives on, crippling the lives of innocents generations after the original sin that created it."[43]

This is just one instance of the weakness of the "revivalist" school — as in the "revival" of religion, of ethnicity, of tribalism — and I am confident that other similar contradictions could successfully be brought to light. One might grant at once that such solidarities have been flourishing without necessarily attributing the phenomenon to qualities inherent in the solidarities themselves, that is, to the fact that they supposedly capture the essence of particular social formations. The causal link, convenient and readily available as it might appear, simply has not been established. It is just as likely that, far from being ahistorical, the solidarities are a function of specific historical factors, cultural influences, economic situations, or strategies.[44]

The same rush to explain a successful phenomenon by its own internal qualities can be found in the "pragmatic" reading of the Third Worldist demise. At issue here is not the Third World's inability to shed its most basic identity but rather its incapacity to ignore for too long the objective laws of economics. The notion, stated long ago by Daniel Bell, is that "ideology, which once was a road to action, has come to be a dead end."[45] At its core is the belief that there is a sharp dichotomy between ideology and science, and that ideology (like politics) is alien to rational economic decision making. Applications to the Third World are relatively straightforward. The revolutionary fervor of the postindependence days is said to have led to harmful delusions, inconsistent with sound economic management. Self-reliance, furious industrialization, the New International Economic Order, and other such gadgets were merely part of a steady ideological diet. Harris, along with so many others in both the North and the South, confidently concludes that the demise of Third Worldism was due to its deceptive, or "ideological," economic postulates. He points to the success of the Asian Gang of Four (South Korea, Taiwan, Hong Kong, and Singapore) as proof that Third Worldism erred and to current moves toward privatization as vindication of pragmatic, neoclassical models of economic growth: "The seventies saw an astonishing victory for counter-revolutionary thought. The neo-classical economists . . . attacked the entire [Third Worldist] system of thought—the idea of the economy as a rigid structure; of the government as a benevolent, strong and rational agent; of industry in general, and heavy industry in particular, having some peculiar merit; of the domestic market being superior to exports, domestic capital to foreign, of self-sufficiency to interdependence. The very idea of conscious long-term direction of the economy by the government was questioned."[46]

The movement was universal, affecting countries as varied as France, Spain, and England. But it hit the Third World (and, though this is a different matter, the Eastern bloc) hardest. I mentioned a few countries earlier in this section, and the list could go on practically without interruption. One after the other, formerly "progressive," "socialist," or "Marxist-Leninist" nations have fallen in line with the IMF and followed its prescriptions. Liberation movements too have learned their lesson well, both the ANC and the PLO doing their best to assuage Western donors. In all these cases, the shift has been interpreted, almost without contradiction or challenge, as the realignment of policy with reality, a move from the ideological to the pragmatic.

Although the deleterious consequences of so many of the policies adopted in the sixties and seventies (e.g., bankrupt agricultural sectors and inefficient and superfluous industries) should not be minimized, it does not take much to realize that the discourse of the eighties and nineties has been just as ideological, just as fraught with preconceptions, hidden agendas, and biases, as its predecessor. In a rather constant way, political leaders see their task as equating decisions with necessity, a course of action with the course of nature. Hence their appeal to outside, quasi-sacred sources: yesterday the revolution and the popular will; today, increasingly, the "objective" rules of economic law. Actions are thus presented as the translation of extrinsic codes that the authorities are said blindly to obey. But that rhetorical effort, in and of itself, does not make the issue one of economic competence and realism versus demagoguery and utopianism. Instead, acceptance or rejection of just such a characterization is one of the principal stakes of political struggle. That the media, academics, and governments in all parts of the world have acceded to the notion that economic "liberalization" (for want of a better word) is the only possible choice simply demonstrates the degree of success the political enterprise enjoys.

Nor will it do to characterize the transition from state ownership to neoliberalism as a straightforward move from coercion to freedom. The characterization generally assumes that there are such things as a "free" market, "real" pricing, and "rational" economics. Yet there is nothing that can be free, real, or rational about any of these. Markets are never free, in the sense that they will always be regulated by a series of permissions and prohibitions (concerning the right to unionize, to engage in secondary boycotts, to strike, to enter and use certain lands, etc.). Duncan Kennedy makes this point clearly in "The Stakes of Law, or Hale and Foucault." As Kennedy shows, one cannot speak of a neutral, natural, much less rational, state of affairs in which the law of the market is given free reign, unrestrained by state intervention. Similarly, the notion of a "freer" market, one that permits all forms of economic activity save those that will cause injury to others, is of little use. As Kennedy writes, "All competition is legalized injury, as is the strike, the lockout, picketing, the consumer boycott, and the leveraged buyout."[47] The question in each instance is which forms of injury to allow and which to forbid.

In like manner, prices reflect a set of background rules reflecting complex political and societal choices. The existence of alternatives to employment, such as welfare payments, the availability of licenses for petty commerce, and the state of tort and antitrust laws affect the relative bargaining power of employer and employee, thereby affecting the price of any given product.[48] That these choices have distributional effects that, in turn, have an impact on overall productivity is quite probable. But that is another matter altogether, independent of the futile quest for truth or rationality.[49]

The point I am trying to make is at once self-evident and yet often ignored. The contemporary economic strategies of Algeria, Ghana, and Egypt, even if they were to lead to higher growth rates than those achieved under the reigns of Boumedienne, Nkrumah, and Nasser, are by no stretch of the imagination "value-neutral." Each policy has unique and important consequences — for income distribution, the availability of social services such as health and education, dependency on (and vulnerability to) the international marketplace — many of which remain unreported. We see this in the repercussions of IMF-imposed austerity (or "stabilization") plans, such as spending and subsidy reductions, wage freezes, the banning of barter agreements, or the dismemberment of local industries under the impact of imported goods.[50] The decision to choose a particular program must be understood as a political one, a decision to benefit, and therefore to harm, certain groups, to emphasize some priorities and therefore to neglect others.

Moreover, the choice of a particular economic program must be understood in the international context as a response to pressures or incentives (as in Argentina's relations with the United States in the early 1990s, or Brazil's, to say nothing of Mexico's). As aid becomes subject to the acceptance of structural adjustment plans, the North is free to export its own economic models and to reorder the Third World's socioeconomic setting, allowing increased dependence to be cast as newfound rationality. Jorge Castaneda puts it this way: "The strongest arguments heard in favor of the free-market radicalism of the late eighties and early nineties consisted precisely in the importance of the foreign constraint. Nothing could be done without external resources; these were more sought after than ever; only certain policies and countries would succeed in attracting them, and consequently there was no alternative to the policies that—it was hoped—would attract funding."[51] True, this growing dependency and the North's ability to impose such plans have been at least in part a function of the dilapidated economies to which a decade or two of Third Worldism had led. But the turn to liberalism, austerity, and privatization cannot be explained as the simple discarding of ideology and the success of scientific economic management. There is ideology in that move as well—which is to say politics, and interests, and conflict.

In short, both propositions suffer from a similar inclination to imagine ideology per se as extrinsic to society, something that can be imposed, resisted, or discarded. Both start from the idea that there is an immutable essence to which Third Worldism is contrasted and to which, inevitably, the underdeveloped world must return: a natural, "nonideological" position, as in Nigel Harris's outlook; an enduring, eternal religious identity, as in Etienne's. The world becomes divided into the ideological and the nonideological, with Third Worldism belonging to one, economic liberalism to the other, and religion, ethnic solidarity, or tribal loyalty fitting uncomfortably between the two—authentic forms of consciousness in the sense that they express the group's genuine identity, yet perilous ones nonetheless. There is an "essence" to economics just as there is an "essence" to social formations, and Third Worldism was neither. Instead, it is portrayed both as an alien implant rejected by an unyielding (Islamic, tribal, etc.) society and as a mythical travesty of economic reality.

Intuitions come easily to essentialists. Faced with a formidable array of events—ethnic conflict, of the kind that tears established sovereignties apart in Central and Eastern Europe, Africa and the Asian subcontinent; the strengthening of religious (especially Muslim) movements from Central Asia to North Africa, reaching even Kepel's "banlieues de l'Islam," the inner cities of Western Europe;[52] the disintegration of state structures, most visibly in Somalia or Liberia, no less impressively in other parts of an underdeveloped world plagued by rampant criminality, famine, disease, and urban overcrowding; and, finally, the tumultuous birth of multiparty systems (I dare not say democracies) in Madagascar, Mongolia, Congo, or Benin, together with the replacement of so-called state socialism by the "sacred principles of free trade, free competition, and freedom of movement for capital"[53] — they grope for an explanation that sounds familiar, matches our preconceptions, fits our expectations.

The explanation in this case, as I have tried to show, exhibited an interesting mix of particularism and universalism. The notion of an essence of the Third World is an instance of the former, for the intensification of tribal, ethnic, or religious strife is attributed to something peculiarly "Third Worldish" (Yugoslavia and other such oddities aside). Then there is the idea of an economic gospel, an example of universalism par excellence. To Europeans and North Americans especially, the particularism of tribalism and the universality of economic prescriptions, understandably, are comforting thoughts. Against all this, ideology stands as an awkward and artificial graft, divorced from the Third World's reality, be it cultural or economic.

I view things from a somewhat different perspective, believing that one cannot sever ideology from society, that cultural and social self-perception always reflect competition between rival discursive systems. Certainly, in any historical period there exists an array of available representations of the world. That some assume a more central role as others move on to the periphery has nothing to do with the so-called "extrinsic" nature of ideology or with a particular society's abiding allegiance to certain sociocultural norms, such as Islam, that, curiously, remain insulated from any kind of change in the domestic or international spheres. Instead, at any given moment, systems of thought interact with both domestic and international socioeconomic factors, contributing to their legitimation or delegitimation. Out of such interactions comes an accepted (or dominant) agenda of public concerns, an outer limit for "responsible opinion," an orthodoxy, and, in fine, the identification of certain groups as the rightful holders of power.

My objection to the predominant post–Third Worldist account is not so much that the leaders of the revolutionary Third World necessarily "believed" in their statements, or that such statements adequately "reflected" reality. There is, of course, a sense in which Third Worldism served the purposes of the various regimes that made it their creed, and I have tried to illustrate how in preceding sections. Nor would I dispute the notion that it has become an obsolete mode of discourse and form of practice, overcome by the influence of economic developments and competing solidarities. But where the essentialists, in their post–Third Worldist incarnation, see immutability and fixedness, I see motion, the dynamic interaction of modes of representation and social condition, the emergence of dominant systems of thought, due not to their inherent truth but to their superior efficacy at particular moments in time. In short, one should be careful to distinguish between the idea that Third Worldism has always been an artificial graft and the idea that it has become an outmoded ideological category; between the belief that religious fundamentalism expresses a core Muslim identity and the belief that prevailing conditions have increased its cultural and social allure; between the view that realism has dislodged ideology and the view that one system of representation simply has taken the place of another.

What, then, happened to Third Worldism? What explains its demise and the concurrent escalation of tribal, religious, and ethnic strife, together with the consensus around free-market values? Third Worldism, I have argued, became an influential ideology or system of representation as a result of a confluence of factors, some domestic, some international. It was, to borrow Elemér Hankiss's term, an "organizational principle,"[54] the paste holding together social, political, and cultural structures. For a time, it helped shape a vision of the Third World that had some coherence and some muscle; that is, it "command[ed] attention," became an "authorized language," so that "the things it designate[d] were] not simply expressed, but also authorized and legitimated."[55] Perceptions of the South, of the North, and of their interaction were affected. But that never was the whole story, for Third Worldism coexisted in uneasy tension with competing pulls that helped structure the international space and inhibit domestic initiatives. Algeria, Libya, Manley's Jamaica, and Ortega's Nicaragua remained pariah states, so to speak. Even from within, Third Worldist countries faced challenges represented by alternative principles that were strengthened or weakened by international developments.

The crisis of Third Worldism can be described as an instance of an ideological language ceasing to command the necessary attention — abroad and in its various homes. Not a matter of truth or falsity per se but one of efficacy, of a capacity to order daily experience. At some point the organizational principle, whatever it might be, can no longer regulate social interactions in a meaningful way; it becomes dysfunctional, discards too many people, leaves too many interests unaccounted for. Then there is a lack of fit between the system of representation and what it is intended to represent. And so the alternatives become the more persuasive discourses.

To this story of ideological ousting and displacement, there is no single starting point, at least not one I am aware of. Untangling the causal relations between these economic, social, and intellectual shifts is a herculean task, far beyond the scope of this book. One of the last sweeping efforts of the kind was the Marxist endeavor to explain changes in the superstructure by changes in the infrastructure and then to fit both within the confines of the class struggle; its misfortune at the very least counsels caution before embarking on yet another. A second point worth bearing in mind is that when we speak of this demise we address a phenomenon that affected countries as disparate as Algeria and Nicaragua, Madagascar and Grenada, along with a specific intellectual discourse. Particular case studies, rather than grand theories, might be more appropriate. For both these reasons, what I propose here is only a rough narrative intended to counter the familiar post–Third Worldist tale. I leave to others the ambition of sorting out precisely how all the various variables fit together, and to the examination of Algeria the formulation of (slightly) more precise hypotheses.

There is no one starting point, perhaps, but an abundance of interesting places to begin nonetheless. Thus, in no particular order, we might consider evolutions on the world stage, for that was the source of so much of Third Worldism's power. Concepts such as "internationalization," "transnationalization," or even "Westernization" tend to be abused; yet there is little doubt that over the past ten or twenty years we have witnessed extraordinary technological changes allowing for the growing dissemination of news, cultural norms, economic perspectives, and political values — especially by Western nations. Independence and decolonization notwithstanding, the Third World remains ever more tributary to these norms, perspectives, and values. Said speaks of "the unprecedented growth in the apparatus for the diffusion and control of information," adding that "we now have an international media presence that insinuates itself, frequently at a level below conscious awareness, over a fantastically wide range." And he continues, quoting Anthony Smith: "The new media have the power to penetrate more deeply into a 'receiving' culture than any previous manifestation of Western technology."[56]

Press agencies (principally, the Agence France Presse, Reuters, and the Associated Press), television, movies, and other like instruments of cultural dissemination give birth to a standardized hierarchy of tastes — in food, clothing, music, even looks — which in turn creates its own hierarchy of power and influence. As Bourdieu convincingly shows, cultural taste is to some degree manufactured; goods are acquired as goods but also as signs, indicators of one's social status, or one's *distinction*.[57] Access to France 2 by residents of Tunis or Rabat, to CNN by practically all, is symptomatic of the South's increasing inability to control the communicational and informational flow. In Algiers, the teachings of the prophet must vie with *Dallas,* while young women demand Pamela and Sue-Ellen hairdos.

The same is true of intellectual proclivities, preys of the reigning orthodoxy, "authorized" truths, or "serious" discourse (to borrow Foucault's words). Increasingly, success in the international realm is contingent upon compliance with exogenous guidelines, national policy becoming, as it were, a subproduct of authoritative international norms. Writing on Algeria, Fanny Colonna evokes a subtle *Dallas–Le Monde* syndrome, with *Dallas* the purveyor of the cultural canon and *Le Monde* of the intellectual.[58] In short, systems of thought struggle to be a part of the acknowledged public space. Progressively squeezed out, Third Worldism could do little more than watch from the sidelines as the media systematically "reorient[ed] international social discourse and process," as the gospel of less government and fewer subsidies, more privatization and unhampered free trade, took hold.[59]

Three caveats: First, there was more to this evolution than just an IMF-ization of discourse, an influx of jeans, Coca-Cola, or *Rambo.* The "Westernization" of cultural exchanges also had the effect of spreading the ideology of human rights, free elections, and multipartyism. As one commentator noted, "The 1980's have seen an unprecedented growth of international concern for human rights — including (prominently) the right to choose democratically the government under which one lives. . . . The growth of democratic norms throughout the world is strikingly evident in the degree to which authoritative regimes find it necessary to wrap themselves in the rhetoric of constitutional democracy."[60]

How deep or lasting these reforms will prove to be is an entirely separate matter, of course. But there is little question that pluralistic institutional arrangements have been multiplying at surprising speed, the result of new demands and new priorities. "It is as if one urgency had replaced another," writes Mahmoud Hussein. "Young people are dying by the hundreds in the name of constitutional principles, a multiparty system, and free elections."[61]

Much of the impetus for democratization came from below, to be sure, yet the degree to which it was pursued and then manipulated by Third World states and elites should not be neglected. At a time of economic hardship, democracy, the creation of multiple parties, and enhanced freedoms of expression were viewed as means of deflecting mounting criticism of the state by minimizing its responsibility. The often risky, sometimes (as in Algeria) desperately dangerous strategy was to unfasten the state from society, the public from the private, in the hope that those at the helm would be spared the people's acrimony.

This brings us to the second, larger point. "Westernization" is not simply a matter of the North peremptorily dictating its rules to the South. Mimicry itself is a strategy rationally adopted by Third World political actors. In other words, a logic is at play, and it is worth spelling out what it is and what it is not. To begin, the "Westernization" of the Third World — an ill-defined concept at best, variously designating secularism or free trade, democracy or pop culture, individualism or modernity[62] — is not a choice made sensible by virtue of its being intrinsically and universally beneficial in a way, say, that Third Worldism was not. Rather, espousal of the West's economic models, of its language, culture, technology, or attire, by the South (portions of the South, I should say) reflects the commonality of interests linking exporter and importer. Bertrand Badie describes the workings of this system in considerable and fascinating detail, but for our purposes a rough summary will suffice.[63] For the elites of the Third World, it makes increasing sense to privatize, liberalize, encourage foreign investment, even align themselves with American diplomatic interests, in order to secure both foreign aid and, perhaps more important, their position as indispensable links to it. In a similar vein, we earlier discussed how the Third World's nation-statist impulse was fueled by the perception that benefits would accrue in the world system. In this case, economic and cultural mimetism are viewed by Third World elites as keys to international aid, to patronage, and, thus, to political survival. Badie goes so far as to suggest that were self-centered economic development possible, it might constitute the greatest peril to the South's rulers in that it might strengthen the role of the technocratic (as opposed to the political) elite and loosen civil society's dependence on the state for the acquisition and disbursement of material resources.[64]

In short, contemporary relations of dependency and the uniformity of economic policies on a world scale reflect, not the handiwork of arrogant Northern imperialists or of impotent Southern puppets, but the common realization by elites of the First and Third Worlds that with resources, knowledge, and technology increasingly concentrated in the North, such choices can serve the interests of both. Which is just another way of saying that for Third World leaders, investment on the international scene — economic, diplomatic, even cultural — is now believed to yield a heftier profit than its domestic counterpart. Consider Badie's explanation of China's position on the Gulf crisis. At first hostile to the idea of military intervention against Iraq, Beijing nonetheless allowed the adoption of Security Council Resolution 618, which authorized it. Not, according to Badie, without a price: a few days after the vote, the United States withdrew its opposition to a $114.3 million loan by the World Bank to China, a token gesture no doubt, but one that signaled the end of Beijing's international isolation. A share of sovereignty, perhaps even of credibility in the eyes of traditional allies, and reluctant participation in Washington's new world order in exchange for renewed membership in the world economy — this was straightforward cost-benefit analysis, which China was as capable as any other to engage in.[65]

None of all this occurred in an ahistorical vacuum, of course. The evolution was closely tied to Europe's and the United States' current superior economic, financial, military, and technological status; to the role of the IMF, the World Bank, and the Economic Bank for Reconstruction and Development (EBRD); and to the debilitated state of Third World economies. There is a snowball effect as well: as country after country adheres to the new economic creed, it becomes increasingly difficult for any one nation to hold out. France learned this the cruel way in the early years of Mitterrand's presidency, as it saw its expansionary economic policy run into the constraints of the international economic and monetary system. So too Tanzania, where "Nyerere's 'experiments' on behalf of a general good were an object of 'outside' scorn while the actual workings of the terms of trade, worldwide, ensured that none of these experiments could do more than limp, or even work at all."[66] Everywhere, the language of "pragmatic development" becomes the only permissible link to the Western world, and so to world markets, and so to financial institutions. With Cuba and Vietnam falling in line, how far behind can North Korea really be?

Third Worldism, with its representation of a world polarized between North and South, its faith in historical progress, and its visions of self-reliant development, had little of consequence to say about this state of affairs. At most, it could bemoan the treachery of a Third World's post-independence leadership found guilty of selling "their souls to the devil at a price that would have shamed Faust."[67] Even that theme became increasingly hollow as the Tunisian betrayal was repeated in Egypt, in China, in the Congo, in Benin, in Somalia, Algeria, or Guinea. Failure to follow the revered model can be imputed to straying disciples for only so long; there inevitably comes a point when the model itself must carry the blame.

The third caveat I want to mention is one to which I have already alluded, namely, that what the globalization of the world economy, the Westernization of taste and of consumption patterns, and the "global village" enjoy in breadth they sorely lack in depth. While political and economic elites of yesterday's Third Worldism, known as the *jeunesse tchi-tchi* in Algeria and as *yummies* (young upwardly mobile Marxists) elsewhere, might well exhibit the traits, habits, or ethos of a transnational class,[68] they nevertheless constitute only a fraction of the population.

This is one of the central paradoxes of the ongoing internationalization: that it comes hand in hand with cultural disparity, not homogeneity, with polarization, not uniformity. The influx of images from the West might create shared wants and desires, but not shared enjoyment. The vast majority of the Third World remains deprived at the same time that a glitzy procession of consumer goods passes nearby. The result is a dualistic culture, with a privileged few participating in the West's cultural universe and the rest left out. If anything, the dissemination of North American and Western European cultural values has had what Badie calls a "boomerang" effect, inspiring anti-Western feeling, a withdrawal into local cultural bonds, and the accelerated cultural disintegration of Third World nation-states. Galissot makes the interesting point, exemplified by Algeria, that the hardest hit are countries with a strong tradition of migration to the North. In recent years, as the doors to Europe gradually have been fastened, those permitted to immigrate increasingly have been persons possessing the linguistic, professional, and cultural tools to adjust. The reaction among those left behind can be a combination of envy and resentment, quickly translating into heightened feelings of indigenous purity and withdrawal into narrow ethnic and communitarian loyalty.[69]

The Third World political and economic leadership's adherence to the West's normative order, meanwhile, further widens the distance separating rulers and ruled, for each seeks sustenance at a different cultural source. Witness the attitude of Morocco, Tunisia, or Pakistan during the Gulf crisis, siding at first with the American-led coalition, providing diplomatic cover and material support, only to backtrack in the face of unexpected popular protest. They had misread the sentiments of their people—assuming, that is, that they had bothered to read them at all.[70] All of which confirms that, far from reflecting the inherent, universal, and irresistible appeal of economic liberalism, North American culture, political institutions, and the like, "Westernization" is the product of so-ber deliberation by elites in North and South who know a good political deal when they see one.

Such cultural divergence has particular significance because it both is nourished by and in turn nourishes a parallel material divide. I am not speaking solely of economic inequity, though there certainly was much of that. Rather, the same logic that induces the Third World's elite to turn over (practically) its economic policy and cultural identity to the North leads it to abandon vast expanses of its domestic social space as well. The logic (which some adopted and others were compelled to fol-low) is the realization that, given scarce resources and a hostile interna-tional economic environment, sources of legitimacy are far more boun-tiful abroad than they are at home. So that it makes political sense to invest in the foreign arena, to seek foreign aid and foreign protection, in short, to become intermediaries rather than producers. What that also means, though, is that not all segments of society are equally useful; indeed, many become, to use David Apter's painfully accurate term, both politically and economically "superfluous." With a shrinking re-source base and the budget-cutting recommendations of the IMF, the consequences are a narrowing of the state's functions and a shortening of its reach. Vital social services, such as education, health, or disaster relief, are curtailed, the ensuing social marginalization of large segments of the population graphically illustrating "where the state leaves off."[71]

Clientelism (or its strengthening) is one outgrowth. Where the pri-mary function of the state ceases to be the organization of society's pro-ductive forces and becomes that of serving as intermediary between foreign and domestic centers, and then as distributor of governmental largess, the key to success is not competence but influence, not expertise but cliental links—for those who govern, links to the outside; for those who are governed, links to those who govern. As Davidson recounts in the case of modern-day Africa, "The actual political content of . . . nation-states narrow[s] into groups and persons with command over, or at least access to, income-yielding resources."[72] The point being, quite simply, that scarcity and the concentration of resources breed vertical relations of fealty: internally through patronage and nepotism, internationally through the mechanism of dependence (though the highly personalized nature of France's relation to certain former colonies in Africa has a tendency to blur the line). At that point loyalty becomes the central currency of all politics.

It needs to be said, too, that for regimes whose legitimacy so heavily depends on their redistributive capacity, times of economic contraction pose particularly acute problems. In the period immediately following independence, indeed, there was much to dole out, economic spoils (when, for example, land had been regained from the *colons*) but also social spoils (the Europeans' departure opening up positions in the civil service). Now, with shortage and scarcity, the very material foundations of legitimacy were at stake. Members of the elite at that point might well find it convenient to seek a renewed legitimacy — say, by appealing to regional, ethnic, or familial solidarity. Thus, the increased demand for cliental links (based on just such ties) emanating from the ruled often is matched by an increased supply coming from the rulers.[73] (Another alternative source of legitimacy, one that has the added advantage of enjoying the West's imprimatur, is democratic elections, the same people who yesterday clamored in favor of the single party becoming, overnight, zealous proponents of multiparty democracy. One observer described this conversion as an instance of elites deciding to "give their people some choice in how they should suffer."[74] Sometimes, of course, the organization of democracy and the manipulation of ethnic loyalties merge, resulting in a partisan system that precisely reflects the country's ethnic makeup.)

These phenomena go well beyond countries of the former Third Worldist universe, but the point is that they affected Third Worldist nations as well, in spite of their earlier ambitious, high-reaching goals. The world balance of power, the state of the international economy, policy choices of the postindependence period (favoring the state-centered urban, the industrial, the large-scale), and the confluence of factors mentioned above, aggravated by the damaging legacy of colonialism, all signified that even "progressive" nations either chose or were forced to redirect their energies to the Western world and its financial institutions. The economic foundations they had begun to set up (with varying degrees of success) had been laid waste, casualties of poor planning, shriveling resources, and a modified international equation, with all the attending consequences: creation of a dual society, disinvestment from areas of critical social import, isolation of the ruling class, reinforcement of cliental ties.

In fact, there is a sense in which countries that fit the Third Worldist mold were peculiarly ill equipped to cope with these changes in the international and domestic arenas. We have seen that the political structure was built entirely around the notion of national unanimity, personalized around a powerful president and a swollen bureaucracy, and supplemented by a feeble partisan organization. As the estrangement between rulers and ruled worsened, the whole edifice crumbled, and the state, which for so long had monopolized public discourse, could offer little in its place. Certainly, to the extent the state had for years made social equality and justice its motto — indeed, had implicitly asked that it be judged on that score — it could hardly claim that it now had what it took to succeed. The point made about the political elites' needing to find alternative grounds of legitimacy is all the more salient here, for Third Worldist leaders had staked their entire fortune on the success of economic development. Narrow ethnic, regional, or clan-based allegiances suddenly looked far more attractive. Though it suffers from his well-known penchant for deterministic and conspiracy-driven explanations, Samir Amin's analysis of Ethiopia's breakup is an interesting illustration.[75]

The job of keeping in place whatever links and channels of communication existed between the regime and the people theoretically should have fallen to the party, but there again the Third Worldist system's penchant for centralization removed this as a viable possibility. Lacking an independent existence, used merely to preach state gospel to the masses, and sheltered from the rigors of pluralistic competition, Third Worldist parties encountered one of two unenviable fates: either they too operated in the constricted circle of the economic and political elites and were, therefore, impotent (in that sense not very different from what had been the original design) or they simply replicated in their midst the cliental patterns that held sway at the state and administrative levels. Elements of both could be found in Algeria, Guinea, Egypt, and Iraq.[76] The pressures of the world economy and, at once cause and consequence, the radical ideological shift caught Third Worldist countries in a state of arrested political development, speaking the words of popular unanimity yet having failed to build the necessary bridges between rulers and ruled, the instruments of popular mobilization, or the means to exercise pressure on an increasingly alien and remote state bureaucracy.

With all this as context, the phenomena popularly identified as religious fundamentalism, tribalism, and ethnic solidarity take on a wholly different meaning. The main thing is that they have a logic of their own, that they appear to be a function of calculated individual and collective choice, that they are not simply a matter of deep, atavistic impulses finally making it to the surface. When the state disengages from society, society disconnects from the state. People seek refuge, protection, and meaning in alternative structures — economic, political, even cultural. The basic organizational principle is perceived as dysfunctional or, worse, irrelevant to the conduct of one's daily existence. To revert to Hankiss's model, there is a lack of fit between the state's resources and society's public needs. "Through the cracks and gaps of the system, alternative organizational principles . . . penetrate it. They beg[in] to regulate social and economic domains . . . which [are] outside the reach of the official institutional system and in areas where this system ha[s] proved inadequate."[77] The time has come to sidestep, to bypass the state.

Economic sidestepping is a familiar concept: we call it participation in the black market, the parallel economy, the quest for commercial venues beyond official channels. Merchandise gets smuggled within boundaries, but across them as well, making a mockery of internationally recognized frontiers and of the states' ability to control them. This is perhaps clearest in the African case, where a dense transnational traffic flourishes between Benin, Togo, and Nigeria, between Sierra Leone, Liberia, and Guinea, oblivious to state, citizenship, or national origin.[78]

Less familiar are political and cultural sidestepping. Yet the parallels are striking: in all three instances, neglect by or frustration with official channels activates parallel ones located at either an infra- or suprastate level. Davidson relies on just such an analogy in his work on Africa: "In periods of breakdown or severe disorder, [tribal] modes of loyalty and self-defense . . . drew back into the defense of individuals or clusters of individuals while at the same time extending their effectiveness in many ways subversive of the state. One can make a comparison between this use of kinship in political contexts . . . and the use of smuggling in economic contexts: each, in its way, acts as a compensation against the weakness or the incapacity of state institutions unable to protect citizens and advance their interests."[79]

Extra-institutional organizations or groupings pick up where the state leaves off, delivering emergency aid to disaster victims (as do Islamic groups in Algeria or Egypt), or free medicine, school equipment, educational support, and administrative advice (again, Islamic militants in Iran under the Shah, Egypt, Algeria, or Tunisia).[80] The proliferation of churches, evangelical sects, and messianic movements in Latin America and parts of Asia, of Hindu movements in India, of clans in Somalia, or of various Islamic brotherhoods in Black Africa, Badie suggests, also should be examined in this light.[81] Indeed, these extra-institutional movements further discredit the state by their mere presence in areas deserted by the authorities and by their ability to provide some of what the state had promised but failed to deliver. Likewise, and in a manner reminiscent of the growth of commercial diasporas, transnational solidarities stand to gain at a time when the central state is viewed as a crumbling, irrelevant, expendable edifice, especially when domestic distress can somehow be tied to the apparent Westernization of the world order. Allegiances and affinities, based on common creed, ethnic origin, and the like, thus cut across state lines. Once more, the links between various Islamic groups are the most visible example. Where once Third Worldism stood, religious connections have stepped in.

It should be noted too that because feelings of social abandonment and of cultural alienation overlap, it becomes difficult to distinguish movements predicated on the assertion of common faith or shared blood from more traditional movements of social protest. Religion, kinship ties, and tribal groupings all capitalize on social privation, cultural frustration, and the absence of the state. Protest thus shifts effortlessly from the social to the cultural. Participants in Morocco's 1990 general strike quickly targeted — and demolished — a luxurious hotel that catered principally to foreign tourists;[82] similarly, impoverished masses in North Africa, the occupied territories, and Pakistan swiftly rallied around Saddam Hussein, who all of a sudden turned into a symbol of the Third World's resistance, of opposition to Western domination, and, in a supremely ironic twist, of Islamic revolt.

In some instances, an embryonic countersociety, based on competing ties, loyalties, and beliefs, might even emerge. The example of the Algerian Front Islamique du Salut (FIS) immediately comes to mind. Another interesting example is that of Hamas and the proto-Palestinian state it has sought to build in the Gaza strip. It is not the financially strapped Palestinian National Authority but the religious movement that provides free health clinics, summer camps, and kindergartens, offers courses in computer science, electrical repair, and sewing, distributes meat to forty thousand families during religious holidays, sponsors sports teams, and runs 80 percent of the mosques.[83] The Palestinian state has yet to see the day, and already its rival-to-be is taking over its putative role.

The more general point is that with the combination, or superimposition, of social and cultural alienation, the temptation is great to seek alternative modes of organization and forms of human interaction and thus to create a separate space with its own set of rules, its own codes, and its own power structure. Consider the case of Islamic movements, where everything from wardrobe to diet to gender relations is methodically rearranged, visible signs of a competing order that one either belongs to or opposes (the ultimate irony being, as Alain Gresh shows vividly in the case of Egypt, that elements legitimated by the state — multipartyism, the welfare state — have no tangible existence, whereas the Islamic movement, which the state does not recognize, is very real indeed).[84] Once more, social and cultural functions overlap: Muslim militants provide free clothing, but it is the strict Islamic garb — the veil, the *gandoura,* and gloves; they provide free transportation to and from school, but gender segregation is imposed; they provide support for the homeless and the unemployed but bring them to a mosque.[85]

In short, one sees a proliferation of political actors, forms of social intercourse, and arenas of power that are detached from any recognized nation-state, being either beneath or beyond it. Badie speaks of a "de-territorialization" of politics, by which he means that the state gradually loses fragments of sovereignty to the informal economy, transnational religious affiliations, or ethnic or tribal allegiances. At various points even its monopoly on the legitimate use of violence might be at risk, which is so manifestly the case in contemporary Algeria.

A final word about tribalism (which I shall use here as shorthand for other forms of parochial solidarities): what the predominant post–Third Worldist view, infatuated with images of awakening identities and colliding civilizations, sees as an irrational withdrawal from modernity or retreat to authenticity, I would interpret as people's coherent and logical reaction to a state of affairs in which such loyalties are the only ones to pay off. Tribalism as a social response is not so very different in this respect from the nationalism (or patriotism) to which the West has become so complacently accustomed. I do not wish to deny the important differences between tribes and nation-states,[86] but a fairly solid argument could be made that each of these modes of social organization is simply a variant of the other, that both depend on arbitrary systems of loyalties, that both summon the same set of myths — regarding a shared ancestry, a shared culture, shared territorial bonds, and privileged rights that accrue from all of the above. The "idioms of organisation," to borrow a term from Richard Tapper,[87] might well differ, but there is common ground in the appeal to an imagined cohesion or homogeneity. Nor ought one accept the notion that the relevant unit in Africa (or elsewhere) is the tribe or the ethnic group. Indeed, people (Africans as well as others) always have a number of pertinent units from which to chose:

the units that grow out of trade patterns, out of the dominant system of political organization, such as the centralized state, out of a shared tongue, or out of myths of common descent. The Third World is no more destined for tribalism or religious fanaticism or ethnic intolerance than Europe or the United States is to nationalism or chauvinism or xenophobia. Instead, all these are reactions that must be understood in context, with a history, social interests, and cultural strains firmly in mind.[88]

What happened to Third Worldism? Changes in the world balance of power, the state's shortcomings, its relinquishment of key social responsibilities, its cultural and economic alignment with the North, the marginalization of ever-expanding portions of the population, and the Third Worldist political system's utter inability to respond to any of the above — these, far more than Huntington's titanic "clash of civilizations," account for the "resurgence" of tribe and faith and ethnicity. The sad irony of it all being that Third Worldism was a victim of those very conditions — dependency, material and cultural inequality, poverty — out of which it originally had grown. And which, foolhardily, it had promised to eradicate.

CHAPTER 6

Turning to Islam

Its beauty endures, but for the time being an eerie look
has come over Algiers. At this hour of its life—late? early? who can
tell?—the look is one of weariness, of helplessness, of one who knows
that the worst lies behind and before it both. It is the look of a city
estranged from itself and its unending violence, a city about ready to
surrender—if only it knew to whom. A few years have elapsed since the
army abruptly canceled the country's first free parliamentary elections.
A temporary move to restore the serenity that predated the rise of the
FIS is how it was described, and when this transient hiatus was over,
people would return to the business of voting and choosing and governing. Yet the electoral process remains in a state of uncertain suspension,
and not a day goes by without an intellectual being killed by so-called
Islamic militants or a suspected FIS sympathizer being arrested, tor-
tured, or shot by the dreaded "ninja" army squads. Algeria finds itself in
the midst of a war that is civil in name only. Three thousand victims in
the first two years, or perhaps two to three hundred a week; thirty thousand killed since 1992, or maybe forty thousand—but who is counting?
Among the casualties, a president, a former prime minister, and thousands upon thousands of ordinary citizens—women too independent to
wear a veil, intellectuals too proud to don a muzzle, foreigners too stubborn to leave, and young men unfortunate enough to fit the Islamist
profile.[1] At the same stubborn pace, grisly rumors fill the city. Algiers,
once confident, once master of its own rhythm, is adrift. Days must
dawn reluctantly on cities like this.

It is January 1994, and the haggard capital is playing host to the state-sponsored and much-trumpeted "reconciliation conference." With a country on the edge of civil war and economic collapse, and hardly a democratic life to speak of, this might seem like curious prioritizing. But legitimacy has become the sole remaining lifeline of the regime, and that is what it is out to get. In vain are memories of the war of national liberation stirred, for most of it is history by now, and what is not, the FLN, methodically, has managed to squander. True to themselves, the authorities also have wasted no time fretting away the slim political capital gained by cutting ties to the Front and ushering in an era of multiparty democracy. For years, in short, the regime has been running on empty. It was high time for a refill, and dialogue was a price well worth paying.

Quite an odd sight it turned out to be: practically all parties were invited to this unprecedented political pow-wow, yet in the end hardly any came. One by one, the FLN, Aït-Ahmed's FFS, former president Ben Bella's Mouvement pour la Démocratie en Algérie (MDA), the Kabilya-based Rassemblement pour la Culture et la Démocratie (RCD), and the "moderate" Islamic organizations decided to boycott the conference. The forum intended to open up the political process had turned into a surreal tête-à-tête between the regime and itself, a bizarre introspective exercise. As the years go by, and in virtual self-parody, the regime gradually takes on the traits of its most vicious caricatures. Having rattled on for so long in a meaningless, vacuous, monotonous idiom, it has ended up splendidly isolated, cloistered, out of touch, with no one left to chat with but itself. Earlier I spoke of the distance between the Third World's civil and political societies, of the alienation, of the disconnection. But in its raw symbolism this was just too much.

Many things have happened since that time, and more is still to come. Attempted dialogues, possibly; political shuffling, predictably; violence, strife, and deaths, certainly. As these pages are written, President Zeroual — Algeria's third since January 1992 — has initiated, then interrupted contact with jailed leaders of the FIS, shifting from a strategy of "reconciliation" to one of "eradication." Parties of the "legal opposition" — principally the FLN, the FFS, and Mahfoud Nahnah's Hamas — reached agreement with the FIS on a peace proposal (instantly rejected by the regime) that called for an end to violence, political negotiations, the release of political prisoners, and the legalization of the Islamic Front. Instead, the regime organized presidential elections in November 1995, which Zeroual handsomely won, reportedly with about 60 percent of the vote — but without the participation of the FIS, the FLN, or the

FFS. The Groupe Islamique Armé (GIA), a more radical splinter group, is vowing to fight any compromise. France is closing its borders to fleeing Algerians. Tensions between Algeria and Morocco are beginning to flare up. Meanwhile, the officially acknowledged death toll has abruptly risen from three thousand to ten. Yet as a weary-eyed and worn-out Algiers looks on, the answers to only two questions really seem to matter: How did we get to where we are? and Where do we go from here?

❖   ❖   ❖

President Boumedienne died in 1978 after fourteen years in office, a surprisingly mysterious, enigmatic man. Certainly, he had not enjoyed the kind of intimate bond with his people that Nasser had in Egypt. Still, Boumedienne had come a long way from his early days as ruler. He had, as it were, grown into the charismatic figure required by his institutional role, albeit with more solemnity than enthusiasm.

The metamorphosis had been political. From the early seventies on, his position gradually became more radical as, one by one, he nationalized French oil companies (1971), embarked on an agrarian reform and recruited student volunteers for its implementation (1971–72), called for a "socialist management of enterprises," and instituted free medical care (1974). The climax came in 1976 with the debate over the adoption of a national charter, which seems to have been the president's most serious attempt to involve the people directly in the radical transformation of society. True, as in all of Boumedienne's other projects, much was inspired from above, and popular participation, however spontaneous, was goaded by the state. Bad habits die hard — especially precautionary ones — but there is little doubt that this was a novelty by Algerian standards and that something was being unleashed that once had been strictly contained. Boumedienne's idea, as Ali-el-Kenz later wrote, was to build a society of militant, salaried workers employed by the state or by its cooperatives, a quasi-egalitarian society in which a strong, centralized state would enjoy the legitimacy of its origins (the war of national liberation) and the support of its social basis (le peuple).[2]

During the same period, the president emerged as a leader of the Non-Aligned Movement. As Peter Lyon put it, "There can be no doubt . . . that it was the fourth Non-Aligned Summit which met in Algiers in August 1973, and Algeria's active chairmanship then and for three years thereafter, which imparted a strong sense of dynamism, purposefulness, and forward-looking momentum to . . . the Non-Aligned Movement."[3] Boumedienne also was the driving force behind his country's decision

to back, some would say to create, the Polisario Front in its struggle for
Western Sahara's independence.

But the metamorphosis also had taken on more personal traits. Observers point to the impact of Fidel Castro's festive visit to the Algerian
capital in 1972, the crowds' enthusiastic response, the bonds that it revealed could exist between a ruler and a people. After that, it is rumored,
Boumedienne was never quite the same. Not that he parted with his
trademark severity or became a crowd-pleasing ruler—a populist in the
ordinary sense of that word. That had been Ben Bella's style and aspiration, and Boumedienne was too much the anti–Ben Bella even to toy
with the thought. Yet the seriousness that continued to carry him along
had a slightly new tinge, as if he finally were reassured that Algerians
were willing to view him as their rightful leader, not quite a charismatic
figure, no longer a mere usurper.

In a sense, then, the metamorphosis had even been physical and
emotional. The frail, dour, "austere," "coarse," "ascetic" Boumedienne
had given way to a sturdier, "warmer," "affable" leader.[4] His had never
been and never would be the grandiloquent style of a Nasser, a Castro,
or an Nkrumah, but the political function had undeniably molded the
man. Indeed, if last offices can be taken as a rough gauge of popular
feeling—and they often can: consider Nasser, remember Sadat—then
Boumedienne's posthumously established his Third Worldist credentials. Writing at the time, Jean-Pierre Durand remarked that "President
Boumedienne's highly popular funeral on December 27, 1978, manifested the people's attachment to Algeria's political conquests (*acquis*)."[5]
Up against initial mistrust, resentment, even bitterness, the image of a
sage, forward-looking Boumedienne eventually won out. Here, for instance, is one of his staunchest opponents, Mohamed Boudiaf: "We considered Boumedienne to be a dictator and his regime to be mined, ready
to blow up at any time. Boumedienne's death and the human tide that
accompanied him to his final resting place—including all those scenes
that illustrated the undeniable bond he shared with his people—proved
that we had been wrong."[6]

There was no clear-cut message in the selection of Boumedienne's
successor other than that the army still had things firmly in hand, that it
was not about to countenance open dissent, and that, as often is the
military's want, it would rather make no decision than have to make a
choice. Two leading contenders emerged: Foreign Minister Bouteflika,
known as a moderate, Western-leaning "liberal," and Mohammed Salah
Yahyiaoui, the head of the FLN apparatus, who enjoyed the combined

support of left-wing radicals and Islamic activists. The army, by far the country's single most influential power broker, passed over both, settling on an apparently neutral figure from among its own ranks. His bland politics and bland personality made Colonel Chadli Benjedid the perfect compromise, and many at the time regarded him as a convenient, transitional figurehead.

Changes were slow to come. From the outset, the new regime's leitmotif was continuity—with Boumedienne's policies, with the spirit of the revolution, and with the legacy of the war of national liberation. Nor was this much of a surprise, considering that Chadli had been a party to, and his legitimacy a function of, all three. Yet, now and then, faint hints of pending policy shifts were dropped in the state-controlled press. The Boumedienne era was subject to severe criticism, and economic decisions made at the time were faulted for much that was wrong in Algeria. By the mid-eighties the hints were coming in droves; soon they would become fact.

Two factors can be said to have precipitated Algeria's transformation. The first was the serious predicaments faced by the Algerian economy. Boumedienne's industrial and state-led growth was achieved at the expense of the agricultural sector—directly through disproportionate investing in industry and indirectly through unfavorable pricing policies.[7] Dependence on food imports during Boumedienne's presidency therefore rose sharply, from approximately 10 percent of overall consumption in 1969 to 75 percent in the early 1980s.[8] By that time, cereal imports amounted to roughly 40 percent of national consumption; dairy products, 50 percent; and sugar, 95 percent.[9] John Entelis notes that "during the early 1970s, [food imports] grew by an average of 31 percent a year, and during the mid-1970s, the growth rate soared to 450 percent."[10] This was only made worse by Algeria's population growth rate, a staggering 3.3 percent per year. From 8.7 million in 1959, the country's population reached 11 million at the time of independence. Today, it is over 25 million (over half of which is under twenty years of age), with an anticipated 35 million by the year 2000 and 57 million by 2025.[11]

For as long as oil prices remained high, however, this was a situation Algeria could afford. But that would not long be the case. From a record thirty-four dollars a barrel in 1982, the price fell to approximately twelve dollars in 1986, resulting in a rapid decline in oil revenues.[12] For a country like Algeria, in which 98 percent of all export revenue derives from the sale of crude oil and natural gas, the consequences were devastating. Boumedienne's massive industrialization program, as well as the twinning of welfare statism and political radicalism, presupposed a steady inflow of oil revenues. As the stream dried up, each ambition would suffer in turn.

In retrospect, far too much had been spent on industrial investment and on importing advanced technology, with the result that countless factories stood idle or underutilized and the foreign debt skyrocketed. Thus, the ratio of debt service to export revenue rose from 33 percent in 1984 to 55 percent in 1987 and 76 percent in 1992. At the same time, the ratio of debt to gross domestic product rose from 41 percent in 1987 to 66 percent in 1992.[13] Less money available meant less to go around, with obvious consequences for the state's ability to dispense benefits, purchase political peace with social largesse, and thus preserve the conditions of its legitimacy. Step by brisk step, the declining oil prices undermined the economic, social, and political predicates of the Algerian system.

Broadly speaking, Chadli's reforms were part of the familiar spectrum of postsocialist cures, what Jorge Castaneda cleverly dubs a form of "Reaganomics in the tropics":[14] privatization and other measures designed to encourage private investment, renewed emphasis on agricultural production and changes in land ownership, the provision of incentives, such as favorable tax laws, to lure foreign investment and joint ventures, and cutbacks in social programs and food subsidies.[15] Many of these policies were given sanction in the new national charter, adopted by referendum on January 16, 1986. The state's gradual withdrawal from the economy was expressed, symbolically, in the 1987 decision to eliminate the ministry of planning. As Entelis put it, "Despite repeated assertions that 'change within continuity' remains the regime's overall objective, the truth is that Boumedienne's form of socialist orthodoxy is being dismantled piece by piece."[16]

Such economic reevaluation could not but have an impact on Algeria's diplomacy. Korany accurately speaks of a "domestication" of foreign policy, by which he means that foreign policy was both "tam[ed]" and "align[ed] . . . with internal or domestic policy."[17] Gradually, the country began to adopt a less activist posture, retreating into a relative self-effacement that was not due exclusively to differences in personal style between Chadli and Boumedienne.[18] Though a reversal remains possible, steps taken toward reconciliation with Morocco raised questions concerning Algeria's continued commitment to the Polisario Front.[19] Writing in 1988, James Markham commented that "a quarter century ago, revolutionary Algeria, having wrenched its independence from

France in a bloody armed struggle, was a heroic beacon to those fighting for freedom elsewhere. . . . This summer a less visionary Algeria, preoccupied with lifting its own living standards, quietly sacrificed an anti-Moroccan guerrilla movement that it had nurtured and armed for more than 13 years."[20]

The second trigger for Chadli's reformist drive had to do with the domestic political situation. I am referring to his efforts, tentative at first, to forsake the monolithic character of the political system and loosen the tight grip the state exercised over it. In this as well, he had good reason for seeking change. As noted above, the proportion of Algerians who had participated in or even remembered the 1954 revolution had dropped dramatically. More than two-thirds of today's citizens were born after independence was proclaimed in 1962; for them, support for the regime depended less on faithfulness to the past then on hope about the future. A discourse laced with references to those days of majestic heroism no longer could command the authority it once enjoyed. As one commentator put it, "The Front's mythology . . . fell victim to the relentless demographics of the Third World."[21] As a result, a degree of freedom was allowed in the state-controlled press — though the fact that so much of it was used to denigrate Boumedienne's legacy leads one to wonder how much actually was state-inspired — and the reputation of a number of former FLN leaders was rehabilitated. (Even this effort had its limits, though. In July 1985 *Algérie-Actualité* published a special report on the history of the MTLD's Organisation Spéciale, whose leaders, one will recall, were Hocine Aït-Ahmed and Ahmed Ben Bella. By order of the state, all issues were confiscated and destroyed.) But the real impetus for change originated in pressures from below.

The mid-1980s proved to be a particularly trying time for the regime. Demonstrations, clashes, and strikes occurred throughout 1985, notably in Kabilya's capital city, Tizi-Ouzou, sparked by demands that the regime respect the rights of the Berber minority. Also centered in Kabilya was the Comité des Enfants de Chouhada (Committee of the Children of Martyrs), an organization that questioned the genuineness of the state's affiliation with the heroes of the war and held unofficial counterceremonies to celebrate the revolution on its own terms. Linking the Berber movement with the struggle for democracy, the Ligue Algérienne des Droits de l'Homme (LADH) was founded in June 1985, principally by Berber militants. Almost from the start, its leaders were subject to arrest, trial, exile, and harassment, while the regime tried to undermine the Ligue by creating its own puppet organization. In December the trial of LADH members and of the "sons of martyrs" began in Medea, generating worldwide attention. For the first time in its history, the Algerian republic was condemned by the U.N. Commission on Human Rights, as well as by other, traditionally sympathetic international human rights organizations.[22] Finally, in the fall of 1986 mass demonstrations swept through eastern Algeria, fueled by dissatisfaction with proposed educational reforms and, more broadly, with worsening living conditions.[23]

But the pivotal events took place in October 1988. On October 4 there began what at that point was the most violent and bloodiest period in Algeria's postcolonial history. In Algiers, a group of demonstrators started attacking shops, government offices, and cars, leading to the destruction of scores of public and private buildings. Targets were chosen with seemingly keen political precision: a city hall, a government office, luxury hotels, and the commercial centers of affluent Algeria, in short, all that symbolized the state, its corruption, and economic inequality. By week's end the unrest had spread to other regions of the country, a state of siege had been proclaimed, the army had intervened, and between five hundred and a thousand people had been killed.[24]

Repression was the first, but not the only, governmental response. For just as violence by and against the French precipitated the birth of Algeria's hegemonic political system, so intra-Algerian violence accelerated its demise. "Repression," concluded Abdelkader Djeghloul, "killed the consensus that had been built on the identification between the party-state and society."[25] In the wake of the riots, a traumatized Parliament agreed to several reforms that freed mass organizations — representing women, workers, the youth — from the FLN's heavy tutelage. By February 1989 Algeria had adopted a constitution that fundamentally modified the political setting. The new version deleted any reference to socialism or to the FLN as a constitutional actor fulfilling a public role. In contrast, it guaranteed the right to establish political associations (Article 40), rights of expression, association, and organization (Article 39), privacy (Article 37), the principle of separation of powers, and protection for private property.[26] In essence, as Daniel Brumberg puts it, the old bargain — absence of political participation in exchange for social welfare — was replaced by the new — acceptance of economic reform in exchange for democratization.[27]

Soon the political field was saturated with close to thirty political organizations, not only such major organizations as the FLN and the FIS but countless others ranging from the social-democratic to the communist. While the law stipulated that "a political association cannot be based on an exclusively confessional, linguistic, regional, gender, racial, or socio-professional basis," this provision proved difficult to enforce. The RCD was an essentially Berber movement opposed to the country's forced Arabization, Aït-Ahmed's FFS also was Berber-centered, and of course the FIS, along with two lesser Islamist parties—Hamas and an-Nahdha—made no secret of its religious platform.[28] (One of the few organizations denied legal certification was the PPA, heir to Messali's old party and headed by his nephew. The decision, another reflection of the regime's tenacious anti-Messalism, was justified by a provision in the law stipulating that no party could be based upon "behavior contrary . . . to the Revolution of November 1954.")[29]

In an attempt to placate the fears of a number of the regime's dignitaries, President Chadli stressed that "the Constitution does not challenge the FLN, insofar as power at every level remains in its hands." But there was no way to dodge the truth that cardinal political axioms were under assault. Indeed, barely four months earlier the president had asserted that a "multiparty system would represent a danger for national unity."[30] Nor did he leave much doubt about the reasons for his sudden conversion: "If the nation wants political associations," he said, "then we must abide by its will."[31]

❖   ❖   ❖

One way of describing the situation is that Algeria's society had outgrown the confining economic and political outfit imposed by Boumedienne's regime. It was finally coming apart at the seams—economically, with the need to open up and allow the private sector some breathing space; politically, with the introduction of a measure of free expression and plural democracy. A widely accepted version takes this analogy a step further. Having rejected its tight and coercive garb, Algeria slipped into a more comfortable, natural apparel—the free market, democracy, or, in a slightly darker variant, Islam and clannism. I will leave the more pessimistic version for later, but, in any event, all share the same essentialist premise. Thus, in view of the deteriorating conditions in Algeria, scholars and politicians were quick to conclude that Chadli's political reforms simply reflected recognition of society's autonomous existence and that their economic counterpart amounted to the unremarkable adjustment of policy to reality. John Entelis argued that

in the five-year period from Chadli's uncontested election to the presidency in February 1979 to the renewal of his five-year mandate in January 1984 . . .

Algeria has evolved away from the ideological militancy and economic aus-terity of the Boumediene era. . . . Chadli Benjedid has taken the Algerian ship of state toward a different, more pragmatically oriented direction. . . . Thus a full two decades after independence Algeria's revolution has been institutionalized with Chadli's no-nonsense, businesslike demeanor repre-senting a new style of governance.[32]

He concludes that "the tilt toward pragmatism . . . has been viewed as an issue of management and administration, not politics."[33] This view is not unique to Entelis, of course. *Businesslike, pragmatic,* and *realistic* are words that are most often encountered in descriptions of Chadli's Al-geria, in which they suggest the self-evidence of his policies.[34] The ad-jectives, by the sheer implication of naturalness they convey, inevitably throw the previous epoch into the separate domain of ideology and de-ception. The path followed by Boumedienne is thus made to appear as a negation of reality, his promises as a hoax.

What concerns me — aside from these hyperbolic characterizations of both Boumedienne's and Chadli's reigns — is the underlying assump-tions regarding ideology and the existence of neutral economic options. Chadli's choices may have been motivated by an economic situation whose gravity one ought not to downplay. But they were choices, none-theless, and political ones at that. Thus, privatization can be safely as-sumed to have represented (in part at least) an effort to shift the spotlight away from the state, which was willing to forgo some of its power if that meant forsaking much of its responsibility and to delegate some of its authority if that meant deflecting most of the blame.[35]

Much the same is true of the turn to "pluralism," which was instantly interpreted as a concession to society's hostility to statist policies and a natural, even healthy stage in the construction of an autonomous civil society. In fact, rather than the state's overbearing presence, it was its disengagement, the end of welfare-statism, of price subsidies and job security, that was at the root of society's anger. For Algeria's leaders, democracy "was not a political ideology aimed at resolving social and economic contradictions but chiefly a discourse aimed at justifying the state's retreat from social obligations it was unable to meet. The demand for democracy came from the state and adjoining classes far more than it did from a majority of the people. The privileged social classes, possess-ing financial or cultural capital, joined hands with state bureaucrats re-cently converted to democracy and free markets precisely because they were better equipped to participate in the race for goods, services, and jobs."[36] In both instances — privatization and democratization — rising social discontent prompted the ruling class to spread out responsibility for the country's (mis)management while at the same time retaining overall control by recycling the state personnel into the private sector and by ensuring that effective political power ultimately remained in the same (military) hands. In neither instance can we say that Algeria bowed to reality; rather, and as a result of an interplay of domestic pressure groups, collective mythology, and international developments, Chadli's Algeria adopted and accepted a particular rendition of it.

From this perspective, Algeria's new orientation is no more natural than was Third Worldism. I do not dispute that the fate of Third Worldism in Algeria can be explained as the attrition of a legitimacy formula bequeathed by the Third World's anticolonial movements in general and, more particularly, by Algeria's nationalist war and post-independence project. At some stage, there was a delinkage between the state's ideology and the social formation it was intended to manage. My point is that there is no natural successor. For in shaping the characteristics of the dominant discourse, historical context—foreign and domestic, including the war of national liberation and worldwide decolonization in one case, fratricidal violence between progressive Third World regimes and the rising influence of Western culture (chiefly, Reaganomics, Thatcherite individualism, and the broad IMF-ization of discourse) in the other—played as much a part for the new as it did for the old. The garb into which Algeria so cozily slipped, in sum, had been meticulously woven, stitched, and tailored.

Another way of putting it is that with Chadli one dominant organizational principle took the place of another. The scope of the changes that followed Boumedienne's death can best be understood by reexamining his policies in some detail. Throughout his regime, the single most important motif remained the war of national liberation. The war *organized* the Algerian polity by inspiring its principal themes: a populist reverence for the *peuple;* an implicit egalitarianism expressed essentially as scorn for ostentatious wealth; and faith in a quasi-military style of politics that took the shape of statism. The evidence for this in terms of the overall political organization was overwhelming. The construction of a centralized, streamlined political system, the negation of all potential differences (between Berbers and Arabs, religious and secular groups, social classes, clans, etc.), the preference for a single party, the personalization of rule and plebiscitarian nature of politics, and the proliferation of national charters—all were in the logic of the revolution (not a neutral denomination by any means), and all were legitimated by reference to the struggle for independence.

The same was true of the regime's economic policies, fashioned in the style of a belligerent, quasi-martial crusade for industrialization and development, a frontal attack on social injustice, a campaign for national pride. The availability of oil and natural gas came in handy, of course, for it permitted the state to generate revenue without having to raise income domestically, that is, it allowed the state to meet various demands without having to make excessively painful redistributive choices.[37] Be that as it may, Boumedienne's Algeria used its export revenue in aid of a statist, activist, "voluntaristic" public policy with several interconnected aims: to build a strong administrative system; to enable the state to supplant the market's accumulative and distributive functions; and to abide by an implicit "social compromise,"[38] a "'social contract' obliging the state to provide a safety net of cheap prices for basic foodstuffs, job guarantees, and cradle-to-grave entitlements."[39]

Lastly, the war had a distinct impact on the cultural mind-set of Boumedienne's regime. In a nutshell, the experience of anticolonialism and of the war of national liberation (which, as we have seen, combined rejection of the colonial order with mimicry of many of its political features), followed by economic growth, suggested a possible synthesis between industrialization, urbanization, and development on the one hand and religious, traditional, egalitarian, and populist values on the other.

In asserting that the most authoritative political metaphor was the war and submitting that Chadli did more than simply surrender to economic and political laws, I have in mind the replacement of this organizational principle, of these themes, by a series of others that were just as mythic, constructed, or ideological. More needs to be said, though, if we are fully to appreciate the startling difference in the makeup, or tenor, of post–Third Worldist Algeria. For the change had a very tangible, palpable dimension that the term *organizational principle,* in its abstractness, imperfectly imparts. It affected many things, among them the principal political imagery, people's self-perception, the realm of accepted discourse (and accepted truths), the country's moral architecture, the very rhythm, geography, and representation of power. When observers oppose Boumedienne's ideology to Chadli's pragmatism, this is what they miss—or obscure.

The Algerian sociologist Ali El-Kenz developed these thoughts in his essay "Phenomenology of National Consciousness." What I find most interesting is the way he traces the transformation of Algeria's self-representation. Since independence, he argues, there have been two "historical moments," each with its own "morphology" and its own "self-awareness."[40] The first, roughly corresponding to Boumedienne's era, was dense (his way of saying that it abounded in theoretical analysis and ideological production), homogeneous (meaning monolithic, single-mindedly focused on a handful of core questions, such as economic development), and dynamic (optimistic, forward-looking). The result was an Algeria in which individuals were meant to think of themselves as equal participants in a vital historical process, as members of the *peuple,* the masses — preferably revolutionary, popular, or toiling. El-Kenz makes the point that throughout the 1970s these masses often took to the streets in ritualized processions — commemorating the launching of the revolution, Independence Day, May 1, the agrarian revolution, and so on. The link to the war, to the vision of an ongoing, progressing march, to its populism and implicit egalitarianism, is plain. The positive hero is one who selflessly accepts his or her role in the revolution while renouncing any personal glory. The idea of "the masses" itself, as El-Kenz explains, is less important for its sociological than for its political, and ultimately moral, content. In Third Worldist Algeria the outsiders are those who purposely remove themselves from the *peuple,* either by collaborating with the external enemy — otherwise known as "imperialism" — or by signaling their difference through ostentatious displays of wealth.

Boumedienne's era also was associated with a particular political mapping. In Algeria's political imagery, the dominant sites were the factory, the city, the university, and the "villages of the agricultural revolution," all of which symbolized the promise and goals of the revolution: urbanization, industrialization, and development more generally. At the center of this particular topography were the *entreprises nationales,* mammoth state-owned factories. (The most impressive was SONATRACH, the national oil and gas company, which employed roughly one hundred thousand workers and controlled the mineral rights to an area approximating 1,085 million square kilometers.)[41] Indeed, the *entreprises* embodied the revolutionary ideal of a homogeneous, cohesive whole, in which political, social, and cultural attributes all merge.[42] For there was more to these factories than sheer economic production. Their function was to create a miniature model for Algeria in which everything would be provided — ideological indoctrination, cultural activities, food, lodging, transportation, vacation, childcare, athletics. Employees were encouraged to identify with their factory by all sorts of means — special uniforms, insignias, and sports teams. And employment was offered preferentially to veterans of the war (the *mujahideen*), their widows, and their children, such being the prerogatives of a group of citizens whose political origins were so much a part of the factories' (and, it follows, Algeria's) self-definition.[43]

The redrawing of the political landscape was dramatic, full of rhetorical winks and subtle verbal operations. The *entreprises nationales,* centerpieces of Third Worldist Algeria, were quick to lose not only their former status and power but their purpose and even their very names. Split up and reorganized along functional and geographic lines, they became "regional" companies with a single mission: production.[44] The only investment worth speaking of being economic, one began to hear how wasteful and inefficient it was to dispense housing, nourishment, transportation, or cultural outlets. At the same time, new rules for managing the workforce were introduced, linking salary to performance and making it easier to discharge unwanted workers.[45] All in all, as Hugh Roberts comments, "the main aim . . . was to make the state sector conform to capitalist criteria of efficiency and profitability."[46]

But this was only one instance of a far more general pattern. By highlighting the differences between so-called economic and political rationales and carving out distinct spheres for each, the new discourse excluded a whole range of pivotal issues from the realm of legitimate discussion: issues of equality, of redistribution, of socioeconomic priorities. Insofar as they were deemed to interfere with matters of efficiency and productivity, they were branded as hostile to the exclusive purpose of the economic sector. To evoke any of one them was to improperly inject ideology or politics into economics — the decision to maximize "efficiency" and "profit" at all cost being defined, naturally, as both nonideological and apolitical. Yet the apparently unassailable logic of the new orthodoxy, its self-evident character, the sense that economic rationality finally was being set free, masked an intense, at times fiery debate (which took the shape of a journalistic feud between the more Boumediennist *Révolution Africaine* and the more "centrist" *Algérie-Actualité*) brimming with normative and doctrinal assumptions — on all sides.

This propensity to segregate and partition intellectual fields is typical of post-Third Worldism. Where Third Worldism generated images of oneness, of absolute equivalence — between executive power, legislative power, the party, the popular will, economics, the normative order, and so on — its successor is all about disconnection and segmentation. In the system of knowledge that followed Third Worldism, not only is politics divorced from economics but the state is separated from civil society. To repeat: the notion of a unanimous popular will, of the possibility of recognizing and even unearthing it, formed the basis of the Third Worldist understanding. Everything was connected because it had to be: the people, from whom the will emanated; the state, which was both guide and faithful follower; and within the state, the branches that passed, implemented, and interpreted the rules. There could be no separation of powers, since power by definition was one, but only a separation of functions—between the party, mass organizations, and the executive, legislative, and judicial branches.[47] To speak of a political order detached from its social basis was to betray the principles of the revolution and pervert its original promise.

The vision of the state as external to the social order rests on vastly different premises. Of these, the most important is the notion of the "limited," "impartial," or "impersonal" state, whose role is to institute neutral procedural rules, to guarantee the smooth and orderly operation of social interactions, and to respect the current, albeit transient, majority will. No longer expected to represent the univocal popular aspiration, but rather to juggle competing group demands, the state must remain at some distance, an observer instead of a participant. Separation of powers, checks and balances, and multiparty elections, all of which are at least somewhat at odds with the Third Worldist representation of the world, are other familiar hallmarks of this universe. Note that like Third Worldism, which conveniently brushed aside a number of vexing questions (regarding, for example, absolute state power and social diversity), the vision that succeeded it had hidden costs as well. In this instance, there was a disturbing tendency to overlook the background rules and social context (often one of sharp social stratification, political imbalance, and uneven access to information and to the media) within which the plea for state noninterference is made. So that the state's outwardly passive decision not to get involved more often than not conceals an active decision to ratify the status quo.

Algeria's conversion, in short, could not be achieved without prior acceptance of a new organizational principle, or as El-Kenz would put it, a different "self-awareness." The adoption of various laws aimed at encouraging private entrepreneurs (e.g., by easing access to credit or facilitating imports), privatizing agriculture, abolishing the formerly "irreversible conquests" of the revolution, opening the country to foreign investors, allowing the creation of independent political associations, or reducing food subsidies[48] all in their own way presupposed a novel set of values, a different imagery, and another jargon. (One minor, but symbolic, change comes to mind: Whereas during Boumedienne's tenure the president vowed to protect "the fundamental rights and liberties of the *people*," he now pledged to protect the "fundamental liberties and rights of *man* and of *citizens*.")[49]

That Western Europe, the United States, and financial institutions generally lent the weight of their authority to laud Algeria's newfound "wisdom" played no small part in this regard.[50] The international reference points became perestroika, economic adjustment, Chinese pragmatism, and Eastern European reformism, the key terms *economic logic* (as if there were but one), *deregulation, de-bureaucratization,* and, most valuable of all, *crisis,* a word that, while never precisely defined, magically validated all that was performed in its name.[51] The "bourgeoisie" — together with notions of individualism, competition, and wealth — had been rescued from political and moral condemnation, for the relevant distinction no longer opposed the egalitarian masses to the elite, but rather profit to waste. Of the once suspect private employer, El-Kenz writes that he "has today become someone who is looked up to, a 'maqla' with a high social visibility, who lives in a rich villa in the old colonial quarter, who marries off his children in sumptuous ceremonies and contributes to the building of a mosque. . . . [Previously,] an employee of the National Steel Corporation would have been considered a good match by parents in search of a son-in-law. Nowadays, matrimonial alliances have changed their objectives, and nothing can match a good private capitalist."[52] In the words of *Algérie-Actualité,* "Making money has never been an immoral activity."[53] From the mid-eighties on, increasing (and increasingly confident) displays of wealth could be seen in Algiers — luxury cars, villas, elegant nightclubs, and so on. As a consequence, what once had been the glorified "popular masses" became a crowd of unenterprising social parasites; the welfare state, once celebrated as political mentor, dispenser of both wisdom and wealth, now was condemned as incompetent and inefficacious; what had been considered priorities were decried as waste.

Perhaps the most vivid symbol of this ideological remodeling is Riadh El-Feth, what Joelle Stolz describes as the "new Mecca of a golden youth": one hundred forty-six hectares containing one hundred sixty modern boutiques, forty restaurants, and three movie theaters, with the latest American and West European rock music as background. Riadh El-Feth is the new experimental space, under the joint patronage of the public and private sectors, manufactured for a new ideological "people," the chi-chi population, the "golden youth that drives its Kawasaki and borrows dad's BMW."[54] How remote, in contrast, the *entreprises natio-nales* now appear!

Consider some of the articles published by *Algérie-Actualité*, the news organ most closely associated with the "pragmatic," "liberal" trend. One piece in particular stands out, perhaps because its remarkable title so viv-idly captured — better yet, framed — the terms of the debate: "Le social-isme de la mamelle," that is "Breast-fed Socialism." The article dubbed the FLN the "ministère de la parole," the department of rhetoric, and characterized its militants as "men with an ambiguous profile and of du-bious competence, whose sole expertise is in the art of empty oratory."[55] In other columns, *Algérie-Actualité* lamented the use of "old ideological refrains" and stressed the "shortcomings" that were bound to result from "populist discourse," which "has led to all of the defects provoked by a rigid, dogmatic language." Algeria, the magazine concluded, was in need of an economic environment in which "efficiency and seriousness would be the dominant values." If the aim was to inject political considerations into economic management, he reasoned, so be it. But in that case, firms ought to be evaluated according to the "quality of their discourse" and not the quality of their output, a prospect he clearly held in derision.[56] In this stark opposition between ideology and commerce, between rhet-oric and production, left out are the inevitable repercussions of privati-zation or "liberalization" on, say, the social distribution of work and wealth, job security, the status of employer, employee, technocrat, and peasant, or lifestyle in a more general sense. For once one accepts and internalizes the central premise — that the domains of the political and the economic can be compartmentalized strictly and that the one ought to leave the other alone — all else follows smoothly.

Another item in *Algérie-Actualité* helps to further clarify this point. In 1986 it advertised the publication of a new magazine, *Algérie-Economie*, whose purpose was to become the "vector of economic information . . . partner of creators of wealth and of jobs, companion to the spirit of initiative and barometer of social, economic activity. . . . Its features in-clude: 'your money,' 'economic climate,' 'life of the firm,' 'careers and prospects.'"[57] To an American or European audience, there is nothing particularly noteworthy here. But read in the context of pre-Chadli Al-geria, the ad's ordinariness dissipates. For it would have been unthink-able or, to borrow Bourdieu's terminology, "inaudible," absent the un-derlying cultural shift that followed Boumedienne's death. Who indeed is expressing this pressing need, and what group of people can offer a legitimate response? The point is that both utterance of the message and receptivity to it required that certain social desires be legitimated and certain social classes ideologically destigmatized.

What happened to the politics of opposition is especially interesting. In the era of Third Worldism, as I earlier remarked, dissent was patterned after the state's own ideological model, displaying a remarkable gift for political imitation. Opponents asked for different policies, a different state, and a different party, but populist policies, a centralized state, and a single party all the same. Yet, as the techniques and morphology of power change, so do the techniques and morphology of protest. From this perspective as well one can observe the demise of Third Worldism, for new forms of opposition began to emerge — regionalism, black marketeering, human rights activism, the women's movement, street violence, and urban protest. True, as I soon will discuss, the FIS retains much of the holistic, centralizing nature of the FLN. But even the Islamists tapped into methods of protest exemplifying an alternative politics.

In the preceding chapter, I described in general terms the sidestepping of a state that itself has chosen to step aside. That is precisely what we see happening in Algeria. As the state recedes, especially a state that has so completely monopolized the social, economic, and political scenes, people tend to seek alternatives, to organize themselves according to competing allegiances. This by no means is a negligible point, since it registers a change in what El-Kenz calls society's self-awareness from (relatively) confident, united, and homogeneous to insecure, diffuse, and diversified. At its apex, Algerian Third Worldism exuded a sense of coherence, of a shared and integrated project, of a collective history. Yet as social and ideological ties loosened, one witnessed the atomization and fragmentation of the social fabric. All of which is to say that where the state no longer fulfills its prior cultural and economic roles, alternative channels of support, scriptures, symbolic orders, and symbolic spaces are set up and are called upon. "What is most important is to be able to weather history's spiraling decline, and people know that this can only be done as a group, using informal tools of social intercourse that once were trivial but that, given the novel situation, must be summoned up from collective memory."[58]

One obvious index of the state's retreat is the growth of the underground economy. When the state neglected prior economic and social responsibilities, the black market gradually emerged as a central regulator of economic life. It made up for the lacunae of official mechanisms of exchange. "If you want to build a house," one taxi driver explained, "it takes two years. Pay a colonel, it takes two weeks."[59] According to the IMF and the World Bank, the parallel economy represents roughly 10 percent of the official economy.[60] Using more informal statistical tools, Ahmed Henni estimates it to be closer to 50 percent.[61] For his part, Mahfoud Bennoune argued that by the end of the 1980s "the black market account[ed] for 80 percent of all goods exchanged in the country."[62] Society was assembling an economic life that had its own codes, its own rules of behavior, its own vocabulary — *trabendisme* was the term coined to describe participation in this parallel economy — and its own geographic space, as official boundaries were ignored and tradesmen freely crossed into Morocco or Tunisia.[63]

Not that state actors were wholly removed from the parallel economic universe or lacked any responsibility for its creation. Far from it: members of the state apparatus used whatever connections and influence they retained to insinuate themselves within its nooks and crannies, to take as much advantage of its rich possibilities as they possibly could.[64] In a sense, Algeria's informal economy spawned two specimens of black marketeers. One is an offshoot of the administrative state, comprising the recycled state bureaucrats and technocrats who enjoy access to international finance and state capital. The other, which gravitates around street traders and the bazaar economy, is viewed by the state as "transgressive," depicted all at once as irrational, disorderly, and a foe of modernity, and, because it is concealed, feared as a potential financier of Islamist forces. Even in this age of economic liberalization, as Deborah Harrold writes, "the dominant Algerian economic discourse still invokes an aesthetic that places the orderly, the planned, the modern in a mythic binary opposed to the informal, the traditional, the Islamic."[65] But the point is that even the former category — the "sanctioned" one — realized that the state-run economy was becoming ancillary and that the relevant activities were occurring elsewhere. The point is also that by contributing to this second economy, the recycled bureaucrats further destabilized the public sector, undermined the national treasury and currency, and turned any form of planning into a futile and frustrating exercise.[66]

A perplexing confusion of social roles ensues. Hankiss develops this theme in his study of "socialist" Hungary: company managers must adapt to the rules of the state bureaucracy, compete on the market, and adjust to the second economy.[67] In Algeria, social actors may work for the state bureaucracy or state-owned companies in the morning, adjusting to the rhythm and requirements of the administrative economy, and then become "private" actors in the afternoon, at which time they might resort to the market and to *trabendisme*. One's social role may also be tied to varying functional needs, ordinary citizens using official channels for certain goods and services (e.g., health care or education), semioffi-cial, cliental channels (e.g., for housing) or underground channels (e.g., for certain imported products) for others.

Other practical extensions of the state's disengagement and ideologi-cal burnout are not difficult to divine. As the quest for alternative socio-political venues goes forth, forms of clientelism and subnational solidar-ities naturally take on increased importance. I do not wish to leave the impression that client-patron relations were unknown in pre-Chadli Al-geria, for they have long been a feature of Algerian politics.[68] But they took on a renewed urgency with the decline of the state and of state-sponsored programs and with the strengthening of a local elite that displayed more open economic and cultural ties to the West. Loyalties based on clan, region, language, residence, or family become the new social cushion, the new cultural anchor, not through some sort of rever-sion or relapse to society's natural ways, but out of necessity and strate-gic choice. One of the most vivid examples is the Berber movement, which asserted itself with increased vigor in the 1980s.[69] According to Hugh Roberts, "With the loss of *élan* in the regime's economic devel-opment strategy, popular discontent has tended increasingly to surface in the form of competing claims to representation in the state apparatus expressed in terms of cultural identity and legitimacy, and a growing disposition to contest the prerogatives and legitimacy of the state appa-ratus when these claims are frustrated."[70] Family ties also take on far greater importance as individuals find that they must share their income, or a roof, or a meal.[71]

But resistance and protest are not always so subdued. The effect of the state's gradual removal from the economy and its abandonment of its prior Third Worldist discourse was not only to disrupt customary economic structures, encourage the organization of a parallel economy, or activate alternative political and cultural channels. For one thing, it also dramatically enlarged the ranks of the unemployed and underem-ployed. By the end of the 1980s roughly a quarter of the active popula-tion reportedly was out of a job. Indeed, Rachid Tlemçani has estimated that if women are included, approximately two-thirds of the Algerian labor force has been "marginalized."[72] Marginalization "show[s] where the state leaves off"; it provokes feelings of exclusion, or, to use David Apter's phrase, of social "superfluousness."[73] We should expect its victims to be particularly receptive to antistatist discourse and to be easily mobilized by dissident groups, for, as Apter also writes, these are the conditions under which "a sub-society, becoming an anti-society, define[s] what was being lost while seeking redemptive solutions."[74] And, indeed, evidence of such a trend has been noted not only in Algeria but in much of the Maghrib and Egypt as well. "When there are no longer sufficient resources to provide for and satisfy those expecting minimal gratification (the impoverished peasantry, the urban sub-proletariat, unemployed skilled workers, those with decreasing spending power) the state becomes the target of manifold discontent . . . : the excluded . . . reject the system that no longer has the means to integrate them into the allocation process."[75]

Urban phenomena of exclusion and revolt are particularly acute in this context and can reach very deeply; the October 1988 events in Algeria are a good example. The city—whether Cairo, Tunis, Casablanca, or Algiers—gradually becomes the focal point of social contradictions and discontent. This is in part because there is a specific "ideology of the city,"[76] born of the dual experiences of colonialism and independence, both of which invested urban centers with a new and pivotal meaning. As a result, the city becomes the harbor of society's basic tensions, such as the opposition between conspicuous consumption and glaring impoverishment, between traditional culture and Western influence, rising unemployment, the formation of a marginalized underclass, and the housing crisis. "We should not therefore be astonished," writes Michael Gilsenan, "to find that in times of crisis the modern city is itself called in question, taken to symbolize forces of oppression or a non-Islamic way of life. In this context the hotels, nightclubs, and cinemas that are attacked and burned down have a greater symbolic weight than their apparently banal function might merit them."[77]

All of this gets magnified when, as in Algeria, a populist, quasi-egalitarian ideology yields to the mythology of economic logic, profitability, and freedom of the market. The complexion of the city changes, reflecting the modified structure of power and the new boundaries of legitimate discourse and behavior. Class separations are exhibited more openly and more confidently in the city's very physical appearance. As El-Kenz observed, real estate activity in Algiers, and in particular the marked differences between neighborhoods, some possessing the best schools and the most modern private clinics, mirrors a pattern of sharpening social differentiation.[78]

Indeed, by encouraging the development of a consumer mentality, the importation of Western cultural products, and the flaunting of private wealth at a time of scarcity and rising unemployment, the new ideological system runs a serious risk of self-defeat. While one segment of society calls for even finer consumer goods, an increased ability to pass its wealth along to the next generation, free enterprise, and free expression, another clamors for such basic goods as jobs, food, housing, sports facilities, and the like. In terms of what they own, demand, and expect, the two groups grow further apart. And as inequities in the distribution of material, cultural, or intellectual capital intensify, so must the frustration, and the anger.[79] All of which — the sense of material and cultural deprivation, feelings of marginalization and of exclusion, the state's abandonment of vital social tasks, and, more generally, the absence of a common ideological mooring to compensate for Third Worldism's debacle — bring us to the central question of contemporary Algerian politics: the question of Islam, or Islamism.

In the 1960s and 1970s, amidst the exuberance of decolonization and beneath the shadows of Che, Mao, Nasser, and Ho Chi Minh, a dream now and again would form in the minds of Algerian — and other — militants: their country, awakening from over a century of foreign occupation, would become the revolutionary center of the Third World, a place one would look to for inspiration, guidance, and support, in a word (and it is a word that often was bandied about), a new Mecca.

They were right on one count. By the 1990s Algeria was well on its way to becoming just that — though it almost certainly was not what those young rebels had had in mind. Now, nights were filled with talk of a different Mecca, the literal one, the original. As the allegory turned into reality, the aged revolutionaries looked down to examine their purported creation yet failed to recognize their work. Instead, they saw unfamiliar, turbaned faces, or perhaps they were familiar ones after all — those of workers, peasants, members of the middle class — cast in unfamiliar roles.

The Front Islamique du Salut was officially founded on February 18, 1989, in the wake of October's momentous events and the political opening to which they led. The regime had the authority to refuse to accredit the FIS, for the law barred the creation of parties based on religion. President Chadli decided otherwise, however, asserting that "it is not conceivable to apply democracy to Communists and to deprive the current which preaches spiritual belonging."[80] In September 1989 the FIS received official recognition—a first in the modern Arab world for a religious party.

From the start the FIS was a semiclandestine organization, overt and covert in (more or less) equal parts. The subtle combination of legalism and political radicalism was embodied in its two principal leaders, Abbassi Madani and Ali Belhadj, and in their deft division of labor. Born in 1931, Madani had lived through years of French colonialism and of autocratic rule at the hand of the FLN, his legitimacy deriving in part from having opposed the two and from having been imprisoned by both—by the French in 1954 and by his fellow Algerians in 1982. Madani had come to Islamism by way of Messalism (not an unusual path by any means), having been a member of the PPA/MTLD before joining the FLN. By the time Algeria gained its independence, Madani could be heard denouncing the FLN's "anti-islamic drift."[81] At age fifty-nine, after years spent in the shadow of leaders of the religious opposition to Boumedienne and Chadli (mainly sheikhs Abdellatif Soltani and Ahmed Sahnoun), he became the FIS's spokesperson and de facto president.[82]

If Madani represented the FIS's legitimate, lawful side, Belhadj personified its more fiery, radical facet. Unlike Madani, he was too young to take part in the war, had an exclusively religious education, and had never lived abroad—indeed, had never set foot in a non-Muslim country.[83] In a way, much of Belhadj's notoriety in the West derived from the fact that he so readily accommodated its Orientalist stereotypes: the Arab as zealot, hothead, terrorist, crudely provincial. So much of it was purely rhetorical, and sheer theatrics, but it served Belhadj well with some of his constituents, and the Western media with some of their own.

Madani explained the choice of the movement's name as follows:

C'est un "front," parce qu'il affronte; et parce qu'il a un large éventail d'actions et de domaines; c'est le front du peuple algérien avec toutes ses couches, et sur son vaste territoire. . . .

Il est "islamique" d'appellation, parce qu'il a un contenu, une méthode, une fonction historique islamiques. L'islam est un but auquel nous empruntons un modèle de changement et de réforme, et ou nous puisons notre raison d'être et les raisons de la continuité de notre être, l'être de la meilleure des nations. . . .

Quant au "salut," il est representé par la fonction apostolique, en tant que salut de la foi, celui qui méne à la voie droite et empêche l'erreur; et par la fonction historique, économique, sociale, culturelle et civilisationnelle. C'est le salut de tous pour être tout.

[It is a "front" because it confronts, and because it is involved in a wide range of actions and of domains; it is the front of the Algerian people, of all its layers and throughout its vast territory. . . .
We call it "Islamic" because its content, method, and historical functions all are Islamic. Islam is a goal from which we borrow a model for change and for reform, and out of which we draw our raison d'être and the reasons for the constancy of our spirit, the spirit of the best of nations. . . .
As for "salvation," it is incarnated in the apostolic function, the salvation of faith, which leads onto the righteous path and prevents deviation; and in the historical, economic, social, cultural, and civilizational functions. It is the salvation of everyone so that they may be everything.][84]

In no time, the streets would belong to the Islamic Front. Over and over it would prove to be the most effective and most popular of the numberless parties (soon to reach fifty) that came into being. The principal symbolic moments occurred during its mass demonstrations, raw displays of organizational, ideological, and rhetorical power—marches in favor of the application of Koranic (*shari'ah*) law, electoral rallies, and so forth. If there was something strangely familiar in their self-assurance and poise, that really was no surprise. For their behavior mirrored the confidence and composure that once had been the hallmark of that other organization with aspirations to hegemonic status, the FLN. True, elections stood in the FIS's way, and then the government, and then the army. But what did they amount to when the people, history, and God were on its side?

The first pluralistic elections in Algeria's postcolonial history were scheduled for June 12, 1990. This was a time of worldwide "ballot chic," as Ajami nicely puts it, and Algeria conformed.[85] Of course, these were merely local, municipal elections, but they would provide the first measure of the parties' respective strength and constituted an invaluable dress rehearsal for the parliamentary counterpart that was to follow. This being so, observers were prepared to inspect the results closely, searching for subtle political messages or possible electoral fraud.

There was no need. Sophisticated analyses were unnecessary, for voters left no doubts about their inclination; and even if there had been irregularities, the lopsidedness of the outcome suggested that they really could not have made much of a difference. The FIS captured over 54 percent of the popular vote—64.18 percent in Algiers, 70.57 percent in Oran, and 72 percent in Constantine. Of 1,551 communes, it controlled 853, and of 48 *wilayas* (departments), it was in charge of 32.[86] Overall, some 4 million Algerians cast their ballot for the FIS. The FLN, in contrast, was the choice of 2 million Algerians, attracting only just over

28 percent of the popular vote. In less than a year and a half the Islamic
Front had essentially conquered Algeria before its former masters' eyes.

I do not intend to recount in detail all that ensued, but a few high-
lights are worth noting.[87] The FIS's electoral and ideological dominion
over Algeria did not go uncontested, and elements within the FIS itself
were not willing to abide by the state-imposed political calendar. In June
1991, just a few weeks before legislative elections were to be held, the FIS
called for a general strike. Ostensibly triggered by what the FIS claimed
to be an unfair electoral law, the strike was designed to overthrow the
regime. It evoked a territorial conquest of sorts, Islamism taking hold of
one site after another: mosques, streets, hospitals. City sounds also were
appropriated, as loudspeakers filled the air with speeches and sermons.

But violence soon would erupt between FIS supporters and riot police. Both sides resorted to arrests, interrogations, and brutality.[88] Once
again a state of siege was decreed, elections were postponed, and Madani
and Belhadj were arrested on charges of "armed conspiracy against the
state."[89] But history was interrupted for only so long; soon President
Chadli announced that the state of siege was being lifted and that two-
round National Assembly elections would be held in December 1991 and
January 1992.

At about that time, I returned to Algiers. I had not been there since
July 1990, but except for a few more veils and a few more beards, little
on the surface appeared to have changed. Yet the depth of the cultural
and political divide soon became shockingly apparent — as did the depth
of popular support enjoyed by the FIS. Senior leaders of the FLN saw
things quite differently. Exuding customary assuredness, they would
mention the Islamists' purported inability to manage the communes and
city halls, their distasteful contempt for individual rights, and the emergence of more moderate Islamist alternatives (not without some help
from the regime), throw in some polling data, and conclude that the FIS
could not capture more than a third of the vote, with the FLN doing
the same or even slightly better. Thanks to the winner-take-all, majority electoral system imposed by the regime, that would leave a political
field polarized between the FIS and the FLN, with smaller secular parties gravitating toward the latter. All things considered, such a situation
would suit the FLN bosses quite well.

It was hard, given all one could see and hear, to understand what they
were expecting. But then again, they had made an art of neither watch-
ing nor listening. True, the FIS inspired fear among many, especially
among women and the Berber minority (and who could blame them?),

the upper class, and the Westernized elite. Equally true, municipal and communal administration by the Islamists had fallen short of their exorbitant promises. But how a discredited party, ideologically bankrupt and politically broke, or a handful of inexperienced democratic parties operating in an environment that for so long had been hostile to any hint of pluralism could capture either the apprehension or the disillusionment was a question these FLN elders never explicitly confronted.

On December 26, 1991, Algeria voted again. And again the FIS emerged as the uncontested winner. Its total number of votes won had declined from 4 million to 3 million, but with 47 percent of the popular vote, the Islamist party had captured 188 of the 231 seats that were decided in the first round. The FLN's 23 percent of the vote gave it a mere 15 seats, while Aït-Ahmed's FFS, taking advantage of an electoral system originally designed to benefit the ruling party, captured 25 with 7.45 percent of the vote.[90] The outcome of the second round was hardly in doubt, since the FIS needed to win only 27 of the remaining 199 seats in order to control the new National Assembly.

With tensions mounting, calls by members of the secular opposition to halt the electoral process, and the regime sharply divided between those who wished to see it continue and those who wished to see it stopped, the army stepped in—though, in typical Algerian style, under cover. On January 11, in what Lahouari Addi calls an "electoral holdup," Chadli Benjedid appeared on television to announce his resignation and then was quickly put under house arrest.[91] A day and a few constitutional contortions later, the Haut Conseil de Securité (HCS), a presidential advisory body, proclaimed that it was taking charge, canceled the second round of the elections, and created a five-member Haut Conseil d'Etat (HCE) to assume all presidential powers. As Fouad Ajami would describe the peculiar sequence of events, "Algeria had seen it all by then: The rulers launching an electoral process whose verdict they could not honor; the Islamicist challengers prevailing in a democratic process of sorts while running down democracy as a Western imposition; the Algerian bourgeoisie, its professional associations and "modernist" women coming out into the streets to hail the armed forces, cheer them on, and plead with them to protect the cultural freedoms of a Mediterranean society caught between an Islamic calling from below and a history of exposure to the fashions and the ways of Europe—principally the ways of France."[92] The cancellation of the elections was a prelude to other steps aimed at "de-Islamicizing" Algeria. The regime outlawed the FIS and its related Islamic associations, dissolved city halls the FIS had conquered in 1990, fired workers who had gone on strike in June 1991, and attempted to wrest control of insubordinate mosques.[93]

There would be more to come, just as anomalous and in a way just as desperate. Seeking "to perfect the illusion of a new start," the regime turned to a seventy-three-year-old veteran of the war of national liberation, one of the original founders of the FLN, who for the previous twenty-eight years had been living in exile in Morocco.[94] Once condemned to death and pardoned neither by Boumedienne nor by Chadli, Mohamed Boudiaf returned as president of the HCE. Six months later he was assassinated — by the FIS? by members of the old regime threatened by his reformist pledges? — a pawn in a game he had joined midway and now was forced to leave unfinished.

Since then Algeria has been the scene of perpetual and ghastly violence and counterviolence, a battle between governmental and Islamist forces at the very least, although involvement by splinter groups on both sides, of organized crime, and of disorganized gangsterism simply could not be ruled out. At first there were few casualties, though isolated acts of terror did occur. Later, however, the bloodletting began, as extremists on one side mirrored extremists on the other in their obdurate refusal to compromise or negotiate. The government on occasion evinced an apparent willingness to negotiate with the FIS, most notably in the fall of 1994. Each time, however, it swiftly recanted, presumably under pressure from military hard-liners.[95] The FIS, for its part, seemed increasingly unable to control the situation on the ground. Competition from the extremist GIA was compounded by the FIS's clandestine status and the ensuing impossibility to convene its *majlis al-shura* (consultative council) to bring discipline to its fractured organization.

Nor has the so-called democratic center been of much use, hamstrung as it has been by its own internal contradictions. On one side was the odd coalition of the Berber-based RCD and the Tahaddi movement, heir to the former communists. Dubbed "eradicators," they backed the interruption of the electoral process and the all-out war against the Islamists, defending democracy against the religious threat — by any means, even antidemocratic ones, and with any ally, even if it happened to be the army. On the other side were the secular parties and moderate Islamic organizations — the FLN, the FFS, Hamas, and others. They condemned the 1992 coup in the name of democracy and called for the inclusion of the antidemocratic FIS in a nationwide dialogue.[96]

Days limp on, and the ancien régime keeps on fighting, invoking imaginary plots — Iranian, French, Saudi, Sudanese — increasingly remote from everything that surrounds it, as if the myths of the past had robbed it of any connection to the present. Meanwhile, journalists, local officials, farmers, shopkeepers, and foreign tourists are being killed with frightening regularity.[97] Beirut-like car bombings, Afghan-like warfare, beheadings, mutilations, torture, and rape are becoming Algeria's daily fare. If this is the road to Mecca, it is rough indeed, more muddy than pure, more soulless than saintly, more unmerciful than compassionate.

The "return of Islam" is a catchy phrase but, or rather therefore, a misleading one. It suggests, first, that Islam somehow had cleared out and, second, that what we are witnessing in Algeria today is essentially a religious phenomenon — two propositions that I find neither particularly helpful nor very accurate. Before exploring these two thoughts, however, I would like a word about words. I have deliberately chosen to use the term *Islamism* in discussing events in Algeria because, strictly speaking, we are not dealing with fundamentalism. There is considerable overlap, of course, since in both cases the demand is for renewed respect for sacred texts. But we should not misinterpret these rough similarities. Unlike fundamentalism, Islamism is concerned with the political, economic, and social spheres, not exclusively the moral. Nor is traditionalism really the issue, for the political instruments, activities, and goals of Algerian Islamism are neither traditional nor in any sense sheltered from the influence of European or American culture. Considerable nostalgia is involved, to be sure, but so are utopia and a plan for the future that is far more than a sheer retreat into the past. The French like to use the term *intégristes,* but the concept's close ties to Christianity hardly makes it an appropriate alternative.[98] I have settled, then, for *Islamism* as defined by François Burgat: "the recourse to the vocabulary of Islam, used in the post-colonial period to express within the state, or more often against it, an alternative political program that uses the heritage of the West as a foil, but allows nevertheless the reappropriation of its principal references."[99]

The appearance of a strong Islamist movement in Algeria is neither a resurgence nor a return, for Islam never left the Algerian stage. A quick survey of Algeria's modern history ought to make that plain, whether one chooses to look at the years of colonial occupation (when Islam often provided the sole refuge for the local population), the interwar period (during which Ben Badis's *ulémas* played a considerable ideological role, both directly and by influencing other nationalist parties), or the war of national liberation (where Islamic and nationalist discourse often intersected, the FLN's first proclamation vowing to restore the Algerian state "in accordance with the principles of Islam"). Even under Ben Bella's and Boumedienne's regimes, the nation's Islamic character never strayed far beneath the surface. The constitution established Islam as the state's religion and required that it be the president's as well. Throughout those years, the country was regulated by a distinctly Islamic temporal rhythm: religious holidays of the Hegirian calendar punctuated the year, Friday became the weekly day off, and, when necessary, working hours were modified to accommodate the rigors of Ramadan. There are more obvious signs as well, such as the colors of the national flag (green and white) and its symbols (a red crescent and a star), the recurring veil, and the muezzin's daily invocations. In one of the most extended analyses to date, Henri Sanson describes this as "Islamic secularism," but whatever the case might be, it is Islamic all the same.[100]

Nor was that the only form that Islam took during Algeria's Third Worldist years. The religious association Al Qiyam (values) made itself known as early as 1964, when it engaged in a succession of mainly verbal clashes with the secular Left and, more generally, took issue with what it considered to be Ben Bella's socialism. Although Boumedienne was viewed more favorably at the start, by the seventies his brand of socialism too was coming under sustained attack. The agrarian revolution, and particularly the nationalization and redistribution of privately owned lands that it entailed, was denounced on various religious grounds, as was the regime's central ideological manifesto, the national charter of 1976.[101] Some version of Islam also was enlisted in battles surrounding linguistic and familial policies. Finally, in the aftermath of Boumedienne's death, religious opposition became altogether more open and more violent. There were demonstrations, strikes, attacks against left-wing students and stores selling alcohol (followed by arrests, repression, and the like), and, most important of all, the birth in 1982 of the Islamist Movement of Algeria, an underground armed organization led by Mustapha Bouyali. Five years and many deaths later, Bouyali was gunned down in a deadly ambush.[102]

The question, then, is not where Islam went but what form it took, and why. A useful way of thinking about it is as a vocabulary or medium out of which emanates a variety of idioms, dialects, and jargons.[103] To say of something that it is "Islam" or "Islamic" is in this sense quite useless since these concepts encompass so wide a range of diverse, more often than not conflicting (even irreconcilable) practices, beliefs, and aspirations. In *Recognizing Islam,* Gilsenan illustrates this by recounting the fluctuating meaning of Islam among groups within Egypt, a meaning that changes with time and across social strata — in the colonial, Nasserist, or *infitah* (i.e., "open door") stages of Egyptian history, from the perspective of the Muslim Brotherhood, Sufi sects, state officialdom, petty bourgeoisie, lumpenproletariat, or technocrats. Thus, the central question, in the Algerian case as in all others, is why Islam has taken on one of these multitudinous forms, how it came to be assimilated that way, and by whom.

Reasons for my discomfort with the second proposition now should be apparent. What matters in the triumph of the FIS and of Islamist discourse generally is less that it is a phenomenon involving Islam (yet that is what is implied by reference to a "turn to Islam") than that it is a rebellious, populist Islam, one that has been appropriated by a movement of violent and absolute opposition to the state. In short, it is not Islam that has spawned the FIS, but specific social dislocations, class frustrations and class strategies, cultural anxieties, ideological pulls, and global power relations. This is not at all to say that religion is unimportant or that faith is mere pretense. The belief remains — what changes is its manifestations, and from our perspective, they are everything.

Thoughts such as these have been with us for some time now, which is why it is particularly distressing to note how hard it has been for them to register, how little of an inroad they seem to have made in the popular media in Europe and the United States. Observers holding such widely divergent views as Fouad Ajami and Michael Gilsenan at the very least would agree on the basic proposition that there exists a link between particular social and historical conditions on the one hand and the shape taken (or role played) by Islamic discourse on the other. Even among contemporary followers of Islamist movements — Hamas in the occupied territories, the Muslim Brotherhood in Egypt, or the FIS in Algeria — there are widely divergent experiences of Islam. To quote Gilsenan, "Different and sometimes mutually exclusive apprehensions and practices of Islam are emerging that separate societies and classes as much as they unite them. Rhetorical unity may be easily achieved, but in the subterranean world there are social forces that push and thrust at the shell of dessicated formulas."[104]

Yet far from being uncontroversial, this view is forced to contend with the standard notion that, minor variations aside, Islam by essence is an all-encompassing worldview, ordering the social, the moral, and the political, and therefore inherently totalitarian and, when resisted, most likely violent. As a result, events in Algeria are depicted as a "turn to Islam," meaning a turn to those purportedly core characteristics of the faith — intolerance, fanaticism, reactionary opposition to modernity, to progress, and to the West.

There are some ready explanations for the peculiar hold this view exercises on the West. For there is a sense in which Islam is indeed distinctly receptive to, and an apt vehicle for, such radical and sweeping protest. From the outset, as Maxime Rodinson has remarked, and unlike Christianity, Islam presented itself as a politico-religious structure with the ability to establish equitable institutions on earth. The Prophet was at the head of a community of believers but also of a state; his message is theistic but also political and social; Islam is all at once *din* (religion) and *dawla* (government).[105] Burgat complements this view by stating that "the totalizing pretensions of monotheistic religions carry a potential for totalitarianism that is all the stronger in Islam since, at least in principle, it refutes the barriers of secularization."[106]

To this one might add the important fact that Islam for some time now has been viewed by its followers as a dominated, and oppressed, religion, that is, a religion of the Third World. Beginning in the era of colonialism and continuing up until the current epoch, the "enemy" unfailingly has been non-Muslim, distinctions between anticolonial, Arab, and Muslim nationalism thereby having a marked tendency to blur. As Rodinson comments, "Even beyond the boundaries of the Muslim world, Islam has acquired the prestige of being and of consistently having been at the forefront of resistance to a Christian and expansionist Europe, both missionary and imperialist."[107]

I am willing to concede much of this, but I would rather put it as follows: Islam, as a result of conditions surrounding its advent, development, and status within the world, has been readily translated into a medium of political and social protest and a concrete blueprint for the future perhaps more readily than its religious counterparts. It possesses, as it were, an *efficacy* as a language of radical insurgency that others do not. But Islam offers more than enough latitude to justify social protest *and* political immobilism, progress *and* retrogression, militancy *and* quietism. To tax Islamic tenets with responsibility for the terrorism and the bigotry and the extremism is thus both inaccurate and unfair. The point being that one ought not confuse the content of a particular dogma with the conditions under which it is being invoked and the uses to which it is being put.

Nor has the West been alone in failing to come to terms with the inherent multiplicity of Islam. Efforts by states in contemporary Algeria or Egypt to co-opt movements of Islamic protest (in essence by catering to some of their demands and sprinkling official discourse with more frequent "Islamic" references) are other instances of this complete misunderstanding, albeit in another one of its variants. In conditions of severe social and cultural polarization as exist in Egypt and, increasingly, Algeria the demands of militant Islamists cannot be satisfied by the state's sudden religious rebirth. For by that point, the state has come to symbolize one extremity of the divide — the foreign, corrupt, and exploitative. Nothing short of its deposal will do, certainly not the state's abrupt and ostentatious embracement of the Islamists' version of Islam, which, if anything, will be taken as further evidence of its hypocrisy. Gilsenan shows this in the Egyptian case, where "state support for what might crudely be called a cleaned-up version of the 'religion of the streets' can be *more* productive of contradiction than state disapproval or even quasi-repression."[108] The mingling of state and religion under these circumstances thus ends up as treacherous business indeed: instead of religion's cleansing the disreputable state, it is the state that sullies religion, or at least that part of religion which it has been able to recuperate.

Let me come, then, to the question with which we started out: how did radical Islamism come to take up residence at the heart of Algeria's polity? Some general answers propose themselves. First, the absence of democracy and of any mass-based political party, let alone bona fide political pluralism, led to a vacuum that Islamic discourse alone was able to fill. While successive governments silenced all dissident political speech, Islam enjoyed the use of an inviolable space (the mosque), a tribune (the preacher's pulpit), and a sacred public language (religious discourse). Forms of public discontent thus tended to take on religious accents; that, in turn, "facilitated the advent of preachers solidly anchored in civil society."[109]

A similar situation was noted in Egypt under Nasser, as well as in Baathist Iraq and Syria. In all three, the price of ideological control — some would say the price of Third Worldism — included the stifling of genuine mass political participation in the name of political orthodoxy. "Devastating, as they do, other channels of opposition, [states] leave men with that one thing that the elites cannot monopolize: religious devotion doubling as piety and as a political instrument."[110]

That is but one manner in which the state's own discourse smoothed the way for religious forms of opposition. The Algerian regime projected a moralistic image of politics and a moralistic image of governance that went hand in hand. The moralistic politics is that there exists only one genuine path, that all ideological debate is between a "right" and a "wrong," and that the wrong, by definition, is betrayal, disloyalty, apostasy. The moralistic notion of governance is simply an extension, the idea that disagreements over economic or social policy belong not to the realm of legitimate argument nor even to the realm of class conflict, but rather to the domain of the ethical. Little wonder that Algerians would interpret rising poverty, worsening living conditions, and the shortage of housing, goods, and employment less as indicators of misguided management than as symptoms of a moral failing of the state. The crisis, though experienced most immediately at the socioeconomic level, was met by calls for a remedy on the moral plane. From there to religious salvation was but a small step.

This helps explain a paradox I referred to briefly above: that while the FIS has one foot in the post–Third Worldist era, feeding on forms of allegiance and forms of protest (such as black-marketeering) that are inherently antistatist in nature, its other foot remains planted firmly in the age of Third Worldism. Gone is the socialistic, progressive, state-centered lyricism of the FLN and its earlier Third Worldist critics (the Boudiafs or Aït-Ahmeds in their 1970s incarnation), but the political absolutism, the Manicheanism, the negation of any private sphere, and the belief that all dissent was treachery endure. The FIS's ideology, like similar expressions of exclusionary identity politics elsewhere, thus thrived on the very Third Worldist heritage against which it rose. It is true that democratic movements and human rights associations also are beneficiaries of Third Worldism's collapse, including in Algeria, but they are maneuvering on unfamiliar ground and can hardly rely on a civil society disabled by years of mistreatment at the hands of the Algerian state. The FIS's ability to capture both popular opposition to the state and popular thirst for the type of absolute, moralistic project the state once embodied was the more potent.

Second is the paradoxical situation involving the state's attempted co-optation of Islam. Reacting to growing discontent in the postindependence period, the Algerian state undertook to appropriate Islamic discourse to enhance its own legitimacy. Algeria's religious identity increasingly was emphasized, Friday became the weekly day off, bets and the breeding of pigs were prohibited.[111] Algeria's "Arabization" policy also can be considered part of this trend, given the close relationship between language and Islam.[112] Overall, the state appears to have viewed Islam as an effective ideological resource that it was free to manipulate.

Thus, it was used both to counteract the influence of leftist militants (on the rise since the launching of the agrarian revolution) and to placate the demands of radicalized Islamic groups.[113]

As we saw earlier, such efforts are likely to backfire, and backfire they did. The disquiet that spoke with an Islamic accent essentially was directed against the state, a manifestation of society's growing sense of alienation from it. The state-sponsored, highly "bureaucratized" Islam (both the recruitment of *imams* and the construction of mosques fell under strict governmental control) hardly can be expected to mollify these feelings.[114] As things stood, Algeria's two-track strategy (political repression of the Islamic movement's leadership and ideological appropriation of elements of its discourse) achieved precisely the opposite of what had been intended: it undermined the state's ideological legitimacy while strengthening the political status of its religious-based opposition. The state's close identification with the project of Third Worldism made it a poor candidate for promoting a distinct worldview. Having encouraged an ideological demand it was unable to satisfy, the state was forced to face the consequences.

Other aspects of the state's policy — rather than an enduring Islamic hostility to central power or to modern forms of political organization — help explain the recent upsurge of religious opposition. François Burgat points to the state's deliberate suppression of Algeria's Berber identity as one reason for the vigor of Arab-Islamic sentiment.[115] Along the same lines, the government's indecisive and waffling family policy (involving, importantly, the status of women) angered habitual supporters while emboldening traditional opponents.

All this goes some way toward explaining why opposition to the state assumed a religious guise, but it leaves us with the task of accounting for the particular sort of Islam that took hold. Islamic opposition, as I have said, has been a regular feature of the Algerian landscape, from Ben Badis to his contemporary heirs, Abdelaziz Soltani or Mahfoud Nahnah. But for quite some time it was of only sporadic importance, confined chiefly to the moral sphere, "attack[ing], above all, the degradation of morals as the supreme evil, of which the consumption of alcohol, the mixing of sexes, the lack of consideration for religion or even the cult of pre-Islamic Roman ruins were the expression."[116] Islamic opposition under Boumedienne also preserved within it the basic socioeconomic conservatism of the former *ulémas,* so that it remained a favorite of landowners threatened by the regime's agrarian policy. Landed interests financed the construction of mosques and the activities of various religious associations while religious spokespeople regularly condemned Boumedienne's policy of land redistribution in the name of respect for private property.[117] Beyond that, however, Islamic opposition lacked social roots and failed to attract a sizable following. Even young Algerians favorably predisposed toward the views of the religious movement were said to have taken issue with its socioeconomic outlook. As one put it, "One of our slogans was: 'With the agrarian revolution and against Communism.' . . . we said that we could not be against the distribution of land because we could only benefit from it. Most of us were from peasant origins. We were even more proletarian, in the end, not even proletarian, but frankly without anything."[118] Without an effective social foundation, Islamism lacked credibility as a language of political protest.

What planted radical Islamism firmly at the core of oppositional politics by the early 1990s was the encounter between religion and social discontent. The conjunction of the two lent to the former a power base and to the latter a channel of communication as well as a voice that was relatively unrestrained. Indeed, and at that point, the factors that made Islamic discourse a superior medium of protest—the nature of Islam, which provided it with a comprehensive project to match the state's own all-embracing ideology; its ability to capitalize on the perceived polarization between Muslim and non-Muslim nations, the religious resonating particularly well with the geopolitical; the fact that it was the only non-official discourse licensed by Algerian Third Worldism; and the availability of a sacred forum of expression that even the state was reluctant to muzzle—helped disseminate the sociopolitical message at an exceptional pace. As soon as the mélange caught on, it achieved remarkable and, in the state's view, unmanageable success.

That the voices of social dissatisfaction and religious defiance should blend into one calls for some elucidation. Some possible reasons suggest themselves instantly. The vocabulary of Islam is rich enough, as I earlier stated, to welcome both a language of social conservatism and one of social progress—and that is one explanation. Islam's often austere moral climate is particularly well suited to circumstances of sharp social inequality, in which luxury and deprivation live side by side. Indeed, notions of equity and social justice are not foreign to Islam and can be made part of its agenda without much effort.[119] This is all the more true when privatization replaces public ownership, the state elite and segments of the private sector begin to form de facto alliances, and corruption—or, far more importantly, its effects—becomes increasingly visible. At such times, Islam's normative language about right and wrong lapses into a political discourse on justice and inequality.

Earlier I mentioned that Islam was perceived as a religion besieged by the West — much like the Third World as a whole. In Algeria today this identification between Islam and the Third World is compounded by an association, warranted or not, of conspicuous consumption and widening inequality with Algeria's apparent cultural Westernization — and that is a second reason. Calls for a break with the "West" fell on receptive ears insofar as inaccessible Western goods, CNN, nightclubs, foreign education, luxury hotels, injustice, and faithlessness all got lumped together with a social elite "doubly condemned for its economic privileges and its cultural proximity to the former colonial power."[120] Language politics also played a part. Arabization efforts notwithstanding, power remained in the hands of French-speaking Algerians, thereby adding to the less privileged and less educated classes' sense of cultural and economic marginalization. "Employ[ing] French to manage a country it destined for Arabic, and ceaselessly denounc[ing] the very language it used," the elite was viewed as denying to others the tools of successful integration in a Western-dominated world.[121] From social displeasure to anti-Westernism and then to religious zealotry and intolerance, the progression was a logical, if unfortunate, one.[122] Rached Al-Ghannouchi, a Tunisian Islamist leader, put it very plainly: "The secularism or Westernization did not anyway represent a popular movement. It was an effective minority, which had been able to marginalize the majority because it could understand the West, and understand foreigners, and communicate with the new international order. The majority did not have that knowledge so it was intellectually marginalized."[123] One might discern, as is customary in such instances, an interesting mix of envy and distaste, of desire and repulsion. But the interplay between the two, as also is usual, only serves to exacerbate the sense of alienation. In Algeria, the situation is made worse by unrelenting Western (especially French) attacks against the FIS. As Burgat remarks, "The supreme paradox was that the FLN in its battle against the FIS found itself constantly placed in a position of paraphrasing the French media," hardly an ideal position from which to recapture a squandered popular legitimacy.[124]

Other, slightly more subtle reasons help account for the juxtaposition of cultural and social claims. Some forms of disruption — the lack of social infrastructures, such as sports facilities or movie theaters; unemployment and the resulting idleness — are experienced at the levels of both material discomfort and cultural challenge. One good illustration is the housing crisis, for along with it come the destabilization of urban family patterns, acute overcrowding, and delayed marriages. That some young Algerians might react by seeking refuge in a more conservative and puritanical version of Islam should come as no surprise.[125] The social origins of the problem and its apparent cultural resolution rapidly get confused, to the point that the state's own attempted cultural synthesis between industrialization, urbanization, and development, on the one hand, and religious, traditional, and populist values on the other, is called into question. In this sense, the FIS is born of the meeting between social restlessness and a tailored religious script.

The next question I wish to address concerns the practical means Islamism used to set foot in Algeria. What were its points of entry? its passageways? The mosque was one. If we agree to think of Islam as a vocabulary and as a language, then the mosque stands out as one of its essential terms—a hallowed, untouchable arena in which inner spirituality and outward sociability intersect, and piety as well as collective norms, social etiquette, and social status are continuously defined and redefined.[126] Above all, it is the symbolic expression of the Islamic community, or *umma,* coming together. A mosque is, in Michael Gilsenan's words, a "vital [signifier] of the identity of a particular community in a particular space. [It] is more than the frame within which that community as a congregation of Muslims meets. It is a sign of the constitution of a number of people as a community and not merely as an agglomeration of individuals that has neither corporate existence nor claims to it."[127] Not for nothing, then, did the independent Algerian state strive to maintain tight control over this space, regulating everything from the construction of mosques to the recruitment of preachers and the content of their sermons.

One way to view the Islamists' rise to prominence is as a process through which they both took possession of this sacred site and radically inverted its meaning. This is another instance of space and its definition being central. Not only did the center of the nation's cultural life shift from the institutions of Third Worldism—public schools, universities, national enterprises, and so on—to the mosque but the mosque itself changed. Previously a symbol of the rulers' legitimacy, it became an index of their discredit and of the Islamists' own markedly different stature. Where religion and the mosque once marked the boundary between the pure and the impure, they now marked the frontier between state power and popular defiance.

It is important to bear in mind that, like all other Islamic signifiers, mosques are polysemous. They can take on a whole range of meanings and associations—with the state or against it; with one social group or with another; as instruments of the status quo or agents of revolutionary

challenge. Gilsenan, again, does a masterful job of illustrating the phenomenon as it occurred in Egypt. The transplantation of a Sufi mosque
from a popular quarter to Cairo's most fashionable district, he shows,
went hand in hand with a change in the nation's sociopolitical makeup
(Nasser had gone, Sadat had come) and with state efforts to enlist support from a neutralized ("cleaned up") version of "street Sufism" — both
events the ornate new mosque was intended to signify.[128]

Seen in such a way, the actions of Algerian Islamists' were highly subversive and, from the state's perspective, profoundly threatening. Friday
sermons became occasions for battles over politics and state power pos-
ing as theological dispute. Defending the right to mix religion and politics, FIS leader Abbassi Madani explained: "If the mosques are not there
for that, what purpose do they serve? . . . [The mosque] is the place for
all the acts of good, in which all the affairs of the Umma are treated. It is
in the mosque that the Caliph was designated and pronounced his political discourses. It is from there that the armies left to confront the
enemy."[129] Islamists also began building what are known as *ash-sha'b*
(popular) and *hurra* (free) mosques, makeshift constructions that lacked
the required official permit. "The organizers would then invite the inhabitants of the neighbourhood to bless the site with their prayers. Only
then, after the improvised, often ramshackle, building had been conse-
crated would the leaders go to the official authorities requesting authorization to complete a proper mosque on the site."[130] By then, popular sanctification made it all but impossible for the state to say no as it
helplessly watched these semiofficial mosques turn into focal points of a
spreading counterculture.[131]

The challenge to the state is thus directly physical. The space on which
unofficial mosques are built is seen as having been abandoned by the
authorities or, worse, conquered by the Islamists. In the manner of Muslim armies taking possession of territory, each new mosque is a new conquest, a *foutouh* (literally, "opening"), every inch of space "liberated" territory, protected against state intrusion. Sometimes this occurs in a very
concrete way: where the state's economic rationale might require tear-
ing down a dilapidated, run-down housing complex, residents have been
known to set up makeshift mosques as symbolic bulwarks. How dramatic, then, when a mosque actually breaks loose and extends, both
physically and symbolically, beyond its allotted space. The sacred zone
might "reach out into the streets, settle in public fora, fasten itself to the
workplace."[132] Improvised mosques might be created in the most ordinary, mundane places — a basement, a cellar, a garage, a room. As Ali

Belhadj, the FIS's second in command, proclaimed: "Toute la terre est une mosquée" [The earth in its entirety is a mosque].[133] In some factories, Abderrahmane Moussaoui notes, Islamic militants imposed their own sense of space and time, incorporating the mosque, its rituals, and its rhythm into everyday social life. "The state-controlled economic timetable is superseded by a spiritual timetable," in this context a rebellious one.[134] As the religious realm branches out, and sacred zones proliferate, time and space literally slip away from the state. They become, so to speak, uncontrollable.[135]

(Uncontrollable, but only so far as the state was concerned. Having painstakingly emancipated numerous mosques from state control, the FIS was not about to let them go. The unruliness was only relative, that is, and the chaos tightly supervised, as one hegemony quietly replaced the other. *Imams* had to be approved by the FIS; in disregard of the law, lists of candidates who prevailed in the 1990 local elections were presented to the public in FIS-controlled mosques; candidates backed by the FIS pledged to resign from their official positions if they ever were to be ejected from the party, and they also vowed to conduct discussions of sensitive issues in mosques.[136] The FIS had mastery over rituals, personnel, and the contents of religious discourse—it had learned its lesson well.)

There were other logical points of entry for Algerian Islamism. Having once monopolized the political, social, and cultural fields, and now being in the midst of gradual but steady disengagement, the Algerian state left behind a great vacuum. Islamism had little difficulty in connecting with social distress, for it involved itself precisely where the vacuum and the attendant need were experienced most severely.

The evidence for this effort abounds. Describing the situation in North Africa generally, Burgat explains that the Islamist movement gained access to "the heart of civil society . . . with methods of social and educational action that took advantage of the weaknesses of state policy," including "free medicine; distribution of school equipment; legal and administrative advice; the organization of youth in scouting and militant outings; the taking charge of civil and religious festivals."[137] Islamist militants also helped with garbage collection and were at the forefront of efforts to provide medical and other basic services to victims of the 1989 earthquake.[138] All in all, "the Islamist militants began to weave the fabric of a veritable 'counter-society.'"[139]

The FIS was banned, civil strife intensified, and the army, more openly than ever before, entered the picture. Still, little changed, and all kinds of behaviors were administered by the Islamists' shadow power. While some regions remained under exclusive state control, others reportedly fell to Islamist groups (not necessarily the FIS), near the capital, on the eastern coast, and in the West. In between, one found territories with overlapping jurisdictions, where the state was master of the physical land, but the FIS, its military offshoots, or splinter groups were in charge of all manner of domains, relating to culture, the economy, and social interaction. Reacting to a combination of intimidation and public pressure, a number of towns thus proscribed the sale of alcohol and canceled concerts featuring "sacrilegious" European artists. Enjoined by the Islamists, some vendors ceased selling cigarettes or newspapers; tax collectors refused to do their job; and public transportation was increasingly segregated along gender lines, men in front, women behind (and more and more often behind a veil as well).[140] In a throwback to the wartime FLN, armed Islamic groups have been known to threaten and punish those who violated their injunction to boycott tobacco, other products of mass consumption, even schools.[141] Meanwhile, responding to a wave of targeted terror, Algeria's foreign community began to flee in droves, changing in almost physical ways the country's relation to the world.

The roots of contemporary Algerian Islamism, its ideological content, and the manner in which it came to be embedded in social relations help shed some light on the social background of its followers. Recall, for example, what earlier was said about the urban masses, "part of the ever vaster world of bidonvilles, slums and densely packed 'old cities' that so mark [the Middle East] as a whole."[142] At the symbolic center of the state's collapse was the city. Large-scale unemployment and a dramatic housing shortage led to the marginalization of vast segments of the Algerian people and signaled the troubled passage from a rural to an urban society. Deprived of traditional modes of social intercourse, yet without any access to new ones, many city dwellers found themselves adrift in a state of increasing isolation and exclusion. Islamism offered comforting social norms — dress codes, ritualized prayers — and a sense of collective purpose to young, disaffected, and marginalized Algerians in desperate search of both. As might be expected, Algiers, Oran, Constantinople, and, within them, large numbers of displaced rural migrants became the carriers and the conveyors of a radicalized religious message of opposition to corruption, injustice, foreign capital, and foreign culture.

But that is not all. The urban young and unemployed might well constitute the FIS's main human reservoir,[143] yet its financial backers and much of its leadership come from very different origins. Benefactors have included members of the Algerian middle classes, who finance the construction of unofficial mosques, and the movement also has a strong merchant component.[144] Nor was the state able to satisfy the demands of large segments of the intelligentsia, who were by-products of pressure for Arabization yet victims of the economy's maladjustment to this evolution. The Algerian example thus draws our attention to the important role in the growth of Islamist militancy of the intellectuals, the petite bourgeoisie, and the middle strata, threatened by the contraction of the political and cultural elite, by the loss of opportunity, and by the internationalization of the domestic economy.

Moreover, it draws our attention to the crucial fact that neither the FIS nor, for that matter, Islamism constitutes a uniform movement. In the Algerian case, a variety of social groups and manifestations of social discontent gradually latched onto the FIS. Indeed, the success of Islamism in Algeria can be attributed in part to its ability to weave together disparate, and even competing, religious and social threads. The FIS is an aggregation of antagonistic religious traditions: urban reformists; rural traditionalists; "algerianists" (so called because of their belief in Algeria's specificity, they represent the moderate branch of Algerian Islam, generally composed of French-speaking members of the country's intellectual elite, educated by the state only to be neglected by it); and "salafists" (the plebeian, tradition-oriented, and Arabic-speaking branch of Algerian Islam, with ties to the broader pan-Islamic movement). The FIS is also a remarkable amalgamation of social groups. By-products of Algeria's truncated urbanization join their fortunes with the middle class, artisans, merchants, small business owners, teachers, and even members of the Arabic-speaking elite. All share a distaste for the state that has abandoned them and an attraction to a worldview that, by blaming their situation on that state's moral shortcomings, can help restore their bruised sense of self-worth. As a result, the FIS has become the vehicle of a project that is at once morally conservative and socially progressive, theocratic and yet pseudo-democratic, welfare-statist and laissez-faire. Such latent contradictions between those who seek a different part in the game and those who clamor for new rules entirely, between those with shrinking opportunities and those with none at all, between the Arabic-speaking who feel left out and the French-speaking who feel threatened, inevitably must come to a head.

At one level they already have. Witness for example the tensions between the FIS's more moderate "algerianists," who favor participation in the electoral process and negotiations with the regime, and the more radical *salafiyya* or Afghan branches, dedicated to the violent overthrow of the regime. Labat calls this the struggle between "technocrats" and "theocrats." Witness, too, the sudden emergence of an array of armed offshoots, most notably the Armed Islamic Group, whose loyalty to the Islamic Front is a matter of considerable doubt and whose recourse to urban terrorism a source of deep controversy.[145] Equally revealing was the FIS's attitude during the Gulf war, caught as it was between Saudi financiers and a generally pro-Iraqi mass base. (In the end, and though it condemned the invasion of Kuwait, the FIS staunchly opposed Western military intervention and Arab complicity in it. Dressed in military fatigues, Ali Belhadj proclaimed a *jihad*, or holy war, against European and American invaders and called on Algeria to send troops in defense of its Iraqi brethren.)[146]

❖   ❖   ❖

We come at last to the dismaying question of violence. Between February 1992 and the spring of 1995 the war cost an estimated forty thousand lives. On the one side young men are among the targets; on the other side, intellectuals, women, foreigners, tax collectors, and police constables. The FIS's armed wing, the Islamic Salvation Army (AIS), is said to have counted roughly twenty-five thousand members; the more radical GIA, about half that number.

The history of present-day violence in Algeria begins with Mustafa Bouyali's Armed Islamic Algerian Movement, which for five years led bloody attacks against representatives of the state. Bouyali was gunned down in February 1987, and his guerrilla movement came to an abrupt end. In the intervening years, however, he had become a romantic hero to many Algerians, and a symbol to which they would later turn. Many of Bouyali's followers came together again in the early nineties, in the aftermath of the first clashes between the army and strikers and, subsequently, of the cancellation of the parliamentary elections in 1992. Their relationship with the FIS at this stage was uneasy: the armed groups distrusted the politicians' willingness to negotiate with the regime, and leaders of the Front feared that too intimate an association with the armed movement might tarnish their reputation.

Soon, however, the need for the FIS to take control of the multiplying armed groups, despite the potential harm to its image, became apparent. Indeed, if it failed to exercise such control, the FIS ran the risk of appearing obsolete to its followers and impotent to its foes. In 1994, leaders of the FIS founded the AIS in an attempt to bring together the various armed groups.

They were only partly successful. A number of young Algerians rejected the FIS leadership and, refusing any possible compromise with the impious state, would not join the FIS. The GIA grew out of this sentiment, less as a unified movement than as a collection of scattered groups determined to use violence at all costs. Hence the increase in urban terrorism and the indiscriminate assassination of persons viewed as belonging to the regime's sociopolitical basis: bureaucrats, journalists, foreigners, teachers, magistrates, and even the mothers, wives, and sisters of members of the security forces. Predictably, the GIA recruits most heavily among the disaffected youth of the slums, the unemployed, veterans of the Afghan war, and even members of criminal gangs for whom the politicization of banditry offers a unique means of social rehabilitation. The GIA is an extreme manifestation of Algeria's social and economic failings, the dark underside of uncontrolled urbanization, privatization, and the enrichment of the few.

The fierce violence of the conflict is one of those phenomena for which explanations are both too many and too few. The centralized, centripetal nature of the regime is a potential reason. So many within the system depended on their relationship to the state for their well-being that the stakes of any power struggle automatically were magnified. This was true of the political, administrative, and military elites, direct employees of the state, but also of a vast array of consumers and traders for whom connections to state actors were the chief determinants of success. Add to this that the working class enjoyed a social instead of an economic salary and that, for reasons having to do with the scope of French colonial rule, Algeria's bourgeoisie remained tributary to the state, and one can grasp how difficult it is for power to change hands in a peaceful, consensual manner. In short, there was — is — far too much to gain by conquering power, and far too much to lose by relinquishing it, for such things to happen without a serious fight.

Nor was Algeria's political system particularly adept at coping with dissension. Negating the division between public and private spheres, branding all disagreement as treachery and all politics as good or evil, the state automatically amplified the significance of dissent and managed to turn even its most localized expression into direct (and threatening) challenges to the regime's authority. For this reason as well, nonviolent forms of contest were alien to the political system.[147]

More generally, much of what accounted for the rise of radical Islam also can help explain the resort to violence. That is not to say that all Islam is violent nor that all islamic resistance is a *jihad*. Rather, the same conditions we canvassed in trying to explain the religion are useful clues to understanding the violence. These include years without free expression or even a semblance of democracy and the immoderate moralism of official discourse, both of which contributed to the radicalization — and militarization — of Algerian politics.

That the first signs of violence erupted at a time when steps finally were being taken to loosen the state's and the FLN's grip on power is not as paradoxical as might first appear to be the case. As Addi explains, the habituation to a rigid, centralized system by then had taken place, and apparent efforts by the state to disinvolve itself (politically through democratization and economically through privatization) were perceived as leaving a temporary vacuum rather than representing a lasting transfer of power to the "private sphere" or to "civil society." The vacuum represented both opportunity (to prevail) and peril (to lose out), and the stakes remained access to economic well-being but also resolution of highly charged questions of identity (religion, language, gender roles, etc.). This was a mix almost certain to unleash furious competition.[148]

The ubiquity of violence in Algeria's past is another potential reason for the fierce character of the contemporary struggle. At almost every stage in their recent history, Algerians' relation to the state and to politics generally has been one of coercion, force, and resistance. René Galissot suggests one look as far back as the Muslim conquest or Ottoman rule, but French colonialism suffices as a starting point.[149] Memories of brutal invasion, of Abdelkader's early revolt, and of defiance by acts of sabotage or banditry remain, magnified through the prism of popular legend. The militarization of Algerian politics persisted even after independence. While most states have armies, Algeria's army has a state — a saying borne out by the military's role in Ben Bella's rise and in his fall, by its dominant position under Boumedienne, and by its behind-the-scenes maneuverings under Chadli.

But, without a doubt, the role of the war of national liberation is primary in this respect, as is the mythology it has spun. Algerians have been reminded far too often of the glory of the wartime *mujahid* for them not to feel some degree of reverence, however ill-informed, for violence and guerrilla warfare. To quote Benjamin Stora, "One cannot teach with impunity the principle that armed struggle is central to the nation's construction and then act surprised when that principle is put to use."[150]

Indeed, and paradoxically, the war is the dominant point of reference on all sides: in the French media, for dramatic effect; in the state's discourse, to conjure up images of the *mujahid* defending the legacy of 1954; and in the narrative of Algeria's Islamists, who seek to portray their fight as the final phase of the liberation struggle. For all three, the new civil war is best viewed as the second war of independence, a 1954 redux in which differing versions of the past serve to vindicate conflicting designs for the future.[151]

(But all that is mere irony. The real tragedy is that the guerrilla fighters turned statesmen or army leaders seem to have unlearned the lessons they once so masterfully taught the world: that, absent popular support, military power cannot defeat an armed insurrection and that the search for a moderate "third force" to avoid dealing with one's principal opponent is mere illusion. Instead, they have resuscitated the old folktale propagated by the French — that it would have taken just a little more firepower, just a little less politics, just a trifle more backbone.)

Why, then, the violence? The concentration of power, the inflexibility of the political system, the extreme moralization of politics, and the nation's long history of warfare all no doubt played their part, but even in combination, they take us only so far. The same totalitarian statism and vilification of dissent (only worse) could be found elsewhere, yet change has not always come at such a price — witness the case of so much of the former Soviet bloc. As I stated at the outset, satisfactory explanations are abundant and yet lacking. In the end, the secret may well lie in the crass accidents of history, the clumsy mismanagement of politics — the decision to ban the FIS when no other organization could channel the desperation of those Algerians who felt marginalized and excluded; the refusal to seriously negotiate with FIS leaders early enough to preempt the rise of the GIA; an ill-timed terrorist attack; or perhaps simply a wrong personality at the wrong place at the wrong time.

History handed over to the Islamists an eclectic and apparently limitless supply of social resentment, cultural frustration, and ideological waste. This, I think, is both their blessing and their curse. From one perspective, the FIS (and, more broadly, Islamism) flourishes as a loose assortment of the true believers, the urban underclass, the culturally marginalized, an anxious petty bourgeoisie, and artisans, villagers, or merchants who yearn for the certainty and stability that seems so much a thing of the past. Yet from another, the FIS has been forced to minister to urgent, abundant, and therefore unavoidably inconsistent needs.

In this curious sort of way, the FIS appears to be the worthy descendant of the FLN, which itself tried to don the mantles of the proletariat, the peasantry, the technocracy — all at the same time.[152] Nor is this much of a surprise, really. Having deliberately created a political vacuum, imposed the myth of a unanimous and monolithic people, and suppressed the slightest hint of a democratic opposition, the FLN — once its brand of Third Worldism had become a spent force — cleared the path for an alternative that shared its hegemonic, monopolistic outlook. And what better conveyor of this refurbished, fuzzy blend of populism and messianism than religion — than Islam? A different corps of clerics would be needed, perhaps (though only perhaps), but like Third Worldism, Islamism would have an answer for everything, and for everyone. Several, in fact. And for the time being at least.

Afterthoughts

On the day he was gunned down, Said Mekbel, editor of the Algerian *Matin,* published what would turn out to be his last article. He wrote of leaving home without knowing whether he would get to work and of leaving work without knowing whether he ever would see his home again.[1] Like President Boudiaf's two years earlier, Mekbel's precise, macabre clairvoyance came to symbolize the sorry state of contemporary Algeria, in which words had become routine omens of death waiting to happen.

It was a long way from the postcolonial fervor to this grisly war with an ever-narrowing power apparatus on the one side, Islamist forces increasingly dominated by the extremist GIA on the other, and countless civilian casualties in between. At the end of the road, I would venture to guess, lies an Algeria that, if not "Islamist," at the very least reflects a deal between the army and the FIS.[2] There is too much hunger for power on both sides, and far too little stomach for genuine democracy on either, for it to be otherwise.

But whatever the outcome, this much can be said: Algeria expresses in its most pure and most concentrated form the degradation and repudiation of the Third Worldist ideal it once embodied. After roughly thirty years during which it has had to rub elbows with bureaucracy, corruption, social contradiction, and economic inequity, it has been reduced to a litany of garbled dogmas, neither believed nor practiced. Having failed in Algeria and beyond, Third Worldism leaves little of itself behind. Having chosen history as its sole judge, it has been irreparably disavowed by history's cruel verdict.[3]

❖   ❖   ❖

Progress, I once read, is the record of the deeds of men and women who did not know their place. What was it about Third Worldism that so appealed to intellectuals and militants in both the First World and the Third? Precisely, I suppose, that resistance to rank, to status, and to destiny, the sense of losing one's way, purposely and defiantly, and of wandering where one clearly does not belong. The audacity, the insolence, the impetuousness of it all was what charmed and attracted. Alone, Castro stood up to America and all its might; Algeria defied France; Nasser, a European coalition, and Israel, and Arab reaction. So much of what passes for politics feeds on such crude emotions, and so much of what is achieved, good and bad, is inspired by them.

A book such as this ends up revealing as much about its author as it does about its intended subject matter. Far more, typically. I too was a prey of Third Worldism, one of the seduced and ensnared. Here and there throughout these pages I must have betrayed that sometime existence, those onetime sensations. There is no real cause for regret, though. For as I have tried to make clear throughout these pages, all our visions of North and South — developmentalism, modernization theory, dependency, and, now, democratization and nation-building — are tainted or filtered, products of knowledge and of interpretation, which is to say, of ideology. Erasing the ambiguous, erecting the clear-cut, for the sake of expediency, at the expense of accuracy — such are the ways and the wiles of things ideological. We have no other means of apprehending the social world, really, and though other systems of thought might well have been less obdurate and less constraining, Third Worldism — so captivating, so utopian — was not a bad one to start with after all.

Besides, I had what some might consider the good fortune of catching the dream on its way out. By the time I could make any sense of all this, Castro's beard was graying, Arafat's half-shaved one was beginning to irritate more than it frightened, and Nkrumah was gone — as were Nasser, Lumumba, Sukarno, Che Guevara, and Modibo Keita. I had missed some of Third Worldism's most revered figures; in return, though, my disillusionment was far less painful because the illusions themselves had been so ephemeral.

Like others, nonetheless, I have had to come to terms with what has become of our past. What are we to make of the FIS, of tribalism and nativism, of the mounting despair? What does this say, in fine, about Third Worldism? That it was a slice of history, first of all, a specific ideological and political construct linked intimately to colonialism and its overthrow. It was the paradigm within which individual existences were made collective, a space within which the oppressed (colonized and poor) were able to reappropriate precious means of discourse and of action. Key here is dignity, the yearning for equal status and worth that both was impelled by and grew out of decolonization. In Algeria as elsewhere, Third Worldism translated into independence, a radical reshaping of the world, the attainment of certain basic socioeconomic goals. The new states were demigods of sorts, born out of disjunctive moments, mythical events: violence, wars of national liberation, martyrdom. They became surrogates for theories of social and economic progress and for legends of moral overcoming. Moreover, one should not forget what previously had been in place, namely, colonial rule, which at its worst meant ethnic or racial discrimination and oppression but almost always economic uprooting, political dislocation, and cultural disorientation. That had a lot to do, as I have tried to show, with the establishment of strong, centralized nation-states and of single-party systems, the personalization of rule, the lack of tolerance for dissent — everything that, in hindsight, was wrong and pernicious.

Questions are raised by Third Worldism's demise, as they are by the types of transitions we witness today: from one Mecca to another, from socialism to free-market capitalism, from Ortega to Chamoro, and, far more damaging, from Assad to Assad, and still Assad, and still Saddam Hussein, and still Castro. The permanence of an Assad, the persistence of a Hussein: this, more than anything else, is the real tragedy of Third Worldism. The people were equated with the state, the state with the ruler, the ruler with the dream. Third Worldists, too often, lumped them together and worshiped them all. Under the circumstances, Third Worldism soon found itself at one, then several removes from the beguiling utopia of the beginning. The tendency to idealize both the romantic ends and the grubby means history lends us to accomplish them is one price of ideological myopia. Leon Wieseltier has a nice expression for it: he calls it confusing the status of victim and that of saint.[4] Third Worldist leaders, emerging from decades of colonial oppression, might well have qualified for one, but they never quite made the other.

As I write these words, I have before me a copy of Ernest Gellner's recent meditations on the fall of Marxism in the former Soviet Union. He attributes this "ignominious" collapse in part to the system's "monolithic nature . . . its fusion of the social, economic, political, and ideological hierarchies. . . . The entire structure was so rigid," he concludes, "that when a large part of it went, *everything went*."[5] That pretty much sums up the case for Third Worldism as well. Its system of representation was holistic, centralized, to be sure, but in a way it was more than that: centripetal, as it were, each individual ideological item (the state, the party, history, the economy) referring back to the core, the so-called popular will. One believed in it unconditionally or not at all. Once doubts about the existence of a popular will or about the state's capacity to represent it began to creep in, the whole had nothing more to lean on. So everything went.

I always have been rather skeptical of hasty burials and promises of instant successors. Now that the Third Worldist alien graft is finally out of the way, we are told, countries of the developing world must choose between two "natural" paths: traditionalism and modernity. Religious fundamentalism, ethnic polarization, and tribal solidarities represent the perilous call of cultural essence, leaving as the only other option the summons of pragmatism, or simple reality, that is, political pluralism (or constitutional democracy) and economic liberalism (or market capitalism). My own sense is that this is to look at things upside down and to present as alternatives what are largely causally related phenomena.

The belief underlying the prevailing view is that the transition from Third Worldism, where it has occurred, reflects a categorical rejection of failed state-centered policies. Certainly, this was partly the case, but only partly. For what was rejected was less hegemonic statism than the hybrid offsprings to which it gave way, crossbreeds between market and centralized organizational principles, between state manager and private entrepreneur. What that means is that the "superfluous" class of unemployed juveniles is as much the child of state socialism as it is the progeny of the international marketplace and that "traditionalism" is not the converse of "modernity" but often its other, less seductive side. In other words, nativism, Islamism, and the like have been by-products of—not alternatives to—privatization and the state's overall disengagement.

Let me put this another way: neither Western goods, styles, and culture nor consumerism and private enterprise are instruments in a clash between reason and the underdeveloped world's innate, and stubborn, traditionalism, as some Westerners are prone to see it, and some Third World regimes all too quick to concur. That view assumes away issues of distribution, of unequal access, of uneven information. Jorge Castaneda has noted the results of increased reliance on the private sector and of deregulated markets in Latin America: layer upon layer of poverty, sharpening inequalities, more crime, and less safety.[6] The so-called liberalization of the Third World has meant a social split, a separation, not a merging, nor does it pit modernity against tradition, but wealth against want. It is these inequities, in part, that prompt the ethnic or religious reflex — acts of self-preservation more than of self-delusion.

This raises further questions. As in Eastern Europe and the former Soviet Union, in the Third World economic liberalization and democratization probably are twin goals pursued by some members of the middle class and of the articulate intelligentsia. To many other people, however, one goal has worked directly against the other. Up until now, economic transformations have intensified social polarization and quickened the pace of state disinvestment. As a result, political pluralism and competitive elections have been incapable of performing their regulating function, that is, to transfer social conflicts to a level where they are more easily managed by the state. Instead, they have been a pathway to reborn ethnicism or religious intolerance; they have taken the form of demonstrations, riots, extra-institutional protest, and, in some cases, violence. One commentator observed that "economic liberalism might well exacerbate social tensions that political liberalism, far from taming, might then turn into a general crisis of the political system."[7] Thus, even if we assume that social polarization and marginalization hastened the demise of Third Worldism, it does not follow that economic liberalization and pluralistic democracy will be better able to cope with the public feelings the former have generated or even to withstand them. There is, in short, no necessary congruence between what caused the passing of Third Worldism and the system that took its place.

And then there are all the unaddressed issues with which we began: the Third World's uneven relations with the industrialized world, its hunger, its persistent poverty, its exploitation, some would say. These facts are difficult to get around. In the end, Third Worldism might not have made much difference — who knows? Yet it is scarcely an exaggeration to say that within today's dominant representations of the world such problems, perhaps even the regions in which they arise, appear as mere afterthoughts. Meanwhile, the gap widens, both internally and internationally, both materially and culturally, between haves and havenots, between those who understand the rules of the game and those who hardly are aware the game has been going on in the first place.

In the end, it all comes down to a question of rank, of status, and of destiny, I suppose. A question of progress. A question of men and women forgetting their place. Or rather remembering, again and again, how not to know it.

Notes

Introduction

1. Yves Lacoste, *Contre les anti-tiers-mondistes*, 17.
2. Ernest Gellner, "Unknown Apollo of Biskra," 277.
3. Fouad Ajami, *Arab Predicament*, 68.
4. A further justification for selecting Algeria relates to the paucity of English-language works on the subject. There are some notable exceptions, for example, books by Quandt, Ruedy, and Entelis; but on the whole, there is very little indeed, certainly nothing compared with the vast literature that exists in French. For a country that is so evidently becoming of interest to American scholars and policymakers alike, this is a gap that needs to be filled.
5. The works of Anthony Smith, in particular, provide both enlightening analysis and comprehensive bibliographies on the subject of nationalism; see his *Theories of Nationalism* and *State and Nation in the Third World*. Other works include Karl Deutsch and William Foltz, *Nation-Building;* and Elie Kedourie, *Nationalism*. Concerning the Third World and the international system, Robert Mortimer's *Third World Coalition in International Politics* and Stephen Krasner's *Structural Conflict* are particularly noteworthy.

Chapter 1

1. Edward Said writes: "The history of all cultures is the history of cultural borrowings. Cultures are not impermeable; just as Western science borrowed from Arabs, they had borrowed from India and Greece. Culture is never just a matter of ownership, of borrowing and lending with absolute debtors and creditors, but rather of appropriations, common experiences, and interdependencies of all kinds among different cultures" (*Culture and Imperialism*, 217).

2. Anthony Smith offers useful guideposts for such an enterprise in *Theories of Nationalism.*

3. Eric Hobsbawm, *Age of Extremes,* 200.

4. Smith, *State and Nation in the Third World,* 29. On the nature of the colonial administrative apparatus, particularly in the African context, see also J. F. A. Ajayi, "Colonialism"; Immanuel Wallerstein, "Colonial Era in Africa"; and idem, ed., *Social Change, the Colonial Situation.*

5. Wallerstein, "Colonial Era in Africa," 411.

6. Martin Kilson, "Emergent Elite of Black Africa, 1900 to 1960."

7. See Hobsbawm, *Age of Extremes,* 213.

8. Ibid., 214.

9. On the Pan-African movement, see Colin Legum, *Pan-Africanism;* Du-Bois's quote appears on p. 25.

10. Alexandre Bennigsen and Chantal Lemercier-Quelquejay, *Sultan Galiev: Le père de la révolution tiers-mondiste,* 275.

11. *L'Ikdam,* quoted in *Bulletin de l'Afrique Française,* June 1927. See also Messali Hadj, *Les mémoires de Messali Hadj,* 157.

12. Quoted in Claude Liauzu, *Aux origines des tiers-mondismes,* 31.

13. Basil Davidson, *Black Star.*

14. See, e.g., Jean Ziegler, *Contre l'ordre du monde,* 189–90.

15. See, e.g., Elie Kedourie, Introduction, 81–90.

16. See, e.g., Albert Hourani, *History of the Arab Peoples,* 310, for a discussion of the conflictual relation between Tunisian assimilationists and the French *colons.*

17. Davidson continues, explaining that

> the British were the most systematic in imposing this sentence to nowhere, but at least they were less hypocritical than others. They held out no empty promises of "assimilation" to the white man's condition, and they gave rather few lectures on the universal rights of man. Indulging in both, the French were just as systematic in their racism while camouflaging its reality behind Jacobin verbiage that promised much and meant, in practice, remarkably little. The Belgians took their line from the French, although with less verbiage, while the Italians, Portuguese, and Spanish (with the Germans out of the picture after 1918) generally retired behind a miasmic fog of Christian beatitude which none of them intended to honor, or even thought they should honor. (Basil Davidson, *Black Man's Burden,* 47–48).

The French attitude is confirmed by a 1929 report in the colonial police files castigating the "annoying [*fâcheux*] state of mind among the half-civilized along the West [African] Coast. In daily contact with Europeans, they have acquired ideas about equality that sometimes take the form of demands expressed in an unacceptable tone [*sur un ton déplacé*]" (quoted in ibid., 171).

18. Resistance by traditional Sufi orders in the Arab world is recounted in Hourani, *History of the Arab Peoples,* 312–13.

19. While his analysis arguably understates the indirect role played by traditional ideologies, Hobsbawm notes that "none of the successful movements of liberation in the backward world before the 1970s was inspired or achieved by traditional or neo-traditional ideologies" (*Age of Extremes,* 201).

20. Davidson, *Black Man's Burden,* 48.

21. Ibid., 104–6. Ajayi also emphasizes these points: "Once conquest had

been achieved, it was the submissive chiefs, the custodians of law, order and hallowed custom, rather than radical educated élite, who became the favoured agents of European administration" ("Colonialism," 505; see also Wallerstein, "Colonial Era in Africa," 409).

22. See Samir Amin et al., *Le Tiers Monde et la gauche*, 8.

23. Quoted from Engels's article in the *Northern Star*, January 22, 1848, in René Galissot and Gilbert Badia, *Marx, marxisme, et Algérie*, 26.

24. Maurice Godelier, *Horizons, trajets marxistes en anthropologie*, 2:46; see also Galissot and Badia, *Marx, marxisme, et Algérie*.

25. Samir Amin, *Eurocentrism*, 120.

26. Leon Trotsky, quoted in Jean Ziegler, *Vive le pouvoir!* 225.

27. Tom Nairn, "Marxism and the Modern Janus," 3, 27.

28. Liauzu, *Aux origines des tiers-mondismes*, 55.

29. Bennigsen and Lemercier-Quelquejay, *Sultan-Galiev*.

30. For a detailed, thought-provoking discussion of the appeal of the Russian Revolution, see François Furet, *Le passé d'une illusion*.

31. For a discussion of the origins of the concept, see François Furet, *Penser la révolution française*.

32. Kedourie, *Nationalism*, 9; Alfred Cobban, *The Nation-State and National Self-Determination*, 219; Davidson, *Black Man's Burden*, 10. See also Smith, *State and Nation in the Third World*.

33. This privileging of the territorial link can be traced back to the concept of "autochthony." These notions are discussed in Jean Manas, "This Land Is My Land."

34. See Bertrand Badie, *L'état importé*, 82ff.; see also Paul Alliès, *L'invention du territoire*.

35. Davidson, *Black Man's Burden*, 116–17.

36. Ibid., 49.

37. Badie, *L'état importé*, 86.

38. Hourani, *History of the Arab Peoples*, 343–44.

39. Davidson, *Black Man's Burden*, 115, 116; see also James Coleman, "Tradition and Nationalism in Tropical Africa."

40. Said, *Culture and Imperialism*, 210.

41. Furet makes the interesting observation that in Europe nationalism combined the appeal of modernity with the reassurance of tradition (Furet, *Le passé d'une illusion*, 58). To which one might add, in the case of the Third World, that nation-statism joined the comfort of mimicking Europe to the promise of defying her.

Chapter 2

1. Mohammed Harbi, *1954*, 153–54.

2. William Quandt, *Revolution and Political Leadership;* C. H. Moore, *Politics in North Africa;* Elbassi Hermassi, *Etat et société au Maghreb;* Janet Dorsch Zagoria, "The Rise and Fall of the Movement of Messali Hadj in Algeria."

3. See, e.g., Moore, *Politics in North Africa*, 34–38; Hermassi, *Etat et société*

au Maghreb, 104 – 9; and Zagoria, "The Rise and Fall of the Movement of Messali Hadj in Algeria."

4. As Quandt wrote, the FLN's decision to act "was based on a common agreement that the legal nationalist movement had failed and was disintegrating, that national independence was the primary condition for Muslim Algerians both to regain their honor and to advance socially and economically and that violence was the only way that the French colonial system could be destroyed in Algeria. Beyond these simple perceptions there was little agreement" (*Revolution and Political Leadership,* 93; see also David Ottaway and Marina Ottaway, *Algeria*).

5. This theme is discussed in more detail in part 3.

6. See Benjamin Stora, *L'Algérie en 1995,* 23 – 24.

7. Jean-Claude Vatin, *L'Algérie politique,* 316.

8. Ali Mérad, *Le réformisme musulman en Algérie.*

9. Mustapha Benabdellaziz, "Education et politique"; Gellner, "Unknown Apollo of Biskra."

10. Henri Alleg, ed., *La guerre d'Algérie.*

11. Abdelkader Djeghloul, "La formation des intellectuels algériens modernes (1880 – 1930)"; Gilbert Meynier, *L'Algérie révélée;* Benjamin Stora and Zakya Daoud, *Ferhat Abbas.*

12. See, e.g., Harbi's *Les archives de la révolution algérienne; Aux origines du Front de Libération Nationale;* and *Le F.L.N.* See also Mohamed Guénanéche and Mahfoud Kaddache, *L'Étoile Nord-Africaine;* and idem, *Le Parti du Peuple Algérien.*

13. On the history of this period, see Charles-André Julien, *L'Afrique du Nord en marche;* and Charles-Robert Ageron, *Histoire de l'Algérie contemporaine.*

14. John P. Entelis, *Algeria,* 25.

15. Ahmed Koulakssis and Gilbert Meynier, *L'émir Khaled,* 35.

16. Ibid., 37.

17. See Vatin, *L'Algérie politique,* 139ff. On Abdelkader, see Bruno Etienne, "Abd-El-Kader"; and René Galissot, "Abdel Kader et la nationalité algérienne."

18. Hervé Bourges and Claude Wauthier, *Les 50 Afriques,* 45 – 46.

19. See André Nouschi, *Enquête sur le niveau de vie des populations rurales constantinoises de la conquête jusqu'en 1919;* Xavier Yacono, *La colonisation des plaines du Chétif;* and N. Kielstra, "Was the Algerian Revolution a Peasant War?"

20. See Larbi Talha, "Le dépérissement des classes moyennes pré-capitalistes," 92.

21. Eric Wolfe, quoted in Mahfoud Bennoune, "The Introduction of Nationalism into Rural Algeria," 1.

22. Bennoune, "Introduction of Nationalism into Rural Algeria," 2.

23. See Talha, "Le dépérissement des classes moyennes pré-capitalistes."

24. Pierre Bourdieu and Abdelmalek Sayad, *Le déracinement,* 34.

25. Kielstra, "Was the Algerian Revolution a Peasant War?" 173 – 74.

26. On these and other aspects of French cultural policies, see Mostefa Lacheraf, *L'Algérie;* Yvonne Turin, *Affrontements culturels dans l'Algérie coloniale;* and Fanny Colonna, *Instituteurs algériens, 1883 – 1939.*

27. Michael Gilsenan, *Recognizing Islam,* 145.

28. Vatin, *L'Algérie politique*, 102.
29. Koulakssis and Meynier, *L'émir Khaled*, 29.
30. See Lahouari Addi, *L'Algérie et la démocratie*, 26–27.
31. See Harbi, *1954*, 100–101.
32. Gilsenan, *Recognizing Islam*, 143. Gilsenan explains that the Mahdi "is a member of the Prophet's family who will return at the end of time to establish the reign of social justice on earth and to purify religion" (ibid.).
33. Ibid., 148.
34. Belkacem Saadallah, "The Rise of Algerian Nationalism," 47.
35. Vatin, *L'Algérie politique*, 141.
36. Gilsenan, *Recognizing Islam*, 145.
37. Koulakssis and Meynier, *L'émir Khaled*, 84–86.
38. On the concept of "ethnonationalism," see J. Manas, "This Land Is My Land"; see also the discussion on nation-statism in chapter 1 above.
39. Gilsenan, *Recognizing Islam*, 152.
40. The intellectual reformists are not to be confused with the religious reformists, to whom I will refer later.
41. See "Contribution à la connaissance de l'émir Khaled," *Algérie-Actualité*, March 13–19, 1980.
42. Vatin, *L'Algérie politique*, 168–69.
43. The best biography of Ferhat Abbas is Stora and Daoud, *Ferhat Abbas*.
44. This need to be close to the common people is well documented by Stora and Daoud; see, e.g., ibid., 74.
45. Ibid., 34.
46. Koulakssis and Meynier, *L'émir Khaled*, 219–20.
47. See Djeghloul, "La formation des intellectuels algériens modernes," 73; and Koulakssis and Meynier, *L'émir Khaled*, 6–7. Many would take issue with this comparison between Abbas and Khaled, as well as with the contention that Abbas was not an integrationist. Abbas's now famous article "En marge du nationalisme: La France c'est moi!" written in 1936, has widely been thought to hold the clue to his convictions. In words that would prove so costly to him, he asserted: "I have not discovered an Algerian homeland [*patrie*]. I have questioned history; I have questioned the dead and the living; I have visited the cemeteries; nobody has mentioned it. . . . Would a Muslim Algerian seriously contemplate building the future on the dust of the past?" (reprinted in Claude Collot and Jean-Robert Henry, *Le Mouvement National Algérien*, 65–66. For a discussion, see Stora and Daoud, *Ferhat Abbas*, 73–77; and Koulakssis and Meynier, *L'émir Khaled*, 7).
48. This theme is considered in Djeghloul, "La formation des intellectuels algériens modernes."
49. Emir Khaled, quoted in John Ruedy, *Modern Algeria*, 130.
50. Harbi, *1954*, 107.
51. Koulakssis and Meynier, *L'émir Khaled*, 322.
52. Ruedy, *Modern Algeria*, 129.
53. Jacques Berque, *Le Maghreb entre deux guerres*, 242.
54. Ferhat Abbas, *La nuit coloniale*, 123.
55. Djeghloul, "La formation des intellectuels algériens modernes," 64.

56. Emir Khaled, quoted in Mahfoud Kaddache, *Histoire du nationalisme algérien*, 1 : 183.

57. Ferhat Abbas, quoted in Charles-Robert Ageron, "Ferhat Abbas et l'évolution politique de l'Algérie musulmane pendant la seconde guerre mondiale," 127.

58. Hannah Arendt, *On Revolution*, 88.

59. Ibid., 76.

60. Clifford Geertz, *Islam Observed*, 76.

61. Koulakssis and Meynier, *L'émir Khaled*, 239.

62. Ibid., 54.

63. Abbas, quoted in Stora and Daoud, *Ferhat Abbas*, 32.

64. Abbas, quoted in *La République Algérienne*, no. 10 (December 11, 1953).

65. Abbas, quoted in ibid., no. 9 (December 4, 1953).

66. Emir Khaled, quoted in Koulakssis and Meynier, *L'émir Khaled*, 291.

67. Emir Khaled, quoted in Guénanéche and Kaddache, *L'Étoile Nord-Africaine*, 21.

68. Djeghloul, "La formation des intellectuels algériens modernes," 74–75.

69. Hadj, *Les mémoires de Messali Hadj*, 167.

70. For relevant statistics, see Liauzu, *Aux origines des tiers-mondismes*, 172; and Jean-Louis Carlier, "La première Étoile Nord-Africaine."

71. The first Messalist organization, the ENA, was banned by the French government in 1937. It was followed by the PPA, which, unlike the ENA, was based in Algeria. In 1939 the French banned the PPA, which thereafter became a clandestine movement. In 1945 the PPA's leadership founded the MTLD, which enjoyed legal status. At that time, then, Messalism possessed both a legal and a covert wing.

72. Liauzu, *Aux origines des tiers-mondismes*, 139, 9.

73. See Mohamed Harbi, "Violence, nationalisme, islamisme," 27.

74. Nguyen Van Tao, quoted in Liauzu, *Aux origines des tiers-mondismes*, 22.

75. Liauzu, *Aux origines des tiers-mondismes*, 107.

76. Ibid., 130.

77. Hourani, *History of the Arab Peoples*, 325.

78. Central Committee of the Communist Party, 1931, quoted in Liauzu, *Aux origines des tiers-mondismes*, 56.

79. Hadj, *Les mémoires de Messali Hadj*, 106–7.

80. Messali Hadj, quoted in Liauzu, *Aux origines des tiers-mondismes*, 9.

81. Vatin, *L'Algérie politique*. The following works provide relevant background to the historical controversy: Emmanuel Sivan, "L'Étoile Nord-Africaine and the Genesis of Algerian Nationalism"; André Nouschi, *La naissance du nationalisme algérien*; Hadj, *Les mémoires de Messali Hadj*; Benjamin Stora, *Messali Hadj*; Carlier, "La première Étoile Nord-Africaine"; and Mohamed Lebjaoui, *Vérités sur la révolution algérienne*. For the most part, debates turn on the date of the ENA's creation and the respective roles of Emir Khaled, Messali Hadj, and the PCF. As Vatin comments: "According to some, the ENA is a creation of the French communists, who aspired to control the North African émigré community. According to others, the effort was provided essentially by Algerians and Muslims, the ENA advancing in the PCF's shadow in order to enjoy the required support" (*L'Algérie politique*, 200).

82. Sivan, "L'Étoile Nord-Africaine and the Genesis of Algerian Nationalism."

83. See Emmanuel Sivan, *Communisme et nationalisme en Algérie;* and idem, "'Slave-Owner Mentality' and Bolshevism." See also Saadallah, "Rise of Algerian Nationalism," 352ff.; and Meynier, *L'Algérie révélée,* 703–8.

84. *La Lutte Sociale,* April 30, 1921.

85. Harbi, *1954,* 112.

86. Stora, *Messali Hadj,* 72, 73–74, 77, quotation on 72.

87. In 1932 the PCF explained its approach as follows:

We have seriously looked at our position regarding the ENA and its newspaper, *El-Oumma.* This reformist and religious national organization has had, to this day, a strong influence on our comrades. . . . It is with their help that this organization and its newspaper have expanded. . . . We have decided to abandon this absurd tactic, which has turned our comrades into [the ENA's] instrument. We have decided to struggle within the ENA. Our aim is to . . . use this organization for our own work. We are not at all working to reenforce the organization, but to combat it. . . . As of now, we will create our own newspaper, *El-Hammel* [*sic*]. (Reprinted in Liauzu, *Aux origines des tiers-mondismes,* 39–40. On the PNR, see Amar Ouzegane, *Le meilleur combat,* 181.)

88. See Harbi, *Le F.L.N.,* 17; and Stora, *Messali Hadj,* 167.

89. See Stora, *Messali Hadj,* 167.

90. Harbi, *Le F.L.N.,* 17.

91. From the ENA's first program, presented in 1925, quoted in ibid., 116.

92. See Harbi, *Le F.L.N.,* 25; see also Slimane Chikh, *L'Algérie en armes,* 58.

93. See, e.g., *El Oumma,* August 27, 1938; see also Stora, *Messali Hadj,* 167.

94. Harbi, "Violence, nationalisme, islamisme," 27.

95. See Smith, *State and Nation in the Third World,* 103; Maxime Rodinson, *L'Islam,* 275; and Abdallah Laroui, *L'idéologie arabe contemporaine,* 139.

96. Hadj, *Les mémoires de Messali Hadj,* 33.

97. François Furet, *Le passé d'une illusion,* 41.

98. Smith, *State and Nation in the Third World,* 103, 104.

99. See, e.g., *El Oumma,* no. 1 (October 1930).

100. Stora, *Messali Hadj,* 101.

101. Harbi, *Le F.L.N.*

102. For a recent, more sophisticated rendition of this view, see Paul Thibaud and Pierre Vidal-Naquet, "Le combat pour l'indépendance algérienne," 146.

103. Stora, *Messali Hadj,* 112.

104. Ferhat Abbas, *L'indépendance confisquée, 1962–1978,* 43. A more thorough discussion of Messali's appeals to religion can be found in Addi, *L'Algérie et la démocratie,* 22, 25–26.

105. Rodinson, *L'Islam,* 274.

106. Abdallah Laroui, *Islam et modernité,* 42–43, 33–34, 36.

107. Geertz, *Islam Observed,* 63; Abdallah Laroui, *The Crisis of the Arab Intellectual,* vii.

108. Anouar Abdel-Malek, *La pensée politique arabe contemporaine,* 68–69.

109. Albert Hourani, *Arabic Thought in the Liberal Age,* 141–43; Laroui, *Islam et modernité,* 33–43; Bertrand Badie, *Les deux états,* 86ff.

110. Gellner, "Unknown Apollo of Biskra," 285.

111. This issue is discussed more thoroughly above.

112. Gilsenan, *Recognizing Islam*, 145.

113. See Mérad, *Le réformisme musulman en Algérie*, 73ff.; Fanny Colonna, "Cultural Resistance and Religious Legitimacy in Colonial Algeria"; Vatin, "Popular Puritanism versus State Reformism"; and idem, "Religious Resistance and State Power in Algeria."

114. Gilsenan, *Recognizing Islam*, 145.

115. Ibid., 143–44.

116. Vatin, *L'Algérie politique*, 189.

117. Berque, *Le Maghreb entre deux guerres*, 70.

118. Gellner, "Unknown Apollo of Biskra," 292, 300.

119. Mérad, *Le réformisme musulman en Algérie*, 130, 394.

120. Addi, *L'Algérie et la démocratie*, 20–21.

121. Ben Badis, quoted in Collot and Henry, *Le Mouvement National Algérien*, 68.

122. To quote Gilsenan, the reformist movement "never conquered social and economic power but . . . both appropriate[d] and define[d] the field of religious legitimacy. It became the arbiter of 'true Islam.' It fixed the boundaries of religion in a way that had not previously been possible in Algerian history, and in this sense their version became the established version" (*Recognizing Islam*, 153–54).

123. An early illustration is provided by the words of one of the theoreticians of reformism, Mohammad Rida (1865–1935), who wrote approvingly of the Russian revolution. "Literally," he explained, "bolshevism means 'the majority,'" the liberation of workers from oppression. Therefore, "Muslims hope for the success of socialism, since it will abolish the enslavement of all people. . . . The reader will not be surprised to hear that 99 percent of the world's inhabitants are socialists or bolsheviks. They represent the people whose voice, as the proverb goes, is God's voice. . . . Universal revolution and establishment of a reign of justice and peace depend on the people" (Mohammad Rida, quoted in Abdel-Malek, *La pensée politique arabe contemporaine*, 232–37).

124. Gamal Abdel Nasser, quoted in Paul Balta and Claudine Rulleau, *La vision Nassérienne*, 131.

125. Sukarno, quoted in Geertz, *Islam Observed*, 85. Such a connection between religion and revolutionary politics is by no means singular to Islam. The so-called theology of liberation that has spread throughout Latin America is another variant, though so manifestly different as to make hazardous any attempted comparison.

126. Stora and Daoud, *Ferhat Abbas*, 100.

127. Ibid., 99.

128. See Ouzegane, *Le meilleur combat*.

129. Furet examines the "universal charm of October" in *Le passé d'une illusion*, 78–120.

130. Pierre Vidal-Naquet suggests this interesting idea in Thibaud and Vidal-Naquet, "Le combat pour l'indépendance algérienne," 142. While it is developed in the context of the Algerian war, it is useful for an understanding of the interwar period as well.

131. See Liauzu, *Aux origines des tiers-mondismes*, 58–67.

Part 1 Conclusion

1. David Keen, "In Africa, Planned Suffering," A-15.
2. A fierce critique of the NDI-type "democracy promotion" paradigm can be found in David Samuel's "At Play in the Fields of Oppression."

Part 2 Introduction

1. Thomas Sankara, quoted in Davidson, *Black Man's Burden*, 241.

Chapter 3

1. Edward Said, *Orientalism*, 312.
2. Roland Barthes, *Mythologies*, 142.
3. Alfred Sauvy, in *L'Observateur*, August 14, 1952.
4. Lacoste, *Contre les anti-tiers-mondistes*, 72.
5. See, e.g., Jonathan D. Spence, *The Gate of Heavenly Peace*, chap. 12.
6. Alistair Horne, *A Savage War of Peace*, 130.
7. Jean Lacouture, *Nasser*, 157, 224.
8. For useful background, see Hourani, *History of the Arab Peoples*, 365 – 69.
9. See Lacouture, *Nasser*, 171 – 72.
10. Davidson, *Black Star*, 12 – 13.
11. Ryszard Kapuscinski, *The Soccer War*, 48 – 49.
12. Hobsbawm, *Age of Extremes*, 439.
13. Che Guevara, quoted in Richard J. Barnet, *Intervention and Revolution*, 6, and Hervé Hamon and Patrick Rotman, *Génération*, 94.
14. Jorge G. Castaneda, *Utopia Unarmed*, 80. According to Hobsbawm, "No revolution could have been better designed to appeal to the Left of the western hemisphere and the developed countries, at the end of a decade of global conservatism; or to give the guerrilla strategy better publicity. The Cuban revolution had everything: romance, heroism in the mountains, ex-student leaders with the selfless generosity of their youth . . . a jubilant people, in a tropical tourist paradise pulsing with rumba rhythms" (*Age of Extremes*, 440).
15. For an illustration of this outlook, see Wilfred Burchett, *Vietnam Will Win!*
16. Hobsbawm, *Age of Extremes*, 436.
17. David Apter, *Rethinking Development*, 237, 240.
18. Ania Francos, quoted in Hamon and Rotman, *Génération*, 87 – 94.
19. See Jean Genet, *Un captif amoureux*.
20. Gabriel Almond, in Gabriel Almond and James S. Coleman, *The Politics of the Developing Areas*, 64.
21. S. N. Eisenstadt, *Modernization*, 1; see also Walt Whitman Rostow, *The Stages of Economic Growth*.
22. Frantz Fanon, *The Wretched of the Earth*, 76.
23. Osvaldo Sunkel and Pedro Paz, quoted in J. Samuel Valenzuela and Ar-

turo Valenzuela, "Modernization and Dependency," 544. Other relevant works include Fernando Henrique Cardoso, "Dependency and Development in Latin America"; André Gunder Frank, *L'accumulation dépendante;* Samir Amin, *L'accumulation à l'échelle mondiale;* idem, *Le développement inégal;* and Arghiri Emmanuel, *L'échange inégal.*

24. Of course, if a state violates an international rule, say, by invading or plundering another sovereign, a distinction is easier to make. But that certainly is not all that is meant by *imperialist,* and if it were, a better word would be *unlawful.*

25. Johan Galtung presented one of the most detailed accounts of this perspective in his seminal piece "A Structural Theory of Imperialism."

26. See, generally, Irene L. Gendzier, *Managing Political Change.*

27. See, e.g., Almond and Coleman, *Politics of the Developing Areas;* Talcott Parsons, *The System of Modern Societies;* and David McClelland, *The Achieving Society.*

28. Valenzuela and Valenzuela, "Modernization and Dependency," 538.

29. Julius Nyerere, quoted in Peter Worsley, *The Third World,* 182.

30. Samir Amin, "La stratégie de la révolution socialiste dans le Tiers Monde," 184.

31. Worsley, *The Third World,* 243.

32. Lin Bao, quoted in Edmond Jouve, *Le Tiers Monde dans la vie internationale,* 14.

33. Nyerere, quoted in Worsley, *The Third World,* 244.

34. Amin, "La stratégie de la révolution socialiste," 186-87.

35. Worsley, *The Third World,* 243.

36. Jean-Paul Sartre, in his preface to Fanon, *Wretched of the Earth,* 21.

37. Agostinho Neto, quoted in Aquino de Bragança and Immanuel Wallerstein, *The African Liberation Reader,* 3:212-14. Amilcar Cabral expressed the same view: "Our armed struggle is only one aspect of the general struggle of the oppressed people against imperialism, of man's struggle for dignity, freedom, progress" (*Revolution in Guinea,* 65).

38. See Maria Antonietta Macciochi, *Daily Life in Revolutionary China.* On Maoism's influence in Europe more generally, see Hamon and Rotman, *Génération.*

39. Ziegler, *Contre l'ordre du monde,* 16.

40. Krasner, *Structural Conflict,* 9, 91.

41. The metaphor of the trade union acquired considerable popularity in Third World circles, and it obviously played out well among Third Worldists, who were prone to project the class struggle onto the international scene. Reacting to the actions taken by the Organization of Petroleum Exporting Countries (OPEC) in the early 1970s, the African scholar Ali Mazrui explained that "from the point of view of millions of Asians and Africans, the Arab oil sanctions against select Western countries will probably rank in history alongside Japan's victory over Russia in 1905," OPEC becoming the "equivalent of organized labor in the history of the industrialized countries" and oil resources, "a basis for collective bargaining" ("The Arab Oil Boycott and the New Balance of Economic Power," quoted in Roger D. Hansen, *Beyond the North-South Stalemate,* 22-23).

42. Bandung had antecedents, among them the Pan-African movement and, principally, the emergence of an "Afro-Asian" group at the United Nations. Yet they lacked both the emotional intensity and the practical staying power of Bandung. Studies of this and other forerunners of Bandung and the Non-Aligned Movement can be found in Eugène Berg, *Non-alignement et nouvel ordre mondial*, 11–19; and Pierre Queuille, *Histoire de l'afro-asiatisme jusqu'à Bandoung*.

The various "pan" movements, Pan-Africanism and Pan-Arabism in particular, were caught between the pragmatic reality of the nation-state and the idealistic vision of Third World universalism. I spoke of the former in earlier pages. Regarding the latter, I simply will note for now that Third World solidarity as seen through Third Worldist eyes generally was of the Bandung, not the Pan-African or the Pan-Arab, type, though at one time or another Third Worldism would claim all these as part of its worldview (see Smith, *State and Nation in the Third World*, 55). As Touré asked rhetorically: "Was not Allende closer to the exploited black than certain Afro-Americans or African leaders? . . . Is it not true that our friend, the great revolutionary leader of Cuba, Fidel Castro, is more hated by the imperialists, colonialists, segregationists, and fascists than black leaders who have become the accomplices and devoted and servile agents of those who exploit their brothers and generally scoff at the rights of African people?" (quoted in David Ottaway and Marina Ottaway, *Afrocommunism*, 23).

43. Leopold Senghor, quoted in Berg, *Non-alignement et nouvel ordre mondial*, 22–23; Odette Guitard, *Bandung ou le réveil des peuples colonisés;* Jean Rous, "Bandoung, répétition de l'histoire." For another, similar account, see Mohamed Yazid, "De Bandoung à Alger," quoted in Albert-Paul Lentin, *La lutte tricontinentale*, 23.

44. Hansen, *Beyond the North-South Stalemate*, 89.

45. Details on the AAPSO can be found in Homer Jack, *Cairo;* David Kimche, *The Afro-Asian Movement;* and Lentin, *La lutte tricontinentale*.

46. Mortimer, *Third World Coalition*, 10.

47. Works on the Non-Aligned Movement are legion, and only a handful are referenced here: Berg, *Non-alignement et nouvel ordre mondial;* Peter Willetts, *The Non-Aligned Movement;* and Laurence W. Martin, ed., *Neutralism and Non-Alignment*.

48. Mortimer, *Third World Coalition*, 39.

49. Ibid., 3, 48.

50. See Hansen, *Beyond the North-South Stalemate*, 91.

51. On the NIEO in particular, see Mohamed Bedjaoui, *Pour un nouvel ordre économique international;* Madjid Bencheikh, *Droit international du sous-développement;* and Samir Amin, *La faillite du développement en Afrique et dans le Tiers Monde*, 72–86.

52. See Krasner, *Structural Conflict*, 62.

53. Mortimer, *Third World Coalition*, 34.

54. U.N. General Assembly, quoted in ibid., 53.

55. Mortimer, *Third World Coalition*, 70.

56. Krasner, *Structural Conflict*, 88.

57. Hansen, *Beyond the North-South Stalemate*, 4.

58. Ibid., 39.

59. Hannah Arendt, *On Violence*, 26.

60. See Michel de Certeau, *L'écriture de l'histoire*.

61. Said, *Culture and Imperialism*, 16.

62. Tarif Khalidi, "Palestinian Historiography."

63. Levy-Bruhl, quoted in Etienne, *La France et l'Islam*, 27.

64. de Certeau, *L'écriture de l'histoire*, 176.

65. Variations on this theme can be found in Julius Nyerere, *Ujamaa*, 11; and Ahmed Sékou Touré, *The Doctrine and Methods of the Democratic Party of Guinea*, pt. 2, 20.

66. Nyerere, quoted in Ottaway and Ottaway, *Afrocommunism*, 17.

67. Cabral, *Revolution in Guinea*, 56, 68.

68. Amilcar Cabral, *Unité et lutte*, 1:224.

69. Touré, quoted in Yves Benot, *Indépendances africaines*, 1:60.

70. Fidel Castro reportedly told a French journalist that "Jean-Jacques [Rousseau] had been his teacher and that he had fought Batista with the *Social Contract* in his pocket" (Lucio Colletti, *From Rousseau to Lenin*, 143–44).

71. Albert Memmi, *Portrait du colonisé*, 40–42.

72. Davidson, *Black Man's Burden*, 164–66.

73. Abdel-Malek, *La pensée politique arabe contemporaine*, 11.

74. Ben Barka, quoted in ibid., 126.

75. Bragança and Wallerstein, *African Liberation Reader*, 3:215. Examples include Algeria's Front de Libération Nationale and Angola's own Popular Movement for the Liberation of Angola.

76. See Abdel-Malek, *La pensée politique arabe contemporaine*, 114 (Nasser); and S. Neil McFarlane, *Superpower Rivalry and Third World Radicalism*, 84 (Ho Chi Minh and Dos Santos).

77. White Paper issued in 1967 and quoted in Bragança and Wallerstein, *African Liberation Reader*, 1:108.

78. Touré, quoted in Benot, *Indépendances africaines*, 1:77; see also Jean-Jacques Rousseau, *Du contrat social*, 102.

79. Mona Ozouf, "De thérmidor à brumaire"; see also idem, *La fête révolutionnaire*.

80. See Jean Starobinsky, *J.-J. Rousseau*.

81. Gamal Abdel Nasser, quoted in Balta and Rulleau, *La vision Nassérienne*, 65.

82. Mao, quoted in Leszek Kolakowski, *Main Currents of Marxism*, 3:513.

83. Quoted in Bragança and Wallerstein, *African Liberation Reader*, 1:113–14.

84. Arendt, *On Revolution*, 183.

85. Said, *Culture and Imperialism*, 270. See also Ziegler's discussion in *Contre l'ordre du monde*, 321.

86. Fanon, *Wretched of the Earth*, 73.

87. Ibid.

88. See Cabral, *Unité et lutte*, 1:202; see also Benot, *Indépendances africaines*, 2:17.

89. Amilcar Cabral, quoted in Davidson, *Black Man's Burden*, 300.

90. Quoted in Abdel-Malek, *La pensée politique arabe contemporaine*, 116.

91. See John W. Amos, *Palestinian Resistance*, 34–35, 132; and Edward Said, *The Question of Palestine*, 158.

92. For a discussion of the meaning and uses of political violence, see David Apter, "Thinking about Violence." Apter applies his theoretical analysis to the case of the Japanese Sanrizuka movement in *Against the State* (with Nagayo Sawa).

93. Jean-Paul Sartre, *Critique of Dialectical Reason*, 724.

94. Chikh, *L'Algérie en armes*.

95. See Jacques Vergès, *Le salaud lumineux*.

96. See Arendt, *On Violence*, 19 – 20. Arendt acknowledges that Fanon was "much more doubtful about violence than his admirers" (ibid., 14 n. 19).

97. Davidson, *Black Man's Burden*, 301.

98. Said, *Culture and Imperialism*, 275.

99. Colletti, *From Rousseau to Lenin*, 145.

100. Touré, quoted in Benot, *Indépendances africaines*, 1 : 78.

101. Georges Balandier, *Sens et puissance*, 280.

102. See, e.g., Mohamed Heykal's defense of the army's role in Egypt in Abdel-Malek, *La pensée politique arabe contemporaine*, 189 – 95.

103. See John Davis, "Qaddafi's Theory of Non-Representative Government"; Jean Gueyras, "Dix ans de pouvoir populaire en Libye"; Davidson, *Black Man's Burden*, 299 – 300, 308.

104. For the quotation from Egypt's 1962 charter, see Balta and Rulleau, *La vision Nassérienne*, 123; on Nkrumah's attacks against party bureaucrats and careerists, see, e.g., Kapuscinski, *Soccer War*, 36.

105. Pierre Bourdieu, *Ce que parler veut dire*, 224.

106. Raoul Girardet, *Mythes et mythologies politiques*, 61.

107. Arendt, *On Revolution*, 91.

108. Lynn Hunt, *Politics, Culture, and Class in the French Revolution*, 43.

109. François Furet, *Penser la révolution française*, 78.

110. Nyerere, quoted in Guy Hermet, "State-Controlled Elections," 12 – 13.

111. Michel Camau, *La notion de démocratie dans la pensée des dirigeants maghrébins*, 287 – 88.

112. See Hanna Pitkin, *The Concept of Representation*.

113. Juan Linz, "Non-Competitive Elections in Europe," 44.

114. Apter, *Rethinking Development*, 297.

115. See, e.g., Gérard Chaliand, *Les faubourgs de l'histoire;* idem, *Mythes révolutionnaires du Tiers-Monde;* and Lacoste, *Contre les anti-tiers-mondistes*.

116. Bourdieu, *Ce que parler veut dire*, 137.

117. Philippe Braillard, *Mythe et réalité du non-alignement*, 13.

118. Cabral, *Revolution in Guinea*, 67 – 68.

119. Guevara, quoted in Castaneda, *Utopia Unarmed*, 80.

120. See "Le Ché est Mort," *Le Monde*, August 27, 1987.

121. Arendt, *On Violence*, 21 n. 37.

122. Hobsbawm, *Age of Extremes*, 443; see also 447.

123. Said, *Culture and Imperialism*, 195.

124. To quote Said again:

The sense for Europeans of a tremendous and disorienting change in perspective in the West–non-West relationship was entirely new, experienced neither in the European Renaissance nor in the "discovery" of the Orient three centuries later. Think of the differences between Poliziano's recovery and editing of Greek classics in the 1460s, or Bopp and Schlegel reading Sanskrit grammarians in the 1810s, and a French political theorist or Orientalist reading Fanon during the Algerian War in 1961, or Césaire's *Discours sur le colonialisme* when it appeared in 1955 just after the French defeat at Dien Bien Phu. Not only is this last unfortunate fellow addressed by natives while his army is engaged by them, as neither of his predecessors were, but he is reading a text in the language of Bossuet and Chateaubriand, using concepts of Hegel, Marx, and Freud to incriminate the very civilization producing all of them (ibid., 195–97).

Chapter 4

1. Founded in 1944, the AML was not, strictly speaking, a political party, but rather a loose association that brought together the main nationalistic currents in Algeria, with the exception of the communists.

2. For a discussion of this period, see Stora and Daoud, *Ferhat Abbas,* 122–48.

3. Horne, *Savage War of Peace,* 25. See also Julien, *L'Afrique du Nord en marche,* 262–66; and Stora and Daoud, *Ferhat Abbas,* 146–47.

4. Harbi, *1954,* 16; Horne, *Savage War of Peace,* 26.

5. See Vatin, *L'Algérie politique,* 276.

6. See, generally, Harbi, *Le F.L.N.*

7. Ibid., 117.

8. Horne, *Savage War of Peace,* 77.

9. Ibid., 27.

10. Vatin, *L'Algérie politique,* 278.

11. Kateb Yacine, quoted in Horne, *Savage War of Peace,* 77.

12. Irene L. Gendzier, *Frantz Fanon,* 125.

13. Translated in Horne, *Savage War of Peace,* 94–95.

14. Harbi, *1954,* 69.

15. See ibid., 37.

16. See Kielstra, "Was the Algerian Revolution a Peasant War?" and Harbi, *1954,* 24.

17. Quoted in Harbi, *1954,* 35.

18. See ibid., 146; see also Martha Crenshaw Hutchinson, *Revolutionary Terrorism,* 50.

19. Said, *Culture and Imperialism,* 185. Said devotes many interesting pages to Camus (see 172–85).

20. Albert Camus, *Essais,* 1012–13, translated in Said, *Culture and Imperialism,* 179.

21. Mouloud Feraoun, *Journal, 1955–1962,* 42, 47 (1955 entry).

22. Pierre Bourdieu, *The Algerians,* 163; see also Slimane Chikh, *L'Algérie en armes,* 318.

23. Harbi, *1954,* 146.

24. Quoted in Chikh, *L'Algérie en armes,* 307.

25. The best (and for a long time the only) account of this quasi civil war can be found in Harbi, *Le F.L.N.*

26. Jean Leca, "Algérie," 641.

27. For an interesting essay exploring Algeria's history along these lines, see Stora, "Algérie."

28. Quoted from Vatin, *L'Algérie politique,* 282; and Harbi, *1954,* 154.

29. Reprinted in *El Moudjahid,* the FLN's press organ, no. 4 (emphasis added).

30. Harbi, *1954,* 159; see also Stora, "Algérie," 65.

31. Harbi, *Le F.L.N.,* 172.

32. *El Moudjahid,* no. 30 (October 10, 1958).

33. Ibid., no. 25 (June 13, 1958).

34. Ibid.

35. See Monique Gadant, *Islam et nationalisme en Algérie,* 149–50.

36. *El Moudjahid,* no. 22 (April 16, 1958).

37. Ibid., no. 15 (January 1, 1958).

38. See "L'Algérie fête ses 25 ans d'histoire," *Libération,* July 6, 1987.

39. Fanon, *Wretched of the Earth,* 47.

40. See Mahfoud Bennoune, "Socioeconomic Changes in Rural Algeria, 1830–1954," 12; Bourdieu, *The Algerians;* Bruno Etienne, "La paysannerie dans le discours et la pratique"; and Addi, *L'Algérie et la démocratie,* 46–47.

41. As asserted by one of the FLN's historical leaders, Larbi Ben M'Hidi (see Chikh, *L'Algérie en armes,* 378).

42. See Said, *Culture and Imperialism,* 270; Fanon, *Wretched of the Earth,* 30; Kateb Yacine, *Nedjma;* and Jacques Berque, *Déposséssion du monde,* 156.

43. Hocine Aït-Ahmed, quoted in Harbi, *Les archives de la révolution algérienne,* 36–37.

44. Amar Ouzegane, *Le meilleur combat,* 159, 203.

45. Ibid., 147.

46. See Chikh, *L'Algérie en armes,* 224–25.

47. Rachid Mimouni, *Tombéza.*

48. Tahar Ouettar, *L'As,* 127.

49. See, generally, Etienne, "La paysannerie."

50. Kielstra, "Was the Algerian Revolution a Peasant War?" 181–82.

51. Harbi, *Le F.L.N.,* 317.

52. See Gadant, *Islam et nationalisme en Algérie,* 130.

53. Harbi, *Le F.L.N.,* 302; see also 171. Addi explores Algeria's relationship with the idea of multipartyism in *L'Algérie et la démocratie,* 58.

54. Harbi, *Le F.L.N.,* 176. For quotes from the so-called Tripoli Program, see Chikh, *L'Algérie en armes,* 357–73.

55. *El Moudjahid,* no. 9 (August 20, 1957).

56. Ibid., no. 11 (November 1, 1957).

57. See Addi, *L'Algérie et la démocratie,* 46.

58. See ibid., 56–58; and Jean Leca and Jean-Claude Vatin, *L'Algérie politique: Institutions et régime,* 383. See also, generally, Harbi, *Le F.L.N.*

59. See S. Chikh, *L'Algérie en armes,* 254–56; see also J. Charby, *L'Algérie en prison.*

60. Bourdieu, *The Algerians,* 156.

61. See Bennoune, "Introduction of Nationalism into Rural Algeria."

62. Gilsenan, *Recognizing Islam,* 15.

63. See Frantz Fanon, *L'an V de la révolution algérienne,* 42; and Philippe Lucas, "Déchiffrement dialectique de l'histoire et libération de la connaissance." Susan Slyomovics analyzes the various cultural and political uses of the veil in "Hassiba Ben Bouali, If You Could See Our Algeria."

64. See Kaddache, *Histoire du nationalisme algérien*, 1:550–52.

65. See Harbi, *Le F.L.N.*, 307.

66. Ibid., 6, 148.

67. Messali Hadj to the leaders of the MNA, reprinted in Harbi, *Les archives de la révolution algérienne*, 129–30.

68. Quoted in Harbi, *Le F.L.N.*, 149.

69. Harbi, *1954*, 155; see also Benjamin Stora, *Messali Hadj*.

70. Horne, *Savage War of Peace*, 409.

71. Chikh, *L'Algérie en armes*, 421.

72. Frantz Fanon, *Pour la révolution africaine*, 167–72, originally published in *El Moudjahid*, no. 31 (November 1, 1958), under the title "La guerre d'Algérie et la libération des hommes."

73. Chikh, *L'Algérie en armes*, 198–99.

74. Horne, *Savage War of Peace*, 68.

75. Mendès-France, quoted in ibid., 98 (emphasis added).

76. See André Burguière, introduction to Amin et al., *Le Tiers Monde et la Gauche*, 20.

77. Chaliand, *Mythes révolutionnaires du Tiers-Monde*, 12.

78. Daniel Guérin, *Ci-gît le colonialisme*, 330.

79. Chaliand, *Les faubourgs de l'histoire*, 30.

80. Jean-Paul Sartre, preface to Fanon, *Wretched of the Earth*, 26.

81. Robert Davezies, quoted in Hervé Hamon and Patrick Rotman, *Les porteurs de valises*, 380.

82. Hamon and Rotman, *Les porteurs de valises*, 380.

83. Horne, *Savage War of Peace*, 523.

84. Quoted in ibid., 530.

85. Horne, *Savage War of Peace*, 531 (emphasis in the original).

86. Charles Gallagher, *The United States and North Africa*, 115.

87. See Horne, *Savage War of Peace*, 536.

88. Harbi, *Le F.L.N.*, 372.

89. Bourges and Wauthier, *Les 50 Afriques*, 51.

90. Horne, *Savage War of Peace*, 540.

91. Kapuscinski, *Soccer War*, 110.

92. Destanne de Bernis, quoted in Entelis, *Algeria*, 113–14.

93. Maxime Rodinson, in a study of Marx's sociological and economic theories, makes this point (see Rodinson, *De Pythagore à Lénine*, 136).

94. Boumedienne, quoted in M. E. Benissad, *Economie du développement de l'Algérie*, 33, 21.

95. Ibid., 22–23.

96. Guérin, *Ci-gît le colonialisme*, 339–40.

97. Ibid., 356–64.

98. Gellner, "Unknown Apollo of Biskra," 278.

99. See, generally, Serge Koulytchizky, *L'autogestion, l'homme et l'état;* and Ian Clegg, *Workers' Self-Management in Algeria*.

100. Chaliand, *Les faubourgs de l'histoire*, 88.

101. Ibid., 86.

102. See Bruno Etienne, *L'Algérie, cultures et révolution;* and Nicole Grimaud, *La politique extérieure de l'Algérie*.

103. Grimaud, *La politique extérieure de l'Algérie*, 30.

104. See, generally, Philippe Lucas, *Problèmes de la transition au socialisme*.

105. See Karl Mannheim, *Ideology and Utopia*.

106. Paul Balta and Claudine Rulleau, *L'Algérie des algériens, vingt ans après*, 192.

107. On this notion of foreign policy "spheres," see Chikh, *L'Algérie en armes*; and Grimaud, *La politique extérieure de l'Algérie*.

108. See Robert Mortimer, "The Algerian Revolution in Search of the African Revolution," 372; Hubert Michel, "La politique africaine des états du Maghreb," 45.

109. Baghat Korany, "From Revolution to Domestication," 121.

110. Ben Bella also was deeply interested in the African arena, in which he detected substantial revolutionary potential. Together with Nasser, Nkrumah, Modibo Keita, Sékou Touré, and Julius Nyerere, he entertained the hope of uniting the forces of progress in an anticolonial and anti-imperialist crusade. By the time Boumedienne came to power these hopes had not been realized, and the focus shifted toward other horizons (see Grimaud, *La politique extérieure de l'Algérie*, 266–74).

111. John P. Entelis, "Algeria in World Politics," 73.

112. See Robert Mortimer, "Algeria and the Politics of International Economic Reform," 677, 679.

113. Ben Bella shared this vision: "To be nonaligned does not mean to withdraw into oneself, remain at an equal distance between East and West, or engage in perpetual acrobatics vis-à-vis the superpowers. . . . Nonalignment must be expressed by a constant struggle for national independence and against foreign domination" (quoted in Grimaud, *La politique extérieure de l'Algérie*, 276).

114. See Korany, "From Revolution to Domestication," 120.

115. Boumedienne, quoted in Grimaud, *La politique extérieure de l'Algérie*, 294.

116. Entelis, "Algeria in World Politics," 71.

117. Mortimer, "Algeria and the Politics of International Economic Reform," 671.

118. On the summit generally, see Bruno Etienne, "L'Algérie et la IVe Conférence des Non-Alignés."

119. See Korany, "From Revolution to Domestication," 138; and Grimaud, *La politique extérieure de l'Algérie*, 307–13.

120. Earlier, France had proposed that the United Nations organize a conference devoted to energy. Scoring an initial tactical victory, Boumedienne was able to widen the agenda to include the issue of raw materials and, more generally, economic development.

121. Boumedienne, quoted in Jouve, *Le Tiers Monde dans la vie internationale*, 96.

122. Mortimer, "Algeria and the Politics of International Economic Reform," 691.

123. Korany, "From Revolution to Domestication," 138. Under Bouteflika's presidency, South African participation was suspended and Yassir Arafat was invited to address the General Assembly (see Dominique O'Cornesse, "Le rôle de l'Algérie à l'Assemblée de l'ONU").

124. Etienne, "La paysannerie," 40.

125. Ibid., 42.

126. Leca and Vatin, *L'Algérie politique,* 265; see also Ahmed Rouadjia, "Du nationalisme du FLN à l'islamisme du FIS."

127. *La charte d'Alger,* 42-43.

128. *El Moudjahid,* September 24-25, 1972.

129. Ibid., April 26 and March 19, 1971.

130. Henri Sanson, "Le peuple de la révolution socialiste algérienne," 87.

131. Ibid., 85.

132. *La charte d'Alger,* 42-43.

133. B. Amazit, "L'alphabet de l'indépendance."

134. Koulakssis and Meynier, *L'émir Khaled,* 318.

135. Ibid., 12.

136. *La République,* February 26, 1971; *El Moudjahid,* May 28, 1971; *An-Nasr,* June 26, 1971.

137. Mohamed Chérif Sahli, *Décoloniser l'histoire.* See also Vatin, *L'Algérie politique;* and idem, "Histoire en soi et histoire pour soi."

138. Ahmed Taleb Ibrahimi, *De la décolonisation à la révolution culturelle,* 217-18.

139. Sami Kuider Nair discusses the official suppression of Berber identity in "Le peuple exclu," 42-43. See also Smail Aouili and Ramdane Redjala, "La Kabylie face à la dérive intégriste," 200-202.

140. Taleb-Ibrahimi, *De la décolonisation à la révolution culturelle,* 217-18.

141. See Addi, *L'Algérie et la démocratie,* 84-89; and Lucille Provost, "L'économie de rente et ses avatars."

142. See Camau, *La notion de démocratie.*

143. Leca and Vatin, *L'Algérie politique,* 74-75.

144. See Sanson, *Laïcité islamique en Algérie,* 53.

145. Boumedienne, quoted in ibid., 83.

146. Jean Leca and Jean-Claude Vatin, "Le système politique algérien (1976-1978)," 16.

147. Leca and Vatin, *L'Algérie politique,* 61-62.

148. Michel Camau, "Caractère et rôle du constitutionnalisme dans les états maghrébins," 394.

149. Leca and Vatin, "Le système politique algérien," 35.

150. Boumedienne, quoted in *Annuaire de l'Afrique du Nord* 20 (1981): 55.

151. Boumedienne, quoted in Leca and Vatin, "Le système politique algérien," 22; in Hugh Roberts, *Political Development in Algeria,* 138; and in *Annuaire de l'Afrique du Nord* 13 (1974): 310.

152. *La charte d'Alger,* 104, 107.

153. Zoubir Zemzoun, "De la démocratie."

154. See Leca, "Algérie," 642.

155. John Nellis, "Comparative Assessment of the Development Performances of Algeria and Tunisia," 372.

156. Leca and Vatin, *L'Algérie politique,* 99.

157. Leca and Vatin, "Le système politique algérien," 48.

158. Ibid., 47.

159. Ibid., 16.

160. Bernard Cubertafond, "Réflexions sur la pratique politique algérienne," 30.

161. See Ramdane Redjala, *L'opposition en Algérie depuis 1962*, 13.

162. Harbi, *Le F.L.N.*, 376; see also Redjala, *L'opposition en Algérie depuis 1962*, 22.

163. Hocine Aït-Ahmed, *La guerre et l'après-guerre*, 117–22.

164. For Boudiaf, see *Le Monde*, June 24, 1963; for Khider, *Jeune Afrique*, March 25, 1963, and *Le Monde*, April 21, 1963; for Abbas, *Jeune Afrique*, May 20, 1963, and, generally, Abbas, *L'indépendance confisquée;* and for Aït-Ahmed, *Annuaire de l'Afrique du Nord* 2 (1963); and, generally, Aït-Ahmed, *La guerre et l'après-guerre.*

165. See *El Djamahir*, July 3, 1963, quoted in *Annuaire de l'Afrique du Nord* 2 (1963): 244.

166. Ben Bella, quoted in *Annuaire de l'Afrique du Nord* 2 (1963).

167. Tract distributed by Boudiaf's PRS on September 22, 1962.

168. According to then minister of information Belaouane, quoted in *Annuaire de l'Afrique du Nord* 1 (1962).

169. "A propos du parti unique," reprinted in Redjala, *L'opposition en Algérie depuis 1962*, 181–82. Mohamed Boudiaf's position regarding the single party is discussed on 81–83.

170. *Annuaire de l'Afrique du Nord* 3 (1964): 119.

171. Abbas, *L'indépendance confisquée*, 14.

172. Aït-Ahmed, interview by *El Badil*, no. 30 (December 1986).

Part 2 Conclusion

1. Anouar Abdel-Malek, introduction to *La pensée politique arabe contemporaine*, 35–36.

2. Ibid., 36.

3. See ibid., 293–98.

4. Smith, *Theories of Nationalism*, 49.

5. Lacouture, *Nasser*, 312, 319.

6. Ibid., xiv.

Part 3 Introduction

1. Said, *Culture and Imperialism*, 302.

2. Fidel Castro himself is said to have quipped that "someday the whole world will be socialist. Of course, we always will need one capitalist country to provide us with economic aid."

3. Badie, *L'état importé.*

4. See James Clifford, *The Predicament of Culture;* Gérard Leclerc, *L'observation de l'homme;* and Laurence Tribe, "The Curvature of Constitutional Space."

5. Ernest Gellner, "Homeland of the Unrevolution," 147.
6. Said, *Orientalism,* 15.
7. Gilles Kepel, *La revanche de Dieu.*

Chapter 5

1. Nigel Harris, *The End of the Third World.*
2. Davidson, *Black Man's Burden,* 234.
3. Ibid., 263.
4. Ibid., 235.
5. Africa's global debt has tripled since 1980 and is now close to $200 billion. Servicing alone costs African countries an annual $10 billion, "four times more than they all spend on health and education" (John Darnton, "In Poor, Decolonized Africa Bankers Are New Overlords," A-8).
6. Krasner, *Structural Conflict,* 30, 80, quotation on 30.
7. Chaliand, *Mythes révolutionnaires du Tiers-Monde,* 73.
8. On the concept of African "state-socialism," see in particular Ottaway and Ottaway, *Afrocommunism.*
9. Davidson, *Black Man's Burden,* 263–64.
10. Said, *Culture and Imperialism,* 219.
11. On an intellectual's journey from enthusiasm to disenchantment, compare Maria Antonietta Macciochi's *Daily Life in Revolutionary China* with her subsequent works. See also Perry Anderson, *In the Tracks of Historical Materialism,* 72–73.
12. Michel Foucault, "L'esprit d'un monde sans esprit," 230–33, 241.
13. Rodinson, *L'Islam,* 301.
14. Introducing his work on nationalism, *Imagined Communities,* Benedict Anderson somberly observes that "a fundamental transformation in the history of Marxism and Marxist movements is upon us. Its most visible signs are the recent wars between Vietnam, Cambodia and China. These wars are of world historical importance because they are the first to occur between regimes whose independence and revolutionary credentials are undeniable" (11).
15. Lacoste, *Contre les anti-tiers-mondistes,* 11–12.
16. Burguière, "Introduction," 32.
17. The articles are reprinted in Amin et al., *Le Tiers Monde et la gauche.*
18. Edward Said, *Covering Islam,* 36.
19. Jacques Julliard, "Le Tiers Monde et la gauche," 39.
20. Furet, *Penser la révolution française,* 42.
21. Bernard-Henry Lévy, *La barbarie à visage humain,* 65–67.
22. Said, *Culture and Imperialism,* 315.
23. See, e.g., Chaliand, *Les faubourgs de l'histoire;* René Galissot, "Les empires se portent bien"; and Jean Ziegler, *La victoire des vaincus.*
24. Galissot, "Les empires se portent bien," 62; Chaliand, *Les faubourgs de l'histoire,* 47.
25. See generally Michel Foucault, *La volonté de savoir;* André Glucksman, *Les*

maîtres penseurs; and Lévy, *La barbarie à visage humain.* There is a critique of the *nouveaux philosophes* in François Aubral and Xavier Delcourt, *Contre la nouvelle philosophie.*

26. Foucault, *La volonté de savoir;* the quotation is translated in Ajami, *Arab Predicament,* 20.

27. Lévy, *La barbarie à visage humain,* 30.

28. See, e.g., Fernand Braudel, "Interview."

29. Maxime Rodinson, "Pas de solution au conflit israélo-arabe."

30. Chaliand, *Mythes révolutionnaires du Tiers Monde,* 256.

31. Alain Touraine, "D'un coup de pied, le plongeur."

32. Julliard, "Le Tiers Monde et la gauche," 145.

33. Ibid., 38, 145.

34. Harris, *End of the Third World,* 182.

35. Robert Frost, "A Semi-Revolution," in *The Poetry of Robert Frost,* 363.

36. See Darnton, "In Poor, Decolonized Africa Bankers Are Overlords," A-8.

37. For a more detailed and comprehensive treatment of these images, see Said, *Covering Islam.*

38. Patricia Crone, *Slaves on Horses,* 84.

39. Bruno Etienne, *L'islamisme radical,* 108.

40. Michael Gilsenan, "Apprehensions of Islam," 34.

41. Sami Zubaida, "An Islamic State?" 3.

42. Yahya Sadowski, "The New Orientalism and the Democracy Debate," 16–18.

43. Ibid., 19, 20.

44. For an argument along these lines, see Samir Amin, *L'ethnie à l'assaut des nations.*

45. Daniel Bell, *The End of Ideology,* 393.

46. Harris, *End of the Third World,* 28.

47. Duncan Kennedy, "The Stakes of Law, or Hale and Foucault!" 91.

48. Ibid., 98.

49. The interplay between changes in legal ground rules, bargaining power, distributional consequences, and, ultimately, violence is illustrated vividly in Joe Stork, "Egypt's Factory Privatization Campaign Turns Deadly," 29.

50. For a quick overview, see Robert S. Browne, "The IMF and the World Bank in the New World Order," 117; Eduardo Galeano, *Open Veins of Latin America,* 240ff.; and Castaneda, *Utopia Unarmed,* chaps. 13 and 14.

51. Castaneda, *Utopia Unarmed,* 422.

52. Gilles Kepel, *Les banlieues de l'Islam.*

53. Galeano, *Open Veins of Latin America,* 242.

54. See Elemér Hankiss, "In Search of a Paradigm." Hankiss bases his work on the efforts of Jürgen Habermas and Claus Offe; see, e.g., Habermas, *Legitimation Crisis;* and Offe, *Contradictions of the Welfare State.*

55. Pierre Bourdieu, *Outline of a Theory of Practice,* 170.

56. Said, *Culture and Imperialism,* 291, 292. The quotation from Smith is from Anthony Smith, *The Geopolitics of Information,* 176.

57. Pierre Bourdieu, *Distinction.*

58. Fanny Colonna, remarks delivered at a seminar held in London on May 10,

1986. The impact of *Dallas* in Algeria has been noted by others as well; see, e.g., Serge Latouche, *L'occidentalisation du monde,* 7; and Omar Aktouf, *Algérie,* 133.

59. The quotation is from Said, *Culture and Imperialism,* 309. See also René Galissot, "La transnationalisation à l'oeuvre sous le modèle de l'état-national"; and Christian de Brie, "Champ libre au modèle libéral et démocratique," 22.

60. See L. Diamond, J. Linz, and S. Lipset, eds., *Democracy in Developing Countries,* 2:ix–x.

61. Mahmoud Hussein, *Versant sud de la liberté,* 7; see also John Darnton, "Africa Tries Democracy, Finding Hope and Peril," A-1.

62. Consider, for example, the uses of the word *Westernization* in the debate surrounding Samuel P. Huntington's "Clash of Civilizations" (see Fouad Ajami, "The Summoning"; and Robert L. Bartley, "The Case for Optimism").

63. See Badie, *L'état importé.*

64. Ibid., 30.

65. Ibid., 56–57.

66. Davidson, *Black Man's Burden,* 222.

67. Galeano, *Open Veins of Latin America,* 14.

68. See Paul Vieille, "Du transnational au politique-monde," 315.

69. René Galissot, "La purification communautaire," 110–11.

70. See Badie, *L'état importé,* 290.

71. Apter, *Rethinking Development,* 315–22.

72. Davidson, *Black Man's Burden,* 209.

73. On this point see Amin, *L'ethnie à l'assaut des nations.*

74. Quoted in Joe Stork, "North Africa Faces the 1990s," 8.

75. Amin, *L'ethnie à l'assaut des nations,* esp. 77–97.

76. Badie, *L'état importé,* 188.

77. Hankiss, "In Search of a Paradigm," 192.

78. In the mid-1980s, "unofficial" trade "reached the astonishing but believable proportion of *nine-tenths of all the trade* of the republic of Benin" (Davidson, *Black Man's Burden,* 213, citing Chris Allen et al., *Benin, the Congo, Burkina Faso,* 134 [emphasis in the original]; see also Robert Kaplan, "The Coming Anarchy," 48).

79. Davidson, *Black Man's Burden,* 224–25.

80. Alain Gresh, "Quand l'islamisme menace le monde," 9; François Burgat and William Dowell, *The Islamic Movement in North Africa,* 93; Kepel, *La revanche de Dieu,* 45.

81. Badie, *L'état importé,* 259ff.

82. Ibid., 233.

83. See Amy D. Marcus, "Going to Extremes," A-1.

84. Gresh, "Quand l'islamisme menace le monde," 9.

85. Kepel, *La revanche de Dieu,* 47, 59–60.

86. For a useful discussion of tribalism in the context of the Middle East, see Philip S. Khoury and Joseph Kostiner, eds., *Tribes and State Formation in the Middle East.*

87. Richard Tapper, "Anthropologists, Historians, and Tribespeople on Tribe and State Formation in the Middle East."

88. According to Davidson, "Much was written on the supposed miseries of

this incorrigible 'tribalism,' and most of what was written, as may now be seen, completely missed the point. Not until years later, when a lot of damage had been done, was it understood that precolonial tribalism was no more peculiar to Africa than nineteenth century nationalism was to Europe. The one, like the other, might be useful and progressive; or according to circumstance, it might be neither" (*Black Man's Burden*, 75).

Chapter 6

1. See Amnesty International, *Repression and Violence Must End,* news release, October 25, 1994.

2. Ali El-Kenz, "La société algérienne aujourd'hui," 10.

3. Peter Lyon, "The Emergence of the Third World"; see also chapter 2 above.

4. Ania Francos and Jean-Pierre Séréni, *Un algérien nommé Boumediène,* 260–61.

5. Jean-Pierre Durand, in *Annuaire de l'Afrique du Nord* 18 (1979): 515.

6. Mohamed Boudiaf, "Interview," 16.

7. The industrial sector received 51 percent of total investment between 1967 and 1973, while agriculture received only 15 percent (see Entelis, *Algeria,* 137; and Jean-Pierre Durand, "L'agriculture sacrifiée," 76). A World Bank study noted that "increased Algerian demand for food . . . did not cause agricultural producer prices to increase which would have stimulated production. Instead, producer prices were kept artificially low by Government, and demand satisfied by imports" (Kevin M. Cleaver, *The Agricultural Development Experience of Algeria, Morocco, and Tunisia,* 8).

8. Jean-Pierre Durand, "Le redressement de l'agriculture," 36. In a well-known political cartoon, an Algerian bureaucrat proudly announces that the nation's "dependence on other countries for food is around 80 percent. But, *hamdou lillah* [thank God], the stomach remains 100 percent Algerian" (reprinted in Arun Kapil, "Algeria's Crisis Intensifies," 6).

9. Durand, "Le redressement de l'agriculture."

10. Entelis, *Algeria,* 133.

11. Nassib Fayçal, "Algérie"; Bruno Frappat, "Démographie," 10; Jacques Girardon, "L'Algérie et nous," 24.

12. Etienne, *L'islamisme radical,* 115; Zakya Daoud, "Algérie," 22.

13. Abderrahim Lamchichi, *L'Algérie en crise,* 175ff., 216; Patrick Eveno, *L'Algérie,* 97, 96.

14. Castaneda, *Utopia Unarmed,* 255.

15. On measures to encourage private investment, see Djillali Liabes, *Capital privé et patrons d'industrie en Algérie.* By 1989 the private industrial sector represented more than 40 percent of the national value added outside agriculture (see Rachid Tlemçani, "Chadli's Perestroïka," 16).

On renewed emphasis on agricultural production and changes in land ownership, see Hugh Roberts, "In Troubled Waters," 52. By early 1981 Algeria had begun lifting several restrictions on the private ownership of land, and some lots were restituted to their original owners. In 1983 Algeria's parliament adopted a law allowing individuals to purchase certain public lands for a symbolic dinar. For a discussion of land privatization in Algeria, see Durand, "Le redressement de l'agriculture."

On incentives and cutbacks, see Entelis, *Algeria*, 128.

16. Entelis, *Algeria*, 148.

17. Korany, "From Revolution to Domestication," 103.

18. Grimaud, *La politique extérieure de l'Algérie*, 313; Roberts, "In Troubled Waters."

19. Roberts, "In Troubled Waters."

20. James Markham, "Where Liberation was a Dream, Other Visions Ascend," sec. 4, p. 1.

21. "Perestroïka in Algiers."

22. Salem Chjoke, "Les droits de l'homme sont-ils murs en Algérie?"

23. "Algérie: Les droits de l'homme."

24. *Le Monde*, December 15, 1988. For an account of these events, see also *Octobre à Alger*, 32ff.

25. Abdelkader Djeghloul, "Fin du populisme en Algérie," 14. See also Mohammed Harbi, "La fin d'une époque," 8.

26. Lamchichi, *L'Algérie en crise*, 290.

27. Daniel Brumberg, "Islam, Elections, and Reform in Algeria," 59.

28. Albert Bourgi, "Algérie."

29. Robert Mortimer, "Islam and Multiparty Politics in Algeria," 582.

30. Chadli Benjedid, quoted in *Le Monde*, November 11, 1988.

31. Benjedid, quoted in *Agence France Presse*, March 29, 1989.

32. Entelis, *Algeria*, 63.

33. Ibid., 125.

34. See, e.g., Frédéric Fritscher, "Le temps du réalisme et du pragmatisme."

35. Jean Leca makes this point in "Social Structure and Political Stability," 186, and in "Etat et société en Algérie," 29.

36. Addi, *L'Algérie et la démocratie*, 133–34; see also idem, "Violence et système politique en Algérie," 56–57, 63–66.

37. The political and social uses of oil revenue are discussed in Giacomo Luciani, "Allocation vs. Production States."

38. Leca, "Social Structure and Political Stability," 159–62.

39. John P. Entelis, "Algeria under Chadli," 51.

40. El-Kenz, "La société algérienne aujourd'hui," 1.

41. "L'énergie entre hier et demain," chap. 5 in Agence Nationale d'Edition et de Publicité, *Algérie*.

42. This idea is also developed in Djillali Liabes, "L'entreprise entre économie politique et société," 224.

43. See El-Kenz, "La société algérienne aujourd'hui"; and Said Shikhi, "L'ouvrier, la vie, et le prince, ou la modernité introuvable," 178–79, 186.

44. See, generally, "Le pari du président Chadli," *Le Monde*, July 2, 1987; "Algeria: Looking Forward to the Next Quarter Century," *The Middle East*, July 1987; "Une stratégie pour l'an 2000," in Agence Nationale d'Edition et de Publi-

cité, *Algérie;* Nasreen Blaschke, "How to Do Business (or Not) in Algeria"; and Entelis, *Algeria,* 126.

45. Liabes, "L'entreprise entre économie politique et société," 214–15.

46. Roberts, "In Troubled Waters," 53.

47. On this point, see Leca, "Etat et société en Algérie," 22; and Addi, "Violence et système politique en Algérie," 59.

48. Lamchichi, *L'Algérie en crise,* 216ff.

49. See *Algérie-Actualité,* no. 1238 (1989); the emphasis is mine.

50. Ali El-Kenz, "Les enjeux d'une crise," 23.

51. See Liabes, "L'entreprise entre économie politique et société," 238.

52. Ali El-Kenz, *Monographie d'une expérience industrielle en Algérie,* 252, translated in Leca, "Social Structure and Political Stability," 162.

53. Quoted in Fritscher, "Le temps du réalisme et du pragmatisme."

54. Joëlle Stolz, "La nouvelle Mecque de la jeunesse dorée."

55. "Le socialisme de la mamelle," *Algérie-Actualité,* no. 1061 (February 13, 1986).

56. *Algérie-Actualité,* nos. 1054 (December 26, 1985); 1065 (March 13, 1986); and 1105 (December 18, 1986).

57. Ibid., no. 1061 (February 13, 1986).

58. El-Kenz, "La société algérienne aujourd'hui," 25. See also Shikhi, "L'ouvrier, la vie, et le prince," 205; and Zakya Daoud, "La frustration des classes moyennes au Maghreb," 6.

59. Quoted in Gary Abramson, "Raising the Stakes," 55.

60. Deborah Harrold, "The Menace and Appeal of Algeria's Parallel Economy," 22.

61. Ahmed Henni, *Essai sur l'économie parallèle,* cited in Harrold, "Menace and Appeal of Algeria's Parallel Economy," 22.

62. Mahfoud Bennoune, "Algeria's Facade of Democracy," 9.

63. Daoud, "La frustration des classes moyennes au Maghreb," 6.

64. On the economic "reconversion" of state-actors, see Liabes, "L'entreprise entre économie politique et société," 236.

65. Harrold, "Menace and Appeal of Algeria's Parallel Economy," 22.

66. El-Kenz, "La société algérienne aujourd'hui," 27.

67. Hankiss, "In Search of a Paradigm," 197–98.

68. See Etienne, *L'Algérie, cultures et révolutions,* 58 and passim; and idem, "Clientelism in Algeria." By *clientelism* I mean the process by which the status of political representative is granted in exchange for goods and services (see John Duncan Powell, "Peasant Society and Clientelist Politics").

69. See Hugh Roberts, "The Politics of Algerian Socialism," 41.

70. Ibid.; on this point, see also Mohammed Harbi, *L'Algérie et son destin,* 202–3.

71. Abdelmajdid Messaoudi, "Chômage et solidarité familiale," 197ff.

72. Tlemçani, "Chadli's Perestroïka," 16.

73. Apter, *Rethinking Development,* 317, 318.

74. Apter with Sawa, *Against the State,* 244.

75. Leca, "Social Structure and Political Stability," 185.

76. Gilsenan, *Recognizing Islam,* 210.

77. Ibid., 214. On the notion of the city as "strategic political arena," see also Abderrahim Lamchichi, *Islam et contestation au Maghreb*, 91–92; Mohamed Naciri, "Espace urbain et société islamique," 127–37; and Claude Liauzu, "L'impossible modèle urbain dans le Tiers Monde." Eric Hobsbawm makes the broader point that urban masses have reemerged as major political actors at the end of the twentieth century after a long eclipse during which revolutions were made principally in the countryside (see *Age of Extremes*, 456–60).

78. El-Kenz, "La société algérienne aujourd'hui," 23.

79. Leca, "Etat et société en Algérie," 52.

80. Chadli, quoted in Burgat and Dowell, *Islamic Movement in North Africa*, 274. Many observers have speculated that Chadli's design in legalizing the FIS (constitutional provisions to the contrary notwithstanding) was to use the Islamic Front as a counterweight to his left-wing foes. The most comprehensive and documented account of the origin of the FIS can be found in Séverine Labat, *Les islamistes algériens*, 95–102, 105–27.

81. Abbassi Madani, quoted in Mustafa Al-Ahnaf, Bernard Botiveau, and Franck Fregosi, eds., *L'Algérie par ses islamistes*, 69.

82. See Burgat and Dowell, *Islamic Movement in North Africa*, 275–76.

83. Ibid., 276.

84. Madani, quoted in Al-Ahnaf, Botiveau, and Fregosi, *L'Algérie par ses islamistes*, 31.

85. Ajami, *Arab Predicament*, 247.

86. Burgat and Dowell, *Islamic Movement in North Africa*, 279.

87. A brief political history from Chadli's rise to power to 1992 is provided in Mohand Salah Tahi, "The Arduous Democratization Process in Algeria."

88. Events are described in ibid., 140–44. For a fictionalized version of these events, see Rachid Mimouni's *La malédiction*.

89. Human Rights Watch, *Human Rights Abuses in Algeria*, 13.

90. Ibid., 14; Addi, *L'Algérie et la démocratie*, 176. In 1990 the FFS had boycotted the elections.

91. Lahouari Addi, "Algérie: Le dérapage."

92. Ajami, *Arab Predicament*, 247–48.

93. See Aissa Khelladi, "Les islamistes algériens à l'assaut du pouvoir," 148–49.

94. Burgat and Dowell, *Islamic Movement in North Africa*, 303.

95. See Kapil, "Algeria's Crisis Intensifies"; and Addi, "Dynamique infernale en Algérie." For details of the government's contacts with Madani and the FIS leadership, see Ahmed Rouadjia, "L'armée et les islamistes," 114–16.

96. See Kapil, "Algeria's Crisis Intensifies"; see also Addi, *L'Algérie et la démocratie*, 171–74. For analyses of the democratic parties, see Monique Gadant and Mohamed Harbi, "Quel pôle démocratique?" 119; and Aissa Khelladi and Marie Virolle, "Les démocrates algériens ou l'indispensable clarification," 177. Despairing of the regime's disingenuous efforts to promote a dialogue, these and other parties met with the FIS in Rome under the aegis of the Catholic association Sant'Egidio. Out of these meetings came the January 1995 peace proposal urging negotiations between the government and all opposition parties—including the FIS.

97. See, generally, Human Rights Watch, *Human Rights Abuses in Algeria.*

98. For a discussion of these distinctions, see François Burgat, *L'islamisme au Maghreb*, 28–49; idem, "De la difficulté de nommer"; and Lamchichi, *Islam et contestation au Maghreb*, 39–50.

99. See Burgat and Dowell, *Islamic Movement in North Africa*, 41.

100. Sanson, *Laïcité islamique en Algérie.* See also Rouadjia, "Du nationalisme du FLN à l'islamisme du FIS," 129–32.

101. In 1974, speaking in Lahore at the second Islamic summit, President Boumedienne stated: "I do not wish to philosophize about Islam. . . . I believe that if there exists a spiritual link between us, it must be made concrete and include a material aspect. . . . With all due respect for the Koran, which I learned when I was ten years old, a hungry people has no need to listen to verses" (quoted in Sanson, *Laïcité islamique en Algérie*, 64).

102. Burgat and Dowell, *Islamic Movement in North Africa*, 250–69; Al-Ahnaf, Botiveau, and Fregosi, *L'Algérie par ses islamistes*, 23–29.

103. Many students of Islam have made use of this metaphor. See, e.g., Jacques Berque, "Que veulent les islamistes au Maghreb?" 20; and Gilsenan, *Recognizing Islam.*

104. Gilsenan, *Recognizing Islam*, 265.

105. Rodinson, *L'Islam*, 244–45, 249, 325; Mohammed Arkoun and Louis Gardet, *L'Islam, hier-demain;* Etienne, *L'islamisme radical;* William Zartman, "Pouvoir et état dans l'Islam."

106. Burgat and Dowell, *Islamic Movement in North Africa*, 40.

107. Rodinson, *L'Islam*, 279.

108. Gilsenan, *Recognizing Islam*, 241.

109. Etienne, *L'islamisme radical*, 122. Similar ideas are developed in Ahmed Rouadjia, *Les frères et la mosquée;* and Mohammed Harbi, "Un F.I.S. enfanté par le F.L.N."

110. Ajami, *Arab Predicament*, 214.

111. Sanson, *Laïcité islamique en Algérie;* Etienne, *L'islamisme radical*, 126; Daniel Junqua, "Algérie."

112. For a discussion of this relationship, see Gilbert Grandguillaume, *Arabisation et politique linguistique au Maghreb.*

113. Burgat, *L'islamisme au Maghreb;* Rouadjia, *Les frères et la mosquée*, 35; Entelis, "Algeria under Chadli," 56.

114. See Burgat, *L'islamisme au Maghreb*, 97–98; and Rouadjia, *Les frères et la mosquée.*

115. See François Burgat, "Sous le 'voile' de l'Islam algérien."

116. Burgat and Dowell, *Islamic Movement in North Africa*, 250.

117. Ibid., 255; Al-Ahnaf, Botiveau, and Fregosi, *L'Algérie par ses islamistes*, 25.

118. Quoted in Burgat and Dowell, *Islamic Movement in North Africa*, 256.

119. Lahouari Addi, "De la permanence du populisme algérien," 40.

120. Burgat and Dowell, *Islamic Movement in North Africa*, 282.

121. Khelladi and Virolle, "Les démocrates algériens ou l'indispensable clarification," 191.

122. See Rouadjia, "Du nationalisme du FLN à l'islamisme du FIS," 135. Recall also Galissot's observation that exclusionary identity politics and emigration

patterns go hand in hand, the former being more likely to prosper in countries that, like Algeria, have a tradition of migration to Europe, especially at times when borders become closed to all but the elite. The association between economic privilege and the West becomes all the more intense, as does the ensuing withdrawal into ethnic and nationalist isolation (see Galissot, "La purification communautaire," 110–11).

123. Rached Al-Ghannouchi, quoted in Burgat and Dowell, *Islamic Movement in North Africa,* 55.

124. Ibid., 282.

125. Ahmed Henni, "Le malaise de la jeunesse maghrébine," 200–202.

126. Abderrahmane Moussaoui, "La mosquée au péril de la commune," 81–82.

127. Gilsenan, *Recognizing Islam,* 178.

128. Ibid., 237–43.

129. Madani, quoted in Burgat and Dowell, *Islamic Movement in North Africa,* 90.

130. Mortimer, "Islam and Multiparty Politics in Algeria," 577.

131. At various times the state did try to restrain the proliferation of unofficial mosques. In 1986 President Chadli insisted that "in constructing a mosque, we must guarantee all the conditions necessary to see that it can fulfill the important role for which it was built. We cannot leave it to the mercy of certain pernicious elements who would use it for destructive ends. . . . The demagogic policy which leads the wilayas and the communes to give authorization to those who construct alone and without any planning must disappear" (quoted in Burgat and Dowell, *Islamic Movement in North Africa,* 89). Later, in 1992, laws were passed to tighten the state's control over the "administration [of] buildings and men" (ibid., 90).

132. Moussaoui, "La mosquée au péril de la commune," 83–84.

133. Ali Belhadj, quoted in Khelladi, "Les islamistes algériens à l'assaut du pouvoir," 141.

134. Moussaoui, "La mosquée au péril de la commune," 83–84.

135. A similar process appears to be under way in Gaza and the West Bank, where Hamas has taken control of a majority of the mosques. Although the new Palestinian Authority banned all political statements from mosques, the rule is neither heeded nor enforced (see Marcus, "Going to Extremes," A-5).

136. Moussaoui, "La mosquée au péril de la commune," 85–89.

137. Burgat and Dowell, *Islamic Movement in North Africa,* 93. See also José Garçon, "L'Algérie à la dérive sur un baril intégriste," 35.

138. Mortimer, "Islam and Multiparty Politics in Algeria," 579.

139. Burgat and Dowell, *Islamic Movement in North Africa,* 93.

140. José Garçon, "L'islamisation forcée de toute une société," 20; *Le Monde,* February 22, 1994, 6; Rouadjia, *Les frères et la mosquée,* 269–71.

141. Kapil, "Algeria's Crisis Intensifies," 3; Benjamin Stora, "Deuxième guerre algérienne?" 248–49. In 1956 the FLN had ordered all students to stay away from high schools and universities.

142. Gilsenan, *Recognizing Islam,* 256.

143. See Jacques Fontaine's instructive study of voting patterns in Algiers, "Quartiers defavorisés et vote islamique à Alger," 141.

144. Mohammed Harbi, "Entretien," 12.
145. Gilles Millet, "La genèse des groupes armés qui ont débordé le FIS," 21; Labat, *Les islamistes algériens*, 129, 227–43.
146. Al-Ahnaf, Botiveau, and Fregosi, *L'Algérie par ses islamistes*, 35.
147. See Addi, "Violence et système politique en Algérie," 63–65.
148. Ibid., 65.
149. Galissot, "La purification communautaire," 103–4.
150. Stora, "Algérie," 67.
151. See, generally, Stora, "Deuxième guerre algérienne?" 242.
152. On the similarities between the FIS and the FLN, see Ammar Koroghli, *Institutions politiques et développement en Algérie;* and Lahouari Addi, "Religion and Modernity in Algeria."

Afterthoughts

1. *Le Matin,* December 3, 1994.
2. See Kapil, "Algeria's Crisis Intensifies," 2–7.
3. Cf. Furet, *Le passé d'une illusion,* 571.
4. Leon Wieseltier, "Bloodlust Memories," 13.
5. Gellner, "Homeland of the Unrevolution," 147.
6. Castaneda, *Utopia Unarmed,* 420–26.
7. Leca, "Etat et société en Algérie," 32–33.

Bibliography

General Literature

Abdel-Malek, Anouar. *La pensée politique arabe contemporaine.* Paris: Seuil, 1970.

Addi, Lahouari. "L'état politique devant l'état économique." *Projet,* no. 193 (May–June 1985).

Ajami, Fouad. *The Arab Predicament.* New York: Cambridge University Press, 1992.

———. "The Summoning." *Foreign Affairs,* September–October 1993.

Ajayi, J. F. A. "Colonialism: An Episode in African History." In *Colonialism in Africa: 1870–1960,* edited by L. H. Gann and P. Duignan. Cambridge: Cambridge University Press, 1970.

Allen, Christopher, et al. *Benin, the Congo, Burkina Faso.* New York: Pinter, 1989.

Alliès, Paul. *L'invention du territoire.* Grenoble: Presses Universitaires de Grenoble, 1980.

Almond, Gabriel, and James S. Coleman. *The Politics of the Developing Areas.* Princeton: Princeton University Press, 1960.

Almond, Gabriel, and G. Bingham Powell. *Comparative Politics: A Developmental Approach.* Boston: Little, Brown, 1966.

Althusser, Louis. *Essays on Ideology.* London: Verso, 1984.

Amin, Samir. *L'accumulation à l'échelle mondiale.* Paris: Anthropos, 1970.

———. *Classe et nation.* Paris: Minuit, 1979.

———. *Le développement du capitalisme en Côte d'Ivoire.* Paris: Minuit, 1969.

———. *Le développement inégal: Essai sur les formations sociales du capitalisme périphérique.* Paris: Minuit, 1973.

———. *L'ethnie à l'assaut des nations.* Paris: L'Harmattan, 1994.

———. *Eurocentrism.* New York: Monthly Review Press, 1989.

———. *La faillite du développement en Afrique et dans le Tiers Monde.* Paris: L'Harmattan, 1989.

287

———. "La stratégie de la révolution socialiste dans le Tiers Monde." In *Connaissance du Tiers Monde,* edited by Catherine Coquery-Vidrovitch. Paris: 10/18, 1978.

———, ed. *Mondialisation et accumulation.* Paris: L'Harmattan, 1993.

Amin, Samir, et al. *Le Tiers Monde et la gauche.* Paris: Seuil, 1979.

Amos, John W. *Palestinian Resistance: Organisation of a National Movement.* New York: Pergamon Press, 1980.

Anderson, Benedict. *Imagined Communities.* London: Verso, 1983.

Anderson, Perry. *Considerations on Western Marxism.* London: Verso, 1979.

———. *In the Tracks of Historical Materialism.* London: Verso, 1984.

———. *Sur Gramsci.* Paris: Maspéro, 1978.

Ansari, H. N. "The Islamic Militants in Egyptian Politics." *International Journal of Middle Eastern Studies* 16 (1984).

Apter, David. "The New Mytho/Logics and the Specter of Superfluous Man." *Social Research* 52 (summer 1985).

———. "The Passing of Development Studies." *Government and Opposition* 15, nos. 3–4 (1980).

———. *The Politics of Modernization.* Chicago: University of Chicago Press, 1965.

———. *Rethinking Development.* London: Sage, 1987.

———. "Thinking about Violence." N.p., n.d. Typescript.

———, ed. *Ideology and Discontent.* New York: Free Press, 1964.

Apter, David, with Nagayo Sawa. *Against the State.* Cambridge: Harvard University Press, 1987.

Arendt, Hannah. *On Revolution.* New York: Penguin, 1985.

———. *On Violence.* New York: Harcourt Brace Jovanovich, 1970.

———. *The Origins of Totalitarianism.* London: André Deutsch, 1986.

Arkoun, Mohammed, and Louis Gardet. *L'Islam, hier-demain.* Paris: Buchet-Castel, 1982.

Aron, Raymond. *Dix-huit leçons sur la société industrielle.* Paris: Gallimard, 1962.

———. *Les étapes de la pensée sociologique.* Paris: Gallimard, 1967.

———. *L'opium des intellectuels.* Paris: Calmann-Lévy, 1986.

Aronson, Ronald. "The Individualist Social Theory of Jean-Paul Sartre." In *Western Marxism: A Critical Reader,* edited by Fareth Stedman Jones et al. London: Verso, 1978.

Aubral, François, and Xavier Delcourt. *Contre la nouvelle philosophie.* Paris: Gallimard, 1977.

Badie, Bertrand. *Les deux états: Pouvoir et société en Occident et en terre d'Islam.* Paris: Fayard, 1986.

———. *L'état importé.* Paris: Fayard, 1992.

Balandier, Georges. *Sens et puissance: Les dynamiques sociales.* Paris: P.U.F., 1971.

Balandier, Georges, and Alfred Sauvy, eds. *Le Tiers Monde: Sous-développement et développement.* Paris: P.U.F., 1956.

Balta, Paul, ed. *L'Islam dans le monde.* Paris: La Découverte, 1986.

Balta, Paul, and Claudine Rulleau. *La vision Nassérienne.* Paris: Sindbad, 1982.

Barnet, Richard J. *Intervention and Revolution.* New York: Meridian, 1972.

Barthes, Roland. *Mythologies.* Paris: Seuil, 1957.

Bartley, Robert L. "The Case for Optimism." *Foreign Affairs,* September–October 1993.

Baudrillard, Jean. *Amérique.* Paris: Grasset, 1986.

———. *Pour une critique de l'économie politique du signe.* Paris: Gallimard, 1972.

Bayart, Jean-François. *L'état en Afrique.* Paris: Fayard, 1989.

Bell, Daniel. *The End of Ideology.* Cambridge: Harvard University Press, 1988.

Bencheikh, Madjid. *Droit international du sous-développement.* Paris: Berger-Leurault, 1983.

Bennigsen, Alexandre, and Chantal Lemercier-Quelquejay. *Sultan Galiev: Le père de la révolution tiers-mondiste.* Paris: Fayard, 1986.

Benot, Yves. *Indépendances africaines: Idéologies et réalités.* 2 vols. Paris: Maspéro, 1975.

Berg, Eugène. *Non-alignement et nouvel ordre mondial.* Paris: P.U.F., 1980.

Berlin, Isaiah. *Four Essays on Liberty.* Oxford: Oxford University Press, 1984.

Bettleheim, Charles. *Planification et croissance accélérée.* Paris: Maspéro, 1971.

Birnbaum, Pierre, and Jean Leca. *Sur l'individualisme.* Paris: Maspéro, 1971.

Blanchet, Pierre, and Claire Brière. *Iran: La révolution au nom de Dieu.* Paris: Seuil, 1979.

Boudon, Raymond. *L'idéologie.* Paris: Fayard, 1986.

Bourdieu, Pierre. *Ce que parler veut dire.* Paris: Fayard, 1982.

———. *Choses dites.* Paris: Minuit, 1987.

———. *Distinction: A Social Critique of the Judgement of Taste.* London: Routledge & Kegan Paul, 1984.

———. "The Force of Law: Toward a Sociology of the Juridical Field." *Hastings Law Journal* 38 (July 1987).

———. *Outline of a Theory of Practice.* Cambridge: Cambridge University Press, 1977.

———. "La représentation politique: Eléments pour une théorie du champ politique." *Actes de la Recherche en Sciences Sociales* 36–37 (February–March 1981).

———. *Le sens pratique.* Paris: Minuit, 1980.

Bourges, Hervé, and Claude Wauthier. *Les 50 Afriques.* 2 vols. Paris: Seuil, 1979.

Bouvier, Pierre. *Fanon.* Paris: Editions Universitaires, 1971.

Bragança, Aquino de, and Immanuel Wallerstein. *The African Liberation Reader.* 3 vols. London: Zed, 1982.

Braillard, Philippe. *Mythe et réalité du non-alignement.* Paris: P.U.F., 1987.

Braudel, Fernand. "Interview." *Le Magazine Littéraire,* no. 212 (November 1984).

Brauman, Rony. "Le tiers mondisme contre le Tiers Monde." *Géopolitique Africaine,* June 1986.

Browne, Robert S. "The IMF and the World Bank in the New World Order." In *Altered States,* edited by Phyllis Bennis and Michael Moushabeck. Brooklyn: Olive Branch, 1993.

Broyelle, Jacques, and Evelyne Tschirhard. *Deuxième retour de Chine.* Paris: Seuil, 1977.

Bruckner, Pascal. *Le sanglot de l'homme blanc.* Paris: Seuil, 1983.

Burchett, Wilfred. *Vietnam Will Win!* New York: Guardian, 1970.

Cabral, Amilcar. *Revolution in Guinea*. London: Stage 1, 1979.
―――. *Unité et lutte*. 2 vols. Paris: Maspéro, 1975.
Camau, Michel. *Contrôle politique et régulations électorales en Tunisie*. Aix-en-Provence: Edisud, 1981.
Cardoso, Fernando Henrique. "Dependency and Development in Latin America." *New Left Review*, no. 74 (1972).
Carnoy, Martin. *The State and Political Theory*. Princeton: Princeton University Press, 1984.
Cassirer, Ernst. *The Myth of the State*. New Haven, Yale University Press, 1946
―――. *Le problème Jean-Jacques Rousseau*. Paris: Hachette, 1987.
Castaneda, Jorge G. *Utopia Unarmed*. New York: Knopf, 1993.
Chaliand, Gérard. *Les faubourgs de l'histoire: Tiers-mondismes et Tiers-Mondes*. Paris: Calmann-Lévy, 1984.
―――. *Mythes révolutionnaires du Tiers-Monde*. Paris: Seuil, 1979.
Clastres, Pierre. *La société contre l'état: Recherches d'anthropologie politique*. Paris: Minuit, 1974.
Clifford, James. *The Predicament of Culture: Twentieth Century Ethnography, Literature, and Art*. Cambridge: Harvard University Press, 1988.
Cobban, Alfred. *The Nation-State and National Self-Determination*. London: Collins, 1969.
―――. *Rousseau and the Modern State*. London: George Allen & Unwin, 1934.
Cohn-Bendit, Dany. *Nous l'avons tant aimée la révolution*. Paris: Bernard Barrault, 1986.
Colletti, Lucio. *From Rousseau to Lenin*. New York: Monthly Review Press, 1972.
Coleman, James. "Tradition and Nationalism in Tropical Africa." in *New States in the Modern World*, edited by Martin Kilson. Cambridge: Harvard University Press, 1975.
Connolly, William, ed. *Legitimacy and the State*. Oxford: Basil Blackwell, 1984.
Coquery-Vidrovitch, Catherine, ed. *Connaissance du Tiers-Monde*. Paris: 10/18, 1978.
Cot, Jean-Pierre. *A l'épreuve du pouvoir: Le tiers-mondisme pour quoi faire?* Paris: Seuil, 1984.
Crone, Patricia. *Slaves on Horses: The Evolution of the Islamic Polity*. Cambridge: Cambridge University Press, 1980.
Cudsi, Alexander, and A. E. H. Dessouki. *Islam and Power*. London: Croom Helm, 1981.
Dahl, Robert. *Regimes and Opposition*. New Haven, Yale University Press, 1973.
Darnton, John. "In Poor, Decolonized Africa Bankers Are New Overlords." *New York Times*, June 20, 1994.
Davidson, Basil. *The Black Man's Burden*. New York: Random House, 1992.
―――. *Black Star*. London: Allen Lane, 1973.
Davis, John. "Qaddafi's Theory of Non-Representative Government." *Government and Opposition* 17, no. 1 (1982).
Debray, Régis. *La critique des armes*. Paris: Seuil, 1973.
―――. "France, fille du souvenir." *Le Nouvel Observateur*, no. 1149 (November 1986).

————. *La puissance et les rêves*. Paris: Gallimard, 1984.

————. *Révolution dans la révolution?* Paris: Maspéro, 1967.

de Certeau, Michel. *Arts de faire*. Paris: 10/18, 1980.

————. *L'écriture de l'histoire*. Paris: Gallimard, 1975.

Deutsch, Karl. *Nationalism and Social Communication*. New York: Technology Press of MIT and Wiley, 1953.

Deutsch, Karl, and William Foltz. *Nation-Building*. New York: Atherton, 1963.

Diamond, Larry, Juan J. Linz, and Seymour Martin Lipset. *Democracy in Developing Countries*. Boulder: L. Rienner, 1990.

Dreyfus, Hubert, and Paul Rabinow. *Michel Foucault: Beyond Structuralism and Hermeneutics*. Chicago: University of Chicago Press, 1982.

Les droits de l'homme et le nouvel occidentalisme. Paris: L'Harmattan, 1988.

Dumont, René. *Pour l'Afrique, j'accuse*. Paris: Plon, 1986.

Dunn, John. *Modern Revolutions: An Introduction to the Analysis of a Political Phenomenon*. Cambridge: Cambridge University Press, 1972.

Eisenstadt, S. N. *Modernization: Protest and Change*. Englewood Cliffs, N.J.: Prentice-Hall, 1966.

Eliade, Mircea. *Le mythe de l'éternel retour — archétypes et répétition*. Paris: Gallimard, 1949.

Emmanuel, Arghiri. *L'échange inégal: Essai sur les antagonismes dans les rapports économiques internationaux*. Paris: Maspéro, 1969.

Evans, Peter, Dietrich Rueschmeyer, and Theda Skocpol, eds. *Bringing the State Back In*. Cambridge: Cambridge University Press, 1985.

Fanon, Frantz. *Pour la révolution africaine*. Paris: Maspéro, 1964.

————. *The Wretched of the Earth*. Harmondsworth: Penguin, 1967.

Faye, Jean-Pierre. *Langages totalitaires*. Paris: Hermann, 1972.

Fei, John, and Gustav Ranis. *Development of the Labor Surplus Economy: Theory and Policy*. Homewood, Ill.: R. D. Irwin, 1964.

Ferry, Luc, and Alain Renaut. *La Pensée 68*. Paris: Gallimard, 1986.

"Fin du National?" *Peuples Méditerranéens*, nos. 35–36 (April–September 1986).

Flory, Maurice, and Robert Mantran. *Les régimes politiques des pays arabes*. Paris: P.U.F., 1968.

Foucault, Michel. "L'esprit d'un monde sans esprit." Afterword to *Iran: La révolution au nom de Dieu*, by Pierre Blanchet and Claire Brière. Paris: Seuil, 1979.

————. *Language, Counter-Memory, Practice*. Edited by Donald F. Bouchard and Sherry Simon. New York: Cornell University Press, 1977.

————. "Omnes et singulatum: Vers une critique de la raison politique." *Le Débat*, no. 41 (September 1986).

————. *Power/Knowledge*. Brighton: Harvester, 1980.

————. *La volonté de savoir*. Paris: Gallimard, 1976.

"Foucault: Du monde entier." *Critique*, nos. 471–72 (August–September 1986).

Foucault: Une histoire de la vérité. Paris: Syros, 1985.

Francos, Ania. *La fête cubaine*. Paris: Julliard, 1961.

Frank, André Gunder. *L'accumulation dépendante*. Paris: Anthropos, 1978.

Friedland, William H., and Carl G. Rosberg, eds. *African Socialism*. Stanford: Stanford University Press, 1964.

Frost, Robert. *The Poetry of Robert Frost*. London: Cape, 1971.

Furet, François. *Le passé d'une illusion*. Paris: Robert-Laffont, 1995.

———. *Penser la révolution française*. Paris: Gallimard, 1978.

Galeano, Eduardo. *Open Veins of Latin America*. New York: Monthly Review Press, 1973.

Galissot, René. "Les empires se portent bien." In *Le Tiers Monde et la gauche,* by Samir Amin et al. Paris: Seuil, 1979.

Galtung, Johan. "A Structural Theory of Imperialism." *Journal of Peace Research* 2 (1971).

Geertz, Clifford. "Ideology as a Cultural System." In *Ideology and Discontent,* edited by David Apter. London: Free Press, 1964.

———. *The Interpretation of Cultures*. New York: Basic Books, 1973.

———. *Islam Observed: Religious Development in Morocco and Indonesia*. New Haven: Yale University Press, 1968.

———, ed. *Old Societies and New States*. New York: Free Press, 1963.

Gellner, Ernest. "Homeland of the Unrevolution." *Daedalus* 122, no. 3 (1993).

———. *Thought and Change*. London: Weidenfeld & Nicolson, 1964.

———. "Tribalism and the State in the Middle East." In *Tribes and State Formation in the Middle East,* edited by Philip S. Khoury and Joseph Kostiner. Berkeley: University of California Press, 1990.

Gellner, Ernest, and G. Ionescu, eds. *Populism*. London: Weidenfeld & Nicolson, 1969.

Gellner, Ernest, and Jean-Claude Vatin, eds. *Islam et politique au Maghreb*. Paris: C.N.R.S., 1981.

Gellner, Ernest, and John Waterbury, eds. *Patrons and Clients in Mediterranean Societies*. London: Duckworth, 1977.

Gendzier, Irene L. *Frantz Fanon: A Critical Study*. London: Wildwood House, 1973.

———. *Managing Political Change: Social Scientists and the Third World*. Boulder: Westview Press, 1985.

Genet, Jean. *Un captif amoureux*. Paris: Gallimard, 1986.

Geremek, Bronislaw. "Between Hope and Despair." *Daedalus* 119, no. 1 (1990).

Gilsenan, Michael. "Apprehensions of Islam." *Merip Reports,* July–August 1988.

———. "Culture and Symbolic Violence." Oxford, January 1987. Typescript.

———. "L'Islam dans l'Egypte contemporaine: Religion d'état, religion populaire." *Annales,* nos. 3–4 (May–August 1980).

———. *Recognizing Islam*. London: I. B. Tauris, 1992.

Girardet, Raoul. *Mythes et mythologies politiques*. Paris: Seuil, 1986.

Glucksmann, André. *Les maîtres penseurs*. Paris: Grasset, 1977.

Glucksmann, André, and Thierry Wolton. *Silence, on tue!* Paris: Grasset, 1986.

Godelier, Maurice. *Horizons, trajets marxistes en anthropologie*. 2 vols. Paris: Maspéro, 1977.

Gordon, David C. *Self-Determination and History in the Third World*. Princeton: Princeton University Press, 1971.

Gramsci, Antonio. *Gramsci dans le texte*. Paris: Editions Sociales, 1975.

———. *Selections from the Prison Notebooks*. Edited and translated by Quintin Hoare and Geoffrey Nowell-Smith. New York: International Publishers, 1971.

Greimas, A. J. *Sémiotique et sciences sociales*. Paris: Seuil, 1976.

Gresh, Alain. "Quand l'islamisme menace le monde." *Le Monde Diplomatique,* December 1993.

Gueyras, Jean. "Dix ans de pouvoir populaire en Libye: Le théatre d'ombres de la Jamahiriya." *Le Monde,* March 3, 1987.

Guitard, Odette. *Bandoung ou le réveil des peuples colonisés*. Paris: P.U.F., 1961.

Habermas, Jürgen. "Une flèche dans le coeur du temps présent." *Critique,* nos. 471–72 (August–September 1986).

———. *Legitimation Crisis*. Boston: Beacon Press, 1975.

Halliday, Fred. "Tunisia's Uncertain Future." *Merip Reports,* March–April 1990.

Hamon, Hervé, and Patrick Rotman. *Génération: Les années de rêve*. Paris: Seuil, 1987.

Hancock, Graham. *Lords of Poverty*. New York: Atlantic Monthly Press, 1989.

Hankiss, Elemér. "In Search of a Paradigm." *Daedalus* 119, no. 1 (1990).

Hansen, Roger D. *Beyond the North-South Stalemate*. New York: McGraw-Hill, 1979.

Harris, Nigel. *The End of the Third World: Newly Industrializing Countries and the Decline of an Ideology*. Harmondsworth: Penguin, 1987.

Held, David. *Models of Democracy*. Stanford: Stanford University Press. 1987.

Hermet, Guy. "State-Controlled Elections: A Framework." In *Elections Without Choice,* edited by Guy Hermet, Richard Rose, and Alain Rouquié. New York: Wiley & Sons, 1978.

Hertz, F. *Nationality in History and Politics*. London: K. Paul, Trench, Trubner & Co., 1944.

Hobsbawm, Eric. *The Age of Extremes*. New York: Pantheon, 1994.

Hourani, Albert. *Arabic Thought in the Liberal Age: 1798–1939*. London: Oxford University Press, 1970.

———. *A History of the Arab Peoples*. Cambridge: Harvard University Press, 1991.

Hunt, Lynn. *Politics, Culture, and Class in the French Revolution*. Berkeley: University of California Press, 1984.

Huntington, Samuel P. *American Politics: The Promise of Disharmony*. Cambridge: Harvard University Press, 1981.

———. "The Clash of Civilizations." *Foreign Affairs,* summer 1993.

———. *The Soldier and the State*. Cambridge: Harvard University Press, 1957.

Hussein, Mahmoud. *L'Egypte, lutte de classes et libération nationale*. 2 Vols. Paris: Maspéro, 1975.

———. *Versant sud de la liberté*. Paris: La Découverte, 1989.

Jabber, Fuad, Ann Mosley Lesch, and William B. Quandt. *The Politics of Palestinian Nationalism*. Berkeley: University of California Press, 1973.

Jack, Homer. *Cairo: The Afro-Asian Peoples' Solidarity Conference. A Critical Political Analysis*. Chicago: Toward Freedom, 1958.

Jacquemot, Pierre, ed. *Economie et sociologie du Tiers-Monde*. Paris: L'Harmattan, 1981.

Jalée, Pierre. *Le pillage du Tiers-Monde*. Paris: Maspéro, 1975.

Johnson, Nels. *Islam and the Politics of Meaning in Palestinian Nationalism*. London: Kegan Paul International, 1982.

Jouve, Edmond. *Le Tiers Monde dans la vie internationale*. Paris: Berger-Leurault, 1986.

Julliard, Jacques. *La faute à Rousseau*. Paris: Seuil, 1985.

———. "Le Tiers Monde et la gauche." In *Le Tiers Monde et la gauche,* by Samir Amin et al. Paris: Seuil, 1979.

Kaplan, Robert. "The Coming Anarchy." *Atlantic Monthly,* February 1994.

Kapuscinski, Ryszard. *The Soccer War.* New York: Vintage, 1992.

Karnow, Stanley. *Vietnam.* New York: Penguin, 1984.

Kedourie, Elie. Introduction to *Nationalism in Asia and Africa.* New York: World, 1970.

———. *Nationalism.* London: Hutchinson & Co., 1961.

Keen, David. "In Africa, Planned Suffering." *New York Times,* August 15, 1994.

Kennedy, Duncan. "The Stakes of Law, or Hale and Foucault!" In *Sexy Dressing, Etc.* Cambridge: Harvard University Press, 1993.

Kepel, Gilles. *Les banlieues de l'islam: Naissance d'une relgion en France.* Paris: Seuil, 1987.

———. *La revanche de Dieu.* Paris: Seuil, 1991.

Khalidi, Tarif. "Palestinian Historiography: 1900–1948." *Journal of Palestine Studies* 10, no. 3 (1981).

Khoury, Philip S., and Joseph Kostiner, eds. *Tribes and State Formation in the Middle East.* Berkeley: University of California Press, 1990.

Kiernan, V. G. *Marxism and Imperialism.* London: Edward Arnold, 1974.

Kilson, Martin. "The Emergent Elites of Black Africa, 1900 to 1960." In *Colonialism in Africa: 1879–1960,* edited by L. H. Gann and P. Duignan, vol. 2. Cambridge: Cambridge University Press, 1970.

Kolakowski, Leszek. *Main Currents of Marxism: Its Rise, Growth, and Dissolution.* 3 vols. Oxford: Clarendon Press, 1978.

Koury, E. M. *The Pattern of Mass Movements in Arab Revolutionary Progressive States.* Paris: Mouton, 1971.

Krasner, Stephen. *Structural Conflict: The Third World against Global Liberalism.* Berkeley: University of California Press, 1985.

Laclau, Ernesto, and Chantal Mouffe. *Hegemony and Socialist Strategy: Towards a Radical Democratic Politics.* London: Verso, 1985.

Lacoste, Yves. *Contre les anti-tiers-mondistes, et contre certains tiers-mondistes.* Paris: La Découverte, 1985.

———. "Vocabulaire et problématique du sous-développement." In *Connaissance du Tiers Monde,* edited by Catherine Coquery-Vidrovitch. Paris: 10/18, 1978.

Lacouture, Jean. *Cinq hommes et la France.* Paris: Seuil, 1961.

———. *The Demigods.* London: Secker & Warburg, 1971.

———. *Nasser.* London: Secker & Warburg, 1973.

Laroui, Abdallah. *The Crisis of the Arab Intellectual: Traditionalism or Historicism?* Berkeley: University of California Press, 1976. Translated by Diarmid Cammell. Originally published as *La crise des intellectuels arabes: Traditionalisme ou historicisme?* Paris: Maspéro, 1974.

———. *Histoire du Maghreb, un essai de synthèse.* Paris: Maspéro, 1970.

———. *L'idéologie arabe contemporaine.* Paris: Maspéro, 1967.

———. *Islam et modernité.* Paris: La Découverte, 1987.

Latouche, Serge. *L'occidentalisation du monde.* Paris: La Découverte, 1989.

Leach, Edmund. *Lévi-Strauss*. Glasgow: Fontana, 1985.
————. *Political Systems of Highland Burma*. Norwich: Fletcher & Son, 1954.
Leclerc, Gérard. *L'observation de l'homme*. Paris: Seuil, 1979.
Lefort, Claude. *Essais sur le politique: XIX–XX siècles*. Paris: Seuil, 1986.
Legum, Colin. *Pan-Africanism: A Short Political Guide*. New York: Praeger, 1965.
Lentin, Albert-Paul. *La lutte tricontinentale*. Paris: Maspero, 1966.
Lesch, Ann Mosley. *Arab Politics in Palestine: 1917–1939*. Ithaca: Cornell University Press, 1979.
Leveau, Rémy. *Le fellah marocain défenseur du trône*. Paris: Fondation Nationale des Sciences Politiques, 1985.
Lévi-Strauss, Claude. *Anthropologie structurale*. Paris: Plon, 1958.
————. *Le cru et le cuit*. Paris: Plon, 1964.
Lévy, Bernard-Henry. *La barbarie à visage humain*. Paris: Grasset, 1977.
Liauzu, Claude. *Aux origines des tiers-mondismes: Colonisés et anti-colonialistes en France, 1919–1939*. Paris: L'Harmattan, 1982.
————. "L'impossible modèle urbain dans le Tiers Monde." *Le Monde Diplomatique,* May 1988.
Linz, Juan. *The Breakdown of Democratic Regimes: Crisis, Breakdown, and Re-equilibration*. Baltimore: John Hopkins University Press, 1978.
————. "Non-Competitive Elections in Europe." In *Elections without Choice,* edited by Guy Hermet, Richard Rose, and Alain Rouquié. New York: Wiley & Sons, 1978.
Lipjhart, Arend. *Democracy in Plural Societies*. New Haven: Yale University Press, 1977.
Lipset, Seymour Martin. *Political Man*. Garden City, N.Y.: Doubleday, 1960.
Lowenthal, Abraham, ed. *The Peruvian Experiment: Continuity and Change under Military Rule*. Princeton: Princeton University Press, 1975.
Luciani, Giacomo. "Allocation vs. Production States: A Theoretical Framework." In *The Arab State,* edited by G. Luciani. Berkeley: University of California Press, 1990.
Lukes, Steven, ed. *Power*. New York: New York University Press, 1986.
Lyon, Peter. "The Emergence of the Third World." In *The Expansion of International Society,* edited by H. Bull and A. Watson. Oxford: Clarendon Press, 1984.
Macciochi, Maria Antonietta. *Daily Life in Revolutionary China*. New York: Monthly Review Press, 1972.
MacFarlane, S. Neil. *Superpower Rivalry and Third World Radicalism*. London: Croom Helm, 1985.
MacRae, Donald. "Populism As an Ideology." In *Populism,* edited by Ernest Gellner and G. Ionescu. London: Weidenfeld & Nicholson, 1969.
Mahiou, Ahmed. *L'avènement du parti unique en Afrique Noire*. Paris: Librairie de Droit et de Jurisprudence, 1969.
Malloy, James M., ed. *Authoritarianism and Corporatism in Latin America*. Pittsburgh: University of Pittsburgh Press, 1977.
Manas, Jean. "This Land Is My Land." 1994. Manuscript on file with author.
Mannheim, Karl. *Ideology and Utopia*. London: K. Paul, Trench, Trubner & Co., 1936.

Marcus, Amy D. "Going to Extremes: Islamic Radicals Rival the PLO As Leaders in West Bank and Gaza." *Wall Street Journal,* July 5, 1994.

Martin, Laurence W., ed. *Neutralism and Non-Alignment: The New States in World Affairs.* Westport, Conn: Greenwood, 1973.

Marx, Karl, and Friedrich Engels. *The German Ideology.* London: Lawrence & Wishart, 1970.

McClelland, David. *The Achieving Society.* Princeton: Van Nostrand, 1961.

Memmi, Albert. *Portrait du colonisé.* Paris: Gallimard, 1985.

Michels, Robert. *Political Parties.* New York: Free Press, 1968.

Mortimer, Robert. *The Third World Coalition in International Politics.* Boulder: Westview Press, 1984.

Mouffe, Chantal. "Hegemony and Ideology in Gramsci." In *Culture, Ideology, and Social Process: A Reader,* edited by Tony Bennett. London: Open University, 1981.

———, ed. *Gramsci and Marxist Theory.* London: Routledge & Kegan Paul, 1979.

Naciri, Mohamed. "Espace urbain et société islamique." *Hérodote,* no. 36 (1985).

———. "La mosquée: Un enjeu dans la ville." *Lamalif,* no. 192 (1987).

Nairn, Tom. "Marxism and the Modern Janus." *New Left Review,* no. 94 (1975).

Nettl, J.-P. *Political Mobilization—A Sociological Analysis of Methods and Concepts.* New York: Basic Books, 1967.

Nkrumah, Kwame. *Consciencism.* New York: Monthly Review Press, 1965.

Nyerere, Julius K. *Ujamaa—Essays on Socialism.* London: Oxford University Press, 1971.

O'Donnell, Guillermo, and Philippe Schmitter, eds. *Transitions from Authoritarian Rule—Tentative Conclusions about Uncertain Democracies.* Baltimore: John Hopkins University Press, 1986.

O'Donnell, Guillermo, and Laurence Whitehead, eds. *Transitions from Authoritarian Rule—Comparative Perspectives.* Baltimore: John Hopkins University Press, 1986.

Offe, Claus. *Contradictions of the Welfare State.* London: Hutchinson, 1984.

Ottaway, David, and Marina Ottaway. *Afrocommunism.* New York: Africana, 1981.

Ozbudun, Ergun, and Myron Weiner, eds. *Competitive Elections in Developing Countries.* Durham, N.C.: Duke University Press, 1987.

Ozouf, Mona. "De thermidor à brumaire: Le discours de la Révolution sur elle-même." *Revue Historique,* no. 493 (1970).

———. *La fête révolutionnaire: 1789–1799.* Paris: Gallimard, 1976.

Parsons, Talcott. *The System of Modern Societies.* Englewood Cliffs, N.J.: Prentice-Hall, 1971.

Perlmutter, Amos. *The Military and Politics in Modern Times.* New Haven: Yale University Press, 1977.

Perroux, François. *L'économie des jeunes nations: Industrialisation et groupements de nations.* Paris: P.U.F., 1962.

Piscatori, James P., ed. *Islam in the Political Process.* New York: Cambridge University Press, 1983.

Pitkin, Hanna. *The Concept of Representation.* Berkeley: University of California Press, 1967.

Poulantzas, Nicos. *L'état, le pouvoir, le socialisme*. Paris: P.U.F., 1978.
————. *Political Power and Social Class*. London: Verso, 1978.
Powell, John Duncan. "Peasant Society and Clientelist Politics." *American Political Science Review* 64 (June 1970).
Queuille, Pierre. *Histoire de l'afro-asiatisme jusqu'à Bandoung: La naissance du Tiers-Monde*. Paris: Payot, 1965.
Racevskis, Karlis. *Michel Foucault and the Subversion of the Intellect*. Ithaca: Cornell University Press, 1983.
Rancière, Jacques. *L'empire du sociologue*. Paris: La Découverte, 1984.
Ratsiraka, Didier. *Strategies for the Twenty-first Century*. Paris: Afrique-Asie-Amérique-Latine, 1984.
"Les régimes islamiques." *Pouvoirs*, no. 12 (1983).
Reszler, André. *Mythes politiques modernes*. Paris: P.U.F., 1981.
Ricoeur, Paul. *The Symbolism of Evil*. New York: Beacon Press, 1979.
Rodinson, Maxime. *De Pythagore à Lénine*. Paris: Fayard, 1993.
————. *Islam et capitalisme*. Paris: Seuil, 1966.
————. *Islam et Marxisme*. In *Connaissance du Tiers Monde*, edited by Catherine Coquery-Vidrovitch. Paris: 10/18, 1978.
————. *L'Islam: Politique et croyance*. Paris: Fayard, 1993.
————. *Marxisme et monde musulman*. Paris: Seuil, 1972.
————. "Nationalisme arabe et nationalismes communautaires." *Revue d'Etudes Palestiniennes*, no. 22 (winter 1987).
————. "Pas de solution au conflit israélo-arabe." *Arabies*, no. 1 (January 1987).
Rostow, Walt Whitman. *The Stages of Economic Growth*. New York: Cambridge University Press, 1960.
Rous, Jean. "Bandoung, répétition de l'histoire." *Esprit,* July 1955.
Rousseau, Jean-Jacques. *Du contrat social*. Geneva: Cheval Ailé, 1947.
Sadowski, Yahya. "The New Orientalism and the Democracy Debate." *Merip Reports,* July–August 1993.
Sahlins, Peter. *Boundaries: The Making of France and Spain in the Pyrenees*. Berkeley: University of California Press, 1989.
Said, Edward. *Covering Islam*. New York: Pantheon, 1981.
————. *Culture and Imperialism*. New York: Knopf, 1993.
————. *Orientalism*. New York: Vintage, 1979.
————. *The Politics of Dispossession*. New York: Pantheon, 1994.
————. *The Question of Palestine*. New York: Vintage, 1980.
Samuel, David. "At Play in the Fields of Oppression." *Harper's Magazine,* no. 290 (May 1995).
Sartre, Jean-Paul. *Critique of Dialectical Reason*. London: Verso, 1982.
————. Preface to *The Wretched of the Earth*, by Frantz Fanon. Harmondsworth: Penguin, 1967.
Sayigh, Rosemary. "The Palestinian Identity among Camp Residents." *Journal of Palestine Studies* 6, no. 3 (1977).
————. *Palestinians: From Peasants to Revolutionaries*. London: Zed, 1979.
————. "Sources of Palestinian Nationalism." *Journal of Palestine Studies* 6, no. 4 (1977).
Schmitter, Philippe. "Still the Century of Corporatism?" *Review of Political Science* 36 (1974).

Sklar, Richard L. "The Nature of Class Domination in Africa." *Journal of Modern African Studies* 17, no. 4 (1979).

Skocpol, Theda. *States and Social Revolutions.* Cambridge: Cambridge University Press, 1979.

Smith, Anthony D. *The Geopolitics of Information: How Western Culture Dominates the World.* New York: Oxford University Press, 1980.

———. *State and Nation in the Third World.* Brighton: Wheatsheaf Books, 1983.

———. *Theories of Nationalism.* London: Duckworth, 1983.

Sorel, Georges. *From Georges Sorel.* Edited by John L. Stanley. New York: Oxford University Press, 1976.

———. *Matériaux pour une théorie du prolétariat.* Paris: Marcel Rivière, 1929.

———. *Réflexions sur la violence.* Paris: Marcel Rivière, 1972.

Spence, Jonathan D. *The Gate of Heavenly Peace.* New York: Penguin, 1981.

Starobinsky, Jean. *J.-J. Rousseau: La transparence et l'obstacle.* Paris: Gallimard, 1971.

Stepan, Alfred. *Authoritarian Brazil.* New Haven: Yale University Press, 1973.

———. *The State and Society: Peru in Comparative Perspective.* Princeton: Princeton University Press, 1978.

Stork, Joe. "Egypt's Factory Privatization Campaign Turns Deadly." *Merip Reports,* January–February 1995.

———. "North Africa Faces the 1990s." *Merip Reports,* March–April 1990.

Sweezy, Paul. "China's Economic Strategy." *Monthly Review,* July–August 1975.

Tapper, Richard. "Anthropologists, Historians, and Tribespeople on Tribe and State in the Middle East." In *Tribes and State Formation in the Middle East,* edited by Philip S. Khoury and Joseph Kostiner. Berkeley: University of California Press, 1990.

Therborn, Göran. *The Ideology of Power and the Power of Ideology.* London: Verso, 1980.

———. *Science, Class, and Society.* London: Verso, 1980.

Touraine, Alain. "D'un coup de pied, le plongeur." *Le Monde,* December 30, 1986.

———. "Fanatiques, terroristes, et mercenaires." *Le Monde,* November 11, 1986.

———. *Les sociétés dépendantes.* Paris: Duculot, 1976.

———. *Sociologie de l'action.* Paris: Seuil, 1965.

Touré, Ahmed Sékou. *The Doctrine and Methods of the Democratic Party of Guinea.* Conakry, 1963.

Tozy, Mohamed. *Champ et contre-champ politico-religieux au Maroc.* Thèse d'état de sciences politiques, Université d'Aix en Provence, 1984.

Tribe, Laurence. "The Curvature of Constitutional Space: What Lawyers Can Learn from Modern Physics." *Harvard Law Review* 103, no. 1 (1989).

Valenzuela, J. Samuel, and Arturo Valenzuela. "Modernization and Dependency: Alternative Perspectives in the Study of Latin American Development." *Comparative Politics* 10, no. 4 (July 1978).

Vatikiotis, P. J. *The Egyptian Army in Politics.* Bloomington: Indiana University Press, 1961.

———, ed. *Revolution in the Middle East*. London: George Allen & Unwin, 1972.

Vergès, Jacques. *Le salaud lumineux*. Paris: Michel Lafon, 1990.

Vieille, Paul. "Du transnational au politique-monde." *Peuples Méditerranéens*, nos. 35–36 (August–September 1986).

Walker, Thomas W., ed. *Nicaragua: The First Five Years*. New York: Praeger, 1985.

Wallerstein, Immanuel. *The Capitalist World-Economy*. Cambridge: Cambridge University Press, 1979.

———. "The Colonial Era in Africa: Changes in the Social Structure." In *Colonialism in Africa: 1870–1960*, edited by L. H. Gann and P. Duignan. Cambridge: Cambridge University Press, 1970.

———. "Crises: The World-Economy, the Movements, and the Ideologies." In *Crises in the World-System*, edited by A. Bergesen. Political Economy of the World-System Annuals, 6. Beverly Hills: Sage, 1983.

———. "Dependence in an Interdependent World: The Limited Possibilities of Transformation within the Capitalist World-Economy." *African Studies Review* 17, no. 1 (April 1974).

———. "L'économie-monde." In *Connaissance du Tiers-Monde*, edited by Catherine Coquery-Vidrovitch. Paris: 10/18, 1978.

———. *The Politics of the World-Economy*. Cambridge: Cambridge University Press, 1984.

———. *Social Change: The Colonial Situation*. New York: Wiley, 1966.

———. "Socialist States: Mercantilist Strategies and Revolutionary Objectives." In *Ascent and Decline in the World-System*, edited by Edward Friedman. Political Economy of the World-System Annuals, 5. Beverly Hills: Sage, 1982.

Waterbury, John. *Le commandeur des croyants: La monarchie marocaine et son élite*. Paris: P.U.F., 1975.

Wieseltier, Leon. "Bloodlust Memories." *New Republic*, March 21, 1994.

Willetts, Peter. *The Non-Aligned Movement: The Origins of a Third World Alliance*. London: Frances Pinter, 1978.

Wolf, Eric. *Peasant Wars of the Twentieth Century*. New York: Harper & Row, 1969.

Worsley, Peter. "The Concept of Populism." In *Populism*, edited by Ernest Gellner and G. Ionescu. London: Weidenfeld & Nicholson, 1969.

———. *The Third World*. London: Weidenfeld & Nicholson, 1967.

Zartman, William. "Pouvoir et état dans l'Islam." *Pouvoirs*, no. 12 (1983).

Zghal, Abdelkader. "Le retour du sacré et la nouvelle demande idéologique des jeunes scolarisés: Le cas de la Tunisie." In *Le Maghreb musulman en 1979*, edited by Christiane Souriau. Paris: C.N.R.S./C.R.E.S.M., 1981.

Ziegler, Jean. *Contre l'ordre du monde: Les rebelles*. Paris: Seuil, 1983.

———. *La victoire des vaincus*. Paris: Seuil, 1988.

———. *Vive le pouvoir! Ou les délices de la raison d'état*. Paris: Seuil, 1985.

Zubaida, Sami. "An Islamic State? The Case of Iran." *Merip Reports*, July–August 1988.

———. "Theories of Nationalism." In *Power and the State*, edited by Gary Littlejohn et al. London: Croom Helm, 1978.

Literature on Algeria

Abbas, Ferhat. *Autopsie d'une guerre*. Paris: Garnier, 1980.
———. *L'indépendance confisquée, 1962–1978*. Paris: Flammarion, 1984.
———. *La nuit coloniale*. Paris: Julliard, 1962.
Abdoun, Rabah. "Les déséquilibres de l'économie algérienne." In *L'Algérie et la modernité*, edited by Ali El-Kenz. Dakar: Codesria, 1989.
Abramson, Gary. "Raising the Stakes." *Africa Report*, November–December 1988.
Addi, Lahouari. "Algérie: Le dérapage." *Le Monde Diplomatique*, February 1997.
———. *L'Algérie et la démocratie*. Paris: La Découverte, 1994.
———. "De la permanence du populisme algérien." In *Algérie: Vers l'état islamique? Peuples Méditerranéens*, nos. 52–53 (July–December 1990).
———. "Dynamique infernale en Algérie." *Le Monde Diplomatique*, October 1995.
———. *L'impasse du populisme*. Alger, ENAL, 1990.
———. "Religion and Modernity in Algeria." *Journal of Democracy* 3, no. 4 (1992).
———. "Violence et système politique en Algérie." *Le Temps Modernes*, no. 580 (January–February 1995).
Agence Nationale d'Edition et de Publicité. *Algérie: Guide économique et social*. Algiers, 1987.
Ageron, Charles-Robert. "Enquête sur les origines du nationalisme algérien: L'émir Khaled, petit-fils d'Abdel Kader, fut-il le premier nationaliste algérien?" *Revue de l'Occident Musulman et de la Méditerranée* (Paris), second semester, 1966.
———. "Ferhat Abbas et l'évolution politique de l'Algérie musulmane pendant la seconde guerre mondiale." *Revue d'Histoire Maghrébine*, no. 4 (July 1975).
———. *Histoire de l'Algérie contemporaine*. Vol. 2. Paris: P.U.F., 1979.
———. "Le mouvement 'Jeunes Algériens' de 1900 à 1923." In *Etudes Maghrébines*. Paris: P.U.F., 1964.
Aït-Ahmed, Hocine. *L'afro-fascisme*. Paris: L'Harmattan, 1980.
———. *La guerre et l'après-guerre*. Paris: Minuit, 1964.
———. "L'impact historique du premier novembre." *El Badil*, no. 29 (November 1986).
———. "Interview." *Jeune-Afrique*, no. 1335 (August 6, 1986).
———. *Mémoires d'un combattant*. Paris: Sylvie Messinger, 1983.
———. "Sur le Maghreb et le mouvement national algérien." *Soual* 2 (1982).
Aktouf, Omar. *Algérie: Entre l'exil et la curée*. Paris: L'Harmattan, 1989.
Al-Ahnaf, Mustafa, Bernard Botiveau, and Franck Fregosi, eds. *L'Algérie par ses islamistes*. Paris: Karthala, 1991.
Alexandre, François. "Le P.C.A. de 1919 à 1939: Données en vue d'éclaircir son action et son rôle." *Revue Algérienne des Sciences Juridiques, Economiques, et Politiques* 11 (December 1974).
"Algérie: Les droits de l'homme. Revue de presse." In *Collectif contre la répression en Algérie*. Paris, n.d.

Alleg, Henri, ed. *La guerre d'Algérie.* 3 vols. Paris: Temps Actuels, 1981.

Amazit, B. "L'alphabet de l'indépendance: Du PPA au FLN." *Révolution Africaine,* no. 1203 (1987).

Amin, Samir. *Le Maghreb moderne.* Paris: Minuit, 1970.

Ammour, Kader, Christian Leucate, and Jean-Jacques Moulin. *La voie algérienne, les contradictions d'un développement national.* Paris: Maspéro, 1974.

Aouili, Smaïl, and Ramdane Redjala. "La Kabylie face à la dérive intégriste." *Le Temps Modernes,* no. 580 (January–February 1995).

Balta, Paul. "Houari Boumediène." *Maghreb-Machrek,* no. 69 (1975).

———. "Quel destin pour l'Algérie?" *Arabies,* no. 1 (January 1987).

Balta, Paul, and Claudine Rulleau. *L'Algérie des algériens, vingt ans après.* Paris: Editions Ouvrières, 1981.

Bedjaoui, Mohamed. *Pour un nouvel ordre économique international.* Paris: UNESCO, 1975.

———. *La révolution algérienne et le droit.* Brussels: Association Internationale des Juristes Démocrates, 1961.

Beghoul, Youcef. "La libération nationale par la voie populaire: L'appel au pays réel." *Revue Algérienne des Sciences Juridiques, Economiques, et Politiques* 11 (December 1974).

Bedrani, Slimane. "Bilans et perspectives de l'agriculture algérienne." In *L'Algérie et la modernité,* edited by Ali El-Kenz. Dakar: Codesria, 1989.

Benabdellaziz, Mustapha. "Education et politique: Le cas de l'Algérie colonisée." Ph.D. diss., Yale University, May 1987.

Ben Bella, Ahmed. *Ben Bella revient.* Paris: Jean Picollec, 1982.

Benhouria, Tahar. *L'économie de l'Algérie.* Paris: Maspéro, 1980.

Benissad, M. E. *Economie du développement de l'Algérie: Sous-développement et socialisme.* Paris: Economica, 1982.

———. *Théories et politiques du développement économique.* Algiers: S.N.E.D., 1974.

Bennoune, Mahfoud. "Algeria's Facade of Democracy." *Middle East Report* 20, no. 2 (1990).

———. "Les fondements socio-historiques de l'état algérien contemporain." In *L'Algérie et la modernité,* edited by Ali El-Kenz. Dakar: Codesria, 1989.

———. "The Introduction of Nationalism into Rural Algeria: 1919–1954." *Maghrib Review* 2, no. 3 (1977).

———. *The Making of Contemporary Algeria, 1830–1987.* Cambridge: Cambridge University Press, 1988.

———. "Socioeconomic Changes in Rural Algeria, 1830–1954: A Diachronic Analysis of a Peasantry under Colonialism." *Peasant Studies Newsletter* 2, no. 2 (1973).

Bennoune, Mahfoud, and Ali El-Kenz. *Le hasard et l'histoire: Entretiens avec Belaïd Abdesselam.* 2 vols. Algiers: ENAG, 1990.

Berger, Denis. "Messali Hadj, P.C.F., Mouvement National Algérien." *Soual* 2 (1982).

Berque, Jacques. *Dépossession du monde.* Paris: Seuil, 1964.

———. *Le Maghreb entre deux guerres.* Paris: Seuil, 1979.

———. "Que veulent les islamistes au Maghreb?" *Le Monde Diplomatique,* February 1992.

Blaschke, Nasreen. "How to Do Business (or Not) in Algeria." *The Middle East*, July 1987.

Bonn, Charles. *La littérature algérienne de langue française et ses lecteurs*. Ottawa, Naaman, 1974.

———. *Le roman algérien de langue française*. Paris: L'Harmattan, 1985.

Boudiaf, Mohamed. "Interview." *Algérie-Actualité*, July 20, 1989.

———. *Où va l'Algérie?* Paris: Librairie de l'Étoile, 1964.

Boukhobza, M'hammad. *Octobre 88: Evolution ou rupture?* Algiers: Bouchène, 1991.

Boumedienne, Houari. "Interview." *Revue Algérienne des Sciences Juridiques, Economiques, et Politiques* 3 (December 1965).

Bourdieu, Pierre. *The Algerians*. Boston: Beacon Press, 1962.

———. *Algérie 60: Structures économiques et structures temporelles*. Paris: Minuit, 1977.

Bourdieu, Pierre, and Abdelmalek Sayad. *Le déracinement*. Paris: Minuit, 1964.

Bourgi, Albert. "Algérie: An I de la démocratie." *Jeune Afrique*, no. 1511 (1989).

Bouvreuil, A. G. "Agitation politique et religieuse chez les musulmans d'Algérie." *Bulletin C.A.F.*, November 1936.

Brumberg, Daniel. "Islam, Elections, and Reform in Algeria." *Journal of Democracy* 2, no. 1 (1991).

Burgat, François. "L'Algérie des 'fellaghas' aux 'intégristes.' " In *Le religieux dans le politique*. Paris: Seuil, 1991.

———. "De la difficulté de nommer: Intégrisme, fondamentalisme, islamisme." *Les Temps Modernes*, no. 500 (1988).

———. *L'islamisme au Maghreb*. Paris: Karthala, 1988.

———. "Sous le 'voile' de l'Islam algérien." *Le Monde*, June 17, 1990.

Burgat, François, and William Dowell. *The Islamic Movement in North Africa*. Austin: Center for Middle Eastern Studies, 1993.

Camau, Michel. "Caractère et rôle du constitutionnalisme dans les états maghrébins." In *Développements politiques au Maghreb*, by Jean Leca et al. Paris: C.N.R.S., 1979.

———. *La notion de démocratie dans la pensée des dirigeants maghrébins*. Paris: C.N.R.S./C.R.E.S.M., 1971.

———. *Pouvoirs et institutions au Maghreb*. Tunis: Cérés, 1978.

"La campagne communiste contre l'Afrique française." *Bulletin C.A.F.*, June 1927.

Carlier, Jean-Louis. "La première Étoile Nord-Africaine." *Revue Algérienne des Sciences Juridiques, Economiques, et Politiques* 9 (December 1972).

Chaliand, Gérard. *L'Algérie est-elle socialiste?* Paris: Seuil, 1964.

Chaliand, Gérard, and Juliette Minces. *L'Algérie indépendante*. Paris: Seuil, 1972.

Charby, J. *L'Algérie en prison*. Paris: Minuit, 1961.

La charte d'Alger. Algiers: Front de Libération Nationale, Commission Centrale d'Information, 1964.

Chikh, Slimane. *L'Algérie en armes, ou le temps des certitudes*. Paris: Economica/ O.P.U., 1981.

Chjoke, Salem. "Les droits de l'homme sont-ils mûrs en Algérie?" *Annuaire de l'Afrique du Nord* 24 (1985).

Cleaver, Kevin M. *The Agricultural Development Experience of Algeria, Morocco, and Tunisia: A Comparison of Strategies for Growth.* Washington, D.C.: World Bank, 1980.

Clegg, Ian. *Workers' Self-Management in Algeria.* New York: Monthly Review Press, 1971.

Collot, Claude. "Le Congrés Musulman Algérien, 1937–1938." *Revue Algérienne des Sciences Juridiques, Economiques, et Politiques* 11 (December 1974).

———. "L'Union Populaire Algérienne, 1937–1939." *Revue Algérienne des Sciences Juridiques, Economiques, et Politiques* 9 (December 1972).

Collot, Claude, and Jean-Robert Henry. *Le Mouvement National Algérien: Textes, 1912–1954.* Paris: L'Harmattan, 1978.

Colonna, Fanny. "Cultural Resistance and Religious Legitimacy in Colonial Algeria." *Economy and Society* 3, no. 3 (1976).

———. *Instituteurs algériens, 1883–1939.* Paris: Presses de la Fondation Nationale des Sciences Politiques, 1975.

———. "La répétition: Les Tolba dans une commune rurale de l'Aurès." *Annuaire de l'Afrique du Nord* 18 (1979).

———. "La ville au village: Transferts de savoirs et de modèles entre villes et campagnes en Algérie." *Revue Française de Sociologie* 19, no. 3 (1978).

"Contribution à la connaissance de l'émir Khaled." *Algérie-Actualité,* March 13, 1980.

Courrière, Yves. *La guerre d'Algérie.* 4 vols. Paris: Fayard, 1968–71.

Cubertafond, Bernard. "Réflexions sur la pratique politique algérienne." *Maghreb/Machrek,* no. 69 (1975).

———. *La république algérienne démocratique et populaire.* Paris: P.U.F., 1979.

Daoud, Zakya. "Algérie: Dans l'étau de la dépendance financière." *Le Monde Diplomatique,* February 1992.

———. "La frustration des classes moyennes au Maghreb." *Le Monde Diplomatique,* November 1991.

Darnton, John. "Africa Tries Democracy, Finding Hope and Peril." *New York Times,* June 21, 1996.

De Brie, Christian. "Champ libre au modèle libéral et démocratique." *Le Monde Diplomatique,* November 1991.

Delisle, René. "Les origines du FLN." *La NEF,* nos. 12–13 (1962).

Desparmet, J. "Naissance d'une histoire 'nationale' de l'Algérie." *Bulletin C.A.F.,* July 1933.

———. "Le pan-arabisme et l'Algérie." *Bulletin C.A.F.,* June 1936.

———. "Un réformateur contemporain en Algérie." *Bulletin C.A.F.,* March 1933.

Djeghloul, Abdelkader. "L'Algérie en état d'anomie politique." *Le Monde Diplomatique,* March 1990.

———. "Les défis de la crise." *Le Monde Diplomatique,* November 1986.

———. "Fin du populisme en Algérie." *Le Monde Diplomatique,* January 1989.

———. "La formation des intellectuels algériens modernes (1880–1930)." In *Aspects de la culture algérienne.* Paris: Centre Culturel Algérien, 1986.

Duclos, Louis-Jean, Jean Duvignaud, and Jean Leca. *Les nationalismes maghrébins.* Paris: Fondation Nationale des Sciences Politiques, 1966.

Du Maghreb. Les Temps Modernes, no. 375 (October 1977).

Durand, Jean-Pierre. "L'agriculture sacrifiée." In *L'Algérie*, edited by Patrick Eveno. Paris: Le Monde, 1994.

———. "Le redressement de l'agriculture." *Le Monde Diplomatique*, November 1986.

Einaudi, Jean-Louis. *Pour l'exemple. L'affaire Iveton*. Paris: L'Harmattan, 1987.

El-Kenz, Ali. "Les enjeux d'une crise." In *L'Algérie Incertaine*, edited by Pierre Robert Baduel, *Revue du Monde Musulman et de la Méditerranée*, no. 65 (1993).

———. *Monographie d'une expérience industrielle en Algérie: Le complexe sidérurgique d'El Hadjar (Annaba)*. Thèse de doctorat d'état en sciences humaines, Université de Paris VIII, 1983.

———. "La société algérienne aujourd'hui — Esquisse d'une phénoménologie de la conscience nationale." In *L'Algérie et la modernité*, edited by Ali El-Kenz. Dakar: Codesria, 1989.

Entelis, John P. *Algeria: The Revolution Institutionalized*. London: Croom Helm, 1986.

———. "Algeria in World Politics." *American-Arab Affairs*, no. 6 (1983).

———. "Algeria under Chadli: Liberalization without Democratization, or, Perestroïka, Yes; Glasnost, No!," *Middle East Insight*, Fall 1988.

Etienne, Bruno. "Abd-El Kader." *Parcours: L'Algérie, Les Hommes et l'Histoire*, no. 4 (1985).

———. *L'Algérie, cultures et révolution*. Paris: Seuil, 1977.

———. "L'Algérie et la IVe Conférence des Non-Alignés: De la solidarité des idées à la solitude dans la stratégie." *Maghreb-Machrek*, no. 60 (1973).

———. "Clientelism in Algeria." In *Patrons and Clients in Mediterranean Societies*, edited by Ernest Gellner and John Waterbury. London: Duckworth, 1977.

———. "Eléments d'une recherche sur la dépendance idéologique: Une hypothèse de perception à partir de la consommation et de la pratique idéologique." In *Indépendance et interdépendances au Maghreb*, by Werner Ruf et al. Paris: C.N.R.S., 1974.

———. *L'islamisme radical*. Paris: Hachette, 1987.

———. "La paysannerie dans le discours et la pratique." *Annuaire de l'Afrique du Nord* 14 (1975).

Eveno, Patrick, ed. *L'Algérie*. Paris: Le Monde, 1994.

Fanon, Frantz. *L'an V de la révolution algérienne*. Paris: Maspéro, 1959.

———. *A Dying Colonialism*. New York: Grove Press, 1965.

Faouzi, Adel. "Islam, réformisme et nationalisme dans la résistance à la colonisation française en Algérie (1830–1930)." *Social Compass* 25, nos. 3–4 (1978).

Favret, J. "Le traditionalisme par excès de modernité." *Archives Européennes de Sociologie*, no. 8 (1967).

Fayçal, Nassib. "Algérie: Dynamique démographique, stagnation économique." *Arabies*, no. 4 (April 1987).

Feraoun, Mouloud. *Journal, 1955–1962*. Paris: Seuil, 1962.

Fontaine, Jacques. "Quartiers défavorisés et vote islamiste à Alger." In *L'Algérie Incertaine*, edited by Pierre Robert Baduel, *Revue du Monde Musulman et de la Méditerranée*, no. 65 (1993).

Francos, Ania, and Jean-Pierre Séréni. *Un algérien nommé Boumediène*. Paris: Stock, 1976.

Frappat, Bruno. "Démographie: Une soudaine prise de conscience." *Le Monde*, December 5, 1985.

Fritscher, Frédéric. "L'Algérie malade de la rumeur." *Le Monde*, January 1, 1987.

———. "Le temps du réalisme et du pragmatisme." *Le Monde*, December 5, 1985.

Gadant, Monique. *Islam et nationalisme en Algérie*. Paris: L'Harmattan, 1988.

Gadant, Monique, and Mohammed Harbi. "Quel pôle démocratique?" *Esprit*, January 1995.

Galissot, René. "Abdel Kader et la nationalité algérienne: Interprétation de la chute de la régence d'Alger et des premières résistances à la conquête française (1830–1839)." *Revue Historique*, no. 233 (1965).

———. "Aux origines de l'immigration algérienne." In *Les algériens en France*, edited by Jacqueline Costa-Lascoux and Emile Temime. Paris: Publisud, 1985.

———. "La purification communautaire." *Les Temps Modernes*, no. 580 (January–February 1995).

———. "Les révolutions du Tiers-Monde sont-elles des révolutions contre *Le Capital* de Marx?" *Les Temps Modernes*, no. 477 (April 1986).

———. "Syndicalisme et nationalisme: La fondation de l'U.G.T.A., ou du syndicalisme C.G.T. au syndicalisme Algérien." *Le Mouvement Social*, no. 66 (January–March 1969).

———. "La transnationalisation à l'oeuvre sous le modèle de l'état-national." *Peuples Méditerranéens*, nos. 35–36 (April–September 1986).

———. "Transnationalisation et renforcement de l'ordre étatique." *Peuples Méditerranéens*, nos. 35–36 (April–September 1986).

Galissot, René, and Gilbert Badia. *Marx, marxisme et Algérie*. Paris: 10/18, 1976.

Gallagher, Charles. *The United States and North Africa: Morocco, Algeria, and Tunisia*. Cambridge: Harvard University Press, 1963.

Garçon, José. "L'Algérie à la dérive sur un baril intégriste." *Libération*, April 6, 1990.

———. "L'islamisation forcée de toute une société." *Libération*, March 14, 1996.

Gellner, Ernest. "The Unknown Apollo of Biskra: The Social Base of Algerian Puritanism." *Government and Opposition* 9, no. 3 (1974).

Gellner, Ernest, et al. *Islam et politique au Maghreb*. Paris: C.N.R.S./C.R.E.S.M., 1981.

Ghozali, Nasser Eddine. "Opposition explicite et collaboration implicite: Le Mouvement National Algérien de Messali Hadj." *Revue Algérienne des Sciences Juridiques, Economiques, et Politiques* 9 (December 1972).

Girardon, Jacques. "L'Algérie et nous." *L'Express*, February 17, 1994.

Glasman, Dominique, and Jean Kremer. *Essai sur l'université et les cadres en Algérie*. Paris: C.N.R.S./C.R.E.S.M., 1978.

Grandguillaume, Gilbert. *Arabisation et politique linguistique au Maghreb*. Paris: Maisonneuve et Larose, 1983.

Grimaud, Nicole. *La politique extérieure de l'Algérie*. Paris: Karthala, 1984.

Guénanéche, Mohamed, and Mahfoud Kaddache. *L'Étoile Nord-Africaine: 1926–1937*. Algiers: O.P.U., 1984.

————. *Le Parti du Peuple Algérien: 1937–1939.* Algiers: O.P.U., 1985.

Guérin, Daniel. *Ci-gît le colonialisme.* Paris: Mouton, 1973.

Hadj, Messali. *Les mémoires de Messali Hadj: 1898–1938.* Paris: Lattes, 1982.

Hadj-Sadok, Mohammed. "De la théorie à la pratique des prescriptions de l'Islam en Algérie contemporaine." *Social Compass* 25, nos. 3–4 (1978).

Hamon, Hervé, and Patrick Rotman. *Les porteurs de valises: La résistance française à la guerre d'Algérie.* Paris: Albin Michel, 1979.

Harbi, Mohammed. *Aux origines du Front de Libération Nationale: La scission du P.P.A.-M.T.L.D.* Paris: Bourgois, 1975.

————. "Entretien." *La Tribune d'Octobre,* June 25, 1990.

————. "La fin d'une époque." *Libération,* October 12, 1988.

————. "Un F.I.S. enfanté par le F.L.N." *Le Monde,* June 21, 1990.

————. *Le F.L.N.: Mirage et réalité.* Paris: Jeune Afrique, 1980.

————. "Messali Hadj et la vérité historique." in *Les mémoires de Messali Hadj: 1898–1938.* Paris: Lattes, 1982.

————. "Les nationalistes algériens et le Maghreb: 1928–1954." *Soual* 2 (1982).

————. *1954: La guerre commence en Algérie.* Paris: Complexs, 1984.

————. "Rationalité idéologique et identité nationale: L'Algérie entre le passé et le présent." *Soual* 1 (1981).

————. "Violence, nationalisme, islamisme." *Le Temps Modernes,* no. 580 (January–February 1995).

————, ed. *L'Algérie et son destin: Croyants ou citoyens.* Paris: Arcantère, 1992.

————. *Les archives de la révolution algérienne.* Paris: Jeune Afrique, 1981.

Harrold, Deborah. "The Menace and Appeal of Algeria's Parallel Economy." *Merip Reports,* January–February 1995.

Heggoy, Alf Andrew. "The Origins of Algerian Nationalism in the Colony and in France." *Muslim World* 58, no. 2 (April 1968).

Heller, Yves. "Les bonnes oeuvres des islamistes algériens." *Le Monde,* June 27, 1990.

Henni, Ahmed. *Essai sur l'économie parallèle: Cas de l'Algérie.* Algiers: ENAG, 1991.

————. "Le malaise de la jeunesse maghrébine: L'exemple algérien." In *Maghreb: Les années de transition,* edited by Bassma Kodmani-Darwish. Paris: Masson, 1990.

————. "Qui a legalisé quel trabendo?" *Algérie: Vers l'état islamique? Peuples Méditerranéens,* nos. 52–53 (July–December 1990).

Hermassi, Elbassi. *Etat et société au Maghreb.* Paris: Anthropos, 1975.

"L'Histoire, mémoire des gloires et des peines." *El Djeich,* no. 258 (November 1984).

Horne, Alistair. *A Savage War of Peace: Algeria, 1954–1962.* London: Macmillan, 1977.

Human Rights Watch. *Human Rights Abuses in Algeria: No One Is Spared.* New York, 1994.

Hutchinson, Martha Crenshaw. *Revolutionary Terrorism.* Stanford: Hoover Institution Press, 1978.

"L'Islamisme aujourd'hui." *Soual* 5 (April 1985).

Isnard, Hildebert. "Aux origines du nationalisme algérien." *Annales,* no. 4 (October–December 1949).

Jacquemot, Pierre, and Marc Raffinot. *Le capitalisme d'état algérien*. Paris: Maspéro, 1977.

Julien, Charles-André. *L'Afrique du Nord en marche: Nationalismes musulmans et souveraineté française*. Paris: Julliard, 1972.

Junqua, Daniel. "Algérie: Défendre l'Islam authentique." In *L'Islam dans le Monde*, edited by Paul Balta. Paris: La Découverte, 1986.

Kaddache, Mahfoud. *Histoire du nationalisme algérien: Question nationale et politique algérienne*. 2 vols. Algiers: S.N.E.D., 1980.

Kaïd, Ahmed. *Contradictions de classes et contradictions au sein des masses*. Algiers: Entreprises Algériennes de Presses, 1970.

Kapil, Arun. "Algeria's Crisis Intensifies." *Merip Reports*, January–February 1995.

Kepel, Gilles. *Le prophète et le pharaon: Les mouvements islamistes dans l'Egypte contemporaine*. Paris: La Découverte, 1984.

Khelladi, Aissa. "Les islamistes algériens à l'assaut du pouvoir." *Les Temps Modernes*, no. 580 (January–February 1995).

Khelladi, Aissa, and Marie Virolle. "Les démocrates algériens ou l'indispensable clarification." *Les Temps Modernes*, no. 580 (January–February 1995).

Kielstra, N. "Was the Algerian Revolution a Peasant War?" *Peasant Studies* 7 (1979).

Korany, Bahgat. "From Revolution to Domestication: The Foreign Policy of Algeria." In *The Foreign Policy of Arab States*, edited by Bahgat Korany and Ali E. Hillal Dessouki. Boulder: Westview Press, 1991.

Koroghli, Ammar. *Institutions politiques et développement en Algérie*. Paris: L'Harmattan, 1988.

Koulakssis, Ahmed, and Gilbert Meynier. *L'émir Khaled: Premier za'im? Identité algérienne et colonialisme français*. Paris: L'Harmattan, 1987.

Koulytchizky, Serge. *L'autogestion, l'homme et l'état: L'expérience Algérienne*. Paris: Mouton, 1974.

Laacher, Smaïn. *Réalités sociales et pouvoir*. Paris: L'Harmattan, 1985.

Labat, Severine. *Les islamistes algériens: Entre les urnes et le maquis*. Paris: Le Seuil, 1995.

Lacheraf, Mostefa. *L'Algérie: Nation et société*. Paris: Maspéro, 1965.

Lacouture, Jean. *Algérie: La guerre est finie*. Paris: Complexs, 1985.

Laks, Monique. *Autogestion ouvrière et pouvoir politique en Algérie (1962–1965)*. Paris: E.D.I., 1970.

Lamchichi, Abderrahim. *L'Algérie en crise*. Paris: L'Harmattan, 1991.

———. *Islam et contestation au Maghreb*. Paris: L'Harmattan, 1989.

———. *L'Islamisme en Algérie*. Paris: L'Harmattan, 1992.

Lazreg, Marnia. *The Emergence of Classes in Algeria*. Boulder: Westview Press, 1976.

Lebjaoui, Mohamed. *Vérités sur la révolution algérienne*. Paris: Gallimard, 1970.

Leca, Jean. "Algérie." In *Encyclopaedia universalis*. Paris, 1988.

———. "Etat et société en Algérie." In *Maghreb: Les années de transition*, edited by Bassma Kadmani-Darwish. Paris: Masson, 1990.

———. "Social Structure and Political Stability: Comparative Evidence from the Algerian, Syrian, and Iraqi Cases." In *The Arab State*, edited by Giacomo Luciani. Berkeley: University of California Press, 1990.

Leca, Jean, and Jean-Claude Vatin. *L'Algérie politique: Institutions et régime.* Paris: Fondation Nationale des Sciences Politiques, 1975.

———. "Le système politique algérien (1976–1978)." In *Développements politiques au Maghreb,* by Jean Leca et al. Paris: C.N.R.S./C.R.E.S.M., 1979.

Leca, Jean, et al. *Développements politiques au Maghreb.* Paris: C.N.R.S./C.R.E.S.M., 1979.

Liabes, Djillali. "L'entreprise entre économie politique et société." In *L'Algérie et la modernité,* edited by Ali El-Kenz. Dakar: Codesria, 1989.

Liauzu, Claude. "Etat, ville et mouvements sociaux au Maghreb et au Moyen-Orient." *Maghreb-Machrek,* no. 115 (1987).

Lucas, Philippe. "Déchiffrement dialectique de l'histoire et libération de la connaisance: Fanon et la lutte de libération algérienne." *Revue Algérienne des Sciences Juridiques, Economiques, et Politiques* 9 (December 1972).

———. *Problèmes de la transition au socialisme: Le transformisme algérien.* Paris: Anthropos, 1978.

Lucas, Philippe, and Jean-Claude Vatin. *L'Algérie des anthropologues.* Paris: Maspéro, 1982.

Lyotard, Jean-François. "Le contenu social de la lutte algérienne." *Socialisme ou Barbarie,* no. 29 (December 1959–February 1960).

Mahiou, Ahmed. "Les forces politiques en Algérie entre les deux guerres mondiales." *Revue Algérienne des Sciences Juridiques, Economiques, et Politiques* 11 (December 1974).

Mahsas, Ahmed. *Le mouvement révolutionnaire en Algérie.* Paris: L'Harmattan, 1979.

Mameri, Khalfa. *Orientations politiques de l'Algérie.* Algiers: S.N.E.D., 1973.

Mammeri, Mouloud. *La traversée.* Paris: Plon, 1982.

Mandouze, André, ed. *La révolution algérienne par les textes.* Paris: Maspéro, 1961.

Mariet, François. "Idéologie scolaire et culture en Algérie." *Revue Française de Sociologie* 19, no. 3 (1978).

Markham, James. "Where Liberation was a Dream, Other Visions Ascend." *New York Times,* September 11, 1988.

Maschino, Tarik M., and Fadéla M'Rabet. *L'Algérie des illusions: La révolution confisquée.* Paris: Laffont, 1972.

Mégherbi, A. "La 'acabiyya chez Ibn Khaldoun: Un concept microsociologique." *Algérie-Actualité,* May 2–8, 1971.

Mérad, Ali. *Le réformisme musulman en Algérie, de 1925 à 1940.* The Hague: Mouton, 1967.

Messaoudi, Abdelmajid. "Chômage et solidarités familiales." In *Algérie: Vers l'état islamique? Peuples Méditerranéens,* nos. 52–53 (July–December 1990).

Meynier, Gilbert. *L'Algérie révélée.* Paris: Droz, 1981.

Michel, Hubert. "La politique africaine des états du Maghreb." *Revue Française d'Etudes Politiques Africaines,* no. 27 (1968).

Miett, Roland. "Le système politique algérien." *L'Afrique et l'Asie Modernes,* no. 114 (1977).

Millet, Gilles. "La genèse des groupes armés qui ont débordé le FIS." *Libération,* March 14, 1994.

Mimouni, Rachid. *Le fleuve détourné.* Paris: Robert-Laffont, 1982.

———. *La malédiction*. Paris: Stock, 1993.

———. *Tombéza*. Paris: Robert-Laffont, 1984.

Montagne, Robert. "La fermentation des partis politiques en Algérie." *Politique Etrangère*, no. 2 (April 1937).

Moore, C. H. *Politics in North Africa*. Boston: Little, Brown, 1970.

Mortimer, Robert. "Algeria and the Politics of International Economic Reform." *Orbis* 21, no. 3 (1977).

———. "The Algerian Revolution in Search of the African Revolution." *Journal of Modern African Studies* 8, no. 3 (1970).

———. "Islam and Multiparty Politics in Algeria." *Middle East Journal* 45, no. 4 (1991).

Moussaoui, Abderrahmane. "La mosquée au péril de la commune." In *Algérie: Vers l'état islamique? Peuples Méditerranéens*, nos. 52–53 (July–December 1990).

Musée Central de l'Armée. *Mémoire de l'Algérie*. Algiers, n.d.

Nadir, A. "Le mouvement réformiste algérien et la guerre de libération nationale." *Revue d'Histoire Maghrébine*, no. 4 (July 1975).

Nair, Kuider Sami. "Algérie, 1954–1982: Forces sociales et blocs au pouvoir." *Les Temps Modernes*, nos. 632–33 (July–August 1982).

———. "Le peuple exclu." *Le Temps Modernes*, no. 580 (January–February 1995).

———. "Pouvoir politique et formes de rationalité: L'état algérien." *Soual* 1 (1981).

Nellis, John. "A Comparative Assessment of the Development Performances of Algeria and Tunisia." *Middle East Journal* 37, no. 3 (1983).

Nouschi, André. *Enquête sur le niveau de vie des populations rurales constantinoises de la conquête jusqu'en 1919: Essai d'histoire économique et sociale*. Paris: P.U.F., 1961.

———. *La naissance du nationalisme algérien: 1914–1954*. Paris: Minuit, 1962.

O'Cornesse, Dominique. "Le rôle de l'Algérie à l'Assemblée de l'ONU." *Maghreb-Machrek*, no. 67 (1975).

Octobre à Alger. Paris: Seuil, 1988.

"Ordre et désordre en Algérie." *Projet*, no. 193 (May–June 1985).

Ottaway, David, and Marina Ottaway. *Algeria: The Politics of a Socialist Revolution*. Berkeley: University of California Press, 1970.

Ouettar, Tahar. *L'As*. Paris: Temps Actuels, 1983.

Ouzegane, Amar. *Le meilleur combat*. Paris: Julliard, 1962.

"Les paysans algériens et l'état." *Maghreb-Machrek*, no. 95 (1982).

"Perestroïka in Algiers." *International Herald Tribune*, October 7, 1988.

Pierre, Andrew J., and William B. Quandt. "Algeria's War on Itself." *Foreign Policy*, no. 99 (summer 1995).

Provost, Lucile. "L'économie de rente et ses avatars." *Esprit*, January 1995.

Quandt, William B. *Revolution and Political Leadership: Algeria, 1954–1968*. Cambridge: MIT Press, 1969.

Rabbihi, Abdou. "Histoire, mémoire, et commémoration." *El Badil*, no. 29 (November 1986).

Ramonet, Ignacio. "L'Algérie sous le choc." *Le Monde Diplomatique*, November 1988.

———. "Vents de réforme en Algérie." *Le Monde Diplomatique*, October 1986.

Redjala, Ramdane. *L'opposition en Algérie depuis 1962.* Paris: L'Harmattan, 1988.
Le retentissement de la révolution algérienne. Proceedings of the Colloque International d'Alger. Algiers: ENAL, 1985.
Roberts, Hugh. "In Troubled Waters." *Africa Report.* September–October 1987.
———. *Political Development in Algeria: The Region of Greater Kabilya.* D.Phil. thesis, Oxford University, 1980.
———. "The Politics of Algerian Socialism." In *North Africa: Contemporary Politics and Economic Development,* edited by Richard Lawless and Allen Findlay. London: Croom Helm, 1984.
Rouadjia, Ahmed. "L'armée et les islamistes, le compromis impossible?" *Esprit,* January 1995.
———. "Du nationalisme du FLN à l'islamisme du FIS." *Les Temps Modernes,* no. 580 (January–February 1995).
———. *Les frères et la mosquée.* Paris: Karthala, 1990.
Ruedy, John. *Modern Algeria: The Origins and Development of a Nation.* Bloomington: Indiana University Press, 1992.
Ruf, Werner, et al. *Indépendance et interdépendances au Maghreb.* Paris: C.N.R.S./ C.R.E.S.M., 1974.
Saadallah, Belkacem. "The Algerian Ulémas: 1919–1931." *Revue d'Histoire Maghrébine,* no. 2 (July 1974).
———. "The Rise of Algerian Nationalism: 1900–1930." Ph.D. diss., University of Minnesota, 1965.
Sahli, Mohamed Chérif. *Décoloniser l'histoire.* Paris: Maspéro, 1965.
Sanson, Henri. *Laïcité islamique en Algérie.* Paris: C.N.R.S./C.R.E.S.M., 1983.
———. "Le peuple de la révolution socialiste algérienne." In *Développements politiques au Maghreb,* by Jean Leca et al. Paris: C.N.R.S., 1979.
Shikhi, Said. "L'ouvrier, la vie, et le prince, ou la modernité introuvable." In *L'Algérie et la modernité,* edited by Ali El-Kenz. Dakar: Codesria, 1989.
Sigaud, Dominique. *La fracture algérienne.* Paris: Calmann-Lévy, 1991.
"La situation dans l'Afrique du Nord." *Bulletin C.A.F.,* July–October 1936.
Sivan, Emmanuel. *Communisme et nationalisme en Algérie: 1920–1962.* Paris: Fondation Nationale des Sciences Politiques, 1976.
———. "L'Étoile Nord-Africaine and the Genesis of Algerian Nationalism." *Maghrib Review* 3, nos. 5–6 (1978).
———. "'Slave-Owner Mentality' and Bolshevism: Algerian Communism, 1920–1927." *Asian and African Studies* 9, no. 2 (1973).
Slim. *L'Algérie de Slim.* Paris: L'Harmattan, 1983.
Slyomovics, Susan. "Hassiba Ben Bouali, If You Could See Our Algeria: Women and Public Space in Algeria." *Merip Reports,* January–February 1995.
Souriau-Hoebrechts, Christiane. *La presse maghrébine.* Paris: C.N.R.S., 1969.
Stolz, Joëlle. "La nouvelle Mecque de la jeunesse dorée." *Libération,* September 6–7, 1986.
Stora, Benjamin. *L'Algérie en 1995: La Guerre, l'histoire, la politique.* Paris: Michalon, 1995.
———. "Algérie: Huit clés pour comprendre." *Jeune Afrique,* no. 1539 (1990).
———. "Deuxième guerre algérienne? Les habits anciens des combattants." *Les Temps Modernes,* no. 580 (January–February 1995).

————. *Dictionnaire biographique de militants nationalistes algériens.* Paris: L'Harmattan, 1985.

————. *Messali Hadj.* Paris: Le Sycomore, 1982.

————. *Sociologie du nationalisme algérien.* Thèse de doctorat, 3e cycle, Université Paris VII, 1984.

————. *Les sources du nationalisme algérien: Parcours idéologiques — origines des acteurs.* Paris: L'Harmattan, 1989.

Stora, Benjamin, and Zakya Daoud. *Ferhat Abbas: Une utopie algérienne.* Paris: Denoel, 1995.

Tahi, Mohand Salah. "The Arduous Democratization Process in Algeria." *Journal of Modern African Studies* 30, no. 3 (1992).

Taleb Ibrahimi, Ahmed. *De la décolonisation à la révolution culturelle.* Algiers: S.N.E.D., 1973.

Talha, Larbi. "Le dépérissement des classes moyennes pré-capitalistes: Prélude à l'émigration ouvrière." In *Les classes moyennes au Maghreb,* by Abdelkader Zghal et al. Paris: C.R.E.S.M., 1980.

Teguia, Mohamed. *L'Algérie en guerre.* Algiers: O.P.U., 1980.

Thibaud, Paul, and Pierre Vidal-Naquet. "Le combat pour l'indépendance algérienne: Une fausse coïncidence." *Esprit,* January 1995.

Tillon, Germaine. *Les ennemis complémentaires.* Paris: Minuit, 1960.

Tlemçani, Rachid. "Chadli's Perestroïka." *Merip Reports,* March–April 1990.

————. *State and Revolution in Algeria.* Boulder: Westview Press, 1987.

Turin, Yvonne. *Affrontements culturels dans l'Algérie coloniale: Ecoles, médecines, religion, 1830–1880.* Paris: Maspéro, 1971.

Vandevelde, Hélène. "Quelques signes d'un glissement des notions de 'peuple' et 'citoyens' à celles de 'Umma' et 'Mu'minim' en Algérie depuis l'indépendance." *Revue Algérienne des Sciences Juridiques, Economiques, et Politiques,* special issue, 1982.

Vatin, Jean-Claude. *L'Algérie politique: Histoire et société.* Paris: Fondation Nationale des Sciences Politiques, 1983.

————. "Histoire en soi et histoire pour soi: 1919–1945, et après." *Revue Algérienne des Sciences Juridiques, Economiques, et Politiques* 11 (December 1974).

————. "Nationalisme et socialisation politique." *Revue Algérienne des Sciences Juridiques, Economiques, et Politiques* 11 (December 1974).

————. "Popular Puritanism versus State Reformism: Islam in Algeria." In *Islam in the Political Process,* edited by James P. Piscatori. New York: Cambridge University Press, 1983.

————. "Pour une sociologie politique des nouveaux désenchantements." *Annuaire de l'Afrique du Nord* 21 (1982).

————. "Religious Resistance and State Power in Algeria." In *Islam and Power,* edited by Alexander Cudsi and A. E. H. Dessouki. London: Croom Helm, 1981.

————. "Revival in the Maghreb: Islam as an Alternative Political Language." In *Islamic Resurgence in the Arab World,* edited by A. E. H. Dessouki. New York: Praeger, 1982.

Von Sivers, Peter. "National Integration and Traditional Rural Organization in Algeria, 1970–80: Background for Islamic Traditionalism?" In *From Na-*

tional to Revolutionary Islam, edited by S. A. Arjomand. London: Macmillan, 1984.

Waterbury, John. "La légitimation du pouvoir au Maghreb: Tradition, protestation, et répression." In *Développements politiques au Maghreb,* by Jean Leca et al. Paris: C.N.R.S., 1979.

Yacine, Kateb. *Nedjma.* Paris: Seuil, 1956.

Yacono, Xavier. *La colonisation des plaines du Chétif.* 2 vols. Algiers: Imbert, 1955.

Yefsah, Abdelkader. "L'armée et le pouvoir en Algérie de 1962 à 1992." In *L'Algérie Incertaine,* edited by Pierre Robert Baduel, *Revue du Monde Musulman et de la Méditerranée,* no. 65 (1993).

Zagoria, Janet Dorsch. "The Rise and Fall of the Movement of Messali Hadj in Algeria: 1912–1954." Ph.D. diss., Columbia University, 1973.

Zahouane, Hocine. "Interview sur le nationalisme algérien." *Soual* 1 (1981).

Zartman, I. William, ed. *Man, State, and Society in the Contemporary Maghrib.* London: Pall Mall, 1973.

Zemzoun, Zoubir. "De la démocratie." *Révolution Africaine,* no. 1199 (February 20, 1987).

Zghal, Abdelkader, et al. *Les classes moyennes au Maghreb.* Paris: C.N.R.S./ C.R.E.S.M., 1980.

Periodicals

Africasia
Afrique-Asie
Annuaire de l'Afrique du Nord
El Badil
Bulletin de l'Afrique Française
Jeune Afrique
Libération
Maghreb-Machrek
Le Monde
Le Monde Diplomatique
El Moudjahid
L'Observateur
Révolution Africaine
Revue Algérienne des Sciences Juridiques, Economiques, et Politiques

Index

Abbas, Ferhat: and assimilationism, 45–47, 261n47; and Ben Badis, 65–66; FLN affiliation of, 121, 123; on historical legitimacy, 156; historical role of, 35, 36; and Messali, 65–66; on PPA, 59; role in post-independence conflicts, 134, 155; UDMA of, 117

Abbasists, 115, 117, 119. *See also* Assimilationism

Abdelkader, 37–38, 46, 120, 123, 124, 247

Abdel-Malek, Anouar, 82, 99, 158

Addi, Lahouari, 149, 229, 247

Africa: black market in, 200, 278n78; failed state socialism in, 168–69, 170; global debt of, 169, 276n5

African-Asian Peoples' Solidarity Organization (AAPSO), 90

African National Congress (ANC), 142

Africasia, 137

Afrique-Asie, 82, 137, 157

Agrarian society. *See* Rural society

AIS (Islamic Salvation Army), 245, 246

Aït-Ahmed, Hocine: on historical legitimacy, 156; on revolutionary people, 125–26; role in FLN, 131, 132; role in in post-independence conflict, 134, 148, 154, 155

Ajami, Fouad, 227, 229, 233

Ajayi, J. F. A., 258–59n21

Alawite sect, 184

Algeria: agricultural sector of, 208, 279nn7,8; civil war casualties in, 204, 210–11, 230–31; constitutional system of, 149–52; democratization trends in, 211–12, 213–14, 227–28, 230; economic-order objectives of, 143–46, 273n120; emigration from, 6, 40, 51–52; failed anti-colonial revolts of, 42–43; FIS' electoral success in, 1–2, 227–29; foreign policy goals of, 141, 142–43, 209–10; France's dual image of, 125; French occupation of, 32–33, 37–40, 42–43; industrialization program in, 208–9, 216–17; Islam's constancy in, 231–32, 237–38, 283n101; labor force marginalization in, 223–24, 243; mosques' role in, 240–42, 284n131; 1994 reconciliation conference in, 204–5; in nonalignment movement, 91, 141, 144–45, 206–7, 273n113; oil revenues of, 145, 149, 208–9; opposition politics in, 142, 154–56; post-independence conflicts in, 134–35; scholarship on, 257n4; state disengagement from society, 209, 218–21, 279–80n15; Third Worldism's ties to, 8–10; Third Worldist status of, 5–7, 132–33, 135–39; traditional patterns of authority in, 41–42; transformed self-representation of, 215–18; underground economy in, 221–23; V-E Day reaction in, 116–17, 118–19; violence in, 245–48. *See also* Algerian war

Algerian Communist Party (PCA), 35, 121

"Algerianists," 244, 245

Algerian war (1954–1962): Camus's perspective on, 120–21; construction of

313

237–38; and nonalignment, 144–45; overall policy of, 214–15; political/personal metamorphosis of, 206–7; role in post-independence conflicts, 134, 135
Bourdieu, Pierre, 82, 108, 112, 121, 166, 193
Bouteflika, Abdelaziz, 141, 146, 207, 273n123
Bouyali, Mustapha, 232, 245
Braillard, Philippe, 113
Braudel, Fernand, 174
Brotherhoods, colonialism's disruption of, 41–43, 62–63. *See also* Islam
Brumberg, Daniel, 211
Bugeaud, Robert-Thomas, 38
Burchett, Wilfred, 82, 87
Burgat, François, 231, 234, 237, 239, 242
Burkina Faso (*formerly* Upper Volta), 8, 75–76, 107

Cabral, Amilcar, 11, 22, 81; on national liberation, 87, 113, 266n37; on subjective social class, 98, 99; on violence, 104, 105
Cambodia, 171, 276n14
Camus, Albert, 120–21
Cape Verde, 107
Capitalism: colonialist endeavor and, 25–26, 27–28, 49–50
Carmichael, Stokely, 3
Carter Center, 164
Castaneda, Jorge, 189, 209, 254
Castro, Fidel, 70, 80, 207, 268n70, 275n2
Centralists, 119, 121
Chaabani, 156
Chaliand, Gérard, 136, 140, 172, 173, 176, 178
Chanderli, Abdelkader, 131
Charte d'Alger, 152
Chikh, Slimane, 105
China, 79, 87, 171, 195, 276nn11,14
Cities: as focus of resistance, 43; marginalized migrants in, 21–22, 243; social differentiation in, 224–25, 282n77
Class: as basis for conflict in urban centers, 224–25, 282n77; colonialism's disruption of, 19–20, 28, 39–40; Marxist theory of, 26; popular masses' replacement of, 49–50, 57, 98, 146–47
Cleaver, Eldridge, 3
Clientelism, 197–98, 199, 223, 281n68
Clinton, Bill, 15
Colonialism: and brotherhoods' disruption, 41–43, 62–63; Camus on, 120–21;

capitalism's links to, 25–26, 27–28, 49–50; constitutionalism as response to, 150–51; and economic/social disruption, 19–20, 28, 38–40, 63; European Left on, 27–29, 67–68; ideological reactions to, 23–27, 258nn19,21; and impact on migrants, 20–22; nationalism and nation-statism as reaction to, 31–32, 96–99, 253, 259n41; as North-South interaction, 18–19; PCF's stance on, 53, 54–56, 263n87; as social discrimination, 98; Third Worldism's evolution and, 6, 7, 20–23; transnational struggle against, 124
Colonna, Fanny, 193, 277–78n58
Les Combattants de la Liberté, 121
Comités de Défense de la Révolution (Burkina Faso), 107
Comité des Enfants de Chouhada (Committee of the Children of Martyrs), 210
Comité d'Études Coloniales, 53
Commission Coloniale (1924–34), 53
Communist University of Workers from the Orient, 22
Congrès de l'Autogestion Industrielle (1964), 139
Congress of the People of the Orient (1920), 22
Conseil de la Révolution (Algreia), 150
Constant, Benjamin, 106–7
Constitutionalism: Algerian *versus* Western, 85, 149–52; under Chadli, 211–12; presidential power and, 153–54. *See also* Democratization; Westernization
Costa-Gavras, 82
Crone, Patricia, 184
Cuban revolution, 80–81, 82, 87–88, 265n14

Daoud, Zakya, 36, 65
Dar al-Islam (land of Islam), 30, 41
Darwish, Mahmoud, 105
Davezies, Robert, 133
Davidson, Basil, 22, 82; on African nationalist movements, 98–99; on assimilationism, 24, 258n17; on clientelism, 197; on nation-state ideal, 30–31; on Nkrumah, 80; on state socialism, 168–69, 170; on tribalism, 200, 278–79n88; on violence, 105
Debray, Regis, 82, 113
De Certeau, Michel, 96
Democratization: under Chadli, 211–12;

representation in Algeria, 47–51; and concepts of popular will, 97–98, 99–100, 106–7, 158, 177–78, 218; contemporary demystification of, 177–79, 181; FLN's institutionalization of, 127–31; historical *versus* democratic bases of, 150–53; Islamism and, 235, 236–37; opposition to, 108–9, 130–31, 154–56; religious reformists' conception of, 61–65, 264 n122; Third Worldist perspective on, 95, 99–101. *See also* Dissent

PPA (Parti du Peuple Algérien), 37; banning of, 262 n71; under Chadli's regime, 212; Islamism and, 59; nationalistic outlook of, 51, 56, 57, 130

Privatization: of land, 39, 209, 279–80 n15; state disengagement from society and, 213–14, 218–19

PRS (Parti de la Révolution Socialiste), 154–56

Quandt, William, 35, 260 n4

Rabin, Yitzhak, 15
Rahmania brotherhood, 63
Ramdane, Abbane, 156
Raptis, Michel, 138
Rassemblement pour la Culture et la Démocratie. *See* RCD
Rawlings, Jerry, 76, 164
Al-Razeq, 62
RCD (Rassemblement pour la Culture et la Démocratie), 205, 212, 230
Religious reformists: FLN and, 35, 36, 119, 121; ideology of, 65–66; religious-political reconciliation by, 44, 61–62, 63–65, 264 nn122,123,125
Resistance. *See* Dissent
Revolutionary movements: assumptions on violence of, 104–5; discourse on history and, 34–35, 96–97; displaced center of, 86–87, 132–33; European Left's support for, 67–68, 132–33; international perceptions on, 87, 132; mythic representation of, 77–78; PCF attitude toward, 53, 54–56, 263 n87; and "popular masses," 97–98, 125–27, 146, 147; scriveners of, 81–82; in Third World countries, 75–76, 79–81, 265 n14. *See also* Algerian revolution
Riadh El-Feth, 219–20
Rida, Mohammad, 264 n123

Roberts, Hugh, 217, 223
Rodinson, Maxime, 58, 60, 171–72, 178, 234
Rotman, Patrick, 133
Rous, Jean, 90
Rousseau, Jean-Jacques, 98, 268 n70
Roy, Manabendra Nath, 22
Rural society: as basis for Algerian political discourse, 146; decentralized authority in, 41–42; FLN's depiction of, 125; impact of colonialism on, 38–40, 42–43; industrialization's impact on, 208, 279 nn7,8
Russian revolution. *See* Bolshevik revolution

Saadallah, Belkacem, 42
Sadowski, Yayha, 185, 186
Sahli, Mohamed Chérif, 148
Sahnoun, Ahmed, 226
Said, Edward, 3, 4, 120; on cultural borrowings, 18, 32, 257 n1; on demise of Third Worldism, 171, 172–73; on group identity, 176; on ideological production, 96, 166; on media, 192; on violence, 104, 105; on West/non-West relationship, 114, 269–70 n124
Sakiet Sidi Youssef, 132
Salafiyya, 62, 244, 245. *See also* Religious reformists
Sandinistas, 101
Sankara, Thomas, 75, 76, 101, 108
Sanson, Henri, 147, 232
Sant'Egidio, 282 n96
Sartre, Jean-Paul, 82, 87, 98, 104–5, 133
Sauvy, Alfred, 49, 78
Schwartzkopf, Norman, 163
Second Pan-African Congress (1919), 52
Sénatus-consulte, 39
Senghor, Leopold, 89–90
Servan-Schreiber, Jean-Jacques, 132–33
Sétif, 116–17
Shining Path (Peru), 87
Sidi Bel-Abbes incident, 55–56
Sièyes, Emmanuel-Joseph, 49–50
Sivan, Emmanuel, 55
Smith, Anthony, 19, 58, 192, 257 n5
Socialism: Eurocentric bias of, 25–26, 86; Islamism and, 64–66, 232, 264 nn122,123,125, 283 n101; Messalist ties to, 56–59; relation to other ideologies, 26–27, 29, 65–66, 115; relation to Third Worldism, 11, 98

Compositor: G & S Typesetters, Inc.
Text: 10/13 Galliard
Display: Galliard
Printer and Binder: Thomson-Shore, Inc.